D0154091

WORKING IN METAL

WORKING IN METAL

Management and Labour in the Metal Industries of Europe and the USA, 1890-1914

CHRIS McGUFFIE

MERLIN PRESS
LONDON

First published 1985
by Merlin Press Ltd
3 Manchester Road
London E14 9BD

© Chris McGuffie 1986

jacket design by Louis Mackay

McGuffie, Chris
Working in metal: management and labour in the
metal industries of Europe and the USA,
1890–1914.
1. Metal trade—Europe—Employees—History
2. Metal trade—United States—Employees—
History
I. Title
338.4'7669'094   HD9506.E9

ISBN 0-85036-312-8

Printed in Great Britain by
Whitstable Litho, Whitstable, Kent

Typesetting by Hems & Co.
The Old Brewery, Tisbury, Wilts.

To Helen and Georgia

'One sees a ragpicker knocking against the walls
Paying no heed to the spies of the cops, his thralls,
But stumbling like a poet lost in his dreams;
He pours his heart out in stupendous schemes.

He takes great oaths and dictates sublime laws,
Casts down the wicked, aids the victims' cause;
Beneath the sky, like a vast canopy,
He is drunken of his splendid qualities.'
Charles Baudelaire, 'The Ragpickers' Wine'.

CONTENTS

LIST OF TABLES

ii

PREFACE

Nothing is more central to the successful functioning of modern industry than the use made of human labour power. It is not the fabulous machines, huge factories, complex enterprise organisations and great markets that presuppose its existence. Quite the contrary, its real or material basis, as with all civilisations, is the collective organisation and application of the mental and manual faculties of millions of people who work: as manual workers, supervisors, clerks, designers, technicians, engineers, and as managers and employers. Only as a result of their purposeful endeavours can the machinery be at all operated, the factories built and filled, the special tools made and applied, and the markets served. How people have learned to undertake such tasks is the concern of the pages that follow; and the story to be considered in detail is how people learned to work in the factories of Europe's and America's most advanced capitalist enterprises at the beginning of this century.

This book is also about social classes. That is, it is about how people have *learned* to become workers, managers and employers through the sorts of work they do, their education and practical training, so that they come to be members of either a factory bourgeoisie, factory proletariat, or factory middle class.

The story concerns learning to labour in the metal industries of Great Britain, France, Germany and America in the period from the late 1890s until the outbreak of World War One; and, in weaving together the different strands of this story, I will draw attention to several myths that popular and historical opinion has come to know and love about the rise of modern industry, and how people have learned to work in it.

When the young Karl Marx and Friedrich Engels attempted to describe the underlying character of modern industry in their own age, during the mid-nineteenth century, they saw it as tending towards a 'constant revolutionising of production, uninterrupted disturbance of all social conditions, everlasting uncertainty and agitation'.[1] Such impulses have certainly not been limited to disturbing the technical or objective means of production, the tools, machinery and the factories that house them. There has also been a constant agitation and disturbance of that most precious means of production, the ability and facility to work itself. Traditionally, this has been most poignantly revealed in the memoirs of workers, in many excellent historical works, and in the myriad industrial

iii

experiences and talk of those who labour today. It has generally concerned the specialisation of workers' mental and manual faculties used in production and the associated specialisation of their training, or what they are taught and allowed to do in their work.

That this was keenly sensed by commentators and experienced by workers in the large industrial plants of Europe and America at the turn of this century is an important call on our attention; and this book sets out to explain how workers were made subject to a greater division of labour in their work and training. Yet this is neither the only call on our attention nor the most important one, for during the early 1900s what needs to be explained is a sense of change with a far broader resonance and an experience of much greater historical importance: the specialisation of labour and training in production *and* the professionalisation of how things were to be done in the first place, i.e., the labour of superintendence and management.

The act of labour is, of course, always a purposeful activity requiring the application of specific and qualitative skills. In various tasks very different mental and manual faculties have to be used and these must draw on different forms of training and experience. Only in this way can metal be mixed, a mould made, a lathe formed and itself be used to fashion a steel rod into a shaft for a car or ship. In this story, I will refer to the totality of these mental and manual attributes as the various *compositions* of labour power used in production. It would be foolishly one-sided, however, to consider only the evolving attributes of labour, how it was trained and its various compositions from the point of view of the direct production of useful goods. As will be emphasised throughout this story, for these products to be themselves executed a larger design must be purposively fashioned to arrange, define and plan in advance what is to be produced, how it is to be produced, and what the particular processes of production will be. This larger design is the work of mental labour and, as a result of its applications, particular patterns of social cooperation in production and what Marx called, 'directing authority', take shape. Various horizontal and vertical divisions of labour are established which allow those who carry out the functions of tending a blast furnace, smelting steel or machining steel rods to do so with the right raw materials and correct machines, whether these be iron ore and pig iron or a planer and a slotter. How this distinctly intellectual labour, the labour of superintendence and management, came to be formed, trained and professionalised, and how its changing skills influenced the labour of those engaged in direct production are the central themes of this story.

Perhaps the most important development that highlighted the formation and growing professionalisation of distinctly mental labour in the metal factories of Europe and America in the early 1900s was the creation of schools, colleges and universities to supply enterprises with 'qualified'

iv

personnel to undertake supervisory and technical functions in the workplace. Though never more than a small minority ever obtained access to the ranks of supervisory, technical and managerial labour during the nineteenth century, the various 'learning by doing' or on-the-job training schemes did provide a ladder for internal promotion within an enterprise. The effect of the move to professionalise production management, by contrast, was to bring all this into question and reorientate higher technical and supervisory positions to qualifications obtained outside the factory. These positions were now to be filled horizontally, especially from the technical colleges and universities, rather than vertically or exclusively within an enterprise.

How this affected the overwhelming majority of those engaged in direct production concerned not only their future access to positions in the factory hierarchy and class structures of European and American society, but also what mental and manual skills or faculties they were henceforth allowed to use in their work. The professionalisation movements in Europe and America radically altered and redefined what work was. Yet this was to be no mere 'ideological' exercise, as the popular meaning of the term would have it. This was not just a question of managers, supervisors and engineers beginning to think differently about their place in the enterprise and legitimating their authority by recourse to an ideology of professional training without any obvious impact on the real world of the workplace. These movements may have been eminently ideological, but they were also very practical. In designing training methods for the refinement and expansion of the labour of superintendence and management, the professional architects of mental labour set out to recompose the faculties that were allowed to be used in the actual fabrication of the product. It was not so much that workers were no longer required to think in their work, but rather that their mental and manual faculties were increasingly designed or composed for the exclusive and *specialised* needs of an individual plant. They were now to be 'taught' and 'shown' what to do, rather than be allowed to 'spontaneously' and 'competitively' acquire their training through the *general needs of the trade* in an empirical manner. No longer were they to be allowed to build up formal and not so formal qualifications just as a result of training in the factory. The erosion of existing forms of proletarian apprenticeships and the introduction of new style 'apprenticeship' programmes for new professional employees is an important part of this story, and it was in this context that a new managerial ideology of direct labour took root in Europe and America. Direct labour came to be seen as a more 'physical' activity complemented by the arrival of mental fatigue and 'nervousness'—the last smidgens of mental labour as it were—and was considered to be the inversion of a more 'professional' or intellectual labour of management. How far this ideology bore witness to a real state of affairs in the European and American metal

v

industries on the eve of World War One can only be tested by describing in detail the training methods and production practices of the older grades of labour and comparing these with the experiences of those who came to be employed in the new professional apparatus of mental labour.

It will not be suggested that these changes occurred in a dramatic or revolutionary manner, though at the time they were often spoken of in this way. On the contrary, the transition was a more continuous experience, comprising no immediate break with the past and, in reality, often drew upon methods of training that had long lineages stretching back to the early nineteenth century. It is my view, however, that during the years spanning the late 1890s and 1914 the basic structures for a renewal of learning how to work were all in place—not only in America, but also in Europe; not only in Germany, but also in France and Britain.

This raises the most important question of why such movements should have taken shape at this time and why it was so necessary for enterprises to develop sophisticated programmes for the training of various layers of their workforce both inside and outside the factory. Part of this is to be accounted for by the technical requirements of the industry and the shortages of trained labour power which stretched back to the foundation years of the modern engineering and steel branches. This was particularly the case in France, Germany and America, where the heavy metal industries had required from the outset programmes for training various grades of the labour force, from managers down to workers, whether these were run by enterprises themselves or by governments. In Britain, as well, though the shortages were not so pressing, an extensive private and empirical system of training took shape to meet the relatively sophisticated technical needs of the two branches during the nineteenth century. By the beginning of this century a new wave of expansion and technical change was under way which also placed severe strains on the supply of trained designers, engineers, chemists and technicians, and called for the deployment and expansion of training programmes. By itself, however, a technical explanation sits rather uncomfortably. As my emphasis is on the lineages of learning how to labour and how these lineages were made, such an explanation would have us rooting out professionalisation movements throughout the nineteenth century, particularly in France where the first echoes could be heard as early as the 1850s and 1860s. What needs to be drawn out, instead, is the reason why four advanced capitalist countries, which had taken very different historical paths in the training and formation of their workers and employers, should have begun to share a more unified experience at the beginning of this century; an experience which is strictly not explicable in terms of the industry's technical needs or some logic of innovation. Here, it is necessary to turn to a social and economic explanation.

What this story will show is that the transformation of industrial training during the early 1900s was strictly social in character, economically determined and an important symptom of a once-and-for-all shift to a more monopolistic capitalism amongst the leading firms. Within the factories of these enterprises, the issue turned on the social development of a formal and professionally-trained intellectual labour of management at one pole of the firm and a growing dequalification of manual labour at the other; both of which shaped the technical needs of the industry and its patterns of labour and training. Economically, the story concerns nothing less than a fundamental change to the way in which capitalist profit-making or accumulation took place within the leading firms.

Here, I will describe the growing importance of plant, machinery and equipment (or fixed capital) in the execution of the product and the economic consequences of this for enterprise profitability. I will concentrate on a ten-year period, stretching from the mid-1890s until the mid-1900s, when, as a result of a massive investment boom in all sorts of plant and equipment, a handful of great concerns in Europe and America changed the face of the industry. This decade, which also witnessed a sharp and powerful slump, brought to the attention of the leading firms whether such a huge investment in plant and equipment was actually in their long-term interests unless followed up by changes to plant organisation and management. It was a mood that turned on the relationship between profitability and how intensively plant and equipment could be used; for if it was not used as intensively as possible, then the long-term profitability of a firm could be endangered. The impact of this investment boom and more defensive posture on the workplace proved to be both path-breaking and irrevocable. The composition of the workforce was transformed. Workers were concentrated into fewer and larger establishments. Traditional trade and proletarian apprenticeships were uprooted and recomposed. Large numbers of black-coated or 'white collar' supervisory and technical employees entered the factories, while, as a whole, large concerns sought to introduce systematic methods of production management that would cause workers to increase their rate of use of machinery, plant and equipment, and bring about a greater and more intensive role for management in the planning of production.

As far as changing the existing patterns of learning how to labour were concerned, managements had themselves to learn how to specialise further the uses made of labour power in direct production and more clearly demarcate what workers could and could not do. They also had to introduce and constantly refine more intensive forms of foremanship, supervisory and technical labour, as well as construct more elaborate and sophisticated forms of maintenance work. The problem for managers and employers had as much to do with the planning and direction of production as it did with the actual use made by workers of the expensive plant and equipment; and those who undertook the tasks of supervisory

vii

labour and planning had to be properly trained. As will become apparent, it was in the nexus between the growing intensification of labour and its 'professional' supervision that one finds the material basis for a renewal of learning how to work in modern industry at this time.

It could come as a surprise that this story has not been adequately told before now, especially of how labour power is utilised in the factory and the corresponding class education and training it has received. Yet there is no need to be pessimistic about the fruits it will bear, as the prevailing traditions of popular and historical opinion would have us believe. These traditions, though, do have the power of being persuasive myths and, therefore, must be taken into account.

One writer, Peter Mathias, has provided some insight into the general problem of the myths that surround the history of modern industry. Speaking at the famous engineering and management academy in Britain, The Cranfield Institute of Technology, in 1973, he drew attention to how, 'Every society needs the support of myths which buttress its way of life. The lessons to be learned from the past have to be drawn into this structure of values so that history should not become a source of disaffection, a means or an agency for subverting contemporary values'.[2] Whether 'society' as a whole or just ruling sections of it need the support of myths to support its way of life is a moot point and one which this story will not be silent on. But one thing that is not in doubt is how several myths have come to shape our understanding of modern industry.

The first can be called the myth of national peculiarity and concerns the relative failure of managerial and scientific endeavours in Britain and France when compared with the advances made by Germany and America in the fields of industrial organisation, mass production techniques and the application of science to industry. Though there are several important nuances in this belief, it basically homes in on the alleged weaknesses of the British and French systems of scientific and industrial training for employers and workers in the late nineteenth and early twentieth centuries. At a time when a professionaly-trained, management and a scientifically trained workforce were coming to be seen as essential weapons in the battle to improve or just maintain the international competitiveness of any one nation, it is suggested that the British and French could not live up to the pace set by their powerful foreign rivals across the Rhine or on the other side of the Atlantic. A number of class and national-cultural peculiarities are believed to be responsible for this sad state of affairs in the training of British and French workers and managers, and these are variously to be laid at the feet of an 'aristocratic' ruling class, an 'amateurish' industrial bourgeoisie, or a 'traditional' social structure. Germany, too, has not been without its own domestic critics.

It is difficult to explain why many historians and sociologists have been so struck by the peculiarities of national development over and above their possible common characteristics, but one suggestion can be offered. The history of modern industry, particularly in Europe, has for some time now been tied to a quite myopic vision of national capitalist development and the role of the businessman in it. It is not so much an aggressive vision as a melancholic one, a concern with the inability of formerly 'great' countries to remain on top in the face of expanding industrial capitalism and international competition. As history, it has not so much served the interests of business by glorifying it, as embraced a popular image of its servility. Yet, as I have already suggested, this story will give attention to how metal enterprises in Britain, France, and Germany came to share a tightly woven, *European* experience with regard to the training of their workforces and the professionalisation of their managements; and an intrinsic part of this story is the positive and aggressive manner with which these tasks were undertaken and how comparable this experience proved to be with developments in America.

It is not to be supposed that I will underestimate the real and substantial national differences in the training of Europe's and America's heavy metal industry workforce, either in the workplace or outside it; let alone will I underestimate the differing roles of the various nation states or the social and cultural impact of the various paths that were followed. I will, however, describe what evolved to be held in common and show that this has proved to be of far greater historical importance to us, who are its products, than any real or supposed differences and peculiarities. How we learn to work is very much a product of what our managerial and worker forebears experienced at the beginning of this century, particularly in the European metal industry.

The second myth, or couplet of myths, bears very much on how we now appreciate this experience in our popular consciousness and concerns the sorts of work modern industry has provided the members of the labour force. On the one hand, it is often argued that modern industrial capitalism has tended towards the decomposition or 'de-skilling' of labour. Mechanisation has been held to be especially responsible for this, as it has reduced the need to apply many and varied skills in production. As a result the working class has become more homogeneous as a class, as well as more united. On the other hand, others would suggest that modern industry has tended not so much towards the decomposition and de-skilling of labour as towards its recomposition and constant 're-skilling' or 'upgrading'. In fact, skilled labour has expanded and given rise to higher forms of professional status and greater economic rewards. At the same time, the emergence of semi-skilled labour, in the form of machine tending, has led to the promotion of many millions of workers from the ranks of unskilled hewers and carriers. Far from the working class becoming more homogeneous and unified, it has in reality become more diversified, heterogeneous and disunited. As these beliefs have congealed over time,

ix

they have been frequently used to judge whether America, Britain, France and Germany, or European industry as a whole, lived up to such expectations. In other words, the question is often posed, whether Germany, for example, experienced a 'degradation' or 'upgrading' of its labour force because of the expansion of modern industry during the late nineteenth and early twentieth centuries.

If this book was only able to succeed in creating a mood or a feeling, it would be one of complete disaffection with such lines of questioning and the popular misconceptions on which they are based. Disaffection, because such notions only consider labour as a technical lump which may be broken up or recomposed, diluted or upgraded into further lumps. 'Labour' is, in fact, a *power* comprising qualitatively different activities— on the one hand, the various and qualitative activities of direct production, and, on the other hand, the various and qualitative activities of planning production. Furthermore, by advancing the notion that labour is a lump, such beliefs suppose that the technical and material attributes of labour power can be read as simultaneously showing either the degradation of labour and the increasing homogeneity of the working class, or the upgrading of labour and the growing differentiation of the working class. This is a complete myth, but like all myths it contains an unseen truth, for labour power is both a material and social phenomenon.

It is both a qualitative activity involved in material production and a social activity whereby the skills and faculties of ordinary people are sundered into the competing and antagonistic interests of fundamentally opposed social classes. It is both an activity whereby the means of life are provided for and an activity whereby social classes receive the necessary sustenance for their recruitment and reproduction. Yet, if labour power has to be considered from a material and social point of view, then there is no need to confuse its material characteristics with its social forms. There is no need to confuse the act of labour with its organisation into classes. It is quite possible for the act of labour to become a highly refined and differentiated material activity and also become a formidable vehicle for the formation of social classes around polarised and competing interests.

Such an interpretation is by no means original. It was the characteristic perception of informed observers at the beginning of the century and as such represents a major, though hitherto unexplored, contribution to the sociology of labour in general, and to our historical understanding of the material and social attributes of labour in particular. A major part of this story is devoted to an analysis of the rich insights that can be gained from a study of these contemporary perceptions, especially when measured against the more simplistic interpretations of many present-day historians and sociologists.

For this story, the issue turns on how highly-stratified educational

x

institutions were formed for particular social classes and sections of social classes, in order to teach people the various mental and manual skills of production and management: institutions for factory workers and various grades of skilled labour; for employers and various groups of managers and engineers; and for the factory middle class and its various grades of supervisory labour, foremen and technicians. Institutions which not only came to have a direct bearing on servicing the highly-refined technical needs of the modern factory, but also on underwriting the formation and composition of classes within it.

A further reason for telling the story of how people have learned to work is more closely related to the concerns of those who would emphasise the peculiarities of national capitalist development. For many historians and sociologists, the late nineteenth and early twentieth centuries represent the high summer of European craftsmen's power and influence in the factory, particularly in metal production. Britain is commonly believed to be a special case in point, yet Germany, France, and even America are drawn in. For Britain, it is a question of whether industrialists remained firmly committed, or were forced to commit themselves, to the maintenance of a craft-based, skilled workforce, rather than take advantage of new techniques of production which would require a widespread de-skilling or upgrading of labour. Whether this interpretation is correct or not, and it is considered in some detail, I will again take a different, non-technological, point of departure.

'Craft' work is often only defined in a most elusive manner, especially when seen through the cultural and social attitudes of contemporaries, whether they be workers or employers. Recently, however, attempts have been made to present the economic foundations of craft work in order to provide a more material explanation of the craftsmen's power and influence in production. I will also present some of the economic aspects of craft labour, but it is important to describe the actual content of this labour, see how it was trained and fitted into the overall structure of work in the modern factory at the beginning of this century. Yet to do this, it is necessary to broaden our perspective somewhat.

Employers in the heavy metal industries of Europe and America built up their apparatus of the mental labour of management and learned to train their workforces not just at the beginning of this century, but also during the nineteenth century. And, an important part of this history was how they began to learn to *regulate* the skills of their workforce in a capitalist manner, i.e. how they learned to train themselves and their workers privately inside their factories for the needs of their enterprises. Though this took several decades to learn, and the timing differed for each country, it comprised the break-up or complete by-passing of craft forms of work, so that the managerial, technical and planning skills previously intrinsic to the practice of a group of trades became either the

xi

private property of the employer and his paid managers or were so newly constructed as to be almost unrecognisable to craftsmen. Those who entered the factories as *workers* at various points during the nineteenth century increasingly found that though their craft may have continued to remain the technical basis of work, it was now increasingly fragmented and specialised. Moreover, they were increasingly prevented from undertaking what were now being defined as the exclusive planning tasks of a separately constituted management, even if they could do them and had practised them in the past as craftsmen. By describing this experience during the nineteenth century and explaining how workers reacted to it, I will try to show that in the overall structure of work the role and influence of the craftsman came to be at best negligible or, at worst, completely subordinated to the capitalist regulation of skill.

With these thoughts in mind, the first part of this story sets out the important views of a number of contemporary observers at the turn of the century concerning the changes they saw occurring to mental and manual faculties used in production and how these were trained. I shall then compare these views with the opinions of more general and nationally orientated historians and sociologists. My aim here is to draw attention to several novel concepts that contemporaries worked with in order to evaluate changes to factory work and skills used in production. The historical validity of these perceptions and concepts will certainly need to be tested in later chapters. It is my opinion, however, that they are much more accurate than the views advanced by many historians and social theorists concerned with changes to skills, work hierarchies and class structures in society and the workplace. These later interpretations tend to be far more one-sided and uncritical, appropriating more of the prevailing moods of the time than the substance of what was actually being described. Our story then turns to an evaluation of the realities of craft work in the European heavy metal industry during the nineteenth century while the remainder of this book is devoted to a series of national studies which explore the myths and realities of learning to labour in the leading metal enterprises of America and Europe at the beginning of this century.

Cambridge, April 1983

NOTES

1. Karl Marx and Friedrich Engels, *The Communist Manifesto* (1848), in David Fernbach, ed., *The Revolutions of 1848,* Penguin, London, 1973, p. 70.
2. Peter Mathias, 'Business History and Management Education', *Business History,* Vol. XVII, January 1975, p. 5.

PART I

PERCEPTIONS OF CHANGE AND THE CAPITALIST REGULATION OF SKILL

INTRODUCTION

1. Contemporary commentators

General changes taking place to work and training were closely observed by a number of leading contemporary commentators at the turn of the century. The views of several groups are important to consider, particularly those expressed by practising engineers, managerial 'scientists', workers, and independent middle-class observers. Publishing their findings in the leading scientific, technical, and management magazines of the day, or in well-documented public and private reports, they spoke of a remarkable transformation taking place in European metal enterprises. Whether their individual accounts tended to celebrate this change as leading to a growing differentiation and 'professionalisation' of the workforce, or lament it in terms of the inexorable decline of 'craft' skill and the rise of a more 'pliable' worker, when taken together it is hard to underestimate their richness and complexity.

They saw themselves as witnessing and theorising about the rise of skills which could no longer be considered as either attributes of craftsmanship or evenly spread throughout the workforce in singular, homogeneous blocks. Skills were, in fact, an *ensemble* of qualitative attributes and faculties, ranging from the 'professional' skills of the chemist and engineer to the fine and 'precise' psycho-motor motions of the machine tender. Each required different forms of technical ability and specialised methods of industrial training. Furthermore, this was seen to be a phenomenon perfectly consistent with growing social polarisation, social differentiation and managerial power in the workplace.

(i) The professionalisation of labour

For one of France's leading engineers, A. Abaut, the change to skills and training methods had to be looked at in terms of the rise of the 'modern factory'. In an article entitled 'Factory Workers', published in 1912 in the prestigious technical and management journal, *Revue de Métallurgie*, he described the 'modern factory' as 'a collection of machines put to work by a personnel of engineers, employees, investors and workers'.[1] The factory personnel could be divided into two main groups: the bourgeoisie and the proletariat. The 'bourgeois' group was composed of the 'masters' *(maîtrise):* works managers, foremen, and skilled workers or *ouvriers d'art*. These were the professional workers. The 'proletarian' group, by contrast, was composed of *non-professionals*, who were purely 'labourers'.[2] What impressed Abaut was the growing importance of the professional workers to the proper running of a factory's 'multiple and delicate functions'.[3] Engineers and employees from the laboratory and planning office were seen as essential for the coordination of technical work; white-collar employees for the organisation of buying, selling, accounting, and the determination of the costs of production; and the *ouvriers d'art*, such as turners and machine setters, for ensuring the regular working of machinery.[4]

In contrast to the principal role played by these professionals, who were essential for 'all labour, all progress, all administration', and who were all 'more or less attached to the bourgeoisie', was the non-essential role of the non-professional, proletarian workers: 'the proletarian, properly so-called', was only 'auxiliary to the professional'—the one who just 'feeds the machine tools', undertook some transport and handling, or gave aid to the white-collar employee and technician.[5] For Abaut, the growing importance of professional labour in the factory was associated with the 'development of mechanical labour' and resulted in 'the necessary expansion of the bourgeois group to the detriment of the proletarian group'.[6] To fail to realise this, to lament with *'grande pitié'* the development of machinery against manual labour, was to engage in sentiment, not science. The reduction of the proletarian group to auxiliary service to the machine was only the reverse side of increasing productivity, improvements to machinery, the growth of research and the general augmentation of the bourgeois group.[7] Furthermore, there was a growing need for professional instruction: 'the acquisition of theoretical and practical knowledge' was now 'indispensable to the modern worker and employee'. Hence, all prejudice against this necessary development of the bourgeoisie had to be banished from the factory, for although many non-professional proletarians would 'pass away', new professional workers would rise up to take their place.[8]

Working engineers and observers in other countries were also impressed by what they saw as the growing professionalisation of production and the effects this had had on skill requirements and the composition of the workforce. The American engineer, O.M. Becker, who wrote extensively on new technologies, claimed in 1906 that the greater division of labour and the use of automatic machines had brought about a decline in the proportion of workers with a knowledge of their craft. At the same time, the increasing complexity of machinery required workers with greater 'skill and intelligence'. The complicated machines had to be *supervised* by skilled professional employees, like foremen, supervising unskilled operatives. However, the recruitment and training of professional employees was made more difficult because of the decline in shop skills amongst workers and the breakdown of traditional apprenticeship systems. Yet professional training was becoming available. It appeared in the form of technical colleges, training schools founded close to a factory, and new and methodical works' apprenticeship programmes.[9]

N.B. Dearle was impressed by a different aspect of the same phenomenon in Britain. In his treatise, *Industrial Training,* published in 1914, he wrote that the new production methods, which called forth a 'greater rapidity of execution, fineness, and accuracy', and therefore brought about 'a reduction of manual skill', was 'compensated for by the need for increased intelligence and a higher level of technical and scientific knowledge'.[10]

That precision and more scientific production methods were bringing about a recomposition of the workforce (on the one hand a dequalification of manual labour, on the other hand, an increasing super-qualification of mental labour or professional work), was a major part of Hans Ehrenberg's observations on the German iron and steel industry. Ehrenberg argued that the dequalification of manual labour was linked to the scientific nature of the innovations in the iron and steel industry. 'The more chemical the technique, the less the result of the process depends on the worker.'[11] On the other hand, the level of responsibility had shifted to technicians and foremen, who had become more numerous as the process of dequalification *(Entgeistigung)* proceeded.[12] New posts in the division of labour had arisen filled by highly-qualified and trained technical employees who undertook intellectual work and engaged in the practical supervision of the management of production.[13] Some of the implications of this 'bourgeoisification' or professionalisation of production are apparent in the observations of the liberal German intellectual, Alfred Weber. Describing the destiny of the manual worker in German industry, he observed in 1912 that industrial capitalism was now able to create a hierarchy of labour powers *(Arbeitsakte),* based not on job milieu, custom or heredity, but on physical and nervous capacities, intelligence and general education.[14]

From this vantage point, intellectual labour was not only seen to be playing a greater role in production, it was also seen to be creating a tendency towards continuing and professional *teaching* of the workforce in new methods and procedures of production. This was certainly to be contrasted with the more traditional reliance on *pre-existing* skills empirically acquired in the factory and embedded in the workforce. As Frederick Winslow Taylor's scientific management disciple, C.B. Thompson, claimed, at the time of America's intervention in the European war, there was now a tendency 'to shift the demand from labour which is already skilled to that which is teachable'. The labour supply now could be drawn 'not so much from those equipped with the usual store of traditional knowledge and technique as from those with the aptitude which enables them to respond quickly and effectively to the intensive training in the newer methods'.[15]

As we shall see, from a purely technical point of view, such an emphasis on professional and technical training was by no means new. In fact, the European metal industry's two main branches had established systems of training and education well before the late nineteenth and early twentieth centuries. As far as direct production was concerned, the very success of employing various instruments of labour, such as lathes and blast furnaces, required a workforce that was not only varied and specific to the tasks at hand, but also based on qualitative skills, qualifications, forms of training and experience. With regard to the labour of superintendence and management, a workforce had long been required to plan the product in advance and to direct the various horizontal and vertical divisions of labour through which the product was fabricated. A workforce, in other words, that was capable of implementing and mobilising what the German theoretician, Alfred Sohn-Rethel, has termed an enterprise's collective 'technical intelligence'. This, too, required the application of differential and qualitative skills, formed by previous training or just plain 'know how'. It comprised the labour of the chemist testing metals in the laboratory, in the foundry or at the blast furnace; of the mechanical engineer designing plant and machinery; of the draughtsman designing the product; and the foreman supervising the actual making of the product. Though contemporaries were certainly struck by the refinement and extension of this existing structure of skills and technical training, they were much keener to emphasise its novelties with respect to past practices. This was especially so with regard to the *qualifications* seen to be now needed from the workforce and how these influenced *relations* between workers and employers, the overall *composition* of the workforce and the *nature of the skills* required in production.

Sohn-Rethel's concept of technical intelligence is a useful guide here. In his opinion, all forms of management, capitalist or otherwise, must organise and apply specific bodies of technical knowledge in order for production to take place at all. What is unique to capitalist production, however, is the way in which management seeks to deepen its qualitative and quantitative knowledge over *all* the technical and material aspects of production.[16] Whether this is possible or not, Sohn-Rethel has spotlighted what a number of commentators bore witness to at the beginning of this century: that there was a refinement and extension of managerial power taking shape, which brought with it the introduction of a more malleable workforce; a workforce more subject to management-inspired planning, control, direction and *diktat*.

(ii) Manual skill as a company asset
Certainly this was the view of the independently-minded R.F. Hoxie in his celebrated war-time study of the American scientific management

xvi

movement. Scientific management, Hoxie claimed, sought to gather up and transfer to management appointees all traditional knowledge, judgment and skill formerly controlled by workers, so that all initiative and skill in connection with work was monopolised by management. Thus, professionalisation of production took the form of confining each worker to a particular task, stripping them of initiative in the choice of tools, the determination of methods of working, the laying-out and setting-up of work, and decisions concerning the feeds and speeds of machinery. All these tasks were, according to the doctrine, to be hived off and divided amongst new professionally-trained personnel, such as 'functional foremen'. For scientific management, all this added up to improved and more professional methods of industrial training and an increase of skill in the workforce. As Frederick Winslow Taylor, claimed in 1903 in his treatise, *Shop Management:*

> The demand for men of originality and brains was never so great as it is now, and the modern subdivision of labour, instead of dwarfing men, enables them all along the line to rise to a higher plane of efficiency, involving at the same time more brain work and less monotony. The type of man who was formerly a day labourer and digging dirt is now for instance making shoes in a factory...

For R.F. Hoxie, by contrast, writing from the point of view of the worker, it meant a narrowing of outlook, skill and experience, which made the worker all the more easily displaced by a cheaper and less skilled colleague.[17] In other words, the increasing professionalisation of management went hand in glove with an increasing dequalification of labour.

That manual skill could now be viewed as a more malleable, reproducible and teachable company asset was something stressed by C.B. Thompson when he lambasted the American Federation of Labor's alleged craft restrictions in 1915. He spoke of the growth of new forms of skill which were based on *individual capability* rather than on craft training; forms of skill based on 'individual differences and individual abilities', or on an 'inherent and acquired capacity'.[18] He defined these new forms of manual skill in terms of their specialisation which made possible a high attainment in a specific field of work and which developed the capacity of the worker to the utmost limit. When measured against the 'hazy versatility' of the traditional 'all-round' machinist, who did things only 'half-well', this was 'real' skill.[19]

British observers emphasised much the same general tendency for their own metal industry. One anonymous pre-war engineer noted that:

> Each machinist becomes a specialist. It is not merely that he operates one class of machine, for the older hands did that, but he either seldom does more than one particular class of work on his machine, or else the range of work done lies within very narrow limits. Having a machine of more or less automatic character,

xvii

with special tools and jigs fixed, or instruments of measurement, he becomes a highly skilled specialist. His energies being no longer diffused like those of the old craftsmen, he acquires astonishing facility in one class of work which devolves upon him, and produces results, both in respect of economy and accuracy, which no general hand, however skilful or technically trained can possibly equal.[20]

W.J. Ashley had a similar efficiency conception of skill, as can be seen from his Sidney Ball Memorial Lecture delivered in 1922. Reflecting on the great 'machine questions' which had wracked the British engineering trades since 1852 (where skilled men opposed the introduction of cheaper labour and demanded that new machinery be manned by the existing skilled men at the skilled men's rate of pay), Ashley argued that machinery and specialisation did not replace skill outright. On the contrary, it created 'new types of skill'. Skill was not a 'homogeneous thing' of which there were 'different degrees or amounts'; skill was a term which in fact covered 'things of very different kinds'.[21] In this view, the evolution of machinery and the evolution of labour power were not inversely related on a unilinear scale of dilution. In the nineteenth century, the labour of an engineer could be variously termed skilled or unskilled: the first mainly manual, or tactile skill, was associated with varying amounts of judgment in the choice of work methods and the execution of each part of the task and informed by a judgment tied to manual dexterity or 'machine sense'; while the latter, though requiring some mental qualities such as patience and attention, was mainly a matter of physical strength. In the twentieth century, however, with the appearance of the so-called 'semi-skilled', Ashley believed that this new stratum was not in a situation half-way between the skilled fitter and the machine helper. This was a 'different kind of skill'. The new worker had only enough training and ability to work on a specialised machine and could not readily turn a hand to anything else; but on this work the worker became in a sense more skilled, turning out more in a given time than, say, the all-round skilled worker could by working the same machine.[22] Second, new kinds of skill had been formed at the apex of the skill pyramid. The all-round skilled worker had given way to the specialised skill of the tool-makers and tool-setters, many of whom became leading or charge hands.[23]

This emphasis on 'the tendency of machine production to produce a concentration of skill', so that the work done covered a 'narrower range' but reached a 'higher level', had impressed N.B. Dearle eight years earlier in 1914,[24] and also the French observer of English engineering practice, Paul de Rousiers, as early as 1896.

De Rousiers toured and studied the Oldham textile machinery works of Platt's. He was struck by the 'extremely delicate' nature of the work done, where 'every workman is a specialist' and 'master of his business'; where 'almost every individual employed by the firm is a skilled workman';

xviii

where not a single woman was employed; where there was no place for 'occasional hands or casuals'; where apprenticeship flourished but where there was no trade union; where the master's position was absolute; where if a workman left he would 'find great difficulty in disposing of [his] special skill'; where finally, his 'highly-specialised' skill made him 'so dependent on the great firm' which directed and employed him, that the masters had mastery of the labour market 'in a very unusual degree'. They could, therefore, impose their own conditions on their men, for their firm and its special work was 'the only channel through which work [could] be obtained'.[25]

It was to this sort of skill that the liberal sympathiser of the working class, James Samuelson, referred when he considered boiler work undertaken at John Brown's in Sheffield. With the introduction of hydraulic riveting machines for large boilers in the early 1890s, 'one *skilled* labourer' was able to do the work which formerly occupied nine hand-riveters.[26]

It was against the rise of just this sort of skill that the young worker, J.T. Murphy, sought to make a stand while serving his apprenticeship at Vickers' Sheffield works in the early 1900s:

> It quickly became apparent to me that unless I made a stand for myself I should quickly become a victim of mass production. After a spell on a drilling machine and then a shaping machine I moved onto a miller. In all cases the process was simple and there was considerable repetition in it. I began agitating to be transferred to a universal miller where the work was more varied and skilled. So began the fight for variety of work and training. As soon as I felt I had mastered a particular machine and its class of work, I would politely ask Mr Graham, the foreman, for a move onto another job. Politeness passed into indignant daily protests until in exasperation he would consent. In the course of a few years I had worked on almost every machine in the place and on all classes of work.[27]

Sensitivity to the general tendency of a recomposition of manual skill was equally apparent in Germany. Otto Jeidels in 1906 spoke of the complete 'overturning of qualifications' that was taking place in the Rhineland's metal industry:

> The sharp dividing line between the skilled and unskilled worker is becoming obscured. The practice of the metal industry presumes that the skilled worker can perform his work independently and according to his own ideas. Yet, the skilled worker finds himself restricted to only the isolated parts of production operations. In the engineering industry, the craft-trained worker is sinking to the 'half-skilled' level, while, on the other hand, a section of the unskilled in those areas of production with a pronounced division of labour is elevated to the level of 'semi-skilled' labour. As a result, the position of the apprentice and young worker is being undermined. In many production operations there is nothing more to teach, and, even in the engineering industry, today's apprentice can be placed on lathe by himself even before the end of his apprenticeship. More than ever, the young worker (17 to 21 years old), just like the fully trained worker, is capable of working in many positions.[28]

Fritz Schulte, in his classic study of the Berlin engineering industry published in 1906, placed a similar emphasis on the general tendency towards a greater specialisation and concentration of skill and its tendency to become a company asset. Looking back on the period 1850-1880, he claimed that skilled engineers did have some *Handwerksmässig* (handicraft skill), which was readily exchangeable between the smaller factories and the bigger enterprises such as *Borsig, Wohlert* and *Schwartzkopf.* The types of jobs undertaken in the absence of the full force of the technical means made available by the later period allowed the engineer to use his bodily force and 'dexterity' *(Gewandtheit),* and also to apply a 'higher measure of intelligence'. In his view, 'this gave them the right, as the elite of the labour force, to be respected', especially those who made casts with the use of a chisel or made dextrous use of a file.[29] However, during and after the 1880s increased competition from Great Britain and America, as well as domestic pressures, compelled enterprises to increase to the highest possible level the 'organisation of the useful application of machines and human labour power'.[30] Thus:

> All this causes the position of the worker in the modern engineering works to be completely different from that in the older machine shops. The machine builder in the old, many sided, sense has become extinct. The worker has become a specialist who only learns certain parts of a job, and this he does from scratch again and again.[31]

Such descriptions found an echo in the pages of the *Archiv für Sozialwissenschaft und Sozialpolitik.* This journal was heavily influenced by Max Weber and his colleagues at Heidelberg, and sought to develop an objective sociological critique of modern German capitalism. It paid particular attention to how workers 'adapt' to modern industrial life and the 'choices' they had in their work. The pre-war *Auslese und Anpassung* studies, which were direct products of these concerns, especially those by Max Weber's brother, Alfred, Marie Bernays and Cl. Heiss, sought to demonstrate the fate of the industrial workers under modern conditions Bernays, for instance, drew a distinction between the fate of the traditional 'extensively' trained craft workers and the new, 'intensively' trained, skilled and semi-skilled workers. While the former had generally received an all-round training in their craft which allowed them to take up a lifelong vocation *(Beruf),* the latter now received an intensive training in only one or two aspects of the work. These workers, in contrast to craft workers, such as pattern makers and moulders, would often have to change their vocation or what was left of it, because the growing simplification of the division of labour had increased the range of partial, narrowly-based, easily teachable and *interchangeable* company skills. For example, turners at Daimler Motors were often to be found undertaking highly simplified work in fitting, wood turning, smithing and founding.[32] Heiss in his study of a Berlin precision engineering plant found much the same: smiths coming to work on automatic lathes, using bores, or in the fitting shop.[33]

Similar echoes of the development of a 'highly-specialised' workforce and of its dependency on the great firms which employed it also came from France. When Georges Friedmann looked back on the major transformation that had occurred to industrial training and skill compositions in the French metal industry in his classical work, *Problèmes humains du machinisme industriel,* he spoke of the inexorable tendency towards the 'degradation of craft skill',[34] which expressed itself in a loss of initiative in the methods of work and the parcellisation and specialisation of the division of labour. In place of the traditional 'journeyman' *(compagnon)* turner, who had served an apprenticeship for several years, who was a 'master' of his machine and who 'maintained a certain initiative', came a new category of turner: 'a specialised labourer'—'executing on a lathe a simple, specialised and repetitive job, where all the assemblies are prepared in advance by the planning office. As a result, initiative disappears, as does the personal bond with the machine and the use of the hammer and chisel'.[35] Even when an apprenticeship was available the newly-qualified worker would soon find that his professional career had been arrested, for he could neither leave his employ nor change his craft. Superior employment was increasingly denied to him for this qualification was not informed by a 'sufficient technical knowledge', which was ever more a monopoly of professional engineers and technicians, who formed an 'entirely separate caste' and whose 'professional intelligence' had been formed in the *Ecoles d'arts et métiers.*[36] Friedmann chose the metaphor of 'feudalism' to describe this tendency where access to the rigidly-structured caste of mental labour was by professional training only.[37]

In contrast to the emphasis placed by engineering observers on a *radical* decomposition and recomposition of proletarian skills, iron and steel observers at the beginning of this century were more impressed by the already lengthy existence of non-exchangeable and plant-specific company skills. The worker of the steel age, noted Hans Ehrenberg, had little or no craft heritage. He (and 'he' was invariably male) was always more semi-skilled than formally skilled. Only foundry and technical work required skilled workers with formal training; for the rest, a subtle hierarchy of readily reproducible skill and experience had evolved since 1870.[38]

At the bottom of the hierarchy stood the unskilled and inexperienced labourer who did the back-breaking work of carrying and loading.[39] There was certainly a self-protecting 'art in manual labouring', which workers such as Scotsman, Patrick McGeown, had to develop. It was essential:

xxi

. . . to know the right way to shovel, hammer, hold a wedge or a crowbar, carry loads, and to fill wheelbarrows. There is a rhythm in these actions which protects the heart, the lungs and brings serenity to the mind. Without that rhythm the muscles shriek, the chest is strained and the mind infested with frustration and anxiety.[40]

Yet exhausting drudgery and a continuous fight with shovelfuls of slag, coke and spilt metal was their essential manual vocation.[41] There then came the slightly trained jobs of coke burner, charger and lever operator; jobs where men had accumulated experience and picked up a little knowledge of the technical processes.[42] At seventeen-and-a-half, McGeown found that he could fill long metal boxes with lime, iron ore and scrap, and dispose of these contents mechanically into an open hearth furnace. Known as chargewheeling, McGeown felt that he had 'learned a trade', especially as he was already 'good with a hammer and good with a shovel'.[43] In Ehrenberg's view, there then came those workers with some 'special ability' or accumulated dexterity, with a little more knowledge of technical processes: the behind rollers in the rolling mills and the No. 3 melters at the blast furnace and open hearth furnaces.[44]

When McGeown became a No. 3 melter his work consisted of furiously shovelling alloys into a furnace under instruction, helping to tap a furnace and repairing it when damaged. Again the work was strenuous.[45] Finally, there came the fully experienced worker who knew how to supervise the technical process, and when sudden disturbances occurred knew how to rectify them. Here the 'art' consisted in the accumulation of practical experience and judgment. It was the work of the No. 1 roller, the No. 1 blast furnace smelter and the No. 1 melter at the steel furnace.[46] For the youthful McGeown, watching the work of a No. 1 melter, here was the act of creation. The melter was the one who 'watched the metal stream from his furnace into the waiting ladle'; he was the one with 'an awareness of creation', who for seven or eight hours had tended to solid limestone, steel scrap, and hot iron surging into a white hot liquid; he was the one who 'controlled the huge flame which played over the metal, saw that it did its work, and that it didn't damage the furnace's brick roof or linings'; who for hour after hour 'watched for every change in the liquid, increased the slag contents with more lime, or thinned it out with iron ore'.[47] This was a job where one could be in love with the work, be a 'perfectionist';[48] where if the furnace bath collapsed and a chaotic mass of sparkling molten metal burst onto the floor a melter faced suspension for a week and a complete loss of confidence in his abilities; where he could become a 'bundle of nerves and hesitations'; where he could sometimes do the 'unorthodox' and get away with it; where luck could be with him or against him; where he could measure his own skill against another's and exclaim, '[You] should be making ice-cream!'[49]

The No. 1 melter was also a man who probably had no *knowledge* of what steel actually was, except that it was a 'tough metal'. At least, that was the response of one melter to McGeown's tough questioning.[50] He was also a man ever more dependent on the modern 'samplepasser'—the laboratory chemist. Until the end of the nineteenth century the sample-passer was the foreman, who crystallised in himself the authority and the knowledge of all the steel melting jobs at the furnace. His special task was to assess a sample of the No. 1 melter's work in order to see if the metal was ready to be tapped.[51] By the end of the century, however, McGeown noticed that the samplepasser was more often a 'superintendent' who 'looks to the laboratory to confirm his practical knowledge'; technology in his view was indeed decimating personal skills more and more'.[52]

It is certainly not the case that metal industry observers of the early twentieth century failed to detect a certain continuity of traditional skills. Fritz Schulte, in describing the situation in Berlin, was quite aware of the persistence of the 'old machine shop and machine builder':

> Right in Berlin there is still a whole series of small machine shops where the skill of the hand guiding the tool has to take the place of the skill performed by complicated machine tools in large establishments. With few exceptions, the rule in these small workshops is that always the same machines are made by a group of older, experienced workers with the personal involvement of the factory owner, who is at the same time his own head foreman. The workers carry out the most varied operations, one after another, as they arise in production. In the modern engineering works, by contrast, casts or forgings wander from the bench of one worker to that of another after every single specialised task. A second worker now adds his labour and then passes the piece onto a third worker, who, for his part, knows nothing of the specialised production tasks of his predecessors. His competence does not extend one hairsbreadth further than boring a hole of prescribed diameter into something with a machine at the exact spot designated to him. In this connection, there was, and to a certain extent still is, a greater variety and diversity of separate production tasks in the older machine shops. So far, human labour has not yet become a mere appendage of the machine, which is the case in the machine shops of the large engineering works.[53]

Otto Jeidels' description of the Rhineland's travelling fitters (*Auswarts-monteur*) is another example. Enterprises which built bridges, gas works, and installed plant and equipment for other enterprises, such as Düssel-dorf's *Benrather Maschinenfabrik,* would send off one or several of the experienced fitters to supervise the installation of the equipment. These were men whose work gave them an unusual amount of freedom, respon-sibility, travel, not to say high wages.[54] In pre-war London engineering works, observers like N.B. Dearle noticed a virtual absence of semi-skilled machine workers, as well as an overall continuity of unified skills, such as fitting and turning. In Dearle's view the nature of the engineering industry in London, with its emphasis on ship repairing firms, new ship construct-ion firms in the outer suburbs and in South London, repair and small order shops, and firms under contract to other businesses to keep their machinery in order, meant that there was a great need for all-round engineers, who could turn their hands to both fitting and turning—who could turn and prepare work in the workshop first and then go out onto a ship and fit it up.[55] As well as an awareness of the continuity of traditional metal skills, observers were equally aware of the rise of new, non-managerial and yet professional shop skills: what Georges Friedmann termed for France a *'nouvel artisanat'* (new artisanry). These were workers who, because of rationalisation and the progress of machine-based precision metal work, undertook the task of building into these machines their characteristics of delicacy, precision and 'polyvalence'. They worked in a company's toolshop making jigs and fixtures; or in a highly specialised model shop making models of new machinery; or in steel factories employed as 'electric arc welders, oxyacetylene cutters, machine welders, (and) on electric furnaces for the treatment of special steels etc., . . . or in the job preparation rooms as technicians in charge of studying tools and determining job processes and production times, etc. . .'[56]

These were the workers who were described by Abaut as *'les ouvriers d'art'.* For both Abaut and Friedmann these new artisans increased their relative number, while technical progress disqualified and diminished the number of those engaged in actual manual production.[57] Such sensitivies, however, were overwhelmed by an appreciation of what was seen to be a general tendency towards the decomposition of manual skills by technical change, a diminution of an individual worker's responsibility in the labour process and of its increasing monopolisation by management. Schulte was very exacting in explaining the 'principle' whereby machinery is substituted for human labour. Mechanisation was nearing the point where human labour is theoretically reduced to 'zero'. From a practical point of view, of course, a certain amount of customary work remained: 'namely, fitting up assemblies, setting machinery and starting it up. . . Here one has to work carefully. However, every establishment seeks, if possible, to reduce each individual worker's amount of responsibility'.[58]

(iii) Psycho-physical labour

If there was a concept that tended to sum up the changes many contemporaries saw occurring to the mental and manual faculties used in direct production and its management, it was that human labour was increasingly *psycho-physical* in character. This term requires some explanation, as it has been largely lost to present-day historians of work and has no widespread popular currency. The psycho-physical study of work was first begun by Omer Buyse, who, in pre-war years was head of the University of Labour in Charleroi, Belgium. In 1910 he published in France a major work in the *Revue Psychologique,* entitled, *'Le probléme psycho-physique de l'Apprentissage'.* His collaborator, and the future heir to his work, was Josefa Ioteyko, who was at the same time head of the

xxiv

Laboratory of Psychology and Physiology at Brussels University and during the War ran a course on fatigue at the *Collège de France* in Paris. Both of these *managerial scientists* originally began their work by attempting to explain 'the want of harmony between the old form of apprenticeship and [the] technical capacity requisite at the present day'.[59] They were struck by what they saw as a complete asymmetry between older forms of industrial training and the training that was needed in the new methods of production. Like the American scientific managers, they were concerned not so much with the 'value of workmanship' (which 'always is, and will remain forever, the decisive element in the development of the *capacity* of production'),[60] but rather with the introduction of automatic and semi-automatic tools and of the system of serial operations, which 'profoundly modify the qualities required in a workman'.[61]

These qualities were seen to be a combination of 'refined aptitude' and 'specific physical requirements', which can both be studied and taught.[62] More precisely these were qualities which concerned the study and teaching of workers in the consequences of specialisation: that is, in the 'adaption of a psycho-physical apparatus to certain particular conditions of action', which required training workers in how to economise their 'nervous flux' in undertaking a particular task; in the importance of using small and undeveloped muscles rather than larger and more developed muscles, given the lighter and more precise nature of work; and finally, in the need for voluntary attention and concentration.[63] Overall, the development of a psycho-physical apparatus in a worker consisted in teaching a 'rapidity and precision of movement' and a 'degree of control. . . over his movements and their coordination'.[64] It was a coordination where manual skill was seen not so much in terms of tough and dextrous manual labour, but in terms of its adaptation to repetitive processes, which required a modicum of mental acuity—attention. It was an attention whose point of departure was the substitution of *nervous* for physical *fatigue*. It was in the end, an *'habileté'* or ability, which depended on the psychological characteristics of the individual worker, and whose inversion was the *'habileté professionnelle'* of the white-collar or 'bourgeois' mental labourer—the professional employee.[65]

Such a sense of the growing polarisation of faculties and abilities used in production was definitely not limited to practising engineers, managerial scientists and middle-class observers. In Britain, the working-class poet and rural philosopher, Alfred Williams, gave vent to similar sentiments in 1915, after having worked at Swindon's Great Western Railway Engineering shops for over twenty years:

A decade and a half ago one could come to the shed fearlessly, and with perfect complacence; work was a pleasure in comparison with what it is now. It is not that the toil was easy, though as a matter of fact, it was not so exhausting as it is at present, but there was an entirely different feeling prevalent. The workman was not watched and timed at every little operation, and he knew that as the job had been one day so it would be the next. Now, however, every day brings fresh trouble from some quarter or other. The supervisory staff has been doubled or trebled, and they must do something to justify their existence. Before the workman can recover from one knock he is visited with another; he is kept in a state of continual agitation and suspense which, in turn, operate on his mind and temper and transform his whole character.

At one time old and experienced hands were trusted and respected, both by reason of their great knowledge of the work, acquired through many years, and as a kind of tacit recognition of their long connection with the firm, but now, when a man has been in the shed for twenty years, however young he may be, he is no longer wanted. There is now a real desire to be rid of him. For one thing his wages are high. In addition to this, he knows too much; he is not pliable. It is time he was shifted to make room for someone lower paid, more plastic and more ignorant of the inner working of things.[66]

Across the Channel, the leader of the French Metalworkers' Union, Alphonse Merrheim, forcefully posed what he thought happened to the worker, 'as soon as [he] passed through the gate of the immense factory. He has the impression that his personality disappears'.

His first productive act hurls him into the anonymous crowd of other producers, lost, swamped and automised in the general techniques of production. Labour is just one motion, constant, automatic and repeated and workers accept this most trying condition as imposed on them by their destiny.[67]

2. Present-day findings

If many contemporaries sought to illuminate, in a complex manner, the *ensemble* of skills they saw evolving and describe how these became locked into patterns of class organisation in the factory, historians and social theorists have generally only emphasised one aspect of this relation, often to the exclusion of the other.

The German social theorist, Ralph Dahrendorf, for example, celebrates what he sees as the growing differentiation of the workforce since the end of the nineteenth century in order to substantiate his claim that modern class structures do not have a tendency to polarise around two irreconcilable and antagonistic points, around a bourgeoisie and a proletariat. In his now classic work, *Class and Class Conflict in Industrial Society,* he argues that the development of a labour force in a modern industrial society has taken place in two stages. He takes Germany as a case in point and contends that, in the period up to the end of the nineteenth century, the proletariat had little social, economic or skill differentiations, while in the period of modern and mature capitalism the proletariat has become much more differentiated into layers of status, skill, dexterity and economic rewards.[68] Dahrendorf's explicitly Weberian conception of social and economic differentiation was here mobilised

xxvi

against what he saw as an out-dated Marxist view that modern industrial capitalism tends towards the creation of an economically and technically more homogeneous proletariat.[69]

An interesting response to Dahrendorf's argument came some years ago from the historian, Wolfram Fischer. Fischer did not wish to argue against Dahrendorf's conception of the modern period. Rather, he sought to show an equally well-established, if not more refined hierarchy of training, skill and economic rewards in German industry in the first half of the nineteenth century. Contrary to earlier historians—who saw the first phase of industrialisation in terms of the departure of trained and skilled craft workers and the arrival of the unskilled and untrained, to be followed in the modern period by more skilled and highly-trained workers—Fischer demonstrated the well-rooted social, economic and skill distinctions amongst workers in German industry from the early to mid-nineteenth century. Neither skill nor job hierarchies ever left the scene in order to re-emerge later, he argued.[70] Yet Fischer was as much concerned to smack Marxist historians over the knuckles as he was to wave a finger at excessive Weberianism. From his studies of job and skill pyramids in the early nineteenth-century German metal industry, he wrote that there was 'no unified mass of workers formed in opposition to the employer'. Rather, workers were positioned into a 'graded structure of authority' and integrated into a 'pyramid-like hierarchy of work'.[71]

If we turn to some of the important accounts by Marxist historians, particularly from America, the emphasis is indeed on the general tendency of modern industry to create an economically and *technically more homogeneous workforce,* where any divisions of job skill and status are seen to have been artificially induced by employers in order to dilute the increasing solidarity of workers that is brought about by technical change. This argument has gained particular currency of late through the work of historians such as Katherine Stone and Dan Clawson,[72] both of whom have been inspired by the late Harry Braverman's treatise, *Labour and Monopoly Capital: The Degradation of Work in the Twentieth Century.*[73] This work has resurrected many of the contemporary observations about the destruction of craftsmanship in the late nineteenth century and of the subtle hierarchies of skill, status, economic rewards and political power which were allegedly razed so that a more homogeneous, pliable and less skilled workforce could be formed.

Braverman, for example, not only laments the destruction of craftsmanship and the tendency in the late nineteenth century towards the creation of a more homogeneous proletariat, but also argues that the best formulation for appreciating the changing methods of industrial training and the decline of skill—a formulation which in his view has not been succeeded for fifty years—is that this was a conscious attack by management on the craftsmen and on their working knowledge in the daily practice of their

xxvii

craft.[74] In general terms, this is part of an inexorable tendency, whereby 'new methods and new machinery are incorporated within a management effort to dissolve the labour process as a process conducted by the worker and to reconstitute it as a process conducted by management'.[75] Katherine Stone took up many of these arguments in her study of the American steel industry at the turn of the century. She suggests that during the nineteenth century steel was made by 'highly skilled industrial craftsmen who enjoyed high prestige in their communities'.[76] By the 1890s the mechanisation drive had drastically changed this situation. Traditional skills like 'heating, roughing, catching and rolling were built into the new machines' and supervised by a semi-skilled workforce.[77] The new technology narrowed skill differentials and led to an 'homogenisation' of the workforce.[78] In response to potential and real collective agitations from workers, employers began to stratify this newly homogenised workforce by the introduction of strictly demarcated job ladders which had no basis in the technical criteria of steel production, but which were in fact designed to fend off the 'labour problem' brought about by mechanisation and the dilution of skill.[79] David Gordon, Richard Edwards and Michael Reich, sociologists by profession, are also partisans of this perspective, if only reluctantly so. They too see the formation of an homogenised workforce during this period; though they would add that during the 1920s and 1930s there was a move away from this situation, as labour markets, firms and production processes became more segmented and differentiated.[80]

These concerns with the early composition of the industrial workforce seem to have come a full circle. Several Anglo-American writers and historians, disillusioned with the theses put forward by the late Harry Braverman, have sought to reassert the validity of the traditional Weberian argument from what I term a neo-Taylorist perspective. Charles Sabel, for instance, has convinced himself, after reading about and visiting many factories, that 'workers were neither a homogeneous class united in opposition to management nor a mass of individuals eager for their own reasons to cooperate. . . with the bosses. Rather, it seemed that in factory after factory in different countries and times the workforce was regularly split along skill lines into distinct groups, perpetuating themselves in different ways'.[81] The Weberian colouring of this line of reasoning comes with the suggestion that workers, like other groups in society, such as 'peasants, white-collar workers, upper level managers, shopkeepers, intellectuals, soldiers', 'ambiguously' relate to each other and other groups.[82] The 'progress' of the division of labour furthers the cause of these ambiguities and separate interests, as no 'one type of work' will come to dominate the labour market. Rather, changes to the division of labour 'will alter the mix of jobs in subtle ways, at one and the same time creating unskilled work, blurring the lines between craft and semi-skilled jobs, and

xxviii

creating demand for various new skills'.[83]

Such a view may not be far removed from the conventional sociologies of work propounded by Dahrendorf and Fischer, yet there is a new departure, or more exactly a renewal. Sabel, like the scientific managers R.F. Hoxie described, would have us believe that, 'an increase in the division of labour creates demand for a mixture of new skills even as it destroys old ones'. The expansion of the division of labour may slowly reduce 'the average skill level', but 'some craftsmen', for example, 'will be able to augment their skills', while new possibilities will open up for semi-skilled work at the *middle range* of the blue-collar hierarchy'.[84] These possibilities include the unskilled and semi-skilled gaining access to *'substantial amounts* of skill' and higher positions, which comprise *learning* how to use new machines, gaining knowledge of an individual machine's quirks, and finally learning how to avoid errors or to rectify them. From this vantage point the semi-skilled workers especially have substantial power over the individual employer, particularly when it comes to not disrupting or sabotaging costly machinery. For craftsmen, the possibilities include learning about the abstract and practical principles of new machinery so that it may be installed and repaired from time to time. Overall then, 'technological *progress* leads to an upgrading of the skills of *workers* who service, repair, draw plans for and even participate in the design of new machines'.[85] From this perspective, a material hierarchy of jobs and its corollary, on-the-job-training, are indeed essential for factory management and production. Furthermore, this reality encourages workers to master 'substantial skills', though, in the last instance, this may be subservient to a managerially controlled promotions policy.[86]

The Taylorist foundations of this approach are to be found not only in the emphasis given to technical *progress* opening up new opportunities for the upgrading of the workforce, particularly in the middle range of the production hierarchy and in the servicing and design of new machinery; it is also to be found in the notion of skill as an *amount,* which both has an *average* and is diffused throughout the division of labour in lumps. In later chapters many of these points are taken up in light of the evidence to be presented on changes to industrial training, but some comments are in order here.

In comparison with the observations of contemporaries, what is noticeably missing from this perspective is any idea that the workforce and its division of labour may have more than one, average dimension. There is no conception of the division of labour as an ensemble of applied faculties organised around the labour of planning and direct production. Also, there is no sense that these faculties may themselves be structured and fractured by a social relation between the bourgeoisie and the proletariat, where one party tends to form itself around the labour of superintendence and management and the other around direct production. These comments are equally applicable to the arguments made by the earlier sociologists such as Dahrendorf; but Dahrendorf did have a great respect for the historical process. What is absent from the neo-Taylorist argument, however, is any feel for the historical lineages of training and skill, which is so essential for defining what is or is not 'substantial skill'. This applies not only to the problem of the substance of the previous skills workers may have had but lost in the past; it also applies to a larger historical process, which contemporary observers picked up very quickly at the beginning of this century; the process where a professionalised minority *come to have* and *monopolise* the *really substantial skills* of management, design, engineering, chemistry, commerce and accounting. It would seem to be a complete vulgarisation and degradation of the term 'skill' to hold on the same plane the 'substantial skill' of *not doing something,* such as not sabotaging or disrupting a machine, with the truly substantial skill of its positive design. By defining skill in such a derogatory fashion, it becomes very difficult to assess what impact the formation of these larger skills had on the vast majority of workers engaged in direct production, especially on what they really learnt or were allowed to learn.

This can be called a qualitative perspective, in contrast to the quantitative perspective of neo-Taylorism. Where the latter has a quite myopic vision of an 'average skill level', the former raises the possibility of a qualitative polarisation of faculties used in production. Where the latter has a one-dimensional view of technical *progress* opening up new possibilities for the upgrading of the workforce, even if only for a few, the latter raises the possibility of a *progressive* differentiation of the workforce opening up new possibilities for the *up*grading of management, the extension of its hierarchy within the workplace, and the *de*grading of faculties workers use in direct production. In contrast to the potential richness of this perspective, all neo-Taylorism has to offer is a blinkered, anti-historical approach, quantitative in character and empirical only in form: 'Industrialists create different kinds of jobs'[87]; not one that explains for what reasons, how, why or when.

3. The national question
How have more nationally-orientated studies come to grips with these issues? It can be readily shown that in Britain, many contemporaries and historians alike, have been struck by the relative failure of British enterprise to adapt to the new methods of industrial training or to undertake the task of recomposing skills in a progressive manner. Two reasons have generally been put forward for this: the absence of a structural commitment to mechanise and specialise production because of the existence of a workforce highly trained in manual handicraft skills; and associated with this, an absence of formal, state, professional and industrial training programmes in the new methods and techniques of

production.

The first line of reasoning was well expressed in a series of articles published in late 1899 and early 1900 in the technically progressive journal, *Fielden's Magazine*. 'It must be remembered', claimed the leader article for January 1900, 'that the producing industries of this country have been founded for many years upon accomplished manual labour, replenished by apprentices. In the past, British producing industry has been made and founded upon craftsmanship'.[88] This foundation of technical practice on craftsmanship was discussed in some depth by the magazine's famed engineering correspondent, Ewert C. Amos, some months before. 'Why do we not encourage the automatic machine to the same extent?', he asked in comparison with what he saw as occurring in America.

> There is probably more than one answer to this question, but the first one that occurs is, that the present position of our labour question is against the extensive use of those machines which require little attention and unskilled artisans to work them.

Though Amos looked forward to this being only 'a transitory state of things', he still gave voice to the 'old idea, so prevalent in this country and in Europe generally, that machinery should assist rather than supplement the skilled worker'. This had its advantages, for it enabled 'the European to completely oust the American from the market in those products which still are and probably always will be, dependent upon skilled labour'.[89]

Whether seen with some optimism or with outright pessimism, such impressions have formed the raw material for the conclusions of historians,[90] and, if anything, the drift of much recent historical work has been to draw out of Britain's 'relative backwardness' the relative advantages of her long-standing commitment to a highly-trained handicraft workforce. This is especially apparent in the work of Pollard and Robertson on the shipbuilding industry, of Saul's work on the engineering industry, and in a general commentary by C.K. Harley.[91]

Harley's work, because it provides an overview of the situation in the shipbuilding, engineering and iron and steel industries, requires some attention. Being concerned with the economics of skilled labour and the 'choice of technique', Harley suggests that Britain's relatively slow drive to replace skilled craft labour with machinery operated by semi-skilled labour was because it was not only cheaper than its American and German counterpart, but also because many of the modern technical processes which Britain took up required a highly-skilled workforce. A relative abundance of such labour existed in Britain, he argues. Referring to the British steel industry's early commitment to the open-hearth process, Harley suggests that the process was not an irrational choice. It is true that the open-hearth process relied on a relatively skilled and highly experienced

xxxi

workforce. Also the steel could be economically produced in small plants, without the integration associated with the Bessemer process—i.e. mechanical handling, large blast furnaces and by-product recovery equipment. However, the products from this process were of superior quality. And, it was precisely these products which supplied the rapidly-advancing heavy engineering and shipbuilding trades, which were themselves reliant on a highly-trained and skilled workforce. Far in advance, then, of the French, German and American steel trades in the field quality output, the British steel industry can be seen as progressively exploiting its natural advantage of skilled labour.[92]

A younger generation of historians have further developed this line of reasoning, and sought to demonstrate its social and political consequences. This is particularly so of the work of Charles More, Alistair Reid, Jonathan Zeitlin, and Joseph Melling. As much of their work remains in the form of unpublished dissertations, especially Reid's important study already referred to, it would be unfair of any writer to enter into a public debate given the status of their work at the present time. Some of it is available, however, in the form of journal articles and, in More's case, a book on skill itself. The centrepiece of Charles More's work is a study of craft skills and whether these can be seen as either the product of restrictive practices by workers with or without managerial collusion, i.e. socially-based skills, or really 'genuine': being part and parcel of work and the practice of a trade.[93] On the issue of the actual role of craft skill in the engineering industry, he suggests, in light of allegedly *profound* changes to the division of labour during World War 1, that engineering workers' skills were 'considerable' and 'genuine'. Certainly, this was what employers *believed* when they referred to the major changes required to put less skilled men and women to work during the war. Furthermore, these dilutees never took over the whole of a skilled craftsman's job anyway. They were limited to work that was revolutionised by the introduction of semi-automatic machinery affixed with jigs and stops, so that the operative did not have to change the tools or adjust the pieces being machined.[94] From this vantage point he believes that before the war a combination of technical and market constraints in the engineering industry prevented a recomposition of skills and methods of industrial training. The industry, in reality, 'encouraged diversified rather than standardised output; (and) the result of this was that the technology of the industry demanded the skilled, all-round worker, and the all-purpose lathe which could be switched to different types of production'.[95] The bulk of work, therefore, required a very high degree of skill, and it was only economic that skilled workers with an all-round training be employed.[96] The implication here is that only with mass production techniques could one expect radical changes to skill compositions and training methods.[97] In this context, other historians consider 'the widespread survival of craftsmen in engineering. . .

xxxii

particularly striking'.[98] In fact, they occupied a 'dominant position in the division of labour'.[99] When the full force of this argument is brought to bear on the work of the late Harry Braverman, it is affirmed that he was quite wrong to believe that skills and training methods could be unilaterally decided by employers. 'Management had little control. . . over skill levels', according to More.[100] At the same time, neither could unions regulate skills required in production. Thus the only possible explanation is a purely technical one: it was just not possible for any party to regulate skill compositions and training methods at this time given the fractured state of the markets and the nature of the technologies in use.[101] Joseph Melling has taken up many of these same themes in his own work, especially the 'contrary to Braverman' idea, that there was 'no simple pattern of de-skilling in modern industry'. The workforce was both upgraded and degraded.[102] Whether Braverman needs to be criticised from this point of view will be considered at various points in this story, but what cannot go unnoticed are the similarities between these arguments and those put forward by Sabel. There is, in the first instance, a common emphasis on the diffusion of considerable or substantial skills amongst the workforce, whether these be craft-based or not; second, there is a singular or quantitative emphasis on the characteristics of the workforce as such, independent of any qualitative fissures that may shape the organisation of mental and manual labour or the formation of social classes within an enterprise. In other words, there is no way of telling whether such skills, if they did 'genuinely' exist, were anything more than a specialised competence subject to managerial design and effectively subordinate to managerial control. There is, lastly, no analysis of managerial skills, as such, or how an examination of these would affect the understanding of skills in general. Overall, it seems that the fissures and divisions in the market place are more important than those intrinsically generated by the workplace.

The second line of reasoning which seeks to address Britain's relative failure to absorb new methods of industrial training and recompose skills can be gleaned from the contemporary observations of Charles Hobson, a Sheffield cutler by trade and for a time a leader of the International Metalworkers' Federation. Speaking on the advantages that continental countries had in their methods of production over the British, Hobson noted that their success was 'mainly the result of their having a better system of technical education, specially directed to the teaching of trade, coupled with a better system of apprenticeship or indenture, and compulsory attendance at school during the apprenticeship period, the sole purpose being to thoroughly teach a trade, including its organisation in production and distribution of manufacture'.[103] The role of the state was seen to be crucial in the promotion of technical education on the Continent, with the result that 'the working classes have moved up from the bottom all along the line; the congested surplus of unemployed non-

xxxiii

skilled labour has disappeared, and at the top a well-employed and numerous set of skilled workmen are busy at work'.[104]

Perhaps the most famous critique of British industrial training from this point of view is that of David Landes. For him the British education system was never intended to systematically 'find and advance talent'.[105] Referring to the Education Act of 1870, he argues that it was designed to 'discipline a growing mass of disaffected proletarians and integrate them into British society'.[106] This primary education system left a lot to be desired. Technical training also in the late nineteenth century was uneven and inadequate, and too dependent on the meagre resources of private initiative.[107] Whether this took the form of gruelling evening classes for the working class or of establishment and business contempt for graduates in science and technology, the sum effect was an education system which could neither advance social mobility nor technical and vocational talent.[108] According to Landes, Britain therefore lacked the skills and knowledge which would have enabled her to absorb the major technical and organisational changes that were occurring in European industry.[109]

Many other historians have taken up and developed these themes. A.L. Levine laments the 'cult of amateurism', empiricism, and the general neglect of scientific training and technical education in industry at apprenticeship, entrepreneurial and professional levels.[110] P.W. Musgrave's study of the British steel industry is a catalogue of lamentations about the low prestige of science, the poor supply of trained chemists and teachers, the absence of any organic continuity between primary and secondary education, and the industrial middle class's imitation of the non-scientific manners of the upper class.[111] Trade unions also cannot be allowed to escape their share of the blame, at least according to Levine. In his view, they blocked off potential changes to industrial training and the introduction of new skills by their restrictive practices and attempts to 'follow the machine'.[112] Eric Hobsbawm, though, seeks to chide 'the deficiencies of the private enterprise mechanism' itself for failing to bring about the necessary changes, due to the consequences of a pioneering bourgeoisie resting on its laurels and supinely imitating truculent 'anti-intellectual, anti-scientific, (and) games-dominated tory imperialism'.[113] 'The British', in his view, 'therefore entered the twentieth century and the age of modern science and technology as a spectacularly ill-educated people'.[114]

Professor François Crouzet offers a French perspective on this theme. Summarising all the recent work which constitutes the 'decline of Britain' debate, he claims that of all the explanations advanced, the one that emphasised the 'human factors' has the greatest claim on our attention, i.e. the 'outlook, attitudes and social values' of Victorian society.[115] In a society run by 'civilised amateurs', with none of the 'harsh character and rough manners' of their grandparents, they could not 'achieve the marriage of science and industry', nor could they provide an educational system which could 'give the entrepreneurs, managers, executives, foremen and operatives the scientific and technical training which they needed'.[116] In a society formed around the 'mystique' of 'practical experience' and contemptuous of technical or scientific training for those who ran the industries, it is hardly surprising that the national state would also mirror these values, with its 'policy of parsimony and *laissez-faire* in the fields of education and research'.[117] In contrast to Germany, where technical and scientific education were held in high esteem at this time, Britain 'cut a poor figure'.[118]

If there is, then, a fair amount of unanimity amongst British contemporary observers and historians concerning a blockage to the recomposition of skills and to new methods of industrial training, opinion in Germany is divided. This division is concerned with whether German employers, especially in the engineering industry, took their labour force as given and unchangeable or whether in collaboration with the state they actively shaped and directed the making of a trained workforce at all levels of production.

The first impression is apparent in the views of contemporary managerial ideologists and rationalisation theorists, such as George Schlesinger, who sought to use the yardstick of pure Taylorism in order to measure the presence or absence of change in German industry. Schlesinger forcefully conveyed to the 54th Assembly of the German Engineers' Association in 1913, the lamentable fact that employers continued to treat the labour force as given and 'unalterable' *(unabänderliche)* and that too much attention had been given to the improvement of techniques of production.[119] Integral to this view was a belief that a stratum of skilled craft workers played a leading and apparently unalterable role in the labour process because of their technical knowledge of production. Writing at the beginning of the twentieth century on the state of the German engineering industry, Paul Steller claimed that 'the skilled engineering workers have always formed an elite of factory workers':

> This derives from their technical training, upon which the greatest value is placed by enterprises. This is why the apprenticeship system in engineering has great economic significance and why nearly all the large engineering establishments train many apprentices.[120]

A number of English-speaking historians have developed these impressions. Peter Stearns has argued that the expansion of the German engineering industry after 1895 led to an increase in skilled labour rather than to a decline.[121] J.J. Lee, more cautious, but equally unambiguous, argues that the 'available evidence scarcely sustains the cataclysmic visions of the massive technological obsolescence of skilled workers', which in his view many of the 'hysterical' accounts of the *Auslese und Anpassung* surveys sought to present by 'generalising impressionistically from spectacular but extreme instances'.[122] Though there was a major rise in the number of white-collar workers, German industry was stood in good stead by the 'reservoir of skilled labour' that had been formed in the nineteenth century, whose 'very quality may have helped to delay the adoption of assembly-line techniques and the conversion of production processes to techniques suitable for unskilled and semi-skilled workers'.[123]

Two German Marxist historians have gone even further. Karl Heinz Roth and Eckhard Brockhaus, inspired by the work of the Italian 'mass worker theses',[124] stress the rigid continuity in the engineering industry of a 'craft mode of production', where a stratum of highly skilled, 'professional-technical workers' *(Facharbeiter-Techniker)* was integral to the technical structure of production and worked in 'direct cooperation' with their similarly highly trained 'employer-technician' *(Unternehmer-Erfinder)*. Occupying a 'professional position' in production, at least until the war, it was impossible for any engineering enterprise in the investment goods industries to assume a dominant position for any length of time without calling on these workers' 'spirit of discovery' *(Erfindungsgeist)* and without cultivating their full identification with the technical aims of production.[125] Why? Because this 'pre-formed stratum of craft workers' brought to the factory their knowledge and dexterity as their own personal properties. In these direct producers was united knowledge, creativity and dexterity that was so essential for continuous production.[126] Only in the non-craft industries, such as the steel industry, could one detect a radical recomposition of skills and methods of training, where labour was being reduced to a more homogeneous, semi-skilled level, to a more 'abstract labour-power'.[127]

The work of David Landes, however, begins from a completely different point of departure. He emphasises the consequences of continental countries such as Germany, having to import skills and techniques from abroad during the nineteenth century. In his view the various German states, private associations and enterprises all cooperated in facilitating both 'man-to-man transmission of skills on the job' and in the creation of formal training programmes for mechanics and engineers: at the highest level *Hauptbergwerks-Instituten* for professional engineers; mechanical training schools for technicians and skilled workers; 'and at the bottom a heterogeneous group of local courses sometimes private, sometimes public, in manual arts, design, and the rudiments of calculation'.[128]

Lacking the necessary skills and scientific knowledge which would underwrite economical production, Germany undertook policies of imparting to its workforce: '(1) the ability to read, write, and calculate; (2) the working skills of the craftsman and the mechanic; (3) the engineer's combination of scientific principle and applied training; and

xxxvi

(4) a high level scientific knowledge, theoretical and applied.'[129] Far from taking the labour force as given and unalterable, far from relying on a pre-formed stratum of craft workers and far from relying on their spirit of discovery, the implication of Landes' work is that the German state, private associations and business enterprises *made* their own labour force at all levels, and were consciously aware of their doing so in a continuous manner. It is Landes' emphasis on the active 'imparting' of skills and knowledge to a workforce through a process of 'cultural diffusion'[130] which suggests a radically different formation of the labour force in Germany to that suggested by the craft historians. *Prima facie* his argument is more in tune with the general observations of Marie Bernays, Schulte and Jeidels concerning the rise of a more activist management, where the training of labour and the use of skills were becoming teachable company assets rather than the integral properties of a privileged group of workers. Landes' argument here will hold a special place in this work, for it is not only an accurate pointer to how the metal industry's workforce was formed in Germany, it also has a lot to say about the formation of the French and British metal workforces. Though, as we shall see, the *particular* patterns of historical development differed in all three countries.

Debate in early twentieth-century France on the level of its adaptation to new methods of training and on the introduction of new skill compositions had many similarities to that going on in Britain at the time. In a series of articles published between January and November 1906, the *Revue de Métallurgie* took up the cudgels to promote the virtues of professional technical education, because of the widespread 'lack of interest' in movements developing in America, Britain and Germany, such as the growth of works laboratories and of scientific universities, like that at Sheffield.[131] While for many years Germany had been perfecting its system and while England had been revamping its own over the previous twelve years, French industrialists demonstrated more interest in improving their tools and machines rather than in improving the 'intelligent tool', the engineer.[132] Such 'indifference' to such a 'vital question for the industry of our country' was 'incomprehensible'.[133] Concerned with its own claim that French industry could absorb three times the number of professional technical personnel than was taking place at the time, the *Revue* took a great interest in the weaknesses of enterprises led by the sons of founding fathers, who with just some 'knowledge of the initial techniques (of production) would avoid an over-expenditure of energy in getting to the top of their occupations'.[134] If 'a very great number of industrialists' gave 'insufficient attention to the importance of technical training', then so also did the education system.[135]

Technical education in the schools by itself is incapable of training engineers or foremen ready to perform useful labour in the factories. Everyone agrees on this point today. Theoretical instruction facilitates the acquisition of practical knowledge, but cannot supply it. It is an absolute necessity then for the personnel running the factories to receive a two-fold education: a theoretical education in the schools and a practical education in the factories.[136]

Such impressions have provided the necessary grist for the mills of English-speaking and French historians. The American historian, A.L. Dunham, looks as far back as the 1820s in order to reveal that French engineers, though very well trained in theory, 'lacked practical experience'.[137] The French historian, Guy Palmade, when seeking to describe the tendency of French business to 'cling to traditional practices and to show intolerance to new ideas', is equally concerned with the problem of scientists 'too obsessed by theories' and technologists who 'did not pay enough attention to their [the scientists] research work'. 'Scientific discoveries', especially in the chemical industry, 'were seldom put into practice. . . In the key sectors of the industry no one seemed to favour a close collaboration with the pure scientist or an intimate liaison between the laboratory and factory'.[138]

With regard to the training of the manual workforce contemporary and historical observations are even more stinging. Senator Astier, President of the Commission on Technical Education in France, writing in *Le Journal* in May 1917, looked back on why technical education reform had stagnated since 1905 when it was officially recognised to be in need of radical change. The reason, he argued, was the widespread custom in France to look down on manual work as demeaning. Manual labour was seen as 'servile work' by the middle class who wished their sons to enter the professions, and by the working class who wished to scale the heights into the middle class.[139] In a recent study, Yves Lequin has sought to place responsibility for this situation at the feet of the ruling classes who 'were indifferent to the needs of the economy and failed to understand its dynamic. . . Everything combined to bring about a general downgrading of the French workforce at all levels on the eve of the First World War'.[140]

Both of these lines of reasoning are part of a larger criticism of the blockages to rationalisation in French industry due to the dominance of social and economic values which laid emphasis on taste and skilled craftsmanship. Tom Kemp in his studies of the stagnation of the French economy in the nineteenth century argues that the French ruling class's predilection to satisfy their high 'quality' tastes after the work of skilled craftsmen choked off the development of low-cost production and machine technology.[141] According to François Crouzet, this meant that successful French manufacturers were prone to take advantage of specialising in products where 'quality, fashion, (and) luxury' had a market premium placed on them, especially when the labour supply was 'both skilled and cheap'.[142] In a context where there was no structural shortage of skilled labour and where upper-class markets seemed to be guaranteed, there seemed little need for the introduction of sophisticated training methods, let alone any realisation of them.[143]

This long, international dialogue on the alleged failings of French business and education, which has been running hot ever since the last war, has been rounded off most recently by Clive Trebilcock, who considers that 'elusive influences', such as 'French value patterns, French tastes, [and] the heterogeneous nature of France's cultural heritage. . . 'might well bear reintroduction into French economic studies'.[144] From this vantage point one can explain how the French education system at all levels became suspect after 1850; how the elementary education sector stagnated; why advances in practical technological education were questionable; why the *grandes écoles,* like the *Polytechnique,* with its emphasis on mathematics and 'military and honorific attachments was sufficient to appropriate most management posts that were not filled by nepotism'; why the training of an intermediate range of managers and NCOs was 'not convincing'; and why, finally, functionaries were held in high regard to the detriment of those who had a practical and vocational form of training, but whose supply remained 'meagre and erratic'. All this is placed at the feet of a national culture 'tipped towards conservatism'.[145]

Interestingly, though there is general agreement on the plight of industrial training and the reactionary continuity of traditional skill compositions at the end of the nineteenth century, one historian, Rondo Cameron, has sought to restore some credibility to the high quality of France's technical education system for the bourgeoisie, at least for the early nineteenth century. No other European country, either before the Revolution or until 1850, could compare with the technical and scientific instruction that was available for professional engineers at the *Collège Royal, Jardin du Roi, École des Ponts et Chaussées,* the *Observatoire,* and *Ecole des Mines.*[146] Cameron, in what can only be considered as a first-rate analysis of French industrial training at the higher levels of mining and engineering, argues forcefully and convincingly that, though 'the honour of successfully harnessing science and technology in the pursuit of common goals belongs to the nineteenth century. . . the work of Frenchmen occupies a prominent place'.[147]

As distinct then from those observers of the general tendencies who emphasised a recomposition of skills and the introduction of new methods of training, most national observers and historians have been impressed by the relative unevenness of their own nation's development and of the relative absence of success in absorbing these general changes. They also tend to emphasise the success of their competitors in coming to terms with these changes in order to highlight weaknesses in their own countries and hopefully spur on the process of change. In Britain it was seen to be the presence of problems associated with a free-wheeling pioneer constrained by a frozen and reactionary social structure and a well-trained, though technically anachronistic, craft-based workforce. What has been added most recently to this viewpoint is the idea that there may also have been distinct technical and market obstacles to any major re-composition of the labour force, especially in the engineering industry. In Germany and France the observations were similar, with the former supposedly taking its labour force as given and unalterable, and the latter, for one reason or another, tied to a backward-looking cultural heritage and a 'traditional' social structure.

There are some exceptions to these views however. In Germany some have seen the state as seeking to play a leading role in the technical training of the workforce at all levels, while in France there may have been a period when systematic and professional technical training was available for the industrial bourgeoisie, even though the workforce as a whole, may have been neglected. There is, of course, a certain amount of national *pique,* not to say inverted national chauvinism, in all these observations. But their emphasis on uneven development at a national level and between nations should draw attention to the necessity of examining the formation of a labour force in terms of its national-historical experience rather than in purely general or technically neutral terms.

Such an over-generalised technical perspective has been the hallmark of much American post-Second World War historical sociology. This emphasises the common technical problems of all nations in creating a trained workforce, imparting skills, organising work discipline, and establishing an advanced technical division of labour. A major failure of this perspective, as shall be seen, is that the formation of a workforce is as much a political and economic process as it is a technical one. Clark Kerr and Abraham Siegel, for instance, have sought to assess the formation of a labour force in the broad context of industrialisation rather than in the specific context of *capitalist* industrialisation, or in any national setting. They claim general rules apply to the formation of any workforce in an industrial society, which can be conceived of as technical problems concerning training, the division of labour, discipline, and so on. Yet their argument has a two-fold weakness. First, it is impossible to reveal anything of significance about the structuring of a workforce without describing the content of that experience either generally or nationally; second, they falsely think that the training of industrial *workers* can be conceived independently of their relationship to the ownership and control of the means of production, either personally or collectively. The implication of their work concerning the technical determination of a labour force is the *normative judgment* that social structures and power arrangements inside and outside of the factory are irrelevant to any study of the formation of a trained industrial workforce.[148]

This does not mean that a general perspective is unwarranted. These national experiences have to be located at a general level so that the overall trajectory of the formation of a labour force in the metal industries of Western Europe may be both described and understood. It does mean, however, that emphasis must be given to the political, economic, cultural, and technical lineages of a trained workforce in its particular national setting.

Such an approach needs to be distinguished from that of three French writers on this subject, Messrs Maurice, Sellier and Silvestre.[149] They combine a national and cultural approach to industrial training in light of the evolution of labour markets. A comparison between present-day Germany and France forms the heart of their study. Their approach certainly escapes the *pique* so often associated with national studies of training and education, and emphasises that the formation of a labour force cannot be understood without an appreciation of the larger social and cultural environment in which this takes place. A distinct 'social effect' *(effet sociétal)* gives the labour force of any one country its peculiar character and shape.

In the case of French methods of training in the metal industry, they suggest that these are generally more elitist and 'guided' *(dirigés)* than those in operation in German metal factories. By this they mean that relations within French enterprises are hierarchically structured, while there is less emphasis placed on the formal acquisition of qualifications and training for the workforce as a whole. In Germany, by contrast, as many employees as possible are encouraged to obtain recognised certificates, diplomas and degrees, and this tends to foment a more co-operative atmosphere in the factories between managers, employees and workers.

According to our authors, the difference here is to be explained by the fact that French industry and its associated labour markets are quite 'Balkanised'. Firms generally produce for very specialised markets and tend to train their employees and workers for their own specific needs and specialised production techniques. Training, in other words, is governed by the special requirements of the firms concerned, and professionally-acquired certificates or diplomas carry less weight. In Germany, on the other hand, firms produce for mass markets and require a fairly homogeneous labour supply, where formally-acquired and interchangeable certificates of instruction are essential. In association with state-sponsored schemes, firms train their workers in general skills, rather than in overly specialised ones so that these may be used in other plants or firms. As a result job turnover can be quite high. This does not mean, though, that there is any instability within an enterprise; rather, it is a sign of the necessary interchange of skills and training required to service a mass product market.

The overall 'social effect' is that there is a greater degree of cooperation within German enterprises and also a greater emphasis placed on the diffusion of functions and tasks; a greater polyvalence of activity as it were. In this context, French plants are seen to be run along the lines of least trust, while German plants are high-trust organisations. In fact, German metal production is allegedly more or less run by workers in association with foremen and chargehands. Promotion is governed by the attainment of certificates, and this encourages a high degree of mobility from the lower to higher grades. Against this, seniority and job experience play a much more important part in French plant management, which often has quite turbulent forms. Employees have to be wrenched from positions and given newer or higher responsibilities without having first obtained the necessary qualifications; whereas in Germany the path of promotion is determined and easily followed by universally recognised slips of paper. The position of foremen is a particular case in point. German foremen are normally trained for their positions in conjunction with the foremen's technical school, while in France such positions are obtained through the path of seniority.

The upshot of this argument is to be found in the suggestion that the *hierarchy of work in German firms is set by qualifications received outside of the factory,* while in French firms the reverse takes place: the hierarchy of work is determined by the division of labour in the factory. In other words, if one becomes a foreman in a German enterprise then this is less a function of the division of labour and more a post whose attributes and responsibilities come from the title *'Meister'* imprinted on a diploma and obtained at a *Werkmeister* school. Thus, as the structure of the work hierarchy has such radically different lineages in France and Germany, there is very little basis for comparing the place and role of German foremen with that of their French counterparts. In fact, these writers would go even further: not only do foremen in France and Germany have radically different lineages, but so, too, do non-manual workers in general. The social differences in the respective formation of the German *Angestellte* and the French *cadres* are so great as to belie comparison.

The consequence of this argument is that one must emphasise the different lineages in the formation of a workforce over and above any apparent similarities, such as the common experience of a capitalist division of labour. These differences, furthermore, are not ones of degree but of 'kind'. They are products of a 'social effect' rather than of a general tendency of capitalist development working itself out in a particular national setting at a particular point in time.[150]

This rather heroic effort to reinterpret the division of labour within an enterprise as a function of qualifications should not be readily dismissed. What is required is an historical study. The qualification fetishism of German industrial training had absolutely nothing to do with a desire to create a cooperative atmosphere at the point of production because of the existence of mass markets. Quite the contrary, it was an attempt to formalise a low trust mode of training that was highly stratified, largely immune to mobility and *in substance comparable* to the forms developed in France and Britain. The actual lineages of this did vary from country to country, but by the early years of this century they were becoming woven into a common European experience. What we shall see is not how the school and its qualifications came to shape the division of labour in the factory, but how the changing needs of the factory were brought to bear on the school, in fact forcing the creation of schools, so that they may *service* a pre-established and factory-based division of labour; not in one country, just Germany, but three—including Britain and France.

The problem to be addressed first, though, is the theme that underlies nearly all the contemporary and historical literature on skills and industrial training at the turn of the century: the craft question. Was a craft-based workforce actually in existence at this time in the European metal industry? And, was it the object of new methods of training and new skill compositions in the various national settings?

NOTES

1. A. Abaut, 'Ouvriers d'Usine', *Rèvue de Métallurgie,* Vol. 9, 1912, pp. 849–64, 891–930.
2. *ibid.,* p. 850.
3. *ibid.,* p. 856.
4. *ibid.,* pp. 856–7.
5. *bid.,* p. 858.
6. *ibid.,* p. 859.
7. *ibid.,* pp. 859, 862.
8. *ibid.,* p. 863.
9. O.M. Becker, 'A Modern Adaptation of the Apprenticeship System', *Engineering Magazine,* Vol. XXXII, No. 2, November 1906, pp. 169–76.
10. N.B. Dearle, *Industrial Training,* King, London, 1914, p. 228.
11. Hans Ehrenberg, *Die Eisenhüttentechnik und der deutsche Hüttenarbeiter,* J.G. Cotta'sche Buchhandlung, Nachfolger. Münchener Volkwirtschaftliche Studien, 80–81, Stuttgart and Berlin, 1906, p. 115.
12. *ibid.,* pp. 115–16.
13. *ibid.,* p. 116.
14. Alfred Weber, 'Das Berufsschicksal der Industriearbeiter', *Archiv für Sozialwissenschaft und Sozialpolitik,* Vol. 34, 1912, p. 318.
15. C.B. Thompson, 'Relation of Scientific Management to Labour', *Quarterly Journal of Economics,* Vol. 30, 1915-16, p. 315.
16. Alfred Sohn-Rethel, 'Technische Intelligenz zwischen Kapitalismus und Sozialismus', in Richard Vahrenkamp, ed., *Technologie und Kapital,* Edition Suhrkamp, Frankfurt-am-Main, 1973, pp. 11–38.
17. See F.W. Taylor, *Shop Management* (1903), New York and London, 1947, pp. 146–7; and R.F. Hoxie, *Scientific Management and Labour,* Appleton,

xliii

New York and London, 1915, pp. 8–11.

18. C.B. Thompson, 'Relation of Scientific Management to Labour', *loc. cit.*, p. 323.
19. *ibid.*, pp. 325-6.
20. Anonymous, 'Interchangeability', *Engineering Review*, Vol. XXIV, No. 5, May 1911, p. 303.
21. W.J. Ashley, *Scientific Management and the Engineering Situation*, Sidney Ball Memorial Lecture, OUP, London, 1922, pp. 23-4.
22. *ibid.*, pp. 24-5.
23. *ibid.*, p. 26. See also A.P.M. Fleming, and J.G. Pearce, *Principles of Apprenticeship Training: with Special Reference to the Engineering Industry*, Longmans, Green and Co., London, 1916, pp. 7-13.
24. N.B. Dearle, *op. cit.*, p. 228.
25. Paul de Rousiers, 'The Construction of Machinery Used in Special Trades', *The Labour Question in Great Britain*, trans. F.L. Herbertson, London, 1896. An extract from de Rousiers' work is now available in Maxime Berg's, ed., *Technology and Toil*, CSE Books, London, 1979, pp. 204-6.
26. James Samuelson, 'The Displacement of Hand Labour in Wood and Iron Manufactures', *Labour Saving Machinery*, (1893); extract in Maxine Berg, ed., *op. cit.*, p. 183.
27. J.T. Murphy, *New Horizons*, John Lane, London, 1942, p. 23.
28. Otto Jeidels, *Die Methoden der Arbeiterentlöhnung in der rheinischwestfälischen Eisenindustrie*, Leonhard Simion, Berlin, 1907, p. 283.
29. Fritz Schulte, *Die Entlöhnungsmethoden in der Berliner Maschinenindustrie*, Leonhard Simion, Berlin, 1906, p. 14.
30. *ibid.*, pp. 15-16.
31. *ibid.*, pp. 16-17.
32. Marie Bernays, 'Berufswahl und Berufsschicksal des modernen Industriearbeiters', *Archiv für Sozialwissenschaft und Sozialpolitik*, Bd. 36, 1912, pp. 890-1.
33. Cl. Heiss, *Die Entlöhnungsmethoden in der Berliner Feinmechanik*, Leonhard Simion, Berlin, 1909, Ch. 1, *passim.*
34. Georges Friedmann, *Problèmes humains du machinisme industriel*, NRF, Gallimard, Paris, 1946, p. 187.
35. *ibid.*, p. 188.
36. *ibid.*, pp. 189-90.
37. *ibid.*, p. 190.
38. Ehrenberg, *op. cit.*, p. 117.
39. *ibid.*, pp. 119-20.
40. Patrick McGeown, *Heat the Furnace Seven Times More: An Autobiography*, Hutchinson, London, 1967, p. 73.
41. *ibid.*, p. 78. McGeown eloquently explained the task of shovelling slag from furnace pockets in order to prepare the furnace for a new heat: 'The slag in the A. furnace pockets proved a far harder task than (was) anticipated. So a fresh gang, myself included, was sent along to work nightshifts on it. There were six of us and as usual we worked in groups of three, and this time we had to fight for every shovelful. There was no smoothness at all in it, and the wedges became blunted with our efforts. Each night we started at six o'clock and worked steadily to first supper at nine. There was an hour break which I spent at home, and would gladly have stayed there. At ten we resumed and worked steadily through till second supper at one in the morning. This was a long affair till two-thirty and really was the boundary of our intense effort. From then on we took it easy, the deadly tiredness of nightshift was upon us, and we bought our ease

xliv

by our earlier efforts'. *ibid.*, p. 78.
42. Ehrenberg, *op. cit.*, pp. 119-20.
43. McGeown, *op. cit.*, pp. 88, 91.
44. Ehrenberg, *op. cit.*, pp. 119-20.
45. McGeown, *op. cit.*, p. 100.
46. Ehrenberg, *op. cit.*, pp. 119-20.
47. McGeown, *op. cit.*, p. 10.
48. *ibid.*, p. 12.
49. *ibid.*, pp. 63-4, 94-6.
50. *ibid.*, p. 30.
51. Ehrenberg, *op. cit.*, pp. 121-2.
52. McGeown, *op. cit.*, p. 11.
53. Schulte, *op. cit.*, p. 16.
54. Jeidels, *op. cit.*, pp. 88-92. A Duisberg bridgebuilding firm paid its travelling fitters about 230 to 300M per month and often a time-saving bonus of as much as 100M would be paid if the installation and construction was done in less time.
55. Dearle, *op. cit.*, pp. 64-5.
56. Friedmann, *op. cit.*, pp. 190, 197.
57. *ibid.*, p. 193.
58. Schulte, *op. cit.*, pp. 16-17.
59. Omer Buyse, 'Le problème psycho-physique de l'apprentissage', *Revue Psychologique*, Vol. III, 1910, pp. 377-99. Josefa Ioteyko, *The Science of Labour and Its Organisation*, George Routledge and Sons, London, 1919, p. 5. Ioteyko's volume brought together a series of articles which appeared in the *Revue Philosophique*, the *Revue Scientifique*, and the *Revue Générale des Sciences* during 1916 and 1917.
60. Ioteyko, *op. cit.*, p. 6. (My emphasis, C. McG.) In all likelihood this is an indirect reference to the role of 'new artisans' in production.
61. *ibid.*, p. 7.
62. *ibid.*, p. 6.
63. *ibid.*, pp. 8-9.
64. *ibid.*, p. 9.
65. See Friedmann, *op. cit.*, pp. 203-6. The study of the psycho-physical apparatus of labour was also related to several other currents of enquiry. This was notably so with the new 'science' of ergonomy, which sought to reveal the laws of 'economical' movement; but it also branched off into the study of human physiology and work, fatigue, motion study, psychology, and the study of concentration. For a description of how such movements developed in France during the early 1900s, see Georges Ribeill, 'Les débuts de l'ergonomie en France à la veille de la Première Guerre mondiale', *Le mouvement social*, No. 113, octobre-décembre, 1980, pp. 3-36.
66. Alfred Williams, *Life in A Railway Factory* (1915), Newton Abbot, 1969, p. 304.
67. Alphonse Merrheim, *La Métallurgie, son origine, son développement*, Paris, 1913, p. 35.
68. See Ralph Dahrendorf, *Class and Class Conflict in Industrial Society*, Routledge and Kegan Paul, London, 1959, *passim;* esp. p. 49.
69. *ibid.*, p. 57.
70. W. Fischer, 'Innerbetrieblicher und sozialer Status der frühen Fabrikarbeiterschaft', *Forschungen zur Sozial- und Wirtschaftsgeschichte*, Vol. VI, 1964, pp. 192-200.
71. *ibid.*, p. 201.

72. See Katherine Stone, 'The Origin of Job Structures in the Steel Industry', in Root and Branch, eds., *The Rise of the Workers' Movement,* Fawcett Publications, Greenwich, 1975, pp. 123-58. Dan Clawson, *Bureaucracy and the Labour Process: The Transformation of U.S. Industry, 1860-1920,* Monthly Review Press, New York, 1980, *passim.*

73. Harry Braverman, *Labour and Monopoly Capital: The Degradation of Work in the Twentieth Century,* Monthly Review Press, New York and London, 1974, *passim.*

74. *ibid.,* pp. 135-7.

75. *ibid.,* p. 170.

76. Stone, *loc. cit.,* p. 125.

77. *ibid.,* pp. 132-3.

78. *ibid.,* p. 135.

79. *ibid.,* p. 142.

80. See David M. Gordon, Richard Edwards, and Michael Reich, *Segmented Work, Divided Workers: The Historical Transformation of Labor in the United States,* CUP, Cambridge, 1982, p. 247, n. 13 and chapters 3-4. Within the time span of this work we cannot enter into this last argument about the segmentation and differentiation of the workforce. We will deal more fully with this view in a later volume, when the rise of Fordism is considered. As will be seen below, however, other writers from different perspectives are quite keen to shift the argument about differentiation of the workforce back into the pre-war period.

81. Charles Sabel, *Work and Politics: The Division of Labour in Industry,* CUP, Cambridge, 1982, p. xi.

82. *ibid.,* pp. 190-1.

83. *ibid.,* p. 11.

84. *ibid.,* p. 57. (My emphasis, C. McG.)

85. *ibid.,* pp. 57, 59, 62, 92-3. (My emphasis, C. McG.)

86. *ibid.,* p. 61.

87. *ibid.,* p. 1.

88. '1899—A Survey', *Fielden's Magazine,* Vol. 2, No. 6, January 1900, p. 4.

89. Ewert C. Amos, 'Machine Tools', *Fielden's Magazine,* Vol. I, No. 1, August 1899, p. 76.

90. Debate concerning the 'relative backwardness' of the British economy in the late nineteenth century is to be found in A.L. Levine, *Industrial Retardation in Britain, 1880-1914,* Weidenfeld and Nicolson, London, 1967; D.H. Aldroft, ed., *The Development of British Industry and Foreign Competition, 1875-1914,* George Allen and Unwin, London, 1968; D.N. McCloskey, ed., *Essays on a Mature Economy: Britain after 1840,* Methuen and Co., London, 1971; and most recently, Roderick Floud and Donald McCloskey, eds., *The Economic History of Britain Since 1700,* 2 vols., CUP, Cambridge, 1981, especially *Volume 2, 1860 to the 1970s* and L.G. Sandberg's essay, 'The Entrepreneur and Technical Change', pp. 99-120.

91. Pollard's early work in the 1950s and his recent collaboration with Paul Robertson assesses how the British shipbuilding industry up to 1914 was not only one of the most competitive sectors of British industry but also the world monopolist on the basis of labour intensive methods and little use of modern machinery. In an article published in 1957 Pollard wrote: 'There is little doubt that much of the equipment found in British yards was less advanced than in America, Germany, and perhaps other countries in this period. British yards had their ancient steam engines to generate power, their lathes and plate-bending machines, but as far as the installation of hydraulic, pneumatic, or electric power transmission was concerned, or the use of mechanical riveters

and drills, crane and gantry equipment, mechanical yard transport, covers for berths, even electric light, most of them were years behind their chief foreign rivals, and visiting experts could seldom conceal their astonishment at this backwardness. . . (yet) . . . there was good reason for the "backwardness" in Britain. Essentially, the reputation of British shipbuilding was based on the skill of its artisans, its boiler makers and shipwrights. In the absence of a pool of skilled labour, foreign shipbuilders were obliged to install expensive equipment, much of which could not pay unless and until all processes had become a true mass production industry.' See Sidney Pollard, 'British and World Shipbuilding, 1890-1914', *Journal of Economic History,* Vol. XVII, No. 3, 1957, pp. 436-7. In their collaborative effort Pollard and Robertson have taken this argument further, especially when they consider the expansion of the shipbuilding industry after 1870, when the use of new materials such as steel 'increased' rather than diluted 'the variety of artisan trades' and brought about an even heavier reliance on handicraft skills. It was in this situation that 'British ship-yard workers consistently produced more than their German or American counterparts'. See Sidney Pollard and Paul Robertson, *The British Shipbuilding Industry, 1870-1914,* Harvard University Press, Cambridge, Mass., London, 1979, pp. 137, 147. A very interesting study of the hand-based division of labour in the British shipbuilding industry up to 1914 is Alastair Reid's, *The Division of Labour in the British Shipbuilding Industry,* Ph.D., University of Cambridge, 1980.

Saul's work, which has concentrated on the heavy capital goods engineering trades, particularly locomotive building and textile machinery, suggests that the possibilities for the development of mass production techniques and for a recomposition of skills was severely limited by the great variation in the markets for these products. Furthermore, many overseas contracts were made on the basis of the world-renown of Britain's skilled fitters who could allegedly file, grind and polish to as close as 0.0005" in order to get fits for the interchange-able parts of textile machines. See S.B. Saul, 'The Market and the Development of the Mechanical Engineering Industries in Britain, 1860-1914', *Economic History Review,* Vol. XX, 1967, p. 114.

92. C.K. Harley, 'Skilled Labour and the Choice of Technique in Edwardian Industry', *Exploration in Economic History,* Vol. XI, 1974, pp. 401-2.

93. See Charles More, *Skill and the English Working Class,* Croom Helm, London, 1980, Preface.

94. *ibid.,* pp. 28-31.

95. *ibid.,* p. 154.

96. *ibid.,* pp. 32, 155.

97. *ibid.,* p. 174 ff. For a similar perspective, pitched at the more general level of how markets and production techniques constrained the recomposition of training and skills, see Sabel, *op. cit.,* pp. 34-7. Sabel speaks of general purpose machinery as being 'a sophisticated version of the artisan's original tools', requiring 'craftsmen to make full use of. . . (their) . . . potential'. *ibid.,* p. 40. See also p. 236, n. 5.

98. See Jonathan Zeitlin, 'Craft Control and the Division of Labour: Engineers and Compositors in Britain, 1890-1930', *Cambridge Journal of Economics,* Vol. 3, No. 3, September 1979, pp. 263, 270.

99. *ibid.,* pp. 263, 270.

100. More, *op. cit.,* p. 167.

101. *ibid.,* p. 167.

102. See Joseph Melling, ' "Non-Commissioned Officers": British Employers and their Supervisory Workers, 1880-1920', *Social History,* Vol. 5, No. 2, May

1980, pp. 194, 219.

103. International Metalworkers' Federation, *Industrial Training also Internationalism, compiled by Charles Hobson, Secretary of the British Section,* Hudson and Son, Birmingham, 1915, p. 7.

104. *ibid.,* p. 11.

105. David Landes, *The Unbound Prometheus: Technical Change and Industrial Development in Western Europe from 1750 to the Present,* Cambridge, at the University Press, 1969, p. 341.

106. *ibid.,* p. 341.

107. *ibid.,* p. 344.

108. *ibid.,* p. 348. See also p. 346.

109. *ibid.,* p. 348.

110. See Levine, *op. cit.,* pp. 70-6. Pollard and Robertson in their discussion of industrial training in the shipbuilding industry argue in a similar vein. For them, despite the advances that were made in the science of shipbuilding and the training of qualified technicians and designers, it was still the case that 'as late as 1914 science and research were still the poor stepchildren of the industry'. Pollard and Robertson, *op. cit.,* p. 136.

111. P.W. Musgrave, *Technical Change, the Labour Force and Education: A Study of the British and German Iron and Steel Industries, 1860-1964,* Pergamon Press, Oxford, 1967, pp. 17, 55, 99.

112. Levine, *op. cit.,* pp. 86-110. This refers to the policy of unions such as the Amalgamated Society of Engineers, who demanded either a skilled rate of pay for a semi-skilled worker attending to a machine formerly the province of a skilled engineer, or that only skilled workers could work new machinery at a skilled tradesman's rate. See also, Maxine Berg, *op. cit.,* p. 170.

113. E.J. Hobsbawm, *Industry and Empire,* Penguin, London, 1974, pp. 187-8, 169, 181 ff.

114. *ibid.,* p. 169. Hobsbawm speaks of the 'virtual absence of university education and the feebleness of formal technological training', and of the fact that Britain in 1913 had only nine thousand university students compared to nearly sixty thousand in Germany and almost thirteen thousand in the USA. *ibid.,* pp. 181-2.

115. François Crouzet, *The Victorian Economy,* translated by A.S. Forster, Methuen and Co. Ltd., London, 1982, pp. 405, 422.

116. *ibid.,* pp. 407, 414-15.

117. *ibid.,* pp. 418, 420.

118. *ibid.,* pp. 420-1.

119. George Schlesinger, Speech to the 54th Assembly of the German Engineers' Association, 1913. *'Verein deutscher Ingenieure, 54, Hauptversammlung in Leipzig, 22 bis 24 Juni, 1913',* in *Stahl und Eisen,* 10 July 1913, Vol. 33, No. 28, 1913, Pt. 2, pp. 1159-60. Schlesinger's speech was reproduced in full under the title: 'Betriebsführung und Betriebswissenschaft', in *Technik und Wirtschaft, Monatschrift des Vereines deutscher Ingenieure,* 6 Jahrg., 8 Heft, August 1913, pp. 525-47. The quote can be found on p. 525.

120. P. Steller, 'Die Maschinenindustrie Deutschlands', *Schriften des Vereins für Socialpolitik,* Bd. 107-108, 1903, pp. 19-20.

121. P.N. Stearns, 'The Unskilled and Industrialisation', *Archiv für Sozial Geschichte,* Bd. XVI, 1976, p. 275. Sadly Stearns never defines what he means by the word 'skill' even though he says that 'In German machine building the skilled increased by 145% after 1895'. *ibid.,* p. 275.

122. J.j. Lee, 'Labour in German Industrialisation', in Peter Mathias and M.M. Postan, eds., *The Cambridge Economic History of Europe, Vol. VII, The*

Industrial Economies: Capital, Labour and Enterprise, Part I, Britain, France, Germany and Scandinavia, CUP, Cambridge 1978, pp. 448, 703, n. 6.

123. *ibid.,* p. 456.

124. Two useful overviews of this work are Red Notes and Conference of Socialist Economists, eds., *Working Class Autonomy and Crisis,* CSE, London, 1979, and Guido Baldi, 'Theses on the Mass Worker and Social Capital', *Radical America,* Vol. 6, No. 3, May-June 1972, pp. 3-21.

125. See Karl Heinz Roth, *Die 'andere' Arbeiterbewegung und die Entwicklung der Kapitalistischen Repression von 1880 bis zur Gegenwart. Ein Betrag zum Neuverständnis der Klassengeschichte in Deutschland,* Trikont Verlag, München, 1974, pp. 23-5, Eckhard Brockhaus, *Zusammensetzung und Neustrucktierung der Arbeiterklasse vor dem ersten Weltkrieg,* Trikont Verlag, München, 1975, pp. 16-18, 28-33.

126. Brockhaus, *op. cit.,* pp. 17-18.

127. *ibid.,* p. 64. See also Sergio Bologna, 'Class Composition and the Theory of the Party at the Origin of the Workers' Council Movement', *The Labour Process and Class Strategies,* CSE Books, London, 1976, pp. 68-91. Bologna's work, originally published in Italy in 1972, provided much of the intellectual framework for the work of Roth and Brockhaus. He was concerned to study those workers whose 'metal work demanded utmost precision', so that 'they directly participated in changing the structure of the product and transforming their own techniques', who had 'a high level of professional ability', were 'engaged in precision work', were 'perfectly familiar with tools (both manual and mechanic)', and who worked 'alongside technicians and engineers in modifying the working process'. *ibid.,* p. 69.

128. Landes, *op. cit.,* p. 150.

129. *ibid.,* p. 340.

130. *ibid.,* p. 148.

131. *Revue de Métallurgie,* Vol. 3, No. 1, January 1906, p. 5.

132. *ibid.,* January 1906, p. 5 and Vol. 3, No. 11, November 1906, p. 585.

133. *ibid.,* November 1906, p. 585.

134. *ibid.,* Vol. 3, No. 2, February 1906, p. 72.

135. *ibid.,* Vol. 3, No. 3, March 1906, p. 107.

136. *ibid.,* Vol. 3, No. 5, May 1906, p. 230.

137. A.L. Dunham, *Industrial Revolution in France, 1815-1848,* Exposition Press, New York, 1955, p. 184.

138. Guy Palmade, *French Capitalism in the Nineteenth Century,* translated with an introduction by Graeme M. Holmes, David and Charles: Newton Abbot, Devon, 1972, p. 208.

139. *Le Journal,* 15 May 1917.

140. Yves Lequin, 'Labour in the French Economy since the Revolution', in Cambridge *Economic History of Europe,* Vol. VII, eds., Peter Mathias and M.M. Postan, *op. cit.,* p. 318.

141. Tom Kemp, *Industrialisation in Nineteenth Century Europe,* Longman, London, 1971, p. 61.

142. F. Crouzet, 'French Economic Growth in the Nineteenth Century Reconsidered', *History,* Vol. 59, 1974, p. 177.

143. Lequin, *loc. cit.,* p. 318. See also J.M. Laux, *In First Gear: The French Automobile Industry to 1914,* McGill-Queens University Press, Montreal, 1967, p. 179, for a similar argument concerning the early twentieth-century French automobile industry.

144. Clive Trebilcock, *The Industrialization of the Continental Powers, 1780-1914,* Longman, London, 1981, pp. 196-7.

145. *ibid.*, pp. 194-6.
146. Rondo Cameron, *France and the Economic Development of Europe*, Princeton University Press, Princeton, New Jersey, 1961, p. 45.
147. *ibid.*, p. 42.
148. Clark Kerr and Abraham Siegel, 'The Structuring of the Workforce in Industrial Society: New Dimensions and New Questions', *Industrial and Labour Relations Review*, Vol. 8, 1955, pp. 147-68.
149. See Marc Maurice, François Sellier and Jean-Jacques Silvestre, 'La production de la hiérarchie dans l'entreprise: recherche d'un effet sociétal', *Revue française de sociologie*, Vol. 20, April 1979, pp. 331-65.
150. A similar line of reasoning is also present in P.W. Musgrave's work on the British and German steel industries, especially on the question of the role of elementary education in the training of their respective workforces during the nineteenth century. In Germany, Dr Musgrave tells us, children learnt literacy and how to 'sit still'. Compulsory military service at a later age also taught 'obedience and duty'. The result was that Germans, as 'citizens' (*sic* subjects of a monarchical empire), were ready to do the government's will and as workers were 'disciplined and docile'. In the absence of such a national and compulsory system of elementary education, the British were forced to rely on *laissez-faire* techniques to train their workforce. Such nationalist caricature may be disappointing to find in a supposedly unbiased study, but from our point of view what is more important is the suggestion that these 'fundamental' differences are explicable in terms of British Benthamite and German Hegelian *philosophies* of the state, rather than in terms of the material and social structures of each country. See Musgrave, *op. cit.*, pp. 41-2, 43, 45.

1

CHAPTER 1: THE CRAFT QUESTION

1. Origins

From the viewpoint of its origins a craft was the material basis upon which was erected a form of urban production dating from the Middle Ages. That form of production was the guild system. During the Middle Ages guilds formed the central focus for the organisation of production into trades, such as pottery, glass and iron wares, and determined the internal social structure within which production could take place. There was a diversity in Europe of legal forms which could endow a guild with titular authority over a craft, but the most common were either endowments by royal charter or by the authority of a town government. In France, for example, the various guilds, or *Communautés d'arts et métiers,* which appeared between the twelfth and eighteenth centuries, were generally either endowed as *Le métier juré* by the crown or as *Le métier réglé* by a municipality.[1] The prescriptions of endowment described in minutia the conditions under which a trade could be carried on, and, though these varied from place to place, they carried the full force of the law behind them. In fact, such regulations sought both to protect the guild from competition from 'outsiders' and 'independents', and the public from 'irregular' production practices by a guild.

Two examples of what Fernand Braudel calls 'the exclusive contiguous monopolies, fiercely defended' and enjoyed by the guilds, may be given from the Duchy of Berg and the Aachen area of the Rhineland in Germany. From the Middle Ages, the sword-makers of Solingen in the Duchy were made-up of three fraternities—the Temperers, Grinders and Sword-Cutlers. Only members of these fraternities were allowed to go abroad as merchants, so as not to bring the trade into disrepute. Furthermore, sword blades had to have the hereditary mark of the maker inscribed on them. In the wool crafts of Aachen the craftsmen of the towns had a monopoly over the use of the fine wool from the region between the Rhine and the Meuse. Every stage of the work, from sorting to pressing, was strictly supervised and regulated. When finished the goods were then authorised by having inscribed on them the trademark of the town, and only those goods so marked could be exported or, indeed, passed straight on to the consumer.[2]

According to Edouard Dolléans, such regulations gave crafts the character of being subordinate to and serving the 'public' interest, a view

1

far removed from that of the early twentieth-century industrial capitalist who saw the public regulation of work and the exercise of a craft as contrary to the social and public interest.[3] The internal structure of a craft, though regulated by the guild, was governed by a master craftsman, in France, the *maître,* in whose industrial household worked his *compagnons* or journeymen, and his apprentices.[4] R.A. Bray's history of boy labour and apprenticeship in Britain, which appeared in 1911, described the medieval apprentice as a boy who had to pay his master a premium and was henceforth indentured for usually seven years. He lived in the master's house, and, in addition to food and lodgings, received wages on a sliding scale. Throughout the course of the apprenticeship he was given, not only practical training into the 'mysteries of a trade, but also that wider training of character and intelligence on which depends the real efficiency of the craftsman'.[5] Mutuality was meant to be the essence of this relationship; the master having engaged a boy to teach him his trade, while the boy promised to serve his master honestly and obediently.[6]

With the end of his indentureship the apprentice became a journeyman. Though his wages rose, little else changed. The journeyman generally still continued to work for his master, and often kept his lodgings in his master's house. At the same time, Bray noted that 'to some extent the master was still responsible for the good conduct of his journeyman'. Also, various regulations forbade a master from enticing journeymen away from other masters and journeymen from combining against the masters.[7] The transition from journeymen to master was a gradual procedure, though it involved no major break in social status because of their mutual ties to one another. Both worked at the craft and before the introduction of merchant middle-men and capitalist production it was relatively easy to start up one's own business or trade.[8]

The guild, in regulating the relationships between a master, journeyman and apprentices, undertook to control the period of apprenticeship, the hours and conditions of labour, wages and premiums: 'The guild visited the workshops, inspected the articles in process of manufacture, satisfied themselves as to their quality, prescribed methods of production and were empowered to confiscate tools not sanctioned by the three classes of persons concerned. Masters, journeymen and apprentices alike benefited by an organisation which was created and controlled in their common interests, while the general public were well served in the system of expert inspection which guaranteed the quality of goods supplied'.[9]

William Sewell has recently described how the French trade corporations supervised the work of their members during the *Ancien Régime:*

> Within the privileged domain defined by its statutes, each trade community was responsible for assuring the honesty of its own members and the quality of the

goods they produced. For this purpose each community had officers chosen from among its members. The officers were called *jurés, syndics, gardes, principals, prieurs, maieurs, consuls,* or *bailles*—the titles varied widely from century to century, from region to region, and from trade to trade. In addition to being charged with a general policing of the trade, they also judged disputes between masters or between masters and workers, represented the trade in relations with local or royal authorities, initiated legal proceedings, and generally tended to the affairs of the community. The *jurés* were usually chosen by election but were sometimes selected by co-option or royal appointment and in a few cases were even chosen by lot. The entire body of masters usually met at least once a year in order to oversee the work of the *jurés* and to discuss and take action on the common affairs of the community.[10]

This role of the urban guild system in articulating the public character and collective control over the regulations governing access to the craft, the conduct of the trade and the training of workmen, remained in force to varying degrees until at least the fifteenth century in England, the eighteenth century in France and the early nineteenth century in Germany. And it is with the internal decay of this system in the face of more capitalistic commercial and production trade practices that a first approximate understanding can be given of the operation, structure and forms of control of those alleged 'craft' practices in operation in the European metal trades during the nineteenth century.

In France during the late seventeenth and eighteenth centuries, the extension and intensification of urban trading placed insuperable pressures on guilds and crafts with respect to the control and regulation of their trades. A growing number of independent competitors were beginning to appear in a trade, while in coal mining and metallurgy large-scale enterprises sprang up which employed several hundred workers, and therefore posed a challenge to those more expensive artisan crafts, such as were carried on in small foundries. Workers also were becoming more mobile, whether in search of higher wages paid by larger enterprises or in search of a place to practise a declining craft. In response to this, crafts became more exclusive by complicating the 'rites' of entrance to the 'mysteries' of the trade and by often limiting entrance to existing family members. It was also often difficult for a guild to adapt itself to the qualifications of workmen who had received their craft training in other regions and towns.[11] The sum effect of this was not only an external erosion of the crafts, but also an increasing stratification within the guild itself. It was increasingly difficult to become a master craftsman; and masters themselves sought to restrict entry to their trade even further.[12]

In Britain during the fifteenth and sixteenth centuries, the supervisory functions of the guilds began to fall into disuse as competition spelt not only the end of quality production, but also led to challenges by independent producers demanding an end to the monopoly privileges of a guild. One early twentieth-century English observer, when referring to the break-up of the guilds in the sixteenth century and the attendant decline of a publicly-regulated craft and apprenticeship system, spoke in terms of the guilds no longer acting as an 'association of equals united by common interests and a common outlook':

> . . . no longer a guarantee of excellence in matters of craftsmanship; no longer the guardian of the interests of the general public, but a narrow sect claiming exclusive privileges—the guilds, rent by strife and envy within, and regarded with open hostility by those outside, drifted slowly towards that inevitable end which awaits those who seek to sacrifice the needs of all on the altar of the selfish desires of the few.[13]

Though this may be a romantic view of the former public virtues of the classical guild, it does express the rise of a more privatised view of the rights to a craft and control over a trade, both within and outside of the guilds. In France, this was expressed in the conflicts and ideological arguments which preceded the passage of the *Loi de la Chapelier* by the National Assembly on 17 June, 1791.

As it became more difficult to become a master, journeymen's organisations, particularly during the early years of the Revolution, became more militant, engaging in industrial actions, street demonstrations and strikes. After a series of agitations the master craftsmen of Paris, led by the carpenters *(maîtres charpentiers)*, appealed to the National Assembly to destroy the 'twin dangers' of corporate association by workers who sought wage rises and forced others to stop work. Yet as Edouard Dolléans notes, it was not just social discontent that led the National Assembly to sift out the earlier rights and privileges of guild organisation so that they became a monopoly of the masters and excluded the journeymen; it was also the desire of the Assembly to consecrate 'the ideology propagated by the physiocratic school'. This was to abolish the privileges of all corporations and introduce juridical equality for all citizens. In other words, what was sought was the legalisation of the capitalist labour contract made between individual and individual. This sounded the real death-knell for the guild-craft system and the associated regulations, rights, privileges and working skills which had provided its bases.[14]

In England this took the form of the state putting into the melting-pot of competition the public regulations which governed apprenticeship and craftsmanship in 1814. Up until then, courts could in theory be used to prosecute employers for failing to observe the Elizabethan Acts, which governed apprenticeships and methods for fixing wages. In the anti-combination atmosphere of the 1790s and early 1800s, however, magistrates in Yorkshire and London were more likely to rule in favour of an employer, especially as Parliament itself had been annually suspending those parts of the Acts dealing with industry since 1802. Also, Lord

Ellenborough's ruling of 1810 took out of the ambit of the Acts all those trades which were considered new or had changed considerably since Elizabeth's rule (the work of an engineer, for example).[15] Hence, an increasing proportion of the workforce had no access to the public regulations governing the conditions of a trade or apprenticeship. Thus, when the Statute of Apprentices was abolished in 1814, the state not only washed its hands of any regulation of craftsmanship and apprenticeship, it also sought to advance the cause of 'competition among workmen'.[16]

The German states between the late 1790s and the 1840s undertook the introduction of similar laws privatising the labour contract, apprenticeship, and regulations governing a trade. At first this was under the impact of the French Revolution and the Napoleonic annexations in the Rhine and northern Germany; yet it soon became an independent movement, spurred on by competition between the states to reap the benefits of large-scale production, whether for military or economic purposes. In a series of measures the guilds gradually lost the right to licence tradesmen, have any jurisdiction over economic policies or to prevent 'citizens' from engaging in several occupations at the same time.[17]

The abolition of guild regulation of a craft and the introduction of a capitalist labour contract did not automatically spell the end of the material basis of the craft, or that ensemble of skills and practices which were applied in production; nor did it supplant the social culture of craft work, particularly the general consciousness of an 'art' for those versed in it. It did not automatically bring about the introduction of a private capitalist regulation of skills. Work still often remained centred on the totality of a craft in metal fabrication and iron work. The workforce in fact remained 'organic';[18] there was little formal division of tasks, simple cooperation still remained dominant and the workforce continued to monopolise 'technical intelligence' or the knowledge and skills of work. Throughout the eighteenth century the English millwright craftsman continued to execute every kind of engineering operation, 'from making wooden patterns to erecting in the mill the machines which had been constructed by their own hands'.[19] With little machinery to aid him, the task of planing surfaces was done by 'chipping and filing', as was 'fitting' the assembly of parts of engines. One mid-nineteenth-century treatise on engineering spoke of the *totality* of skills required from the eighteenth-century millwright:

> . . . the millwright of the last century was an itinerant engineer and mechanic of high reputation. He could handle the axe, the hammer and the plane with equal skill and precision; he could turn, bore or forge with the ease and dispatch of one brought up to these *trades,* and he could set out, and cut in, furrows of a millstone with an accuracy equal or superior to that of a miller himself. . . Generally, he was a fair arithmetician, knew something of geometry, levelling and mensuration, and in some cases, possessed a very competent knowledge of

practical mathematics. He could calculate the velocities, strength and power of machines; could draw in plans and section, and could construct buildings, conduits or water-courses in all their forms and under all the conditions required in his professional capacity; he could build bridges, cut canals, and perform a variety of work now done by civil engineers.[20]

The eighteenth-century French iron industry can provide us with another example of the continuity of an organic workforce. The French iron workers, as one historian explains, 'knew a particular and difficult technique'. They were also united by a strong bond of solidarity.[21] Their 'intolerable independence' from their masters, complemented by a shortage of workers trained in the craft, led one agent for the Committee on Arms and Munitions *(Commission des armes et poudres),* to report to his superiors in the autumn of 1795, that the employers 'are ignorant of how wood is converted into charcoal, ore into cast iron and how this is lastly reduced to iron'.[22] Six years later the prefect of the Cote-d'Or reported that, 'buying and selling' was the totality of the iron masters' 'science'.[23] On the basis of the continuity of traditional techniques of production, iron workers successfully resisted all major attempts by employers to develop an empirical knowledge of the trade. They sabotaged experiments and generally refused to be expropriated of their technical intelligence, 'their technique'.[24] This situation seems to have lasted until the 1850s and 1860s, that is until the age of the mass production of steel.[25] Whether at the blast furnace, foundry, forge, puddling furnace or rolling mill, work was based on a craft *habileté.* It maintained its value and required 'professional qualities'.[26]

Supporting the continuity of such craft practices was a labour supply based on the families of iron workers. Children of the craft workers learnt the trade of their fathers, and though this supplied an employer with a ready source for the reproduction of labour power it was also a 'barrier' to his 'initiative'.[27] Workers could prevent outsiders from entering the trade, as it was often the case that only family members could take up apprenticeships, while simultaneously refusing to co-operate with or instruct foreigners.[28] Denis Woronoff, in seeking to explain the effects of this 'transmission of knowledge and employment by inheritance', speaks of it having created a 'technical inertia' and of forcing the master to remain external to the production process:

Every innovation met with resistance; it was scuttled by 'the routine obstinacy of workers' which was denounced by well-informed employers, scientists and administrators. The master iron makers spoke with pleasure of the smelters, and refiners, 'secrets', together with the tricks of the trade and methods of conduct impervious to any idea of progress and inaccessible to the uninitiated. The industrialists were, in effect, often only the formal coordinators of the production process and largely external to it. The construction of the crucible furnace, the proportions of materials to be used (ore, charcoal, flux), the duration of hammering, as well as the processes of production ultimately depended on the decisions of the workforce. Moreover, the master iron makers were accomplices of their workers.[29]

According to Bertrand Gille, on top of all this, iron workers and founders rarely worked in other provinces. They remained in their own areas because of the privileges they had acquired concerning their knowledge of the disposition of each mine in an area and the internal operations of the furnaces.[30] These were workers who, because of the weight of their qualified labour in the production process, the traditional organisation of production, and their community life, developed a consciousness of their *spécificité* and *supériorité*.[31] It may be said that though craftsmen had been deprived of the means of production their craft still remained the animating principle of the labour process. An employer may have control over the direction of the production process, i.e. over what was to be produced and where, but he still relied on the fact that the *labour process* retained its character as an ensemble of *pre-given cooperative endeavours,* governed more by the organic relationships between craftsmen, journeymen and apprentices than by their real subordination to his capital.

2. The break-up of the crafts

How, then, was the labour process based on the crafts transformed? G.D.H. Cole and Raymond Postgate have suggested that it was only with 'the advent of power-driven machinery' that this 'old social relation of apprentice and master. . . died out'.[32] This is the view of many historians and partly accounts for their emphasis on the existence of craft practices in the late nineteenth-century metal industry until the mechanisation of production. William Sewell, for instance, has described how the workers in the nineteenth-century Marseilles machine and instrument-building trades continued to remain 'proud craftsmen', established in their corporations and bearing little or no resemblance to the 'ill paid and unorganised factory hands in the textile, chemical, or food-processing factories':

> In the days before assembly lines and interchangeable parts, machine construction required great intelligence, judgment, *dexterity,* and finesse— what in the eighteenth century would have been called an "art". . . Many workers in mechanical construction continued to serve their apprenticeship in the traditional metal crafts and continued to call themselves by such titles as *serrurier* (locksmith), or *chaudronnier* (coppersmith), rather than the newer *mécanicien* (machinist).[33]

It is very interesting that Sewell slips in the word 'dexterity' to describe the skills of the Marseilles metalworkers. That 'skill' in this author's mind was seen to combine both the 'art' and *speed* of efficiency suggests that even at this time changes were occurring which normally go undetected by historians attracted to the mechanisation thesis. It can be shown, in fact, that the material basis of the crafts was well and truly being transformed many years before the introduction of mass mechanisation and that the transition was already underway at the end of the eighteenth century, when the trades moved towards principles of production based on *manufacture*. It is in this period of manufacture, I suggest, that employers learnt how to complement their private-capitalist labour contract with a private-capitalist regulation of their workers' skills, and it is by watching how the words 'efficiency', 'dexterity' and 'speed' come to be associated with 'skill' that one gets a clear indication of this process of work.

Marx's argument concerning the nature of manufacture provides a useful starting point for such an enquiry. Manufacture, Marx argued, 'is characterised by the differentiation of the instruments of labour—a differentiation whereby tools of a given sort acquire fixed shapes, adapted to each particular application—and by the specialisation of these instruments, which allows full play to each special tool only in the hands of a specific kind of worker'.[34] Our concern here is with how this form of specialisation affected the craft basis of the labour process and with the kind of worker produced by this change. This problem will be considered from two points of view: from the point of view of the types of skill and training methods introduced for the workforce as a whole, and from the point of view of the development of management skills and training methods.

In Britain, France and Germany the specialisation of production and the development of a specialised workforce took the form of a decomposition and reorganisation of the major crafts in the metal trades, which forced the introduction of a refined division of labour and a fragmentation of tasks, while the 'crafts' themselves still remained the *technical* foundation of work. We will consider developments in Britain first as she was the first country to make the break at the end of the eighteenth century; the situation in France and Germany requires a separate study, as these countries were affected by Britain's early pioneering role and were forced to make the break by taking relatively different roads.

(i) Great Britain

In Britain, the Industrial Revolution led to an enormous expansion of the engineering trades, especially those trades producing coal-mining equipment, textile machinery, steam engines, machine tools and, later, railway equipment, such as locomotives.[35] This expansion also brought about a division of labour in the engineering establishments themselves. The craft of the millwright was broken up into numerous and distinct new 'crafts', such as pattern-makers working in wood, moulders working in iron, boilermakers, fitters working in assembly, turners working on lathes and civil engineers undertaking the work of planning the construction of bridges, canals, factories and machines. The Webbs explained this decline of the millwright's craft in terms of the growth of an 'engineers' economy', where the millwright's trade was parcelled out to specialised workers.[36] A classical example of this was the division of labour and fragmentation of tasks at Boulton and Watt's Soho Engine Manufactory at the beginning of the nineteenth century. The two most important groups of workers in this steam engine works were fitters and turners. In this sense the plant, like many others, had broken with the millwright's craft. Fitters and turners, though, were still working in the craft, even if in only one narrow part of it. The work was still highly skilled and was based on experience that only an apprenticeship could give. In fitting, all filing and chipping was still done by hand and, as Eric Roll notes, 'the fitter had to combine manual skill with a certain degree of empirical technical knowledge demanded by the undeveloped state of both the product and the machinery which produced it':

> In one way, however, the beginnings of modern practice can be seen. Fitting did not remain a general unregulated job. A sub-division had already taken place, and the varieties of fitting work were strictly systematised. To each fitter, or group of fitters, only one article, or group of small articles, was assigned. The nozzles, which demanded a very high degree of skill, were. . . dealt with separately. Similarly all the different valves were fitted by one man and two assistants; and the following are some of the other engine parts fitted separately: parallel motions, governors and throttle valves; working gears; steam cases; the various pumps and so on.[37]

The turners were also a different class of workmen from those general workmen who were typical of the eighteenth century. They too were divided up into different classes and assigned different work.

> So the turning, draw-filling and finishing of pistons and air-pump rods was to be done by William Buxton and John Mincham, while John Allport and John Hunt were detailed to the turning of the heavier parts—cylinders, pistons, rotative shafts, etc.[38]

The utility of Roll's study of the Soho plant (constructed from Boulton and Watt documents from the period 1799–1801), is not so much whether this was typical for engineering establishments at the time, but rather how it anticipates the late nineteenth-century situation at plants such as Platt's textile machinery works and fits in with the observations of contemporaries about the evolution of new and 'different' kinds of skill.[39] The Soho workmen were not craftsmen in the classical sense. They certainly possessed new, and for many, highly-sophisticated skills, which comprised to varying degrees an ability to undertake precision work, manual dexterity and 'judgment'. Yet in a very concrete sense they were new workers whose skills were beginning to be regulated by an employer.

In the first instance, the employers at the Soho plant were attempting to 'increase each man's efficiency in the performance of a particular job', which required the dilution of general skills.[40] The craft was no longer the province of an individual journeyman or artisan but of an inter-dependent collectivity of workers, each specialised in a particular province of the former craft. It may have been the case that the majority had, to varying degrees, a complete knowledge of the craft, but they were essentially disqualified from the complete practice of the craft, and with time this would amount to a dequalification of their labour power. On the other hand, a minority became hyper-qualified not only in all aspects of the craft but also in the preparation and organisation of production[41] —the Boulton and Watt management. According to a management memorandum entitled 'Arrangement of the Engine Manufactory, Soho, December, 1801', all shops either erected or to be erected were specified in terms of the machinery to be found in them, the operations to be performed by each shop, from the drilling shop to the smith's shop; how each shop was relatively situated with regard to the flow of materials and of communica-tions between the shops; and finally, what each machine was required to do in the production process.[42] Hence, those tasks formerly the province of craftsmen, such as the preparation and organisation of work, were now seen as the province of a separately constituted management. Moreover, in taking over responsibility for this work they also sought to use it to systematise the fragmentation of tasks, and to increase efficiency by adapting shops, tools and machines to narrower or more specialised use.[43] The development of new grades of labour, such as planers, was an important aspect of this, as it complemented and deepened the specialisation of the tasks of fitting and turning. William Fairbairn also focuses on comparable developments in the mid-nineteenth century. Speaking of the 'more systematic arrangements' rendered necessary by the introduction of complicated and expensive machinery and how this gradually supplanted the old millwright's trade, he referred to how 'the designing and direction of work passed away from the hands of the work-men into those of the master and his office assistants. This led also to a division of labour; men of general knowledge (millwrights) were only exceptionally required as *foremen* or outdoor superintendents; and the artificers became in the process of time, little more than attendants on the machines'.[44]

This two-fold decomposition of the traditional metal arts, the growth of an 'engineers' economy' and the hyper-qualification of management, led to new definitions and practices of labour in direct production. As can be seen, skill was now being associated with precision, dexterity, and speed, rather than with the older notions of mastery over an art or trade. No longer was 'managerial' or preparatory knowledge to be seen as the exclusive and intrinsic property of immediate production; it was now to be seen as embedded in a separately constituted management hierarchy. No matter how skilful was the precision and dexterity required, this was obviously a different kind of skill, one which was as 'efficient' as it was *degraded*. We will develop this point more fully below and in succeeding chapters, especially as it concerns those neo-Taylorist historians who speak of the 'considerable' and 'genuine' attributes of this 'skill'; for the moment, though, we can more fully explore this degradation of the craftsmanly attributes by turning to a second feature of this 'breach in craft control'[45] —the rise of a primitive, capitalist psycho-physical apparatus of labour.

As Charles Babbage, the famous nineteenth-century mathematical engineer and scientist, noted in his treatise on manufacture of 1832, the new skills that were being acquired were ones based on 'constant repetition of the same process. . . (which) necessarily produces in the workmen a degree of excellence and rapidity in his particular department, which is never possessed by a person who is obliged to execute many different processes'.[46] This induced a new equilibrium in muscular and mental exertion: 'Long habit. . . produces in the muscles exercised a capacity for enduring (physical) fatigue to a much greater degree than they could support under other circumstances. A similar result seems to take place in any change of mental exertion; the attention bestowed on the new subject not being so perfect at first as it becomes after some exercise'.[47]

This specialisation of the psycho-physical attributes of labour points to the third feature of the decomposition of the crafts; the new-found power of the manufacturing employer to go to the market and select with judicious precision the exact nature of the labour power that he required.

As Babbage put it:

> . . . the master manufacturer, by dividing the work to be executed into different processes, each requiring different degrees of skill or of force can purchase exactly that precise quantity of both which is necessary for each purpose.[48]

This was the opinion and practice of one of Britain's largest engineering employers, James Nasmyth, which can be gleaned from his evidence given before the Royal Commission on Trade Unions during 1867–68. Speaking of his antagonism to the Amalgamated Engineers' Society and of their encroachments on his 'liberty' through their apprenticeship regulations, he referred to the fact that during the lock-out of 1852[49] he was determined to introduce a system of remunerating labour which was not conditioned by the length of time a worker took to learn a trade, but 'by their value to me'.[50] By this he meant that because of the advanced division of labour in his Bridgewater works at Patricroft he could employ a youth or a less-skilled adult on processes hitherto controlled by the 'craftsmen' of the Amalgamated Engineers. Asked if a boy of 16 was as useful as a man, Nasmyth replied: 'I was fortunately the contriver of several machines for giving geometrical forms to metal work with such precision and rapidity by certain modifications of the planing machine, that all that class of men who depended upon *mere dexterity* were set aside altogether, and I was able to move on with these lads. Instead of having the old proportion of one boy to four mechanics, I had four boys to one mechanic nearly. There were an immense number of labourers in the neighbourhood, bargemen and others, the Bridgewater Canal Company's Servants, and I got them into my employment, and in a short time they were as good workmen as could be desired'.[51] It was thus with the self-effacement of an irate octopus that he 'rather took the lead in this non-apprentice system', which in the interrogations of his questioners was not conducive 'to the strength of the intellect or the improvement of the artisan', and increased the area from which he drew his labour.[52]

It can be suggested that such a labour market based on the capitalist regulation of skill provides a more exact understanding of why the recruitment of labour did not tax the resources of employers during the nineteenth century. Recent research has tended to emphasise the absence of any real difficulty of finding and recruiting labour. The expanding cotton and metal trades could pick up workers from the declining craft trades, such as iron wares, as well as from the overstocked textile trade, and domestic work.[53] If there was a difficulty it was in the area of work discipline and performance, of obtaining from workers a greater intensity of production, regular and punctual work attendance, acquiescence to a longer working day, and obedience to the employer's instructions. Hence, the need for draconian regulations and fines that governed everyday life in the factory. As Reinhard Bendix argues, 'Given the relative abundance of labour. . . it was sufficient to rely exclusively upon the pressures of the market and the use of coercion to control the workforce'.[54] With time it was hoped that coercion would turn into hegemony, so that an 'ethic of work performance' would develop amongst the workforce itself, an ethic based on 'individual striving and success'.[55] Yet Bendix goes even further when he suggests that, 'In the early phases of industrialisation, the entrepreneurial concern with the workers was not managerial at all, if by "managerial" we mean the deliberate use of means to organise and control the workforce of an enterprise'.[56] However, nothing can be more managerial than the creation of a labour supply inside of the factory by the decomposition of crafts and the associated attempt to regulate skill.

Specialisation of equipment and a fragmentation of tasks enabled 'a mechanic to do more in less time', therefore reducing the scope for applying traditional all-round skills and the time necessary to train workers.[57]

The question is not so much of reducing the importance that employers gave to work discipline and performance, but of complementing it with an emphasis on the equal importance they gave to the organisation and control of their workforce. It was precisely this managerial concern which led Nasmyth in the 1830s to break a strike in his works which sought to compel him to employ only apprenticed labour. Sixty-four 'wheelwrights, carpenters, smiths and stone masons. . . not bred to my business', from Scotland, were enough for him to have his way and for most other machine tool makers to be confident in the expectation that when they needed skilled labour they could easily get it. When it was not needed it could be dismissed and re-employed when trade improved.[58]

It is certainly true that during the nineteenth century the process of change in the metal trades was neither even nor rapid. In the machine building industry there was still a place for 'imaginative artisans to modify old tools and devise new ones'.[59] It is also true that in comparison with the cotton industry machinery was not as extensively applied, with the exception of various sections of the iron and steel trades. The production process, as one historian has noted, still often remained discontinuous, while the role of machinery was often 'ancillary rather than commanding'.[60] Dual technologies, too, often existed together. 'At the Atlas Works, Sheffield', armour plates were tempered in the furnace, in the 1850s, 'but dragged about the factory floor by teams of men in chains'.[61] Yet this does not amount to a labour process dependent for its functioning on 'craftsmanly skill', as Raphael Samuel would like us to believe.[62] The value of Samuel's work is that it provides a huge amount of evidence on the limits of mechanisation in the mid-Victorian economy, the continuity of sweating, often complementing the mechanisation of a part of a trade (as at the Atlas Works), as well as the continuity of heavy, varied and 'skilful' labour. Furthermore, human labour, 'from a commercial point of view', was often cheaper to use than expensive machinery.[63] In comparison with the engineering practices of a later period, it is correct that work was of a 'heavier kind', demanding 'more versatile skills'.[64] But this does not amount to a continuity of craftsmanship. Such a conception confuses craft with skill and the bygone division of labour of artisanal production with a technical division of labour under strong employer control, even though the dextrous and fatiguing use of the hand remained important. In other words, Samuel fails not only to define craftsmanship and its attributes but also to see the process of its decomposition, because *he does not study the evolution of the division of labour.* By confusingly associating hand technologies with 'craftsmanly skill' he cannot appreciate the trajectory of change: the beginnings of the capitalist regulation of skill based on a recomposition of the psycho-physical apparatus of labour.[65] Hence, when he too speaks of the development of over-stocked trades, of Clydeside shipbuilders 'scouring the riverside for work' in 1858, of a fifth of union members in the Sheffield trades out of work and on union relief during the 1860s, of a 'superabundance of labour' being a 'precondition of Victorian economic expansion', he cannot suggest how this was brought about.[66]

Only once does he enter into the topic of the development of the division of labour—with regard to the boot and shoe and riveting trades and Adam Smith's pin-makers[67]—or hint at the evolution of a 'wholly new level of exploitation'.[68] In the end, however, his analysis is quantitative rather than qualitative: 'Nineteenth century capitalism created many more skills than it destroyed'.[69] Yet it is the quality of the change that matters most: the decomposition of skills and training, plus an attempt by employers to regulate them.[70]

If by the mid-nineteenth century employers in the metal trades were seeking to regulate the skills of their workers they developed this ability, and the technical intelligence associated with it, not by formal theoretical and professional training but by practical training and a system of employer apprenticeships. The latter were more common in the engineering and shipbuilding trades than in the iron and steel industry. The famous machine tool maker, Alfred Herbert, did his apprenticeship at Jessops.[71]

Until the late nineteenth century most engineering employers came up through this system, particularly in railway and steam-engine shops. The system produced first-class practical engineers, who as youths mixed their training and public school backgrounds with sports. As S.B. Saul notes, Stoke City Football Club 'was founded by a group of public school boys serving their time in the local railway workshops'.[72]

In no sense was this system a vehicle for skilled workers or their sons to become industrialists. In the steel industry, for example, where the system was rare, only 3% of the sons of skilled workers in 1865 were active managing partners or chairmen of limited companies, vice-chairmen, deputy chairmen, managing directors or other executive directors on the board.[73] The likes of J.M. Allen of Cammell Laird, the son of a skilled worker, were rare. In the normal course of events, partners, owners and directors had a father in this position. According to Charlotte Erickson, some 28% of iron and steel industrialists in 1865 were recruited from this source, by far the largest source of recruitment.[74] In this same period the overwhelming majority did not attend colleges or universities, and when, in 1865, 13% did, it was to Oxbridge, Durham and London.[75] Very few managers came up through the state school system, while only three of Erickson's pre-World War One directors or partners received an academic training in metallurgy at the Royal School of Mines in London.[76] Only 6% of her sample of industrialists in 1865 had received an academic technical training for their future vocation.[77]

The system of employer apprenticeships played a more important part in the formation of Sheffield's steel masters. The town's three leading industrialists of the 1860s, John Brown, Charles Cammell and Samuel Fox, all served apprenticeships: Brown to a factor in the Sheffield file trade; Cammell to an ironmonger in Hull; and Fox to a Sheffield wire-drawer. Both Brown and Fox were either offered money or partnerships from their fathers as soon as their training was finished.[78] By the 1860s these three young 'self-made men' had established leading British enter-prises in rail-making and armaments: Brown coming from crucible steel, files and cutlery; Cammell from foundry work; and Fox from wire work.[79]

As distinct from these founding owners, however, who generally ended up concentrating on the commercial side of the enterprise, the active managers and works engineers, especially in the rising mass production steel industry, were men having had either formal academic technical training or had served employer apprenticeships generally in the *engineer-ing* industry. This is particularly important when one remembers the future links that were forged by the innovating firms, as those in Sheffield, like Brown's, Cammell's and Vickers, between heavy engineering and iron and steel production. Erickson's compilation of the careers of sixty men with leading positions in thirty-one 'innovating' iron and steel firms shows that only four firms did not have men from such backgrounds in these positions from the 1860s onwards. 'All the other firms had a technical man in at least one top position.[80] At least fourteen had a technical training of a formal nature, which included either an academic degree in engineering (6), such as James Ramsbottom from North Western Railways, who was chief engineer; Alexander Wilson, managing director of Cammell's in 1879; Edward Reynolds, managing director of Vickers from 1877; and William Bragge of John Brown's. Twelve of the sixty had completed technical apprenticeships in engineering, and nearly one in three completed their education abroad. Vickers and Cammell's sent their future leading men to branches in America or on the Continent, while others went as independents, such as J.T. Smith who worked at Le Creusot in France, or Samuel Fox who established a firm there.[81] Chemists, as well, were often sent on these sojourns, especially to Germany, where they gained experience, plus their doctorates, in the latest techniques of metallurgical chemistry. Chemists were also imported from Germany, Sweden and Switzerland after being trained at the continental polytechnic schools, in order to meet the shortage of trained chemists in Britain. This did not, though, indicate any *real* British backwardness.[82] As we shall see, Germany and France similarly sent their managers and technical personnel to other countries and imported others as a way of building up an elite of managers and engineers with a knowledge of the latest international techniques of production. Overall, this was one of the earliest signs of an evolving European experience in the metal industries of these countries.

After 1870 these methods of employer training were reinforced by the development of research movements in engineering and metallurgical chemistry. This particularly affected the new university colleges which established laboratories to prove their value to industry. Businessmen, too, became involved by pouring in money and donating resources, if not founding their own 'civic' university, as Thomas Firth did in Sheffield.[83]

Like the alleged continuity of craftsmanship as an integral feature of the skill and training of the workforce in the heavy metal industry, it is hard to substantiate an argument which denigrates the method of training, 'amateurism' and contempt for technical knowledge amongst the British metal industry bourgeoisie. They *may* have been anti-theoretical, they may have distrusted 'science', they may have restricted social mobility, but they were not anti-theory *applied,* anti- the science of engineering, or anti- technical knowledge. To be sure, they were not Taylorian professionals, but to suggest that they *should* have been more than they were would not only be anachronistic but fatuous. In comparison with France and Germany, as we shall see, they had done much since the eighteenth century—they had abolished craftsmanship and its ties to public regulation; they had recomposed and were beginning to regulate skills on the basis of the principles of manufacture; and they had constituted a private, if still empirical, basis for the formation of their own technical intelligence, an intelligence increasingly independent of the knowledge and skills of their workers.

Almost fifty years before 'scientific management' gained wide currency in America, employers in the French and German heavy metal industry were learning, in the words of C.B. Thompson, to 'shift the demand from labour which is already skilled to that which is teachable'. The lineages of this are to be found at the end of the eighteenth century when Britain was going through its Industrial Revolution and the Continent was settling accounts with its feudal past. The period was not one conducive to rapid capital accumulation or industrialisation. By the 1820s, when revolution and revolutionary wars had passed, France and Germany found that they had 'missed' the revolution that had been occurring on the other side of the Channel: the industrialisation of the consumer goods industries—namely, the cotton industry—whose workforce consisted of cheap female and child labour.[84] It is hard to imagine today the significance of Britain's industrial lead over the Continent, which by the 1820s amounted to some sixty years; years of expanding towns, building factories and making machines, as well as making a workforce to operate and service them.[85] But two things were obvious by this time. First, neither Germany nor France could compete with Britain's machine and factory-based cotton industry, either at home or abroad. It was more remunerative for textile and cotton merchants, for that is what they generally were, to exploit putting-out systems so that they could continually reduce the price house-bound labourers received for their work, rather than spend thousands of pounds on imported British textile machinery.[86] Where it was possible to compete was in those branches of industry where Britain had no real *technological* lead: in the iron industry and the machine building trades, i.e. producer goods industries.

It has already been noted that the role of machinery in these trades at this time, was auxiliary to the labour process, rather than its animator, and that what was more important was the division of labour. This raised the second problem. It was work that was heavy, varied, requiring training and qualification, and, for biological as well as social reasons, male. The dimensions of the problem can be readily grasped. What was required was the making of skills involving higher technical attributes than Britain required when its Industrial Revolution began; skills for chemists, metallurgists, engineers, as well as for turners, fitters, millmen, etc., skills in short supply in societies which remained for most of the nineteenth century agricultural and little urbanised.[87] Where Britain's lead allowed it to develop a workforce in an empirical, if not revolutionary fashion, in France and Germany the state and the enterprise would have to provide a public and private educational infrastructure to supply the workplace.

(ii) France

Until at least the introduction of mass-produced steel in the 1870s, French Government reports speak of the shortage of qualified workers for the iron and steel trades.[88] The suppression of guild corporations during the Revolution threw the apprenticeship system into chaos. Revolutionary governments attempted to regulate a new system supervised by the *Chambre des arts et manufactures,* and men such as Talleyrand and Condorcet developed programmes for creating a liberal, democratic and scientifically inclined citizen populace in schools which would be free, secular and open to both sexes. During the Convention, Lakanal and Bourbou developed these ideas into programmes for making a workforce. Manual labour and artisanal skills were given high status. Bourbou, in fact, wanted to turn primary schools into apprenticeship schools for both sexes, while the Convention itself stressed education in mathematics, physics, mechanics and chemistry for artisans and qualified workers. Most of these schemes, however, remained only on paper, victims of political turmoil, bad planning and lack of facilities.[89]

One important source for the recruitment of skilled labour was from Britain itself. Though the Revolution and the wars interrupted the supply of foreign labour (to the extent that officials from the Agency of Mines had to search amongst POW's during 1794-95 for specialists in steel-making and forging to be put at the disposal of employers),[90] in later years it proved essential to get production off the ground and useful for the training of unskilled French workers. In the south and middle regions, enterprises relied heavily on the supply of such labour. Joseph Bessy brought out some forty-two English families to the St Etienne district, most likely to provide skilled supervisors for the work in his plants during the 1820s. At the same time, William Jackson's plant employed English workers under long contracts and for high wages to undertake the difficult task of training French workers and supervising production procedures.[91] In 1825, the Fourchambault iron works employed thirty-five Englishmen; as did Le Creusot and Decazeville. Jacob Holtzer even went to the Ruhr, in Germany, in search of skilled men to work in his Unieux plant.[92] This source of labour, though, proved to be not only expensive, its supply was also too small to fill what one historian calls 'the prevalent lack of skill' at this time.[93] Foreign workers moreover could prove to be too powerful for their employers' liking. Employers would often refer to them as 'masters' in their own right, for they, like the traditional iron workers, still monopolised the 'secrets' of the art.[94] On the whole, however, the iron worker's family was being by-passed in the training of the next generation of qualified workers through a programme which was both plant-based and management-inspired.[95]

Difficulties with recruiting and maintaining a workforce as a whole were equally apparent. The traditional pattern of recruiting from the families of iron workers no longer sufficed as a source of labour, even of the most unskilled kind.[96] Iron masters in the south and Midi regions were often reduced to trying to entice workers away from other local plants either in secret or by directly approaching a company with formal requests for labour. The iron masters at Decazeville and Alais were particularly embroiled in these activities during the 1830s.[97] As well, small population growth, in complete contrast to Britain, and a peasantry tied to the land, meant that French employers could neither rely on a growing reserve army of labour nor on those massive shifts of population from the country to the city to supply their needs.[98] Though a few women and children could be seen making their way to the mills, their role remained marginal.[99]

Two major changes contributed a solution to the problem: some fortunate technical advances which broke the back of strategic crafts in iron and steel production, and allowed for the introduction of less skilled labour; and the concentration of several industries in one area, which allowed for the formation of a large labour force. As this occurred, enterprises were able to build plant training programmes that would both expand their labour supply and allow for the introduction of women and children.[100]

During the first half of the nineteenth century the general structure of the craft system broke down in the iron trades. First, the introduction of coal-fired coke ovens eliminated nearly all those iron craftsmen who operated small, wood-fired furnaces—*bûcherons* and *charbonniers.*[101] Second, the introduction of Bessemer steel in the late 1850s began to throw onto history's technical scrapheap thousands of puddling craftsmen, who traditionally made iron in the same fashion that their wives made bread: with a spoon, a bowl, a hot oven, and reliable ingredients.[102] Both innovations could be operated by semi-skilled workers trained in the factory and supervised by professionally-trained chemists and metallurgists. Related to this also was the growing regional concentration of several industries, especially heavy industries like coal mining, iron, steel, and engineering, centred in the St Etienne coal basin in the south (the Loire area), and the Valenciennes coal basin in the north (the Pas de Calais and the Nord). Workers were generally recruited in the immediate vicinity of the forges, mills, plants and mines: in the north, from Franche-Comté, L'Ariège, and in the south, from the region Lyonnaise.[103] Yves Lequin has calculated that for the years 1850–51 the proportion of workers married in the towns of their birth in the Lyonnaise region was 63.5% for Lyons, 86% for St Etienne, and 74.8% for St Chamond.[104] Employers then were certainly not relying on workers who were *déracinés* or *uprooted.*[105] According to contemporary evidence and historical studies this remained the pattern until World War One.[106] This regional concentration produced some huge mixed enterprises requiring differentially trained workforces, enterprises like the *Compagnie de Commentry-Fourchambault,* which in 1854 comprised coal mines in Commentry, blast furnaces in Montluçon, and factories in Fourchambault. In 1866 it employed some 3,000 workers; *Wendel's* employed 5,000; *Aciéries de la Marine,* 6,000; *Terrenoire,* 1,000; and the giant, *Le Creusot,* 10,000—over half the town's population.[107] It was firms such as these that began to introduce factory-based trade and apprenticeship schools to train workers for their own needs and thereby overcome the twin difficulties of enticing workers away from other plants and having to endure powerful foreign workers. At the Decazeville plant, for example, local apprentices and even labourers *(manoeuvres),* were given 'professional' training by the firm after 1830, while other schools were founded at Hayange, Fourchambault, Alais, Terrenoire, Pont-Saloman and Le Creusot. The system at Le Creusot was developed to such an extent that they were able to train not only their workers, but also their clerks, executives, and engineers.[108] As one historian has so eloquently put it, 'the formula for industrialisation. . . [was the] emancipation of apprenticeship from workmanship *(la fabrication)* so that it became an end in itself.[109] In other words, it was now a company asset, not an organic relationship between the *maître, compagnon,* and *apprenti.* The foreign workers at Decazeville, for instance, began to be displaced in the 1830s, though it is noticeable that this did not affect the position of the foreign engineers, who continued to hold important managerial and technical positions. Locally-trained puddlers were promoted to take the place of the foreign foremen and the English smelters were replaced by the first generation of plant-trained French workers.[110]

It may be true that the state played little role in education for the workforce as a whole, and that, therefore, primary education and general literacy rates developed only slowly, as Lequin suggests.[111] Yet it cannot be accepted that 'the rank and file were completely ignored', or, as Dunham believes, the employer 'had the temperament of a peasant' and found it 'unnecessary to train labour'.[112] Iron, steel and engineering employers, in fact, not only found it necessary to train their labour, they also found that in order to do this and direct their own enterprises, they too had to be trained. They had to develop their own technical intelligence and become hyper-qualified in all aspects of the preparation and organisation of production. They had to build their own structure of conceptual work, know how things were done, who would do them, which means of labour were to be used, and how the object of the work was to be transformed. In other words, they had to learn to programme the actions of an entire labour process. Here the aid of the state was crucial.

If revolutionary governments floundered in providing a system of education and training for the populace as a whole, they did provide a system of lasting value for the training of an industrial bourgeoisie. The period of the Convention and of Napoleon's reign were particularly important. The Convention, in seeking to promote a utilitarian view of science and education over religious and superstitious belief and to supply its own military needs for the liberatory wars, founded in 1794 the *Ecole des Travaux Publics*, the *Conservatoire des Arts et Métiers*, and the *Ecole Normale Supérieure*. In 1795 it founded the *Ecole Polytechnique*. Napoleon extended this work and partly militarised the higher education system. Various *Ecoles d'arts et métiers* were established in 1807, which contained workshops and placed a heavy emphasis on practical work. Military and naval schools were formed, which provided training for military engineers, and students at the *Ecole Polytechnique* were put into uniform. The mining law of 1810 led to the creation of the *Corps des Mines*, composed of state-employed engineers similar to the *Corps des Ponts et Chaussées* which was composed of civil engineers.[113] This system of higher education designed to fill the needs of industry, science, war and government administration produced a social stratum which effectively ran French industrial life on a day-to-day basis.

By the early nineteenth century the *Conservatoire des Arts et Métiers*, for example, was producing the likes of Eugène Schneider, the future iron master, textile industrialists, and others who would become professors and teachers at the *Polytechnique* and the *École des Mines*, etc.[114] The *Polytechnique*, particularly, in the words of Henry Le Chatelier looking back over more than one hundred years of its existence, produced the future heads of 'our great administrations, our great railway companies, and of our most important industries'.[115] Its solidly bourgeois student clientele studied abstract mathematics and science as a foundation for future studies in architecture, civil and military engineering and navigation. It was meant to encourage a disposition towards accuracy and rigorous theoretical method. Its small student population, no more than three hundred to three hundred and fifty students in any one year throughout the nineteenth century, ensured the maintenance of its character as an elitist institution of scientific learning whose students had their career lines feeding into the civil service, ministries of state, the *Ecole des Mines* and the *Ponts et Chaussées*.[116] In the 1820s and 1830s, this college produced the likes of Léon and Paulin Talabot, future innovating metal and railway industrialists, and the heir to de Wendel's iron and steel plants, Charles, François' son.[117] Georges Defaud, a student at the *Polytechnique* in 1794, was responsible for the introduction of puddling in Fourchambault and developed mass production methods in iron making, which brought about the rise of a heavy metal industry in the town.[118]

One of the characteristics of this system was that founding industrialists used it to educate the future heirs to their enterprises—their sons. Charles Martenot, founder of the Commentry works and educated at the *École des Mines,* sent off young Augustin to the same institution in the 1850s. Augustin later administered the Commentry firm himself and built a new works at Ancy-le-Franc.[119] Charrière, the founder of metallurgical works at Allevard, was succeeded during the Second Empire by his son-in-law Pinat, an engineer from *Ponts et Chaussées*.[120] Like Britain, the possibility of artisans, handicraftsmen, and the self-educated rising to become heads of works, like the head forgemen at Jackson's in 1859, was rare.[121] The system was just not designed for them. In comparison with Britain's employer-apprenticeship system and practical training for industrialists, they were even more badly placed. This was a system designed to produce hyper-qualified bourgeois engineers and industrialists.

The expansion of French industry, however, meant that such education could not be limited to founding industrialists and their sons if the needs of expansion were to be met. Therefore, in response to the demand for more engineers the *École Centrale des Arts et Manufactures* was established in 1828-29. Its board of trustees was drawn from the sciences, industry, education, banking and engineering. The school aimed to provide the 'training of civil engineers, factory managers and industrialists'. It ran courses similar to those at the *Polytechnique,* but gave less emphasis to pure science and mathematics and more to applied disciplines and their demonstration. In time it rivalled at home and abroad the reputation of its 'elder sister', and in the years 1832-70 produced some 3,000 engineers.[122] They were the likes of A. Brustlien, technical manager at Jacob

Holtzer's Unieux works in the 1870s, who experimented with chromium and manganese for special steels; Berges, who made inventions in hydraulic power; and the future automobile industrialists like René Panhard, who went through in the 1860s and originally built wood-working machinery in Paris; his classmate, Levassor, who worked at Cockerill's in Seraing before joining Panhard to form the famous automobile firm; André Michelin, who introduced pneumatic tyres; Louis and Emile Mors, who started out in electrical engineering before moving into automobiles; Eugène Brillié, founder member of Gobron-Brillié; as well as the future metallurgical Taylorites, like Léon Guillet, the famous research metallurgist, editor of *Revue de Métallurgie,* and exponent of Taylorism, who installed metallurgical laboratories for special steel making at de Dion-Bouton, makers of tricycles and engines, and Charles de Fréminville, an advocate of scientific management and a future director of *Panhard et Levassor.*[123] It is not an overestimation to say as Cameron does that this was 'an age when the superiority of French science was freely admitted, when scientists wrote even technical treatises with a literary flair, and when practically all educated persons, whether scientists, public officials, or businessmen read and spoke French, [and when] the latest scientific publications from Paris found a ready readership'.[124] This education system became a magnet for foreigners from Germany, Belgium, and other parts of the Continent and provided the models for the establishment of similar schools in Germany, Austria, and America. It was France that provided the model for MIT, the Massachusetts Institute of Technology.[125]

Yet this was not the only source for the training and education of French metal industrialists and managers. In the early period, it was complemented by private travel and work in foreign countries, especially Britain, just as their British counterparts came to France. In the early nineteenth century, for instance, the *ingénieur des mines,* Gallois, discovered that the St Etienne region had adequate iron ore and coal supplies in close proximity to each other. This was unusual in France but in Britain had provided a stimulus for the rise of the iron industry. In 1815–16, Gallois went to England for six months and on his return presented a report on the establishment of plants for the region to the *Conseil général des mines.* He returned to England again in 1820, this time investigating machinery in use in the iron industry. His colleague, Beaunier, a founder of the Béradière steel plant, also travelled to England in 1820 for similar purposes.[126] Joseph Bessy, also from the St Etienne region, who had his works at Firminy, went off to England in 1817 to study the latest techniques.[127] Another Lyonnaise traveller was Denys Benoist, one of the founders of *Drouillard, Benoist et Cie,* a metallurgical plant located at Alais. He travelled to Britain on several occasions during the years 1839–42, visiting iron works at Wolverhampton and Newcastle.[128] Bertrand

Gille goes so far as to suggest, quite rightly, that 'the establishment of large French metal works was preceded by technical voyages to England'.[129] The English, too, reciprocated. Engine builders and iron masters like Wilkinson and Jackson set up their enterprises in France, bringing with them valuable technical knowledge and techniques for making iron and steel, building machines and machine tools.[130]

The most fascinating aspect of this system of higher education is that it underwrote the professionalisation of production management and the transference of directing power in the factories away from supervisory workers, founding industrialists and their sons to white collar *business engineers.* In comparison with today—where the role of the engineer is that of a well-paid *employee-technician,* whose skills do not comprise managerial attributes unless they are obtained independently by pro- motion, and whose work is the object of a very refined division of labour within well *established* enterprises—the engineer of the nineteenth century came to design not only the factory and the machines which would fill it, he also came to run it. Two reasons account for this phenomenon, especially in France. First, the growth and expansion of the metal industry concerned the actual construction of new industries, notably a mass- production steel trade and engineering itself. It also concerned the forma- tion of new enterprises. In other words, technical and scientific attributes were equally as important as business and commercial skills, and in France during the nineteenth century, they came to be formally blended in the same man.

In the first instance, during the 1820s, the products of the engineering schools were brought in as consultants or to install complicated equip- ment. Their role was to select a location for a plant as well as the machinery that would inhabit it. This had to be done with a view to costs of production, markets, and the labour supply. For a new steel enterprise like Decazeville it also meant access to a supply of minerals, especially coal and iron ore, and the costs of obtaining them. It meant coordinating relations and production procedures between shops on the same site and establishments some distance away from each other.[131] By the 1840s, these engineers were being employed on a permanent basis and came to replace the founding capitalist's technical direction of the factory. They at first became the works managers, i.e. *directeurs de hautes fourneaux et de forges,* such as H. Fournel at *Le Creusot,* T.C. de Gargan at *Stiring- Wendel,* Cabrol at *Decazeville,* and E. Martin, Defaud, Saglio, and d'Audincourt at *Fourchambault.*[132] It is true that the consultancy and contract work of engineers did not stop. Once enterprises were established, men who specialised in this work were called in to renovate plants, especially during the 1850s when steel-making technologies changed fundamentally and rapidly. Such engineers were called in to renovate works at L'Orme, de Montataire, Pont-à-Moussan, Denain et Anzin,

Commentry and Montluçon during this time.[133] Also these French engineers were rightly famous and world renowned by the mid-century for their direction of the construction of factories, railways, bridges, engineering plants, and steel mills all over the world, especially in Germany, Russia, Belgium, Austria–Hungary, and Latin America.[134] At the same time though, the internal management of many metal enterprises passed into their hands and were run by them on a day-to-day basis. A railway company, like the *Compagnie du Nord,* hired its engineering plant managers from *Ponts et Chaussées* and the *Arts et Métiers,* while its board of directors came mainly from the *Ecole des Sciences Politiques.* During the 1860s the two groups remained in close contact with one another, but the firm granted a large degree of autonomy to its three major sections, whose day-to-day operations were run by business engineers.[135] According to Claude Fohlen, this role of the engineer within a complex business structure was exceptional for the time.[136] Yet we have already seen that in the heavy metal industry this was not the case, particularly with the development of works manager engineers. Fohlen also draws attention himself to firms like *Decazeville* and *Commentry,* where the engineers were drawn from the *Polytechnique,* the *Ecole Centrale, Arts et Métiers* and the *École des Mines,* and who coordinated diverse operations such as hiring and firing, contracts, production programmes and budgets. Even a middle-size enterprise like the Allevard iron works came to be run by engineers after three generations of dominance by the Charrière family.[137] At the same time, the 1860s saw the title *ingénieur civil* (mechanical engineer) appear frequently against the names of the directors of large engerprises. In an age of expansion the engineer's status grew remarkably: he was both a 'realist and an optimist', 'enterprising and solid', a technician and a businessman.[138] A new type of enterprise leader had come into existence. Their appearance was also marked by the growth of *bureaux de comptabilité,* which employed white-collar administrators and accountants, who implemented their commercial and technical decisions, gradually supplanting the likelihood that these tasks would be undertaken by non-professional supervisory workers in the shop.[139]

A second reason for the growth of the engineer's power in the day-to-day running of the factory was the intensive application of science to industry. This was not just a question of the engineer's monopoly of brainpower, but also of the structural role of science in the production process—of it becoming a productive force, whose agents required intensive, formal training. This was especially true for the higher grades of supervisory labour, such as ordinary foremen, head or section foremen, *chefs de section,* works managers and *ingénieur-mécaniciens* or qualified technical employees in charge of the repair shops. The latter supervised the use of machinery, and directed the work of maintenance crews comprising smiths, pattern-makers and fitters.[140]

The evolution of science as a material force of production, as distinct from just brainpower or institutional knowledge, has been usefully and subtly discussed by Nathan Rosenberg. Commenting on Marx's thoughts about the evolution of science, Rosenberg argues that its tendency to become a force of production is more than a response to the material and productive needs of economic development. Science became a productive force at a certain stage of modern industrial capitalist development: 'Science can only incorporate its findings in impersonal machinery. It cannot be incorporated in human beings with individual volitions; idiosyncracies and refractory temperaments'. It becomes a productive force only when capitalism reaches a stage when the worker and his or her physical and intellectual attributes are 'no longer central to the organisation and arrangement of capital'.[141] Rather, machinery and its scientific development are central. Science, however, as a productive force does not have its full potentialities released until the production of machines themselves is freed from dependence upon human skills, i.e. it is only fully liberated in the period of the *machine* production of machines. In the metal industries of Britain, France and Germany this does not fully occur until the end of the nineteenth century. This is not to say, though, that a favourable social structure can be overlooked. It is enough to compare the situation in France with that of ancient Greece, where the craftsmen, generally slaves, were despised by the ruling class. For Socrates, the 'mechanical arts' had a 'stigma' attached to them, making it illegal at times for a citizen to undertake the trade. In such a case science could not become even a social or institutional productive force, let alone a material force under ruling class direction. Instead, such knowledge survived in the subterranean world of the slave's brain.[142] In France, by contrast, during the 1850s, invention and innovation were becoming factors of production forcing employers to become harbingers of their development. The introduction of Bessemer steel converters, recuperating ovens, lifting and transport equipment, and of works laboratories to study production techniques and the composition of metals, imposed a more scientific basis on management's direction of the labour process. A firm like Jacob Holtzer's Unieux works, near St Etienne, for example, developed extensive works laboratories, staffed by formally trained engineers and designers, which concentrated on research and development into special steels made from nickel, chromium, tungsten, manganese, etc. At first this was linked to the company's arms and munitions production, but by the late nineteenth century the firm began to produce special steels for the nascent automobile industry, with close relations developing with companies like *Panhard et Levassor*. 'The role of scientists grew with the times', according to Vial, and was buttressed by the growth of scientific societies and their publishing outlets.[143] In this respect France took a lead over Britain by its commitment to state and private scientific research and engineering education for the bourgeoisie. The English Industrial Revolution did relatively little to turn science into a productive force, mainly because it was based in the cotton industry rather than in the metal industry. In the cotton industry, the need to mobilise science for industry was not as pressing, whereas in the metal industry its role was crucial. Even the necessary improvements to Watt's steam engine came from engineers with a practical bent, not scientists.[144] Only theoretical scientists with access to works laboratories and an extensive system of higher education could lead the way in the production of special steels. As we shall see below, it was only at the turn of the century that an institutionalised base for scientific and engineering research developed in Britain. Again, this is not to denigrate the achievements of British metal industrialists by the Victorian period; but in comparison with the French their achievement was essentially private and empirical, marked by an early lead and under-written by a favourable social structure, where a peasantry did not act as an obstacle to the formation of a labour force. In France, the achievement was both private and public, empirical and theoretical, at least in the formation of a metal industry bourgeoisie. Yet like Britain, the actual formation and training of the workforce remained in private hands. Both countries also had systematically broken with craft forms of production as their heavy metal industries developed. By turning to Germany we find a similar path of development to France, except that it was a path even more comprehensive in its dissolution of the crafts and in its constitution of a metal industry workforce.

(iii) Germany

When a German engineering industry was being founded in the 1830s and 1840s, neither a trained management nor a trained workforce was in existence or could be seen to have any structural lineages. What was available had to be shaped and what was not available had to be created. In contrast to Britain, and to a certain extent France also, the industry was *new*, both because the major enterprises did not arise out of the traditional metal crafts and because right from the start, its growth was shaped by linkages with heavy industry, notably iron and steel and rail-ways. By this time also, the industry was largely free from the legacies of the restraining guild restrictions imposed on it up to the 1820s and 1830s.[145]

Jürgen Kocka has spoken eloquently of the distinct cultural back-ground which surrounded the rise of modern industry in Germany. The 'old corporate world' had largely collapsed and 'in so far as the traditional expressions, symbols, and life-styles of the crumbling etatist (corporate) society became less strong and less widely accepted, [then] greater scope was offered for individual choice in work and life, for new symbols of individual standing and individual success. . . Economic success now [after 1830] became possible without regard to, or even in defiance of, the inherited guild and class order'.[146] The engineering industry, of course, was neither culturally induced, nor did it grow out of thin air. Textile manufacturers since the late eighteenth century had need of water-wheels, gins, spindles, handlooms and treadmills, often built by instrument makers, clockmakers and 'mechanical artists' *(mechanische Künstler)* in small workshops. Instrument making had long been in existence, which required craftsmen who could build complicated tools and machines. Iron producers too, with their more-or-less fundamental knowledge of metals, had a corresponding knowledge of machine production. Out of this landscape many early engineering firms took shape, at first producing a few machines besides supplying the needs of their own craft, later taking up machine production full-time; or textile and iron producers building the machines they needed in their own repair shops.[147] Yet these origins were not significant in the formation of a fully-fledged engineering industry. If we consider first the formation of an engineering employer class, we can turn to Schröter's survey of the origins of eighty-three engineering firms in the period 1835-1850. Nine firms came from the textile industry (11%), fifteen (18%) were originally iron producers, twenty-eight (34%) came from the crafts, while thirty-one firms (37%) were right from the start, engineering firms.[148] The industry itself therefore did not derive solely from the crafts, but grew out of several areas. Furthermore, though craftsmen were a numerically important group in forming small workshops, the most important group structurally was the middle class.[149]

The middle class had access to money, formal education and practical training in modern metal and engineering production methods, which as a rule, were not available to craftsmen. This also laid the basis for the formation of large enterprises, which quickly came to dominate the industry.[150] These men of the middle class generally came from two backgrounds: from commerce, and therefore functioned in the capacity of raising capital to start an enterprise, and from engineering itself. The latter generally received practical and theoretical training either in existing engineering shops in Germany, or in other countries, such as France and Britain, and later went on to form their own enterprises, most commonly as open partnerships *(offene Handelsgesellschaft)* with a commercial man. The individual owner, like the joint stock company *(Aktiengesellschaft: AG)*, did not play an important role in the formation of an employer class.[151] Two examples from Düsseldorf may suffice. Ernst Schiess was born in Magdeburg in 1840. His father was a banker. The younger Schiess trained to be an engineer at various technical schools in Europe. During the late 1850s and early 1860s, he worked in Manchester's machine tool trade. By 1865 he had returned to Düsseldorf and in cooperation with Alfred

Poensgen founded a small engineering shop, which opened on 1 January 1866, with six workers. The firm concentrated on making machines for shipbuilding and the iron and steel trades, and by the late nineteenth century it was one of the first firms to produce electrically-powered machine tools for specialised mass-production work. After World War One, it went on to join the giant engineering company, DEMAG.[152] Wilhelm De Fries was born in Orsay, a Düsseldorf district, in 1856. He was the son of a coal merchant and wanted to be an engineer at an early age. He took a four-year apprenticeship *(Lehrzeit)* in Duisburg and by 1874 was a fitter at the *Maschinenfabrik von Breur und Schumacher* of Cologne. After more travel and the completion of his military service, he went back to Düsseldorf and for a time joined Schiess, only to move on again to Bechem and Keetman back in Duisburg. By 1891, after many years of travel and working experience he was ready to form his own engineering company with his brother, Heinrich, and Anton Roper, to form De Fries and Company. The firm concentrated on making cranes. This was the origin of the famous *Benrather Maschinenfabrik, AG.,* which by 1910 had also joined DEMAG.[153]

France and Britain were also important influences on the formation of the early nineteenth-century engineering bourgeoisie in Germany. Government officials and future employer-managers were not only sent off to England and France for training, in the hope of bringing back with them technical knowledge and designs for machines to be slightly modified, but also British and French engineers came to such places as Berlin, Chemnitz and the Rhineland to set up enterprises. The celebrated Phoenix works in the Rhineland was originally a French firm.[154] France, too, provided models for the formation of universities, laboratories, and industrial exhibitions. Many of the famous technical colleges were also founded at this time: Stuttgart's in 1832 (from 1840 it became a Polytechnique) Darmstadt's in 1836; Hanover's in 1831; Brunswick's in 1835, and Berlin's as early as 1821.[155]

The making of a trained labour force to work in the engineering establishments raised many acute problems. Two periods need to be discussed here: the period from the early nineteenth century to the late 1850s, and the period from the 1860s till the turn of the century. The first period was effectively the pre-history of the German Industrial Revolution and in the nascent engineering trades was marked by a chronic shortage of trained, skilled labour. Schröter and Becker note that as engineering had been 'alien' *(fremd)* to Germany, a stratum of qualified *Facharbeiter* just did not exist.[156] Those that came from the traditional metal crafts of fitting, smithing and pattern-making had a working knowledge of engineering, but this 'in no way corresponded to the requirements posed by the technical development' of the industry.[157] Journeymen who had obtained their *Beruf* in craft workshops generally had not received essential theoretical and scientific training in engineering. At first, there-fore, they required some extra instruction in some form or another. Moreover, having come from the crafts they were prone to leave the firm once they had obtained this knowledge in order to establish their own independent workshops. Often, in the 1830s and 1840s they would stay only if economic circumstances prevented them from leaving.[158] The prospect of becoming proletarians on a permanent basis did not please them very much.

Like France, such instruction was generally provided by the employer himself, working beside his workers and showing them, or by foreign *Facharbeiter* brought in to fill strategic bottlenecks, train workers and ensure the continuity of a firm's output: such was the early history of firms such as *Gutehoffnungshütte, Harkort's* and *Von Haubold's*.[159] With time a stratum of qualified workers was created who could take over the functions of the employer-educator and the foreign *Facharbeiter*, but in no way can this training be seen as akin to the training of a journeyman under the supervision of a master, or that the labour supply generated had craft attributes. The process was employer-inspired and employer-controlled. Right from the start engineering employers did not take their skilled labour force as given. They had a monopoly over technical intelli-gence and used this to 'allow the workers [to] acquire a certain know-ledge' of the production process.[160] Yet the art of retraining craftsmen in a certain 'dexterity based on experience' or of relying on foreign, skilled workers to work in the new establishments could not overcome the general absence of a reserve army of metal workers.[161]

When Thomas Banfield toured the Rhineland in the 1840s, he was struck by the absence of a fluctuating mass of workers wandering from place to place in search of work.[162] For some Rhineland firms, like *Krupp's, Haniel, Huyssen* and *Jacobi*, the problem was partially solved by the creation of 'labour colonies' *(Arbeiterkolonien)*, which provided housing, factory-schools, pensions, and enterprise savings programmes. This was the case at Essen, Oberhausen, and Hammerstein.[163] Whether it involved this method of recruitment or the more common, though less systematic, method of word-of-mouth and kinship networks the workers were invariably unqualified, coming from general labouring, agriculture, weaving, spinning, tailoring etc.[164] Alfred Krupp's views on his own workforce in the 1840s provide some insight into the frustrations of one heavy metal industry employer:

A. unreal; L. awkward; K. stupid, has improved himself; V. my look-out *(Augen-diener)*; B. still need to look at again; M. lazy; H. runs around aimlessly; S. lazy, doesn't finish much; St. (a master smith) never came again, a drunkard; Bl. return-ing to Elberfeld, conducted himself well here; H. reliable and solid, can be taken on again; L. able builder and an honest man; P. able fellow, ready for anything; C. was drunk, started a fight. . .; W.H. failed to appear; K. driven off for all kinds of things; F. stays away, like one caught out lying and cheating; Sch. stays away, is not to be taken on again. . .; P. good turner, finally however became very lazy; D. came from Düsseldorf dead-drunk, packed off back there. . .; W. was let go; C. carried off by theft; K. an honest man; H. already too old; B. sent away because of unacceptable behaviour towards foreman Hecking. . .; K. a true blue machine assembler *(Montagsman),* was often very late, wanted to leave. . .; P. had a fight with Hecking in a public house, had to be let go. . .[165]

Krupp's chronicle of workers failing to turn up, of drunkenness, of craftsmen leaving, of laziness and of workers showing little flair for the work, need to be taken seriously. Foreman Hecking was obviously an unpopular man, and Krupp was a moralistic, tough, patronising and authoritarian figure. Yet so too were his colleagues. They did not see themselves as having much to work with in building up their enterprises. Even the famous *Maschinenfabrik Esslingen,* which attempted to recruit its workforce from the qualified, was forced to take on, train and discipline for factory production some 31.3% of its workers who were 'unqualified' in any sort of metal work during the period of 1847–60. They included men from agriculture and wine-gardening, and handicraftsmen from other industries, such as weavers and bakers.[166]

Like many enterprises at this time, the machine shop of the Esslingen firm was the only one which extensively used machine tools. It was also the only shop where a broad stratum of technically qualified workers was critically needed and had to be rapidly formed. The firm did not seem to have difficulties in recruiting men for the foundry, assembly shop and smithy, where the work required large amounts of manual dexterity and was *Handwerk* in character.[167] As the firm concentrated on locomotive building, the first section of the German engineering industry to become specialised, the management committed itself to the expansion of the machine shops (the fitting and turning shops), rather than to the handwork shops, like the wagon-building, painting and lacquering shops, which were more and more moved to the periphery of the works. It was precisely in these central machine shops that the firm introduced its own apprenticeship systems, especially in the turning shop. The firm just could not fill all the places in the turning shop without such a system.[168] The expansion of this shop was most rapid. The majority of machines were bought from France, where the firm also acquired some of its skilled foreign labour and had some of its own workers trained. Between 1846 and 1856 the number of workers employed in the turning shop jumped from 48 to 170, an increase of 254%, while the number of lathes in use increased from 21 to 76, or by 262%.[169] A similar picture emerged in Krupp's machine shops during the 1850s. Here, the turners and fitters served no official articles of apprenticeship *(Lehrvertrag).* The apprentices were mere 'novices' picking up a trade. The fitting novices started at filing the right angles of casting boxes so that they could stand side by side, then came a whole series of drills, which ended up with the teaching of some writing. The turning novices started at thread cutting and other jobs arising from this task, and were later transferred to easy jobs, like turning bolts.[170] Already here were shades of what many *Auslese und Anpassung* observers would pick up as a general tendency at the turn of this century. For the untrained labourer *(Hilfsarbeiter)*, work consisted of general labouring around the shop and of the chance of being allocated to a trained *Facharbeiter* who would show him a simple job on a turning or boring machine; and if he had the knack or the 'genius' he could keep this job under the supervision of the *Facharbeiter*. If this supervision was not possible or needed, the foreman was not too far away.[171] Training at Krupp's, therefore, even at this time, was highly specialised. According to Richard Ehrenberg, though a number of fully trained *Facharbeitern* were needed to train other workers, the differentiation of the workforce did not revolve around craft relations; rather, differentiation occurred around specialised tasks on 'the same bank' of machines so that the 'particular dexterity' acquired was 'only rarely exchangeable to another factory'.[172] Ehrenberg went so far as to suggest that it was impossible to distinguish a clear dividing line between the 'skilled' *(gelernt)* and 'semi-skilled' *(angelernt)* workers at this time.[173] A worker from the Chemnitz Machinists' Association similarly drew attention to the evolution of this non-craft differentiation of the workforce in 1847:

> Workers in the machine shops are divided into three classes. The first class consists of those who, due to their trade, are indispensable to the machine shops (smiths, fitters, tool smiths, turners and patternmakers). In the second class I count all those who do not belong to such a trade, but rather to something else. They have come to the factory so that they can secure for themselves an honourable existance through fortunate circumstances, hard work and talent. They call themselves engineers and see no difference between themselves and the first class, since in their opinion a fitter or patternmaker belongs just as much in a factory as a miller or stocking maker. Today, in this class there are people from all the trades: millers, iron makers, spinners, stocking makers, etc. They are to be found usually at a lathe bank and often at a screwing machine and planing machine. They are less often to be found at a furnace. Finally, the third class consists of manual workers and day labourers, who if not the most numerous are certainly the poorest.[174]

It may be true that the situation in Chemnitz, at Krupp's, and at the *Maschinenfabrik Esslingen* was not typical for most engineering firms during the 1840s and 1850s, yet in the years after the depression of 1857–61 it rapidly became so. The depression forced the proletarianisation of many independent craftsmen, driving them into the engineering factories on a permanent basis. The year 1861 also witnessed the end of the last vestiges of guild restrictions on factory work in Leipzig. Craftsmen in small shops could now no longer compete against factory-based engineering.[175] After the depression industrial towns began to grow rapidly, providing a larger reserve army of labour. Many engineering cities, like Chemnitz, registered a doubling of their engineering workforce by 1871. Some sources put the increase in Prussian engineering workers at about 99% between the years 1861-75,[176] while one historian's own calculation is a four-fold increase in the German engineering proletariat as a whole between 1850-71.[177] With the proletarianisation of the crafts and the beginnings of a trained supply of skilled workers in high demand to meet the needs of expansion, workers such as fitters and turners began migrating around the country. Their short supply forced employers to attract them with higher pay, while these workers also saw the benefits in expanding their skills by working in several plants and undertaking a variety of jobs in the course of their working lives.[178] From mining districts, too, came workers with some technical knowledge of engineering, who needed only some extra training to be put to work. But by far the largest source of labour was the unskilled and untrained *Wanderarbeiter*. To the Rhineland and Westphalian industrial region came migrants from beyond the Elbe, particularly Polish peasants who, under the pressure of population growth and agricultural reform (e.g. expropriation of their land), came in search of work. In the region's capital, Düsseldorf, the necessary labour supply, which fed the growing iron, steel and engineering plants, came from Prussia's eastern provinces and the Polish parts of the Empire from the 1870s onwards.[179]

Local supplies of unskilled labour were also generated by the depression and its aftermath. The depression in the cotton industry in the 1860s sent numerous spinners into Chemnitz's engineering plants. Declining cottage trades were also expelling workers, forcing them to seek work elsewhere. In a town like Esslingen, an over-populated construction industry and a contraction in the textile trades provided the metal industry with workers having more than a generation of factory experience behind them, if also without experience in metal work itself.[180] Foreign supplies of skilled labour still remained important, especially in the Rhineland where a growing mass-production iron and steel industry, governed by huge concerns, needed skilled workers from France, Belgium and Britain.[181] Yet such a need was diminishing against a background of changing and more simple manual skill requirements, the expansion of works apprenticeship programmes, the growth of white-collar work, and the rise of trade schools, which stripped away much of the mental labour required from the skilled *Facharbeiter* and met the new commercial and industrial needs of expanding enterprises.

The 1860s also witnessed the widespread application of steam engines and machine tools in the engineering industry. While in the 1840s, a steam engine or machine tool may have been juxtaposed against manufacturing methods in small workshops, by the later period it was becoming more obvious that such machines were only viable in larger factories. Bigger and more powerful machines imposed the necessity of bigger and more powerful associated machinery and a larger place to house them. All this required greater outlays of capital.[182] At the same time, the previous *subjective* combination of the division of labour—where an employer or *Facharbeiter* worked beside the employees cooperating with them in the work—began to give way to a more hierarchical and divided coordination of work, with machinery playing a more commanding role. Though an engineering plant had its skilled workers in the foundry, pattern-making shop etc., the machine shop was more likely to be outfitted with various lathes, boring machines and engines operated by semi-skilled workers. Even amongst the skilled workers it was becoming increasingly unlikely that all would do the same type of work, in all details, even if they could. They too were subjected to a more sophisticated division of labour. The employer himself was more in the position of a non-working commander and director of the labour process, while the factory itself was being broken up into separate departments, from the planning office to the assembly division. Sales offices were being formed, as well as calculation offices in the bigger plants.[183] Factory-based apprenticeship schools were generally formed for the exclusive needs of the firm concerned, as at the *Maschinenfabrik Esslingen* during the 1880s. Though the training in the theory and practice of smithing, fitting, pattern-making and turning obviously varied in quality from firm to firm, even when it was good the training received was unlikely to be transferable to *Handwerksbetriebe*.[184] The emergence of a differentiated enterprise structure and the growth of experimental and construction divisions of firms required the employment of many white collar technicians and employees. At first they came from within the enterprise, especially through the promotion ladder, but by the 1880s they came from the state technical colleges.[185] This latter development especially freed the employer from excessive reliance on the mental labour undertaken by the foreign or factory-trained *Facharbeiter*, such as the labour of planning and the direction of work.

Such policies were supplemented by a growing awareness of the need for trade schools for the training of the higher grades of workers involved in direct production. As was noted earlier, much of the work in the heavy metal trades required quite different skills from those intrinsic to craft workshops, and even though the division of labour fragmented the skills required from the majority, a small minority did require training in scientific knowledge and modern methods of production. As Karl Schröder put it in 1877: 'handicraft workers possess neither technical knowledge, a developed taste, nor the necessary commercial preparation. . . This view. . . has awakened a general desire for industrial continuation schools, in which the future handicraft worker and small trades people generally may secure knowledge and discipline, which is not to be obtained in the

elementary schools or workshops.'[186] In light of this, the major manufacturing states, such as Württemberg, Bavaria, Baden and Saxony, passed
laws and formed Royal Commissions for the establishment of continuation
schools. By 1877, Baden had seventy trade schools in existence, with an
enrolment of some 6,000 pupils; Württemberg had 153 industrial
continuation schools comprising 12,000 pupils and Saxony had twenty-
two such schools and 4,000 students. Prussia, though, remained relatively
retarded. It did have 213 schools covering 21,724 pupils; however, for its
size and wealth this was not equal to what the other states were able to
achieve. Contemporaries placed the blame for this at the feet of the rich
Junker landlords who remained fearful of any movement that encouraged
the growth of manufacturing cities and the depopulation of the countryside.[187]

In general then, the typical engineering worker after the 1860s had no
pre-existing handicraft heritage and education, except that provided by
the employer in the factory or in the trade school. Typically, he no longer
had any universal *Fertigkeit,* as was possible in the early part of the
nineteenth century. He was increasingly trained for *Teilarbeit* (piecework),
whether this was working as an appendage to a machine or with a tool
extending from his hand. This was neither a 'craft mode of production';
nor were employers frequently dependent 'on the ability of craftsmen to
push back the frontiers of their firm's technology';[188] nor, for that matter,
did 'the success and rapidity' with which such a trained labour supply
was created testify 'to the adaptability of the artisanate to the needs of
modern industry'.[189] One historian is quite right to suggest that the
nineteenth-century engineering employer was an 'inventing technician',
but rather than being first among equals, he was more likely to reign
supreme.[190] In contrast to the comparable time in Britain when an
engineering industry was being founded, that is, during the late eighteenth
and early nineteenth-centuries, the formation of an engineering industry
in Germany relied heavily on employers having of necessity to parcel out
their knowledge of the production process rather than dilute or de-
compose the existing crafts. This made the formation of a German
engineering labour force a quite different experience from that of its
counterpart in Britain, particularly the formation of a skilled labour
stratum. The reason for this is largely to be found in the fact that in
Britain the lineages of a trained workforce in the crafts provided a
protective base from which workers could launch struggles against the
capitalist regulation of skill.

3. Workers and counter-regulation

Throughout the nineteenth century all the main unions in the British
metal industry attempted in one form or another to counter-regulate
industrial training and control the allocation of particular jobs. The

Friendly Society of Ironfounders of England, Ireland and Wales had rules against employers using labourers or others who had not served a 'legal' time from being introduced to the art of core-making, even though by the end of the century the work did not require the use of the founder's traditional skills. The Society went even further with the rule that 'all boys coming into the foundry to learn the trade of moulding shall work two years at coremaking, and should then come onto the floor as vacancies occur'. The intention of this rule was to reduce the supply of skilled labour available for coremaking by making the training period as long as possible; again, such a long training period was not technically necessary to learn the 'art'. The Society also attempted to regulate the number of boys who could be allowed into a shop so that their number never rose above the ratio of one boy to three men. As the Society rightly noted, such rules were designed so that 'this important branch of our trade may not be taken out of our hands by those not concerned with the trade'.[191] In the late 1880s, the newly-formed steel smelters' union sought to regulate the time needed and the experience required in order for a worker to move up the job ladder from a number 3 to a number 1 melter. To become a number 2 melter, a worker was obliged to have at least one year's experience as a number 3 melter, while two years' experience was required for a number 2 melter to become a number 1 melter. All this was to be regulated by the local branch of the union, which also determined who would be allocated the jobs after members had done their time.[192]

In the engineering and shipbuilding trades, the boilermakers' union enforced a dual system of training by apprenticeship and job progression from 1882, when the less skilled grades, like 'holders-up', gained admittance to the union. The less skilled could only progress under strict conditions, while skilled platers, angle-iron smiths and riveters were all regulated by the union's universal and strict apprenticeship provisions. A holder-up, for example, could only progress to be a riveter or a plater if no member of a skilled superior grade was out of work in a district. Similarly, a plater, riveter or angle-iron smith was only allowed to work in another branch of the trade if there was no other tradesman from that branch seeking work in the locality.[193] The ASE throughout the century, sought to enforce five to seven-year apprenticeships in order for a youth to fully qualify as a tradesman and to regulate the number of apprentices that could be supervised by a fully-qualified tradesman. When, during the latter part of the century, the union found that it could no longer formally regulate the training of fitters and turners, it sought to demand from employers the right for only its members to operate certain machines and use certain tools at the full trade union rate of wages.[194]

The success of a union at this time in regulating training and who was allowed to undertake particular jobs depended not so much on the craft technique, where the membership had a monopoly over the skill content of the work, but on the power of organisation. The iron founders failed dismally in not recognising this, as an example of an industrial conflict in 1901 shows. In March of that year, the union demanded of the Hull engineering employers that a new type of moulding machine being introduced into the foundries be operated exclusively by their members. The employers refused, arguing that unskilled labour was perfectly adequate to operate the machine. A strike broke out at one firm, with twenty-seven founders coming out. The company broke the strike by hiring black-legs brought in by train and protected by the police. After six months, during which time several workers were either sent to prison or fined for 'intimidation' for attempting to prevent the use of strike-breakers, the union capitulated on 15 August. As the Friendly Society of Ironfounders found out to its cost, an anachronistic, craft-based defence of the skills of its members could not succeed when such skills were rapidly being discounted by employers through the introduction of less skilled labour, which the union refused to admit to its membership.[195]

The smelters' union and the boilermakers were more successful. Unlike the founders, the smelters organised all the furnace workers, including the semi-skilled and foremen, into a tightly-based branch and shop union structure, which gradually gained countervailing powers over training and job progression.[196] Boilermakers successfully used a similar method. Rather than seek to prevent entrance into the trade by less skilled workers, and attempt to enforce restrictions on the basis of a pseudo-monopoly over archaic skills, the boilermakers integrated the less skilled into a tight union structure. This preserved not the reality of a craft hierarchy of work and skill, but its *formalities,* based as this was on the realistic perception that it was the employers who ultimately regulated the skills actually required in riveting, plating and angle-iron smithing.[197]

The engineering employers' spokesman, Benjamin Taylor, recognised that this was the strength and the weakness of the union. In his view, the union as a whole was 'crippled as a militant body', for any general confrontation with the employers as a whole would mean quick defeat by either the strategic use of black-legs or by a prolonged lock-out which would drain the union of its finances. On the other hand, success came by the union enforcing its regulations shop by shop and hull by hull.[198]

The ASE was equally well placed to implement such grass roots tactics and did so. It also had a rather suicidal tendency, however, to allow itself to be placed at times at the centre of generalised confrontations with the engineering employers, when it was neither a general union, and therefore able to take out an entire industry, nor a real craft union, and therefore able to stop production by its members refusing to use their integral skills and be, by definition, immune to blacklegging. This strength and weakness of the ASE was reflected in the origins and aftermath of the engineering lock-out of 1897–1898.[199]

By the 1890s, technical change had made formal apprenticeships irrelevant to the vast majority of engineering workers. 'Progressing' or shop promotion, which is discussed in more depth in a later chapter, was the main form of learning. Yet unlike the boilermakers or smelters, the ASE did not seek to control progressing by allowing the less 'skilled' into the union. As has already been noted, they sought instead to allow skilled tradesmen to 'follow the machine', or at least impose 'skilled' rates of pay for workers who worked on machines formerly the province of a skilled tradesman, while at the same time these workers had to be members of the ASE and not members of other unions, such as the less skilled Machine Workers' Association or the boilermakers' union. This tactic proved very effective for most of the 1890s when used on a shop by shop basis, as the following examples make clear; yet such tactics also tended to isolate the ASE from the other main unions at a time when the employers were building a national organisation, the Engineering Employers' Federation (EEF), to take on the ASE in a national confrontation about who was ultimately to regulate skill and training.

In Hull, at Earle's Shipbuilding and Engineering Co., the ASE in August 1896, claimed the work of 4-inch spindle milling and copying machines. In spindle milling, the union wanted its members on this work instead of the members of the Machine Workers' Association, whom the company preferred because they were cheaper. ASE members went out on strike from mid-August till early November, when the Board of Trade intervened and ruled in their favour. As a result, not only did this company join the EEF to get what it saw as this mess sorted out, but also the ASE handed to the employers a supply of potential 'black-legs' in the form of Machine Workers' unionists.[200] By December 1896, the ASE as a body was agitating against the use of labourers on band saws while at the same time claiming 'all Band Saws as in Engineering shops for our members'. The EEF refused to concede to the ASE the exclusive right to 'any particular class of machines':

> The machines are the property of the employers, and they are solely responsible for the work turned out by them.

Only the employers, the EEF claimed, had the right of discretion about who would do the work and who could work the machines.[201] The ASE however, would not easily give up imposing such claims on a shop by shop basis. An anonymous Leeds electrical engineering employer found himself driven to write to the editor of *Cassier's Magazine* in late 1897 about a situation which had arisen with a painter working on painting machines and undertaking general labouring duties. The painter, he wrote

> . . . was assisting a fitter to fit a flywheel on a shaft; he was simply helping to lift

that onto the shaft; and there happened to be a slight burr on the edge of the keyway which prevented the wheel going right home. The painter happened to be nearest a file, and he took it up with the intention of filing the burr off, when immediately one of the other fitters, who was working at the bench, saw him, and not seeing me took the file away, saying he was not a fitter, and would not allow him to do fitter's work.[202]

An equally anonymous employer from a Sunderland engineering and ship-building firm, in another letter to the editor, complained that:

We recently put down a large radial drilling machine for the purpose, among other things, of drilling, tapping, and studding propellor bosses. This machine is worked by an ordinary driller, who successfully accomplished the work named, but the ASE interfered and demanded the labourer (who was employed along with a driller on account of the heavy nature of the work) be removed and replaced by a member of the ASE. As our work could otherwise be stopped, we had to compromise matters by displacing the labourer by an apprentice fitter.[203]

The Beyer, Peacock employers from the Gorton foundry in Manchester were similarly angry with having to suffer, like 'all other employers':

. . . persistent and. . . vexatious interference with our internal arrangements and management, on the part of the ASE and other Trade Unions, both in connection with the demarcation of work, overtime, the proportion of apprentices, and perhaps most pronouncedly, in the matter of their insisting upon the employment of skilled labour on labour saving tools where high class and costly labour is totally unnecessary, in one case a strike being averted only by our discontinuing to use the machine altogether, as we refused to put a skilled man on and the society would not allow us to put a machine-man or labourer on it.[204]

Throughout 1897 engineering employers felt themselves to be under a general attack from the ASE about the training and skill requirements needed for jobs which were becoming simpler and simpler. In January, the ASE claimed a new boring machine for use only by its members at the Sunderland Forge and Engineering Co., Pallian. The workers on the new machine were non-unionists, with the exception of one who was a member of the Machine Workers' Association. If the company refused the ASE demand, then its members threatened to strike. At the same time, a similar demand was made at the works of the leader of the EEF, Colonel Dyer's Elswick works of Sir William Armstrong and Co. Ltd., who replied in similar terms to the EEF's position of the previous December.[205] By February, ASE members in Barrow were claiming special rates on lathe work in engine shops at the Barrow Naval Construction and Armaments Co., and at the Elswick works ASE members were demanding the removal of 'labourers' from gauge grinding lathes. Again both companies refused, on the basis of the EEF's principle that it would regulate the skills required and the training necessary for the jobs its members undertook.[206] When the crunch finally came with a national lock-out, the ASE found itself with few friends and a tactic which had been largely successful when kept within the bounds of individual shops, but disastrous when generalised into a national conflict. The union, though not quickly defeated, did succumb to the employers' 'treaty' of 1898, known as the 'Conditions of Management mutually adjusted and agreed between the Federated Engineering Employers and the Allied Trades Unions'. The treaty 'established' the principle of 'freedom to employers in the management of their works, and set forth such conditions as to employment. . . the rating of workmen, the training of labourers as operatives. . . as the Trades Unions would not have accepted had they not been beaten'.[207] But 'beaten' the ASE was not; its members returned to shop-by-shop bargaining. Craft *pride,* as one historian has noted, was not so easily thwarted.[208]

The ASE members, as James Hinton observes, continued to 'follow the machine. . . remarkably successfully. . . despite the employers' formal vindication in 1897-1898 of their right to engage whom they chose to work the new machines':

> . . . Though unable to prevent the emergence of a large group of semi-skilled workers paid below the craft rate—about 20% of the workforce were semi-skilled *(sic)* by 1914—the craftsmen were able to wring from the employers recognition that 'special consideration' should be given to the employment of displaced craftsmen. By 1914, a substantial proportion of the work performed by craftsmen, at the craft rate, required little of their skill—a measure of how far the engineers had succeeded in 'following the machine'.[209]

This was also something the Engineering Employers' Federation itself continued to recognise when in 1914 it claimed that 60% of its workforce could still be placed in the category of 'skilled' workers.[210]

It can also be noted that the continuing shop strength of the ASE was registered in the fact that it took until 1907 before the membership of the union actually recognised the employers' victory of 1898. A proposed agreement worked out and provisionally signed in November 1902, was overwhelmingly rejected by the membership of the ASE and the allied trade unions, the vote being 9,714 in favour and 16,652 against.[211] It all must have seemed to be a paper victory for the employers, as it took them until 1907 and the Engineering Trade Agreement to have their management 'rights' recognised, thus rendering 'impossible the recurrence of such vexatious and ruinous interferences with the factory management as preceded the strike *(sic)* of 1897'.[212]

The key clauses of the 1907 agreement which concerned industrial training and skill were points 6 and 7. Point 6 abolished any restrictions on the proportion of apprentices to tradesmen, and point 7 affirmed that 'Employers have the right to select, train and employ those whom they consider best adapted to the various operations carried on in their work-shops, and to pay them according to their ability as workmen'. It also sought to guarantee for employers 'full discretion to appoint the men they consider suitable to work all their machine tools, and to determine the conditions under which they shall be worked', with a view to obtaining 'the most economical production'.[213] On the other hand, the agreement did register the fact that the unions had given *formal, if not real, recog-nition* to the capitalist regulation of skill and to the existence of a psycho-physical apparatus of labour conditioned more by the specific physical and mental requirements of the job and less by custom, job milieu and integral skills.

That in Britain niches of 'craft' *competence* could be, and were, inherited, defended and controlled by metal unions such as the ASE, the boilermakers and the smelters, points therefore not so much to the craft basis of the labour process at this time, but rather to the lineages of the workforce in the crafts. The inheritance of a long tradition of 'public' regulation of a craft and its subsequent dissolution forced the unions to build their own private economic and political bases which would control access to the ranks of skilled labour by union regulations.[214] From this vantage point the role of the engineering bourgeoisie during the nineteenth century was to attempt to *dilute* the control embedded in the *organisa-tions of skilled engineering workers.* The employers could *regulate the actual skills required in the* labour process, but they did not have an exclusive monopoly over who could do the work—an apprenticed trades-man or a semi-skilled labourer. Even so, it is not possible to argue that management 'had little control over skill levels' or that 'craft workers' could maintain a 'dominant position in the division of labour', as two historians would have it.[215] Within the larger structures of contemporary enterprise organisation, the position of even the most skilled workers was defensive and marginal. This applied not only to the question of the organisation and control of the labour of superintendence and manage-ment, but also to the question of who planned the direct production process, particularly the introduction of new machinery. The very attempt by groups of skilled workers to 'capture' the new and more specialised machines reveals this, *especially* as it was partially successful. What workers could not do was to prevent their introduction or the lesser manual and mental skill compositions that their use implied. Whether operated by 'craftsmen' or not, the machines were coming into the plants, and it goes against the evidence, not to say the view of employers them-selves, to suggest that they were as complicated as the traditional ones, or that their 'capture' 'did not mean that crafts(men) actually worked specialised machines requiring little skill, except to an insignificant degree'.[216]

The battles at Beyer, Peacock, in Manchester, and at the Armstrong

Elswick works were about the *removal of labourers* from tasks that re-quired less of the fine and various manual skills traditionally associated with the work. In the case of the Elswick dispute, it concerned not the use of the new gauge grinding machines, but who would use them. The machines were there—though Dr More would have us believe that grinding in general was just as complicated a task as more traditional jobs.[217] Even if there were various grinding machines that required the use of traditional skills, then it is hardly the point. The point is that battle lines were drawn over the issue of who was to use what were considered to be newer, less considerable skills. If this were not the case, then a dispute of this magnitude could not even have been contemplated by employers at the time, let alone joined by the ASE.

For skilled German metal workers, by contrast, the very idea of establishing niches of control which would guarantee tickets of entry to exclusive jobs was generally not relevant. The very newness of the German engineering industry, the absence of any substantial craft heritage in its formation, its early character as an arm of the heavy producer goods industries (rather than an offshoot of the consumer industries), meant that job control in the form of regulating skill and training was even more of an automatic apparatus of management than was the case in Britain. Furthermore, German metal employers were renowned for their often violent opposition to any independent trade union organisation that sought to establish restrictions on the labour supply, training programmes and skill requirements.

As early as the 1840s, the English observer and traveller, Banfield, noted that in the Rhine area the number of apprentices was not limited by any form of worker regulation and that trained workers were generally much younger than their English counterparts, especially amongst moulders. In England, at the time, moulding was a highly restricted job requiring many years of training.[218] Because of the nature of the formation of the engineering industry and the repressive political climate of the Bismarckian period, Germany's metal workers were more likely to find themselves involved in conflicts over the right to strike, to form trade unions, the use of police terror, employer black lists and the introduction of health and safety regulations, than to be involved in continuous skirmishes over the dilution of their trade.

In 1857, for example, police terror destroyed a fitters' strike in Düsseldorf. In this period also workers agitated against compulsory works savings schemes, which were deductions made from wages, in order either to finance the short-term requirements of a firm, and/or arbitrarily tie workers to an individual employer indefinitely. By the late 1860s, agita-tions were taking place over the length of the working day and for the right of engineers to form their own trade unions.[219] It was not until the insurrectionary strike wave of 1905 that employers would deal with

Germany's industrial metal workers' union, the DMV, as a body, and bargain collectively over such issues as guaranteed minimum wages, dictatorial foremanship, sanitation, new methods of pay, such as piece rates, and gang work. Hitherto, such demands had been met with the use of repressive institutions such as the *Berufsgenossenschaften*, an employer-controlled job placement bureau that operated black-lists against active trade unionists and vetted job candidates in regions like Berlin, Hanover, the Rhineland and Bavaria, especially in the heavy engineering and iron and steel trades.[220] Berlin's metal employers, after the strikes of 1889, formed an Association for Protection Against Strikes *(Streikverhütungsvereinigung)*, from which a commission was formed to hear some of the claims of workers, but was mainly aimed at offering advice and counter-measures to employers stricken by an *Ausstandesbewegung* or strike.[221] Against such apparatuses of employer power even the most partisan observers were struck by the weaknesses of organised workers seeking to make a bid against the capitalist regulation of skill and training. Writing on the 1890s in Berlin, Waldemer Follos spoke of how 'big industry creates a ferment in the labour community. In the modern period when most of production is mass produced, when work is done by unskilled workers, women and children, everything is in flux. The individual trained worker feels helpless and is compelled to fasten onto the trade union so that his interests are represented by quite other means than that provided by the *Berufsgenossenschaften*'.[222] Otto Jeidels noted in 1907, after the 1905 strike wave, that there had been very few strikes in the big firms over the previous twenty years, and these were generally lost over issues like wage rises and against wage deductions. Most strikes involved only small groups of workers in small shops and took place in areas outside of the big cities such as Düsseldorf, Cologne and Duisberg.[223]

This is not to suggest that British engineers were any the less involved in such issues in their own country; rather, it is to suggest that the lineages of the British engineering industry in the crafts, like the French iron trade, provided a base for her metal workers to launch defensive struggles against the capitalist regulation of skill, a base which was just not available to German metal workers on a day to day basis.[224]

Perhaps, then, the reason why British engineering workers remained 'skilled craftsmen' was not because they remained craftsmen at all, but because their lineages allowed them to wage class war over skill and industrial training. Joseph Melling has summed this up aptly when he suggests that '. . . new machine skills did not give tradesmen the individual independence of the millwright engineer. . . but depended upon both market conditions and the collectively enforced standards of the craft societies';[225] by which he surely means the politics of organisation. In Germany, by contrast, perhaps the reason why Richard Ehrenberg detected an absence of distinction between the 'skilled' and 'semi-skilled' workers was not because metal work was any the less 'skilful', but because skilled workers and their unions were unable to 'follow the machine' or the course of technical change due to their employers' pre-formed monopoly of technical intelligence and greater organisational strength.

In surveying these separate experiences of Britain, France and Germany, therefore, little has been found to support the view that a 'craft question' played any fundamental role in the formation of Europe's heavy metal industry workforce. In this epoch, which can be described as one of high or competitive capitalism, an employer could not be sustained in ignorance or stupidity by relying on an integrally intelligent and organic workforce. Of course, this is not to suggest that a craft *culture* did not play a role in shaping the attitudes and organisations of skilled workers which could be used to take up the lesser struggle over the supply and distribution of labour power.[226] This also applies to the less skilled, whether they were originally peasants, bakers or gardeners. None of them were blank pieces of paper to be written all over by pen-wielding and regulation-conscious employers. However, from any objective viewpoint, nineteenth-century metal workers could not hope to practise, let alone maintain, either the material integrity of a craft or its integral manual and mental skills. Only the *formalities* of craft labour could be defended, and these could only be held on to as a result of industrial organisation and struggle. It is certainly true that by the end of the century the question of skill was becoming political, a question of the respective powers of labour and capital in production. Yet the terrain had changed, and the conflict now took place on the basis of capital's and not labour's integral ability to regulate the actual skills applied in production.

This transformation, it must be said, was not caused by 'technical progress' or mechanisation, as the French historian, Edouard Dolléans, and others have argued; rather, it was the product of new social and political arrangements of how manual and mental labour were to be organised in the factory. He was certainly accurate when he suggested that the 'technical decomposition of tasks' has been, and will continue to be, 'one of the specific modalities of the industrial division of labour in the large capitalist factory'.[227] It can, however, be added that the historically prior and more important modality was the social and political break with guild and corporate forms of work and skill and the subsequent introduction of a capitalist division of labour itself.

The change was indeed social in character, rather than technical, and comprised the decomposition and recomposition of tasks—both of direct production and planning—in order to facilitate an enterprise's power over the design and composition of the workforce.

If this process of a workforce being made and made subject to a capitalist regulation of skill had been in train since at least the mid-nineteenth century in the European metal industry, then it is difficult to sustain arguments concerning the existence of a craft workforce at the end of the nineteenth century. This is not so much a question of complaining that historians have mistakenly conceived that late nineteenth-century metal workers were medieval relics, freely roaming the factories, proclaiming their independence from the capitalist division of labour. As we have seen, however, some historians do tend towards this view. Rather, it is to suggest that when they speak of 'craftsmen' having 'all-round' or 'considerable' skills through the use of particular technologies, then they remove from their field of vision the larger historical process that provided for the rise of these allegedly 'all-round skills': skills which in fact added up to a qualitative degrading of faculties used in production and the development of skills which became the province of the labour of superintendence and management. The forceful adjectives just do not bear comparison with the force that lay behind the *planning skills* that were formed to design the technologies and the workforce; skills that were not only all-round, considerable and genuine, but also upgraded to the work of management. To fail to realise the considerable significance of this process, as for example the neo-Taylorist perspective does, is to fail to realise the process by which employers formed, reformed and specialised the skills of their workers during the nineteenth century. European metal employers were becoming part of a confident class, and an important aspect of this confidence was the way in which they learned to design and use a labour force in the image of their own intelligence.

In what sense, then, is it possible to speak of a growing European experience amongst metal producers during the nineteenth century? Certainly employers and their managerial personnel were not exclusively trained within national boundaries. Travel and foreign study were important aspects of their formation and provided an arena in which to learn, compare their own experiences, and in turn train their own workforces. They were definitely not parochial. Yet the differences in the lineages cannot be underestimated at this time. Britain's early industrial lead, especially in the consumer industries, far outweighed the fact that she did not have a similarly stupendous technical lead in the rising producer goods industries. Metal producers were readily able to adapt to, and modify where necessary, a workforce already shaped by the experience of the Industrial Revolution. The structure of training, therefore, generally proved to be private and competitive, with the state playing little role. In France and Germany, by contrast, metal industrialists were compelled to develop not only private schemes for the training of their workforce, but also form *rudimentary* relations with their national states for the provision of trained personnel, especially for those who could technically administer the industry. In France, this comprised a state system for the education of a metal bourgeoisie, while in Germany this system was extended down the social ladder to incorporate sections of the new industrial working class who would fill positions in the higher grades of manual labour. Thus, while it is possible to speak of European metal producers having a common experience of private and competitive capitalist methods of training and regulating skills, this experience was primarily shaped by the various *national* roads taken to form a trained workforce.

NOTES

1. See Edouard Dolléans (and Gérard Dehove), *Histoire du travail en France: mouvement ouvrier et législation sociale. Des origines à 1919*. Tome 1, Editions Domat Montchrestien, Paris, 1953, pp. 60-1. On the rise and evolution of the guilds until the eighteenth century, see also p. 64 ff. A useful overview of the developments of guilds within medieval industry and trade may be found in Herbert Heaton's *Economic History of Europe*, Harper and Row, New York, 1969, pp. 190-212. See also William H. Sewell, *Work and Revolution in France, The Language of Labour from the Old Regime to 1848*, CUP, Cambridge, 1982, pp. 25 ff, 37 ff.

2. See Max Harkhausen, 'Government Control and Free Enterprise in Western Germany and the Low Countries in the Eighteenth Century', in Peter Earle, ed., *Essays in European Economic History, 1500-1800*, Clarendon Press, Oxford, 1974, pp. 222, 226-7. The quote from Braudel is taken from his *Capitalism and Material Life, 1400-1800*, Fontana/Collins, Glasgow, 1977, p. 404.

3. Dolléans, *op. cit.*, p. 74. Witold Kula, in his *An Economic Theory of the Feudal System, Towards a Model of the Polish Economy*, NLB, London, 1976, p. 76, also emphasises the corporate and public aspects of the guild: 'The guild, as an element of a social system of corporate bodies, represents an organism that encompasses its own members, their families, and candidate members in an integral fashion, in all their functions, activities, and social needs.' See also Sewell, *op. cit.*, especially p. 27 and p. 32 ff for further examples in France.

4. Dolléans, *op. cit.*, p. 32.

5. R.A. Bray, *Boy Labour and Apprenticeship*, Constable, London, 1911, pp. 1, 5-6.

6. *ibid.*, pp. 5-6, and Sewell, *op. cit.*, pp. 30-1, for France during the seventeenth and eighteenth centuries.

7. *ibid.*, p. 7.

8. *ibid.*, p. 7.

9. *ibid.*, pp. 7-8. By the sixteenth and seventeenth centuries, governments in Britain, France and Germany added an extra arm to this regulation—themselves. The need for uniformity and quality in goods for export led the state to set down trade regulations, which the guilds had to obey. In France, the system was supervised by Colbert and carried out by state-employed factory inspectors who were responsible to the local *intendants*. See Max Barkhausen, *loc. cit.*, p. 265.

10. Sewell, *op. cit.*, p. 29 ff.

11. See Dolléans, *op. cit.*, pp. 81-113, and Sewell, *op. cit.*, p. 32.

12. See Sewell, *op. cit.*, pp. 40 ff and 72 ff.

13. R.A. Bray, *op. cit.*, p. 10. See also E.P. Cheney, *Industrial and Social History of England*, Macmillan, London, 1901, pp. 59-73, 147-54, 159-60.

14. Dolléans, *op. cit.*, pp. 134 and 130 ff. Sewell, *op. cit.*, pp. 40 ff, 72 ff. The possibility of this had already created controversy in 1776, when the Enlighten-

ment's Minister Turgot sought to curtail the activities of trade corporations. It was not, however, met with the same receptivity. The members of the Old Regime's *Parlement* loudly disclaimed the rise of 'undefined liberty', which would turn each 'manufacturer', 'artist' and 'worker' into an 'isolated human being' and destroy 'subordination'. There would be no 'honesty' and the 'entire public' would be the 'constant dupes of artful methods secretly prepared to blind and seduce them'. See Jules Flammermont, ed., *Remonstrances du Parlement au XVIIIe siècle,* Vol. 3, Paris, 1888-86, pp. 312, 315, 347-8, 356-7.

15. G.D.H. Cole and Raymond Postgate, *The Common People, 1746-1946,* Methuen, London, 1949, pp. 175-6.

16. Bray, *op. cit.,* p. 22.

17. See Theodore S. Hamerow, *Restoration, Revolution, Reaction, Economics and Politics in Germany, 1815-1871,* Princeton University Press, Princeton, New Jersey, 1970, p. 22 ff.

18. The concept of an 'organic' workforce was developed by Antonio Gramsci to explain the nature of skill and training at the Ford car factories in Detroit at the beginning of this century. He argued that the Ford plants were built up on the new 'psycho-physical' attributes of labour (specialisation, assembly lines, repetitive precision movements, and the substitution of nervous for physical fatigue). At the same time, high rates of labour turnover tended to disperse the labour force and its psycho-physical skills, which had been 'so laboriously built up' to form an 'organic whole'. See Antonio Gramsci, 'Americanism and Fordism', in Quintin Hoare and Geoffrey Nowell Smith, eds., *Selections from the Prison Notebooks of Antonio Gramsci,* International Publishers, New York 1973, pp. 312, 279-322. A recent assessment of Gramsci's argument, which is a study of the application of Fordist principles in the present-day Brazilian auto industry, argues, on the contrary, that such attributes of labour are not founded on the existence of an 'organic' workforce: 'Most workers', in the Brazilian car industry and the early American industry, 'perform definite and limited jobs, and they are easily replaced'. The 'organic' nature of production is provided by management science and control. The assembly line decreases skill requirements, and skilled workers are only needed for servicing of the machines, construction of tools and dies, and the performance of a limited number of skilled production tasks, such as final assembly mechanics, metal-finishing and hand painting'. See John Humphrey, 'Labour Use and Labour Control in the Brazilian Automobile Industry', *Capital and Class,* No. 12, Winter 1980-81, p. 46. This argument is very useful for our purposes for it provides a theoretical basis for an historical assessment of the transition from an 'organic' to an 'inorganic' workforce; that is, from a labour process where the labourer provides the necessary 'science' for the production process to one where it is provided and monopolised by the mental labour of management.

19. Sidney and Beatrice Webb, *Industrial Democracy,* (1897), Longman, London, 1911, p. 107.

20. Sir William Fairbairn, *A Treatise on Mills and Millwork, Part 1, On the Principles of Mechanism and on Prime Movers,* Longman, Green, Longman, Roberts and Green, London, 1864, pp. v-vi. See also Keith Burgess, 'Technological Change and the 1852 Lock-Out in the British Engineering Industry', *International Review of Social History,* Vol. XIV, Part 2, 1969, pp. 215-19, for further examples. We will speak later of the break-up of this craft and its associated trades and what the author meant by 'work now done by civil engineers'. It should be noted, though, that other crafts were equally important to the traditional 'mechanical arts', especially smithing and wood-working, as Charles More has pointed out. In this light, as we describe the break-up of the mill-

wright's craft it is only to show by way of illustration how one branch of the mechanical crafts was brought within the domain of engineering proper. See More, *Skill and English Working Class*, pp. 146, 195–6.

21. Bertrand Gille, *Les origines de la grande industrie métallurgique en France*, Editions Domat Montchrestien, Paris, 1947, p. xiii. A thorough study of the social and economic situation of the early French iron workers is Gerd Hardach's *Der soziale Status des Arbeiters in der Frühindustrialisierung. Eine Untersuchung über die Arbeitnehmer in der französischen eisenschaffenden Industrie zwischen 1800 and 1870*, Duncker und Humblot, Berlin, 1969. See especially pp. 32–40, 42–6 for a description of the techniques.

22. Quoted in Denis Woronoff, 'Le monde ouvrier de la sidérurgie ancienne: note sur l'example français', *Le mouvement social*, No. 97, October-December 1976, p. 116; Gille, *Les origines. . .*, p. 152.

23. Quoted in Woronoff, *loc. cit.*, p. 116.

24. *ibid.*, p. 116. See also Hardach, *Der soziale Status. . .*, pp. 80–1, 82–3.

25. J. Vial gives several examples of employers and observers at this time referring to being at the 'mercy' of workers, so far as knowledge of the job was concerned. A manager of the Imphy steel works, near St Etienne, claimed that in blast furnace practice: 'we know nothing' of the temperatures required for the fusion of the materials in making pig iron. This knowledge was seen as something which had to be left to the discretion of the head workers. Similarly, forge workers from Champagne were able to maintain and defend the 'secrets' of their trade almost to the end of the nineteenth century. See J. Vial, *L'industrialisation de la sidérurgie française, 1814–1864*, 2 Vols. Thèse pour le Doctorat ès Lettres, Mouton et Cie., Paris, 1967, Vol. 1, pp. 348, n. 7 and 8; 349.

26. *ibid.*, pp. 347–8.

27. Woronoff, *loc. cit.*, pp. 114–15. See also Vial, *op. cit.*, pp. 149–50, and Hardach, *Der soziale Status. . .*, p. 79 ff.

28. Woronoff, *loc. cit.*, pp. 114–15.

29. *ibid.*, pp. 115–16.

30. Gille, *Les origines. . .*, 152. Gerd Hardach, however, has found some seasonal migration, particularly during the winter months when work could be scarce. Hardach, *Der soziale Status. . .*, pp. 62–4.

31. Woronoff, *loc. cit.*, p. 119.

32. Cole and Postgate, *op. cit.*, p. 87.

33. Sewell, *op. cit.*, p. 155. See also p. 157. Joan Scott has given a description of a similar situation amongst the glassworkers at Carmaux during the nineteenth century. These 'highly skilled workers' were able to maintain 'artisan standards and traditions of their trade' even though they worked for an employer. 'They were able to do so because the manufacture of glass bottles depended on their skills. Although they worked for wages in the shops of the employers who owned the means of production, glassblowers nonetheless controlled most aspects of their trade. They alone managed the hiring and training of apprentices and thereby regulated the labour supply. They also set the standards for the quality of the product and the conditions of their work. In addition, the possession of skill and the control of its transmission allowed glassworkers to maintain regular and relatively high wages, to enjoy a social position higher than that of most other workers, and to rest secure about their own occupational futures as well as those of their sons.' See Joan Wallach Scott, *The Glassworkers of Carmaux: French Craftsmen and Political Action in a Nineteenth-Century City*, Harvard University Press, Cambridge, Mass., 1974, pp. 19–20. Scott proceeds to compare the position of the glassblowers with that of the local coal

miners who had no comparable control over their work. In this work the employer monopolised technical expertise *via* his engineers and supervisors, who were seen as the employer's men, unlike the glassworkers' supervisors who were seen as 'men of the craft'—not agents of the company. The glassworker supervisor, *'souffleur'*, was still an artisanal worker with a vested interest in protecting the conditions of work and employment. *ibid.*, p. 61.

The transformation of glass-blowing in the 1880s was to destroy all this. The traditional process of blowing was similar to the crucible process of steel making. At noon the raw materials were placed in crucibles, which took twelve hours to melt. After midnight the blowers began their work. Thus the working day was divided into two parts and two twelve-hour shifts. With the introduction of mechanically-charged furnaces and gas infusion the working day was reorganised. There was now no allocation of melting and blowing into two separate shifts. Both melting and blowing could take place in each shift of eight hours, while the output of bottles increased threefold. The impact of this, according to Scott, was that factories became bigger, small workshops were driven out of the trade, and only less-skilled labour was required, so that a labour market came into operation forcing craftsmen to compete with the less skilled. The craft was further degraded by the introduction of closed moulds, which brought a standard bottle into existence, requiring little judgment from the blowers in their work. See *ibid.*, pp. 74–5, 77.

34. Karl Marx, *Capital*, Vol. 1 (1867), Penguin, London, 1976, p. 460.

35. See David Landes, *The Unbound Prometheus*, pp. 41–123, and Peter Mathias, *The First Industrial Nation: An Economic History of Britain, 1700-1914*, Methuen and Co., London, 1969, pp. 134–44. See also Keith Burgess, 'Technological Change and the 1852 Lock-Out', *loc. cit.*, pp. 222–3.

36. See Sidney and Beatrice Webb, *The History of Trade Unionism* (1894), Longman, London, 1920, p. 205. See also their *Industrial Democracy*, pp. 107–10. For recent studies of the decline of the millwright's craft in the early nineteenth century see R. Gray, *The Labour Aristocracy in Victorian Edinburgh*, Clarendon Press, Oxford, 1976, pp. 37–40 and Keith Burgess, *The Influence of Technological Change on the Social Attitudes and the Trade Union Policies of Workers in the British Engineering Industry, 1780-1860*, Ph.D. Thesis, Leeds, 1970, Ch. 2. Pollard and Robertson in their study of the late nineteenth-century shipbuilding industry describe a similar proliferation of 'crafts' brought about by an expansion of the industry and the decomposition of the traditional crafts: 'In the days of wooden shipbuilding, the shipwrights, assisted by unskilled labourers, formed the main workforce in the yards, and other trades were ancillary. As ships became more complex and machines were introduced, the spectrum of required skills broadened considerably. In time almost all the metal trades came to be represented as well as many other building and engineering trades. . .' Though the authors wish to argue that such a division of labour occurred 'through the addition of crafts new to the industry rather than through the subdivision of traditional shipbuilding trades, they are equally quick to point out the subdivisions which were introduced as the metal crafts were integrated: 'The iron workers, frequently promoted from unskilled labourers, developed into such separate trades as platers, angle-iron smiths, riveters, drillers and their necessary holders-up and assistants; the engineering trades developed independently, yet on a parallel line, into fitters, turners, and drillers. . . in the larger centres the shipwrights split into riggers, mast and block makers, and caulkers. . .' See Sidney Pollard and Paul Robertson, *The British Shipbuilding Industry, 1870-1914*, pp. 151–2.

37. Eric Roll, *An Early Experiment in Industrial Organisation, being a history of*

the firm of Boulton and Watt (1930), Frank Cass and Co., London, 1968, p. 182. A useful extract of this work can be found in Maxine Berg, ed., *Technology and Toil in Nineteenth Century Britain,* pp. 27-35.

38. Roll, *op. cit.,* p. 183.

39. According to Keith Burgess's work, at least, the situation at Boulton and Watt had become quite common amongst engineering firms by the 1850s. See 'Technological Change and the 1852 Lock-Out', *loc. cit.,* p. 228 ff.

40. Roll, *op. cit.,* pp. 182-3.

41. I am indebted to Michel Freyssenent's, *La division capitaliste du travail,* Savelli, Paris, 1977, *passim,* especially pp. 35-8, and Christain Palloix's 'The Labour Process: from Fordism to neo-Fordism', in CSE Pamphlet No. 1, *The Labour Process and Class Strategies,* CSE, London, 1976, pp. 51-2, for the concepts of the dequalification and hyper-qualification of labour as they theorise them for the development of manufacture.

42. See Roll, *op. cit.,* p. 175 ff.

43. Roll summarises the memo as enumerating ten different shops, entitled A to K. These shops and their functions were:

'A. The drilling shop, or rather the heavy drilling shop in which the boring and drilling of such heavy articles as condensors, air and hot and cold water pumps, steam pipes, etc., was done. A large and small drill were used in this shop, and it was provided with a hearth, a convenience for holding grinding and mending tools, and other minor appliances.

B. The heavy turning shop, provided with the great lathe and a second special lathe for turning piston rods, in addition to the usual conveniences. Worthy of mention, among these, is a 'tackle for lifting heavy weights into lathe'. This shop was used for all turning work, such as for pistons, cylinder lids, gudgeons, shafts, piston rods, rotative wheels, etc.

C. The heavy fitting shop, which, in addition to the usual benches and grinding stone, was to have a lapping machine and a small drill. Here the heavier articles were fitted, such as plumber blocks, pistons, glands, etc.

D. The nozzle shop, used exclusively for the fitting of nozzles.

E. The general fitting shop which was intended to be provided with a separate drill and, apart from the usual conveniences, with a 'small portable furnace for heating pins' as well as with a 'crane for lifting heavy weights'. Here, steam cases, inner and outer bottoms and pipes were fitted and the fitting of air pumps was completed.

F. This was a special shop for the fitting of parallel motions and working gears and governors, and had two lathes as well as another smaller lathe for turning pins.

G. This was the next and was called the light fitting shop. Here all the lighter parts—safety, throttle and stop pipes, etc., were fitted.

H. Was the pattern-makers' shop and had the usual benches, grind-stone and a lathe.

I. Was the casters' shop, and for this no particulars are given.

K. The last on the list was the smiths' shop, and was stated to contain a hearth and a vice-bench.' *ibid.,* pp. 172-3.

44. Quoted in Burgess, 'Technological Change and the 1852 Lock-Out', *loc. cit.,* p. 230.

45. The phrase is from Gareth Stedman Jones, 'Class Struggle and the Industrial Revolution', *New Left Review,* 90, March/April, 1975, p. 63. Jones' study is a review of the collapse of craft control in the cotton trade during the Industrial Revolution as presented in the work of John Foster, *Class Struggle and the Industrial Revolution—Early industrial capitalism in three English towns,*

Weidenfeld and Nicolson, London, 1974.
46. Charles Babbage, *On the Economy of Machinery and Manufactures* (1832), John Murray, London, 1846, p. 172.
47. *ibid.*, p. 171.
48. *ibid.*, pp. 175-6.
49. For a survey of the 1852 lock-out in the British engineering industry, see P.J. Murphy, 'The Origins of the 1852 Lock-Out in the British Engineering Industry Reconsidered', *International Review of Social History*, Vol. XXIII, 1978, Part 2, pp. 247-66. See also Keith Burgess, 'Trade Union Policy and the 1852 Lock-Out in the British Engineering Industry', *International Review of Social History*, Vol. 17, Pt. 3, 1972, pp. 645-66.
50. See *Tenth Report from the Royal Commission on Trade Unions, Minutes of Evidence 1867-68*, Cd. 3980-VI, Vol. XXXIX. Evidence from James Nasmyth, 14 July 1868, in *British Parliamentary Papers, Industrial Relations*, Vol. 9, Irish University Press, Shannon, Ireland, 1970, Q. 19, 333 (63), p. 525. An extract of this testimony may be found in Berg, ed., *op. cit.*, pp. 155-9.
51. *ibid.*, Q. 19, 134 (63-64), pp. 525-6. (My emphasis, C. McG.)
52. *ibid.*, Q. 19, 138 (64), p. 526.
53. See Peter L. Payne, 'Industrial Entrepreneurship and Management in Great Britain', *The Cambridge Economic History of Europe, Vol. VII. The Industrial Economies: Capital, Labour and Enterprise, Pt. 1, Britain, France, Germany and Scandinavia*, eds., P. Mathias and M.M. Postan, Cambridge University Press, Cambridge, 1978, p. 189.
54. Reinhard Bendix, *Work and Authority in Industry*, University of California Press, Berkeley, 1974, p. 203.
55. *ibid.*, p. 205.
56. *ibid.*, p. 203.
57. David Landes, *op. cit.*, p. 105.
58. See Evidence from James Nasmyth, *Tenth Report from the Royal Commission on Trade Unions, Minutes of Evidence, 1867-68, loc. cit.*, 14 July Q. 19, 111, (62), p. 524. See also Roderick Floud, *The British Machine Tool Industry, 1850-1914*, Cambridge University Press, Cambridge, 1976, p. 49.
59. Landes, *op. cit.*, p. 105.
60. See Raphael Samuel, 'The Workshop of the World: Steam Power and Hand Technology in mid-Victorian Britain', *History Workshop*, No. 3, Spring, 1977, p. 19.
61. *ibid.*, p. 20.
62. *ibid.*, p. 19.
63. *ibid.*, p. 58.
64. *ibid.*, p. 39.
65. This confusion leads Samuel to misread his own evidence at times. When referring to the nature of work at the Platt Brothers' works in Oldham during the 1890s, he too relies on the evidence of de Rousiers. Yet rather than work through the subtleties of de Rousiers' observations concerning the specialisation and decomposition of craftsmanship, and the subsequent subordination of these workers to a labour market, Samuel leaps to the conclusion that these workers were 'artisans'. See *ibid.*, pp. 40-1.
66. *ibid.*, pp. 47, 50, 51. Some other historians, however, are under no such illusions. Alistair Reid, for example, in his study of the Clyde shipbuilding industry, has found that, though many of its branches were 'skill' consuming or skill intensive, as distinct from being skill or labour saving, this was perfectly compatible with overstocked trades, which led to insecure earnings 'even for the highly skilled trades, and to intense competition between workers, which

divided and weakened their organisational strength'. See A. Reid, 'Politics and Economics in the Formation of the British Working Class: A Response to H.F. Moorehouse', *Social History*, Vol. 3, No. 3, October 1978, pp. 347-61. The quote may be found on p. 360. For a similar perspective see also Keith Burgess, 'Trade Union Policy and the 1852 Lock-Out', *loc. cit.*, p. 658 ff. Burgess argues that there is a strong connection between the Amalgamated Society of Engineers' inability to support unapprenticed labour during the lock-out and the large reserve army of labour covering most grades waiting outside the factory gates: therefore forcing the ASE to concede defeat.

67. See R. Samuel, 'The Workshop of the World', *loc. cit.*, pp. 50–1.

68. *ibid.*, p. 59.

69. *ibid.*, p. 59.

70. Sidney Pollard offers a similar perspective. He quite correctly argues that 'skill in the context of a fundamentally changing technology is not easy to define'. It involved 'manual dexterity. . . knowledge and judgment' from the past, as well as 'a sense of responsibility. . . attendance, a degree of literacy and other abstract knowledge (e.g. 'mathematical knowledge'), required from the new techniques of production'. For Pollard, the 'very many-sidedness of the concept' of skill 'makes it impossible to speak of one-way change. Some skills were driven out and made redundant; others were newly created; others saw their rise and fall within this period; and the status and the role of skilled workers as such changed also'. In fact, he argues, the views supporting the deskilling and reskilling of the workforce are both 'correct'. Again, however, such a point of view may bring together many quantitative and discrete facts, yet it does not address the nature of the changes, their direction and who sought primarily to control them. See Sidney Pollard, 'Labour in Great Britain', *The Cambridge Economic History of Europe, Vol. VIII, The Industrial Economies, Part 1, Britain, France, Germany and Scandinavia,* pp. 118-19.

71. See S.B. Saul, 'The Market and the Development of the Mechanical Engineering Industries in Britain, 1860-1914', in S.B. Saul, ed., *Technological Change: The United States and Britain in the Nineteenth Century*, Methuen and Co. Ltd., London, 1970, p. 166.

72. *ibid.*, p. 169. In the shipbuilding industry before 1890, Pollard and Robertson have found that for employers and managers, 'practical training or an apprenticeship was indispensable and appeared far more important than financial ability': 'The more fortunate started in the yards of their fathers, their families, or their friends; others had to pay heavily to become "premium apprentices". In both cases their future superior position was borne in mind, and after some brief spells in each of the chief branches of the work—woodwork, ironwork, marine engineering—their main instruction was imparted in the drawing office.' Pollard and Robertson, *op. cit.*, p. 74. See also Michael Sanderson, *The Universities in the Nineteenth Century*, Routledge and Kegan Paul, London, 1975, document 35, Fleeming Jenkin to Sir William Thomson, 5 July 1865 (Jenkin advises Thomson about a premium apprenticeship for the latter's son); and also Fleeming Jenkin, *A Lecture on the Education of Civil and Mechanical Engineers*, 1868, for a comparison between premium apprenticeships for future engineers in Britain and college training for engineers on the Continent. The documents can be found on pp. 110–11.

73. See Charlotte Erickson, *British Industrialists: Steel and Hosiery, 1850-1950*, Cambridge University Press, 1959, Table 2, p. 12.

74. *ibid.*, Table 2, pp. 12, 13.

75. *ibid.*, p. 30. The Oxbridge system, in fact, until the 1870s and 1880s, cannot be seen to be attuned to Professor Hobsbawm's 'truculent, games-dominated Tory

imperialism'. Two-thirds of the students at Oxford and Cambridge in the period 1752-1886 went into the church. If these institutions did feed Tory imperialism then it was sustenance based on less than erudite vicars. See Michael Sanderson, *The Universities and British Industry, 1850-1970,* Routledge and Kegan Paul, London, 1972, Ch. 2, and Sanderson, *Universities in the Nineteenth Century,* p. 17.

76. Erickson, *op. cit.,* pp. 31--9.

77. *ibid.,* p. 42.

78. *ibid.,* p. 144 ff.

79. *ibid.,* p. 144 ff; J. Carr and W. Taplin, *A History of the British Steel Industry,* Basil Blackwell, Oxford, 1962, pp. 11-12, 26.

80. Erickson, *op. cit.,* pp. 166-7.

81. *ibid.,* pp. 167-70.

82. See P.W. Musgrave, *Technical Change, the Labour Force and Education,* pp. 34-7.

83. See M. Sanderson, *The Universities in the Nineteenth Century,* pp. 7, 10.

84. Frederick Engels was one of the first observers to draw attention to the fact that female and child labour constituted not only the core of the labour force for the English Industrial Revolution, but also formed the basis of the world's first industrial working class. Quoting Lord Ashley's data from a speech to the House of Commons introducing the Ten Hours Bill on March 15, 1844, Engels pointed out that in 1839, of all the operatives in the cotton factories, 56.5% were female; in the woollen mills, 69.5%; in the silk mills 70.5% and in the flax spinning mills, 70.5%. See Frederick Engels, *The Condition of the Working Class in England in 1844,* in Karl Marx and Frederick Engels, *Collected Works,* Vol. 4, Lawrence and Wishart, London, 1976, p. 436. See also Karl Marx, *Capital,* Vol. 1 (1867), Progress Publishers, London, 1974, pp. 372-80.

85. See David Landes, *op. cit.,* pp. 124-92.

86. See *ibid.,* pp. 142-7, 190-1. See also Claude Fohlen, *The Industrial Revolution in France, 1700-1914,* in Carlo M. Cipolla, ed., *Fontana Economic History of Europe,* Vol. IV, Fontana, London, 1970, p. 26. In the St Etienne hardware trades during the 1820s a similar situation was to be found. According to A.L. Dunham, the workers were illiterate, isolated in the surrounding villages and exploited by city merchants. With growing competition in hardware, this time coming from other parts of France, the merchants did not begin a programme of training the workforce in new methods of production, but cut wages and prices instead—the result being not only greater burdens placed on the producers but also a fall in the quality of the product. See A.L. Dunham, *The Industrial Revolution in France,* p. 185.

87. In comparison with Britain, which by 1891 had only 15.8% of its workforce involved in agriculture and fisheries and 50.2% involved in industry, Germany had 40% of its workforce in agriculture, forestry and fisheries and 33.7% in industry in the period 1895-99. In France between 1866 and 1906, agriculture declined only from 52% to 43% of the workforce, while manufacturing employment grew from 29% to 32% of the workforce. On Britain, see C. Feinstein, *National Income, Expenditure and Output of the United Kingdom, 1855-1965,* CUP, Cambridge, 1972, Table 60, p. T.131 (calculated); Germany, see Walter G. Hoffman (and Franz Grumbach and Helmut Hesse), *Das Wachstum der Deutschen Wirtschaft seit der Mitte des 19. Jahrhunderts,* Springer Verlag, Berlin, 1965, p. 135; and France, see S. Kuznets, 'Quantitative Aspects of the Economic Growth of Nations: II. Industrial Distribution of National Product and Labour Force'; in *Economic Development and Cultural Change,* Supplement to Vol. V, No. 4, July 1957, p. 28. For a discussion of the skills required for an

industrial revolution at a higher level than a predecessor, see Landes, *op. cit.*, p. 150 and A. Gerschenkron, 'Economic Backwardness in Historical Perspective', in B. Hoselitz, ed., *The Progress of Underdeveloped Areas*, The University of Chicago Press, Chicago and London, 1966, pp. 3-29.

88. See, for example, *Statistiques de l'industrie minérale*, Paris, 1840, p. 65, which speaks of the *'Manque d'ouvrièrs qualifiés'* in the iron industry.

89. See J.H. Cagninacci, *L'instruction professionelle de l'ouvrier*, Paris, 1910, pp. 8-9, and F.B. Artz, 'L'enseignement technique en France pendant l'époque révolutionnaire, 1789-1815', *Revue Historique*, Vol. CXCVI, juillet-septembre, 1946, pp. 258-60, 262, 265-70, 276-7.

90. Woronoff, *loc. cit.*, p. 114.

91. A.L. Dunham, *Industrial Revolution in France*, pp. 129, 134; Vial, *op. cit.*, pp. 146-7; and Bertrand Gille, *La sidérurgie française au XIXe siècle, Recherches historiques*, Librairie Droz, S.A. Geneva, 1968, pp. 84-5.

92. Gille, *La sidérurgie française*, pp. 111-12, and Yves Lequin, 'Labour in the French Economy', *The Cambridge Economic History of Europe, Vol. VII, Pt. 1, Britain, France, Germany and Scandinavia*, pp. 299-300.

93. Vial, *op. cit.*, p. 146; the quote is from Dunham, *op. cit.*, p. 130. See also Hardach, *Der soziale Status. . .*, pp. 67-74 for further examples.

94. See Gerd Hardach, 'Les problèmes de main-d'oeuvre à Decazeville', *Revue d'histoire de la sidérurgie*, Tome VIII, No. 1, 1967, pp. 56-8. Hardach is here describing the situation at the Decazeville plant in 1833. See also by the same author, *Der soziale Status. . .*, p. 84.

95. Hardach, *Der soziale Status. . .*, p. 85.

96. Woronoff, *loc. cit.*, pp. 118-19.

97. See Hardach, 'Les problèmes de main-d'oeuvre à Decazeville', *loc. cit.*, p. 59 ff, and Bertrand Gille, 'La formation du prolétariat dans l'industrie sidérurgique française', *Revue d'histoire de la sidérurgie*, Tome IV, No. 4, October–December 1963, p. 249.

98. Guy Palmade, *French Capitalism in the Nineteenth Century*, p. 207. See also, Claude Fohlen, 'The Industrial Revolution in France, 1700-1914', *loc. cit.*, p. 30, and Yves Lequin, 'Labour in the French Economy', *loc. cit.*, pp. 307-8. See also Gille, *La sidérurgie française*, p. 58, who claims this was less of a problem for *'petite métallurgie'*.

99. Vial, *op. cit.*, pp. 335-7; Woronoff, *loc. cit.*, pp. 118-19.

100. See Hardach, *Der soziale Status. . .*, pp. 74-9.

101. Woronoff, *loc. cit.*, pp. 118-19.

102. See Vial, *op. cit.*, pp. 282-7.

103. Claude Fohlen, 'The Industrial Revolution in France, 1700-1914', *loc. cit.*, p. 50 ff; Yves Lequin, 'Labour in the French Economy', *loc. cit.*, p. 307; and Woronoff, *loc. cit.*, pp. 113-14.

104. Yves Lequin, 'La formation du prolétariat industriel dans la région lyonnaise au XIX siècle: approches méthodologiques et premiers résultats', in *Le mouvement social*, No. 97, octobre-décembre, 1976, Table 1, p. 132.

105. *ibid.*, p. 135.

106. See Bertrand Gille, 'La formation du prolétariat ouvrier dans l'industrie sidérurgique française', *loc. cit.*, pp. 248-9. Certainly some geographical mobility was taking place in the last half of the nineteenth century, but this mainly concerned the movement of highly qualified workers. The automobile industry of the early twentieth century also located itself in heavily concentrated regions, especially in the Paris and Lyonnaise regions, to be close to the reserves of skilled and semi-skilled labour earlier brought together by the iron, steel and engineering trades. See Laux, *In First Gear*, pp. 83, 179. The locomotive plant,

Cail à Denain, as well in 1909, could still recruit 80.% of its workers locally. They were, in the words of Louis Chatelier, son of the famous Henry, a manager of the plant, *'racinés dans le terroir'* (workers 'rooted to the soil'); the other 20% were 'nomads'. See Louis Chatelier, 'Les Atéliers Cail à Denain', *Revue de Métallurgie*, Vol. 6, 1909, p. 583. See also Yves Lequin, 'Labour in the French Economy', *loc. cit.*, p. 308.

107. Dolléans, *op. cit.*, p. 274, and Fohlen, 'The Industrial Revolution in France, 1700-1914', *loc. cit.*, p. 60. For an excellent analysis of concentration in the heavy metal industry after the mid-nineteenth century, see J-B. Silly, 'La concentration dans l'industrie sidérurgique en France sous le Second Empire', *Revue d'histoire de la sidérurgie*, Tome III, No. 1, 1962, pp. 19-48; and by the same author, 'Les plus grandes sociétés métallurgiques en 1881', *Revue d'histoire de la sidérurgie*, Tome VI, No. 4, October-December, 1965, pp. 255-72. What is especially interesting of Silly's work is the role of metal industrialists in providing many of the personnel for the great banks, particularly the *Crédit Lyonnaise*, which was staffed by men from the *Commentary*, *Terrenoire*, *Firminy* and *Le Creusot* enterprises. See also Gerd Hardach, *Der soziale Status. . .*, pp. 28-31, 65-6.

108. See Hardach, 'Les problèmes de main-d'oeuvre à Decazeville', *loc. cit.*, pp. 66-7; and Yves Lequin, 'Labour in the French Economy', *loc. cit.*, p. 315.

109. See Vial, *op. cit.*, p. 336; and also Hardach, 'Les problèmes de main d'oeuvre à Decazeville', *loc. cit.*, p. 67, for a description of the situation at Decazeville. Railway companies in the mid-nineteenth century also established their own trade schools, starting with the *Compagnie du Nord* in 1849. See Margot B. Stein, 'The Meaning of Skill: The Case of the French Engine-Drivers, 1837-1917', *Politics and Society*, Vol. 8, Nos. 3-4, 1978, p. 409.

110. Hardach, *Der soziale Status. . .*, pp. 84-5.

111. Lequin, 'Labour in the French Economy', *loc. cit.*, pp. 310-12. See also Hardach, *Der soziale Status. . .*, p. 86 ff, for examples in the iron trades.

112. Lequin, 'Labour in the French Economy', *loc. cit.*, p. 314; Dunham, *op. cit.*, pp. 5, 184.

113. See R. Cameron, *France and the Economic Development of Europe*, pp. 43, 46; Vial, *op. cit.*, pp. 129-30; and F.B. Artz, 'L'enseignement technique en France', *Revue Historique*, Vol. CXCVI, juillet-septembre, 1946, pp. 272 ff, 283-4, and octobre-décembre, 1946, p. 396 ff, Emile Durkheim, *Pédagogique en France*, PUF, Paris, 1969, pp. 334-66; Joseph N. Moody, *French Education Since Napoleon*, Syracuse University Press, New York, 1978, Ch. 1: A. Prost, *L'enseignement en France*, 1800-1967, Librairie Armand Colin, Paris, 1968, p. 301 ff, and F. Ponteil *Histoire de l'enseignement en France; Les grandes étapes, 1789-1964*, Sirey, Paris, 1966, p. 51 ff.

114. Cameron, *op. cit.*, p. 47.

115. Henry Le Chatelier, 'L'enseignement technique dans ses rapports avec l'enseignement universitaire', *Revue de Métallurgie*, Vol. 5, 1908, p. 795.

116. See Cameron, *op. cit.*, pp. 47-9; F.B. Artz, *loc. cit.*, octobre-décembre, 1946, p. 385 ff. See also Adeline Daumard, 'Les Elèves de l'Ecole Polytechnique de 1815 à 1848', *Revue d'histoire moderne et contemporaine*, Vol. 5, 1958, p. 226 ff.

117. Palmade, *op. cit.*, pp. 96, 153. A short biographical sketch of Paulin Talabot can be found in Bertrand Gille, 'Paulin Talabot, Recherches pour une biographie', *Revue d'histoire des mines et de la métallurgie*, Tome II, No. 1, 1970, pp. 49-99.

118. Palmade, *op. cit.*, p. 100. A good biography of Defaud is Guy Thuillier's, *Georges Defaud et les débuts du grand capitalisme dans la métallurgie en Nivernais au*

XIXe siècle, Paris, 1953.
119. See Vial, *op. cit.*, p. 396 and n. 5.
120. Palmade, *op. cit.*, pp. 99-100; and Vial, *op. cit.*, p. 179 and n. 2.
121. Vial, *op. cit.*, p. 379 and n. 9. Maurice Lévy-Leboyer has found that the bourgeoisie formed the overwhelming proportion of students at the four main schools; the *Ecole Centrale*, the *Polytechnique*, the *Ecole des Mines*, and *Ponts et Chaussées*. In the period 1800-70 some 75.9% of students at the *Polytechnique* came from backgrounds in the liberal professions, the industrial bourgeoisie and coupon-clipping *rentiers*. Students with an artisan or commercial background did, though, stand a better chance at the *Conservatoire Nationale des Arts et Métiers* or at the Paris *Ecole des Arts et Métiers*. At the former, 60.2% came from the artisan-commerce stratum in the period 1800-13, while at the Paris *Ecole* 26.8% came from this stratum in the period 1860-75. See M. Lévy-Leboyer, 'Le patronat français a-t-il été malthusien?' *Le mouvement social*, No. 88, juillet-septembre 1974, Table 4, p. 25.
122. Yves Lequin, 'Labour in the French Economy', *loc. cit.*, p. 313; and Cameron, *op. cit.*, pp. 50-1.
123. See J.M. Laux, *op. cit.*, pp. 9-10, 25, 29, 39, 46-7, 116; and Palmade, *op. cit.*, p. 100.
124. Cameron, *op. cit.*, p. 51.
125. *ibid.*, p. 54. See also M. Lévy-Leboyer, 'Le patronat français a-t-il été malthusien?', *loc. cit.*, pp. 26-7, for further examples.
126. Bertrand Gille, *La sidérurgie française*, p. 82.
127. *ibid.*, p. 83.
128. See Robert R. Locke, 'Drouillard, Benoist et Cie', in *Revue d'histoire de la sidérurgie*, Tome VIII, No. 4, 1967, p. 285.
129. Bertrand Gille, *La sidérurgie française*, p. 83.
130. *ibid.*, pp. 83-4; and Claude Fohlen, 'The Industrial Revolution in France, 1700-1914', *loc. cit.*, p. 48. See also Gerd Hardach, *Der soziale Status. . .*, pp. 154-5 for further examples of the English providing many of the early plant engineers to run blast furnaces and construct puddling works.
131. Vial, *op. cit.*, pp. 176-8.
132. *ibid.*, pp. 131-2 and n. 2, 178-9.
133. *ibid.*, pp. 260-1.
134. Cameron, *op. cit.*, pp. 54-61.
135. See François Caron, *Histoire de l'exploitation d'un grand réseau: La Compagnie du Chemin de Fer du Nord, 1846-1937*, Ecole Pratique des Hautes Etudes, Paris, 1973, pp. 241-4.
136. Claude Fohlen, 'Entrepreneurship and Management in Nineteenth Century France', *Cambridge Economic History of Europe, Vol. VII, The Industrial Economies: Capital, Labour and Enterprise*, Pt. 1, Ch. VII, pp. 347-81.
137. *ibid.*, pp. 377-8. The reference to Allevard is on pp. 375-6.
138. Vial, *op. cit.*, pp. 396-7. Vial speaks of this business engineer as *'possédant à fond son métier, attentif à toutes les innovations, à la fois ingénieur et chef d'entreprise capable de diriger les usines et rompu à la pratique'. ibid.*, p. 180. Fohlen also notes this as a tendency, where 'more and more technical tasks were given to engineers who, in fact, under pressure of events, became administrators'. Claude Fohlen, 'Entrepreneurship and Management in Nineteenth Century France', *loc. cit.*, p. 378.
139. Vial, *op. cit.*, p. 176.
140. See Hardach, *Der soziale Status. . .*, pp. 144-53.
141. See Nathan Rosenberg, 'Karl Marx on the Economic Role of Science', *Journal of Political Economy*, Vol. 82, 1974, pp. 713-28 (the quotations may be found

on pp. 720, 721).
142. See S. Lilley, 'Social Aspects of the History of Science', *Archives Internationales d'Histoire des Sciences*, Année 2, 1948–49, pp. 415–16.
143. Vial, *op. cit.*, pp. 257–9; and Laux, *op. cit.*, pp. 89–90.
144. See Lilley, *loc. cit.*, pp. 393–4.
145. See A. Schröter and W. Becker, *Die deutsche Maschinenbauindustrie in der industriellen Revolution*, Akademie, East Berlin, 1962, pp. 26, 48–9.
146. See Jürgen Kocka, 'Entrepreneurs and Managers in German Industrialization', in *Cambridge Economic History of Europe: The Industrial Economies, Capital, Labour and Enterprise*, Vol. VII, Pt. 1, Ch. X, p. 515.
147. See Schröter and Becker, *op. cit.*, pp. 48–9.
148. *ibid.*, pp. 50, 53.
149. Kocka also emphasises that, 'there was only a limited continuity between the pre-industrial period and the industrial revolution, on the level of the institutions and their directors. The new factories were most likely to develop out of earlier putting-out enterprises (i.e. merchants). Less likely to grow out of old manufactories, and still less likely to evolve out of old craftsmen's shops'. See Kocka, 'Entrepreneurs and Managers in German Industrialization', *loc. cit.*, p. 510. See also, pp. 508–9.
150. Schröter and Becker, *op. cit.*, p. 108.
151. *ibid.*, pp. 64, 69. Schröter's survey of the mode of financing of sixty-eight engineering establishments before 1850 has found that only thirteen were formed by individual owners, while eight were constituted as AGs. The remainder were open partnerships. *ibid.*, pp. 73–4. When an early engineering company was formed as an AG from the start, it generally conformed to the pattern of the formation of the open partnership where one of the founders worked in collaboration with commercial men. Such was the case with the foundation of *Maschinenfabrik Esslingen* of Württemberg in 1846. Though underwritten by Württemberg's commercial and financial establishment and a bank, the planning and practical foundation of the firm was undertaken by Emil Kessler. Local government came to Kessler's aid as well, providing him with loans at cheap interest rates and contracts for locomotives without taking a stake in the shares of the company. See Volker Hentschel, *Wirtschaftsgeschichte der Maschinenfabrik Esslingen A.G., 1846-1918*, Ernst Klett Verlag, Stuttgart, 1977, pp. 20–2. See also Kocka, 'Entrepreneurs and Managers in German Industrialization', *loc. cit.*, p. 521. H. Beau's *Das Leistungswissen des frühindustriellen Unternehmertums in Rheinland und Westfälen*, Cologne, 1959, p. 69, contains a survey of the origins of 400 enterprises in the Rhine-Westphalian region during the years 1790-1870 and has come to similar conclusions. The origins of the Siemens and Halske Company were also similar. Johann Georg Halske was often referred to as the *'Mechanicus'*, while Siemens concentrated on the commercial side. See Jürgen Kocka, *Unternehmensverwaltung und Angestelltenschaft am Beispiel Siemens 1847-1914*, Ernst Klett Verlag, Stuttgart, 1969, pp. 56–8. For a contrary view, see Hartmut Kaelble, 'From the Family Enterprise to the Professional Manager: the German Case', Eighth International Economic History Congress, Budapest, 1982, B. 89. *From Family Firm to Professional Management: Structure and Performance of Business Enterprise.* Organiser: L. Hannah, Akadémiai Kiadó, Budapest, 1982, p. 53.
152. See C. Matschoss, *Ein Jahrhundert deutscher Maschinenbau, 1819-1919*, Julius Springer, Berlin, 1922, pp. 281–6.
153. *ibid.*, pp. 185–6; Kocka, 'Entrepreneurs and Managers in German Industrialization', *loc. cit.*, pp. 516–19.

154. Cameron, *op. cit.*, p. 396 ff, 390; Schröter and Becker, *op. cit.*, pp. 37–8, 43; and Kocka, 'Entrepreneurs and Managers in German Industrialization', *loc. cit.*, p. 531 ff.

155. Schröter and Becker, *op. cit.*, pp. 39, 68; Cameron, *op. cit.*, p. 53. Many famous engineering employers attended these model technical schools, such as Borsig, who was a student at one in Breslau. According to Cameron, the French influence on German science was of 'paramount' importance. Great scientists, like Humboldt and Liebig obtained their training in Paris, while scientific textbooks and manuals drew on French research. Cameron, *op. cit.*, p. 45.

For a discussion of the rise of technical colleges during the 1830s and after, see Kocka, 'Entrepreneurs and Managers in German Industrialization', *loc. cit.*, p. 533 ff; on the rise of laboratories see also p. 571 ff. See also P. Lundgreen, *Bildung und Wirtschaftswachstum im Industrialisierungprozess des 19. Jahrhundert*, Berlin, 1973, p. 127 ff. Frank Hauerkamp's *Staatliche Gewerbeförderung im Grossherzogtum Baden unter besonderer Berücksichtigung der Entwicklung des Gewerblichen Bildungswesen im 19. Jahrhundert*, Verlag Karl Alber, Freiburg/München, 1979, p. 19 ff, provides a good description of the origins and development of schools of industrial training in the Baden region and also shows the importance of French influences on the formation of the Karlsruhe Polytechnik at the beginning of the nineteenth century (pp. 30 ff, 90 ff). A less interesting work is Dr Karl-Heinz Manegold's *Universität, Technische Hochschule und Industrie. Ein Beitrag zur Emanziation der Technik im 19. Jahrhundert unter besonderer Berücksichtigung der Bestrebungen Felix Kleins*, Duncker and Humblot, Berlin, 1970, p. 18 ff. Contrary to what the title suggests, this work mainly concentrates on the relations (or conflicts) between the established universities and the new technical colleges. Very little attention is given to the role of industry or firms with regard to the rise of the colleges or the application of science.

156. Schröter and Becker, *op. cit.*, p. 76. Heilwig Schomerus, in a work which complements Hentschel's, has found that in Esslingen, in 1841, a special *Institut* had to be created for the training of mechanics *(Machaniker)* that sought to meet the needs of the railway coming to the town and of the future engineering firms. See *Die Arbeiter der Maschinenfabrik Esslingen: Forschungen zur Lage der Arbeiterschaft im 19. Jahrhundert*, Letta-Cotta, Stuttgart, 1977, pp. 47–9. See also Lundgreen, *op. cit.*, p. 127 ff.

157. Schröter and Becker, *op. cit.*, pp. 228, 65, 77–9, 109.

158. *ibid.*, pp. 76–7.

159. *ibid.*, p. 76.

160. *ibid.*, pp. 228, 230.

161. *ibid.*, p. 228. On the shortages of labour see J.J. Lee, 'Labour in German Industrialisation', in P. Mathias and M.M. Postan, *The Cambridge Modern History of Europe, Vol. VII, The Industrial Economies. . . Part 1. . .*, pp. 450–1.

162. See T.C. Banfield, *Industry of the Rhine*, 2 vols., 1846–48, *Series II, Manufactures*, C. Cox, London, 1848, p. 235.

163. See Richard Ehrenberg, 'Die Frühzeit der Kruppschen Arbeiterschaft', *Archiv für exacte Wirtschaftsforschung*, Vol. 3, 1911, p. 35.

164. Lee, *loc. cit.*, pp. 451–2. See also Schröter and Becker, *op. cit.*, pp. 78–9.

165. Ehrenberg, *loc. cit.*, pp. 47–8.

166. Schomerus, *op. cit.*, pp. 89–90. Schomerus' calculations for the 'unqualified' however, are underestimated, for amongst the 'qualified' workers she includes not only those *Beruf* metal workers, fitters and smiths, etc. but also those who were apprenticed and, therefore, in need of training from the enterprise in

which they worked. See *ibid.*, p. 84, n. 104. See also the same author 'Ausbildung und Aufsteigsmöglichkeiten württembergischer Metallarbeiter 1850 bis 1915, am Beispiel der Maschinenfabrik Esslingen', in Ulruich Engelhardt, Volker Sellin and Horst Stuke, eds., *Soziale Bewegung und politische Verfassung,* Ernst Klett Verlag, Stuttgart, 1976, p. 375 ff. For a similar description of the problems associated with an untrained labour supply at the Siemens plants in Berlin during the 1840s and 1850s, see Jürgen Kocka, *Unternehmensverwaltung und Angestelltenschaft,* p. 65, n. 2 and ff.

167. Schomerus, *op. cit.*, p. 27.

168. *ibid.*, pp. 118-20.

169. *ibid.*, pp. 122-3.

170. Ehrenberg, *loc. cit.*, p. 76.

171. *ibid.*, p. 77. In most of the other Krupp shops, Ehrenberg observed, there were few, if any, *Lehrlinge.* In the hammer shop, apart from the trained hammer-smith, only general labourers were taken on. A labourer who was first taken on to lift and carry could in time move on to a press, and if he was any good could possibly become a 'hammersmith' himself and finally a foreman. See *ibid.*, p. 77.

172. *ibid.*, p. 77.

173. *ibid.*, p. 146.

174. Quoted in Wolfram Fischer, 'Innerbetrieblicher und sozialer Status der frühen Fabrikarbeiterschaft', *Forschungen zur Sozial- und Wirtschaftsgeschichte,* Vol. VI, 1964, pp. 199-200.

175. Schröter and Becker, *op. cit.*, p. 225.

176. See *ibid.*, p. 221 ff. The source quoted by Schröter and Becker is E. Engel, *Die deutsche Industrie 1875 und 1861,* Berlin, 1881, p. 214. See also Schomerus, *op. cit.*, pp. 35-43.

177. Schröter and Becker, *op. cit.*, pp. 221-3.

178. *ibid.*, pp. 226-7, and Schomerus, *op. cit.*, p. 37.

179. See, for example, Jürgen Tampke, *The Ruhr and Revolution: The Revolutionary Movement in the Rhenish-Westphalian Region, 1912-1919,* ANU Press, Canberra, 1978, p. 5 ff. Polish workers were mainly concentrated in the northern Ruhr, often accounting for 50% of the local workforce. They suffered in many ways the worst aspects of proletarian life—poor conditions, subsistence wages, long hours of work, bad housing and tyrannical employers.

180. Schröter and Becker, *op. cit.*, pp. 226-7, and Schomerus, *op. cit.*, pp. 45-7, 87-8. According to Schomerus the firm had been able to recruit much of its labour locally. Even in its founding years, 1847-1848, it was able to obtain over 60% of its workforce from the Württemberg district. Other workers came from outside the district, but their former homes were generally no more than 50km away. In contrast to a region like the Rhineland, where migratory labour played such a large role in the constitution of a workforce, the Esslingen firm found that it could obtain workers locally right up to 1914. See *ibid.*, pp. 65, 69-78. The similarities with the pattern of recruitment in the Lyonnaise region in France are apparent. One of the consequences of not having to rely on uprooted workers for a labour supply seems to have been relatively low levels of job turnover, which characterised the situation in the southern German metal industry as a whole. This question will be explored fully in Chapter 6.

181. Schröter and Becker, *op. cit.*, p. 227.

182. *ibid.*, pp. 190-2, for the increasing fixed capital requirements of big and medium-sized firms and the number of machines and engines in use.

183. *ibid.*, pp. 199-202.

184. Schomerus, *op. cit.*, pp. 151, n. 136, 163. At the Esslingen plant a policy for

training the firm's apprentices had been in existence since its foundation in 1847. See *ibid.,* p. 146. Becker argues that through these training schools a labour aristocracy took shape, which was able to collaborate with management in the direction of the labour process and provide stability in the workforce. See Schröter and Becker, *op. cit.,* pp. 229-30. This is not the place to enter into controversy over the nature of the labour aristocracy and whether it existed or not in the German engineering industry. Let it be said, though, that if one did exist, it was short lived. In Chapter 6 it is shown that at the turn of the century there was little evidence of it, and, by the 1880s the growth of white collar labour was stripping away many of the 'traditional' semi-managerial functions of the *Facharbeiter.* It can also be noted that the very speed and novelty with which an engineering industry and its labour force were created was more likely to have worked against the formation of such a stratum.

185. See Schröter and Becker, *op. cit.,* pp. 228-31.
186. See Karl Schröder, *Hervorragende Förderungsstätten des deutschen Handwerks,* Berlin, 1877, pp. 1-4, 120.
187. *ibid.,* p. 115, and Gustav Schmoller, *Das untere und mittlere gewerbliche Schulwesen in Preussen,* 1881.
188. See J.J. Lee, *loc. cit.,* p. 450.
189. *ibid.,* p. 454.
190. See Eckhard Brockhaus, *Zusammensetzung und Neustrukturierung der Arbeiterklasse vor dem ersten Weltkrieg,* p. 16 ff.
191. District By-Laws of the Friendly Society of Ironfounders of England, Ireland and Wales, Rules V and XII. Source, E.A. Pratt, *Trade Unionism and British Industry,* John Murray, London, 1904, pp. 59-60.
192. See Carr and Taplin, *op. cit.,* pp. 140-1, and also Frank Wilkinson, 'Collective Bargaining in the Steel Industry in the 1920s', in Asa Briggs and John Saville, eds., *Essays in Labour History, 1918-1939,* Croom Helm, London, 1977, pp. 102-32.
193. See Sidney and Beatrice Webb, *Industrial Democracy,* p. 491.
194. See Barbara Drake, *Women in the Engineering Trades,* Allen and Unwin, Fabian Research Department, London, 1917, pp. 10-11.
195. See *Royal Commission on Trades Disputes and Combinations, Minutes of Evidence together with Index and Appendices, Cd. 2826, 1906, in Parliamentary Papers,* Vol. LVI, 1906; evidence by Sir Andrew Noble on 30 November, 1904, p. 160.
196. See sources to footnote 192.
197. Scott, in her study of the unionisation of the French glass workers of Carmaux in the 1890s, provides many points of comparison with the nature of the British boilermakers' union. When a union was formed by Carmaux's glass workers, it did not attempt to prevent the introduction of new techniques of production and maintain older methods of production. Rather, the union's primary aim was to defend the hierarchy of work in glass making. Though mechanisation tended to level skills, the workers sought to preserve the formalities of the traditional craft hierarchy. The union was controlled by *'souffleurs',* the master craftsmen, and all workers with the exception of the auxiliaries were required to join. The organisation of the union followed the structure of the job: a gang of glass workers led by a *souffleur* formed the elemental part of the union. Reluctant unionists found that because of the *souffleurs'* powers in the union, and on the job, they could be 'sacked' by the union or have their apprenticeships extended or promotion up the job ladder denied them. The union also sought to organise employment so that prospective workers had to approach the union first before their employment by a firm could be accepted. Such activities were in marked

contrast to the past when glass workers regulated the work because of the integral power of their skills and their ability to restrict entrance to the trade to only the sons of glass workers. The regulation of skills and of training by the workers before the transformation of the glass-making labour process was therefore largely informal and easily maintained. They did not have to prevent such an occurrence formally where unskilled 'apprentices' could take over the work of the 'skilled' workers. In Scott's view, the instrument was 'the power of organisation':

'Only the political or economic force which the union represented, and *not* the collective skill of its members could ensure their future and protect their jobs.'

From this new strategic position, the union in 1892 attempted to extend the period of apprenticeships, so that, for example, four years of carrying bottles and holding moulds would be the period required before a young man could enter the bottom rung of the 'craft' hierarchy as a *gamin* or *grand garçon,* though there was no real technical need for this in terms of learning anything. Its only aim was to regulate the labour market and prevent the now easily learned skills of the 'craftsmen' from being too quickly acquired. See Scott, *op. cit.,* pp. 99-114. The quote is on p. 106.

198. Benjamin Taylor, 'The Blight of Trade Unionism', *Cassier's Magazine,* Vol. XII, No. 3, January 1898, p. 221.

199. For an evaluation of the lock-out, see R.O. Clarke, 'The Dispute in the British Engineering Industry, 1897-1898: An Evaluation', *Economica,* No. 94, May 1957, pp. 128-37.

200. See the documents in Benjamin Taylor, 'The Machine Question and Eight Hours', *Cassier's Magazine,* Vol. XIII, No. 1, November 1897, p. 97/15. Throughout the 1890s, demarcation disputes with other engineering unions built up a catalogue of bad blood against the ASE. The ASE had taken on the boilermakers by demanding that the assembly and fitting of the new Belleville water tube boilers be hived off to ASE members only. This proved to be an important element in the disunity that occurred in London between the two unions during the lock-out. There were also rebellions by ASE members at Hull and Barrow in the shipyards and the machine shops against members of the Machine Workers' Association working machines which the ASE members claimed as their own. See R.O. Clarke, *loc. cit.,* and Benjamin Taylor, 'The Blight of Trade Unionism', *loc. cit.,* pp. 219-21.

201. Benjamin Taylor, 'The Machine Question and Eight Hours', *loc. cit.,* pp. 97/ 15 to 97/16.

202. Letters to the Editor, *Cassier's Magazine,* Vol. XIII, No. 1, November 1897, pp. 97/11 to 97/12.

203. *ibid.,* pp. 97/12.

204. *ibid.,* c. 22 October, 1897, pp. 97/11.

205. See Benjamin Taylor, 'The Machine Question and Eight Hours', *loc. cit.,* pp. 97/ 16.

206. *ibid.,* pp. 97/16.

207. See 'The Employers Federation and the Amalgamated Society of Engineers Proposed Working Agreement', in *Cassier's Magazine,* Vol. XXI, No. 5, March 1902, p. 522.

208. See James Hinton, *The First Shop Stewards' Movement,* George Allen and Unwin, London, 1973, p. 99. (My emphasis, C. McG.)

209. *ibid.,* p. 61.

210. See Engineering and Allied Employers' National Federation statistics in Committee on Industry and Trade (Balfour Committee), *Survey of Metal Industries,*

H.M.S.O., London, 1928, p. 152.

211. See Anonymous Letter to the Editor, 'The Employers' Federation and the Amalgamated Society of Engineers: Proposed Working Agreement', *loc. cit.*, p. 520.

212. *ibid.*, p. 522.

213. See E.T. Elbourne, *Factory Administration and Accounts (1914)*, Longman, London, 1919, pp. 87–9.

214. I am indebted to Tony Elger, 'Valorisation and "Deskilling". A Critique of Braverman', *Capital and Class*, No. 7, Spring 1979, pp. 87–9 for the original conception of this problem. Sidney Pollard makes a similar point about this when he discusses the rise of the ASE in Britain during the mid-nineteenth century. The ASE, he argues, sought to base its defence of 'skill' not on arcane knowledge, but on organisation and collective bargaining. See Pollard, 'Labour in Great Britain', *loc. cit.*, p. 123.

215. Reference is made here to the views of Charles More and Jonathan Zeitlin already cited on p. 18.

216. See Charles More, *Skill and the English Working Class*, p. 35.

217. *ibid.*, p. 35.

218. See T.C. Banfield, *op. cit.*, p. 41.

219. See A. Schröter and W. Becker, *op. cit.*, pp. 245–9.

220. See Walter Timmerman, *Die Entlöhnungsmethoden in der Hannoverschen Eisenindustrie*, Leonhard Simion, Berlin, 1906. See also L. Schoffer, 'Patterns of Worker Protest: Upper Silesia, 1865–1914', in Peter N. Stearns and Daniel J. Walkowitz, eds., *Workers in the Industrial Revolution*, Transaction Books, New Brunswick, New Jersey, 1974, pp. 324–37. It can also be noted that until 1905 only 60 agreements were in operation in the metal industry covering some 2,530 establishments and approximately 18,270 workers, which was less than 10% of the DMV's membership. See Otto Jeidels, *Die Methoden der Arbeiterentlöhnung in der rheinischwestfälischen Eisenindustrie*, Leonhard Simion, Berlin, 1907, p. 154. See also 'Report of the German Metalworkers' Union to the Sixth Congress of the International Metalworkers' Federation, Berlin, 1913', in International Metalworkers' Federation, *Industrial Training also Internationalism, compiled by Charles Hobson, Secretary of the British Section*, pp. 548–9. On the use of *Berufsgenossenschaften* in Berlin after 1889, see Fritz Schulte, *Die Entlöhnungsmethoden in der Berliner Maschinenindustrie*, p. 75 ff, and on the issues which hit metal workers, see *ibid.*, p. 80 ff, for a description of the foundry strikes in Berlin between 1890 and 1905.

221. See Schulte, *op. cit.*, p. 75 ff.

222. Waldemar Follos, *Lohn und Arbeitsverhältnisse in der Berliner Metallindustrie*, Leonhard Simion, Berlin, 1907, p. 61.

223. Otto Jeidels, *op. cit.*, pp. 148–53.

224. To a certain extent, France lay between Britain and Germany on these questions. Like Britain, it had its 'craftsmen', such as the rolling mill workers of Ardenne who until World War One remained true autocrats in the shop, respected for their secrets of production as well as for their physical strength. On the other hand, trade unions in the metal industry, as in other industries, were liable to instant suppression, unable to organise except in secret or pass beyond the boundaries of a locality to link up into a national body. See M. Verry, *Les laminoirs ardennais. Déclin d'une aristocratie professionelle*, Paris, 1955, and G.D.H. Cole, 'The Genesis of Syndicalism in France', Appendix A, in his *Self Government in Industry*, Bell and Sons, London, 1917, p. 311. See also Jean Latapie, 'Report of the Federal Union of Metal Workers of France to the International Metallurgists' Congress, Amsterdam, 1904', in International

Metalworkers' Federation, *Industrial Training also Internationalism*, pp. 316-17.

225. See Joseph Melling, 'Non-Commissioned Officers: British Employers and their Supervisory Workers, 1880-1920', *Social History*, Vol. 5, May 1980, p. 187.

226. There are a number of very good studies concerned with the influence of craft culture on the formation of industrial working class attitudes and organisations, notably E.P. Thompson's *The Making of the English Working Class*, Penguin, London, 1963. For France, Sewell's *Work and Revolution in France* can be consulted with profit. On Germany, see Theodore Hamerow's *Restoration Revolution, Reaction*. An interesting article on the impact of craft culture on the formation of the Italian working class is Donald H. Bell's 'Worker Culture and Worker Politics: the Experience of an Italian Town, 1880-1915', *Social History*, Vol. 3, No. 1, January 1978, pp. 1-21, which is a study of the town of Sesto San Giovanni.

227. See Dolléans, *op. cit.*, pp. 148-9.

PART 2

THE PROFESSIONALISATION OF LABOUR AND

THE NEW TECHNICAL INTELLIGENCE

CHAPTER 2: THE AMERICAN INFLUENCE AND THE DEVELOPMENT OF A 'UNIFYING IDEA'

From the 1890s a new pattern of uneven development took shape amongst the western economies which brought the experience of European metal enterprises into much closer proximity with each other. If for most of the nineteenth century the main contours of uneven development were located in Europe, with Britain in the pre-eminent position, by the end of the century America had emerged as the new centre of industrial capitalist development, modern mass-production techniques, and huge monopolistic concerns in banking, railways, oil, iron and steel, and engineering. Europe's industrial leaders, including Britain's, had to begin to measure the successes and failures of their own enterprises against what they saw as the 'new' American methods: methods of production management and training that highlighted the growing inadequacies of the private and competitive techniques they had used to build up their own managerial position in the production process.

For many general commentators, independent observers and managerial 'scientists', this was the background against which they sought to describe the changes they saw taking place at the turn of the century to the composition of the workforce and the decline of craft skill. They were concerned not so much to emphasise a non-existent fragility in the position of European metal employers or their inability readily to regulate the skills of workers inside their factories; rather, they sought to highlight the growing *professional qualification* required for new layers of the labour force: a form of qualification that had to be systematically organised both inside and outside of the factory, and especially in conjunction with the state. The reference to a declining 'craft' workforce in this context, was a quite heuristic way of describing how the mass of workers engaged in direct production, whose training normally took place inside the factory, found their already regulated skills undergoing a new and more professional form of de-qualification.

The industrialisation of the American economy after 1850 was an unusual synthesis of European experience. Like Germany and France, industrialisation took place against the background of a structural shortage of skilled labour. Also, the skilled labour that did exist was often very recalcitrant towards any employer who attempted to flood its ranks by reducing training periods and diluting work. Like Britain, therefore, skilled 'workers' sought to regulate the labour supply by 'restrictive practices'.[1]

63

By the beginning of the twentieth century, though, this skilled labour force had been complemented by successive waves of millions of immigrants from southern and eastern Europe who had little experience of factory life, let alone any training in industrial skills.[2] One Government survey conducted after the immigration wave of 1899-1910 found that only 15% of the new immigrants could be classified as 'skilled' labourers, though this was slightly higher than the immigration wave of 1871-82 when only 11.2% of the migrants could be classified in this category.[3]

The combination of each of these developments made the development of a trained labour force in America quite unique. In no other western country were the employers in the leading industries (iron, steel, engineering, meat processing, tobacco, railways and the later automobiles) compelled simultaneously to break the resistance of a well-entrenched stratum of white, skilled labour, organised into exclusive unions, and introduce sophisticated divisions of labour, semi-automatic machinery and new training programmes, so that the incoming millions of Poles, Hungarians, Italians, Portuguese and eastern European Jews could be put to work for cheap wages.[4]

1. Contracting in America and Europe

Until the 1880s and 1890s the recruitment, maintenance, and training of the workforce in the heavy metal industry had been in the hands of skilled 'workers' *via* the system of contracting. A contractor was a person who contracted with an owner to produce by a certain date, a product at a set cost and quantity, while simultaneously hiring his own workers, generally on time wages. The system was rampant in the engineering plants on the north-east coast, in the arms-producing plants of Colt and Winchester, and in the iron and steel mills of Pittsburgh. The company generally undertook the commercial aspects of production; decided on the location of the factory, when it would be open and closed; provided the contractor with company tools, machinery, buildings and power; advanced payment as the goods were produced; hired examiners to check the work; and finally found a market for the finished product. The contractor, on the other hand, gave employment to his workers, sacked them and trained them when necessary, supervised and disciplined them, set their wages, and did not allow them to share in the profits of the job.[5]

The general absence of direct employer control over the recruitment and training of the workforce was checked to a certain extent by local state child labour laws, which if enforced (and they often were not), would restrict the area of selection. The introduction of company pension and accident schemes after 1900 also brought the employers into more direct contact with their workers, as a system of physical examinations run by personnel departments was required; as well, employer associations recruited workers to member firms and limited the competition for labour by the introduction of labour bureaux, which also operated black-lists, promoted open shops and provided strike-breakers.[6] But this cannot be seen as adding up to real employer control over the maintenance and training of a labour force. As Daniel Nelson has noted, apart from the employer selecting the contractors to undertake the work and bargaining a price with them, the system was essentially 'informal', lubricated by personal contacts, queues outside the factory gate and, all too often, racial criteria of selection—'Poles' and 'Hunks' for heavy manual labour, and Italians, Portuguese and Jews for repetition work requiring quick eyes and fingers. At the same time, all this was sustained within the boundaries of the contractor-cum-foreman's 'empire'.[7] Certainly, examples of direct managerial intervention into the control and maintenance of the work-force were apparent during the mid to late nineteenth century, especially in the form of the company town, where provision was made for schools, churches, shops, and 'welfare' services, etc., in order to attract and keep a workforce to operate the steel mills and work in the mines. Yet only a small minority of workers laboured in company towns in the heavy metal industry. Most worked in the big cities, such as Pittsburgh, Chicago, and in the cities on the north-east coast.[8]

The managerial functions of the contractors and their 'quasi-autonomous' powers *vis-a-vis* the owners were underwritten by exclusive union organisations, like the Amalgamated Association of Iron and Steel Workers, which was founded in 1876 as an amalgamation of contracting puddlers (the Sons of Vulcan), and contracting rollers (the Heaters, Rollers Union, and Roll Hands' Union).[9] These unions had a seemingly corporate-guild character, often imposing formal restrictions on output and how machinery and tools were to be used in order to bargain effectively with the owners. The Amalgamated, for example, in making contracts with the iron masters, placed limits on the size of a charge and the number of heats per turn in puddling mills; the number of bars to be rolled per turn in sheet mills; and the number of pounds of tin plate to be rolled in tin plate mills.[10] When a mass-production steel industry was being founded, the Amalgamated transferred these tactics to the steel mills. In the late 1880s, an agreement reached at the Homestead steel plant contained fifty-eight pages of footnotes regulating the work of the Amalgamated's men.[11]

For the emerging masters of the mass-production steel and heavy-engineering trades, however, the position of the contractors and their powers were coming to be seen as a gross interference with the evolution of a more hierarchical and bureaucratic management structure. The introduction of new techniques of steel making, like the Bessemer and open-hearth processes, the extensive use of charging equipment, travelling cranes and 'live' rollers, and the exceedingly large fixed-capital commit-ments that this entailed, placed a low premium on the continuing utility of the contractor.[12] Similar pressures were also at work in the engineering industry from the late 1880s.[13] From the employers' point of view, the contractors had too much knowledge of the ways and means of production. Often an enterprise did not know the income contractors were making on various jobs, or whether they were making a big profit on one job and a loss on another, or whether the job was being done in the most efficient manner. Only by constantly cutting the contractors' prices could an enterprise be sure that costs of production would fall and productivity be increased. One historian has also found that in the engineering industry contractors would often hold back technical improvements as a countermeasure until the price was set, which for the employers meant that reducing production costs and increasing their profits was often a protracted and uneven process.[14] Owners also felt pressed that the existing system was causing overmanning and prevented them from obtaining exact knowledge of their 'true' costs of production, especially their labour costs, which were allegedly only known to the contractor. The contractors' position, therefore, was seen as a threat to company profitability, as well as an obstacle to economical production.[15] In this context, employers sought to introduce more hierarchical and less contradictory accounting procedures, put an end to profit-sharing with the contractors, introduce salaried foremanship and direct employment of the workforce, establish company-controlled training schemes, and finally seek government sponsorship for the training of managers and engineers.

In order to appreciate the intensity of employer feeling against the position of the contractors and their programme for change, it is first necessary to compare the American system with the European systems of 'sub-contracting'. The systems of piece-wage foremanship or subcontracting that could be commonly found in the European metal industry until the 1890s bore many *prima facie* similarities with the American version. The British iron and steel industry was, of course, renowned for the widespread systems of contracting which existed in the latter half of the nineteenth century. Here, groups of workers were organised into gangs by a 'subcontractor', generally a skilled worker, such as a head roller, puddler or smelter. He was then given a contract price or 'tonnage rate' (a rate for so many tons of puddled iron, for example), out of which he paid his time-wage underhands. The contractor in these cases kept the balance of the contract price after deducting the wages of his underhands. As in the German iron and steel industry, contracting was still in existence at the turn of the century. When researching his book on methods of pay in British industry, David Schloss visited a Midlands iron and steel plant in 1892. He found that every operation was performed by subcontractors employing their own workers from puddling through rolling, sheetmilling, hammering, and also in the company's coal and ore mines.[16] Two years before, an iron workers' union leader reported on the widespread basis of subcontracting in the Midlands' plate rolling mills. Of 145 mills, 113 were run by contractors, while 99 of these were let out to subcontractors.[17] The system could also be found in the Bessemer steel factories of Barrow in the 1870s and to a lesser extent in the newer Siemens-Martin plants in South Wales and some areas of Scotland.[18]

According to the evidence of Government enquiries, especially the 1892–94 Royal Commission on Labour, when contracting went into decline in the late 1880s amongst the iron trades it continued to remain virulent in the steel sections, and perhaps nowhere more so than in the forge and armour-plate plants of Sheffield and Rotherham.[19] As Duncan Burn has noted, the system was certainly 'a long time a-dying' in the British steel industry, and was only finally abolished in 1911 at John Summers' sheet rolling mill.[20]

Evidence of contracting in the British engineering industry during the late nineteenth century is sketchy and fragmentary, though David Schloss did suggest that in the 1890s, 'a very large part of the work in many branches is commonly conducted upon this plan'.[21] Again it was a question of a leading worker contracting with an owner for a piece of work, for example, fitting up a number of machines, while the owner advanced payments on account and a lump sum on completion of the work. In this case, however, the underlings, though still paid time wages, were in fact hired by the firm and drew their wages from the owner. In terms of the historical development of contracting systems, this version is best seen as the final form before the introduction of modern salaried foremanship. It was also the version to be found in the German metal industry until the late 1890s.

It was here called the *Zwischenmeistersystem*, literally an arrangement between foremen or 'masters'. A contractor in a shop brought together a group of workers at his own discretion and arbitrariness to undertake a certain job. He then appointed a 'gang leader' *(Kolonnenführer)*, who was given a price for the job, while the underhands were paid time wages. This was a most hated form of wage payment, as only the gang leader shared in the bonus for completing the job on time or doing it in less time, while the underlings were sweated. The system was widely based in the most technically advanced sections of the German engineering industry, especially in the machine, machine tool, railway, ship and electrical branches. Martin Segitz, in his confidential report to the International Metalworkers' Congress held in London in 1896, put it this way:

> The heavy industry is prevalent: machines, tools, railway buildings [sic.], ship-buildings [sic], electro-technical products. There is specially contract work being done by which the workers are being very much robbed, or by which great profit is being got from the workmen.

As well, 'only the most qualified workmen receive a wage of more than

20 marks' (approximately 20 shillings, a very poor wage even by the standards of the day).[22] Segitz's comrade at the congress, J.A. Theodor, who represented the Moulders' Union, complemented this with a telling description of the plight of skilled workers.

> The German Moulders' Central Society has set itself the task to draw into the society the great number of struggling moulders and foundrymen. Under the prevailing circumstances the work of organisation is extremely difficult, on account of the despotic authority of the contractors and their ever willing foremen, the workmen have been degraded to will-less slaves.[23]

This method of labour organisation was also common in the iron and steel trades, especially in the production of pig iron. In 1906 it was still possible to find a blast furnace foreman on a contract premium for a job while his underlings were paid pure time wages. A similar situation was to be found in many unmechanised rolling mills, as at Krupp's in the Ruhr, in the Siegerland iron works and in Rhineland rolling mills.[24]

A common characteristic of all these systems was that the contractor or piece-rate foreman did not just supervise the work of unskilled labourers; he also supervised skilled workers. The German Moulders' Union was not alone in drawing attention to this and neither was it alone in speaking of the degradation of skilled workers into 'will-less slaves'. Amongst the skilled steel workers of Rotherham, near Sheffield, it was regarded as a 'great grievance' in 1892.[25] In the steel industry, particularly, the position of the number 2 and 3 steel melters, or the tappers at the blast furnace, was by no means incomparable to the skill composition of their respective contractors, yet these skilled workers were an essential component of the contractor's 'underhands'. Recent studies on the American metal industry have also drawn attention to the fact that contractors were often spread right throughout the plant supervising all aspects of production and directing the work of skilled as well as unskilled workers, as at the Whitin Machine Works and in the iron and steel trades.[26]

Contractors certainly undertook work of a highly skilled and specialised nature, but it is not the case that they were only used on work that was too difficult for the employer to organise.[27] It was also common practice for the contractors to be selected by the employer and not by the workers.[28] They were invariably men of 'experience' and 'rare value', at least for the Rhineland's *Gutehoffnungshütte*, during the late nineteenth century;[29] and in recognising this situation in their own shops, Berlin's moulders, for example, sought to form their own work gangs and negotiate directly with the contractor as to how much the job was worth. If the job took too long, or the quality of the mould varied then post mortem negotiations took place.[30] The force of this evidence suggests that contracting, on both sides of the Atlantic, was structured within the labour of superintendence and management; yet if we briefly consider the dominant opinion of historians on this question, it is suggested that contracting represented either a 'backward' form of labour organisation or a 'craft mode of production', where skilled workers enjoyed the fruits of their dominant position in the division of labour.[31] There is no need to go over the craft question again: we need only ask why skilled workers, if they allegedly had a large degree of control over the labour process, were so concerned about the position of the contractors and, in fact, sought to establish countervailing powers against them. The answer is to be found in the underlying *employer-inspired* rationality of the entire system. David Schloss put the matter succinctly with regard to the British engineering industry:

> . . . the faster the subordinate members of a contract group get through their work, the smaller will be the amount deducted from the contract price in respect of the time wages of these workmen, and the larger will be the balance (of this price) which constitutes the remuneration of the leading man—the contractor.[32]

In other words, the faster a group could be made to work the greater was the contractor's profit. The slower the group worked the quicker did the contractor approach 'losing on the job'.[33] The owner lost nothing, as he had already made a contract price which had guaranteed his profit. As one historian has recently put it: 'Plainly, contractors have to be seen as participating to a significant degree in the exploitation of their employees.'[34]

In this period, enterprise policy was generally designed to keep down labour costs and extract the maximum amount of labour from workers, and this had to be done by 'highly skilled and experienced men', as Patrick McGeown described them in his memoirs of life in the British steel industry.[35] The supervisors, as we have seen, were selected for their knowledge of both the work to be done and the abilities of the workers who would do it. In such a situation, managerial authority had to be constructed along lines that were flexible, fragmented and decentralised. Moreover, in order for the job to be done in the required time and for the maximum amount of labour to be extracted, higher management had to make it in the contractor's interest to keep down the wages share of the cost of the product. Thus his incentive not only ensured a profit for him, but also ensured a reduction in the overall costs of production for the enterprise and a defence of its profitability.[36] Men who could effectively undertake such tasks were truly men of experience and rare value for any enterprise, and it is no wonder that they 'grew into such gentlemen, attending race meetings and even owning race horses'.[37] At the Whitin Machine Works they earned substantial profits from their work.[38] Direct authoritarian rule was the basis of their power and also the political dimension of the company's real control over the production process. Of course, the owner had not completely subordinated the contractors to a managerial division of labour. He had, on the contrary, to enter into a profit-sharing relationship with them. Yet in every crucial respect, these 'gentlemen' constituted the first intermediate stratum of underling managers formed for the specific purpose of undertaking the labour of superintendence within a capitalist division of labour. Their history is the pre-history of foremanship. Gerd Hardach has given us eloquent testimony of this in his study of the early French iron industry. Contracting was again common here, especially in the southern firms located in Le Creusot, Decazeville and Aubin. The height of its influence was in the period from the 1830s until the 1850s, and the contractor was often the foreign skilled worker brought in to train the labour force. With time, though, the position was filled by locally trained men. The functions of these 'overseers' or 'contract foremen' concerned the 'administration and control of production, the recruitment of a suitable workforce and the control of production costs'.[39] As a result, they entered into a profit-sharing arrangement with higher management for the exploitation of their workers. Like their American counterparts their powers were enormous within the confines of the workshop and included fining workers for unpunctuality, ill-discipline, drinking, or for just not working hard enough. They were the organisational form of the constantly ringing bell, the ubiquitous clock, and the deduction made at the end of the month.[40]

The usefulness of this French example is that it allows us to highlight both the underlying rationale of all the contracting systems referred to and see where the American version differed. All the systems were animated by the desire of higher management to provide their workshop supervisors with a profit incentive, in order to get the job out on time, contain labour costs and facilitate the driving and organisation of the workforce. Where the American system evolved differently, however, was with respect to the training and recruitment of the workforce. In Britain, France, and Germany these activities were already being actively organised by higher management, at least by, if not before, the 1850s. It will be remembered, for example, that many of the southern French enterprises were organising the training and recruitment of their workforces from the 1830s. In America, by contrast, these activities appeared to remain the prerogative of the contractors until the very end of the nineteenth century. In fact, at this time, the system appeared to develop a novel and quite modern variation. In the engineering industry, at least, contractors occasionally took over from an owner the running of a whole concern. One or several of them would bring in their own men and in the event of a disagreement between either of the parties or with the termination of the contract, the contractors would take these men with them to the next shop they were about to take over. As one English observer of the practice put it in

1901: 'Many of the best known American shops are run along this system'.[41] A further difference in the American and European systems, and one which came to be of great concern to the employers, was the virulent ideology that was associated with it. In Europe, as we have seen, it was very unlikely that the contractor would see himself, or be seen, as anything other than a driver of workers, irrespective of his 'independence' from higher management or his 'skill' at work. In America, on the other hand, these supervisors-cum-managers saw themselves, and were often seen by their employers, as 'craftsmen', while their unions and associations were informed by an ideology of 'producerism', which defined all those engaged in production as members of the same 'industrial' bloc, whether they were 'workers', 'capitalists', or contractors.[42] As an ideology, such an outlook constructed an entire image of industrial society out of the position of only one stratum of it. As an expression of industrial realities it was a pure myth. The contractors were not craftsmen operating within a 'craft system' of production sustained by mutualistic ties with their journeymen and apprentices on one side, and with the merchant, on the other side. A craft heritage just had no pre-history in America. There had been few guilds, and there were no 'corporations', except in the capitalistic sense, and the contractors were an intrinsic part of these corporations.[43] That this stratum sought to maintain and defend its privileged position both against employers and workers by recourse to a mythical past said more about its position as a *petite bourgeoisie* than it did about its 'productive' labour or its 'corporatist' restrictions on production. As members of a *petite bourgeoisie*, the contractors sought to combine the contradictory interests of labour and capital in a universalist ideology that would keep their feet 'firmly' planted in both camps.[44]

Yet such a contradictory class position was no longer sustainable at the beginning of the twentieth century. With the blowout in the reserve army of immigrant labour, the increasing availability of technologies that could put this labour to work, and the changing economic climate, employers had only one choice before them: to destroy contracting.

2. Fixed capital and the intensification of labour

The main features of this changing economic climate concerned the commitment to mechanise the producer goods industries, of which the metal industry was the most important branch. Throughout the latter half of the nineteenth century, but especially after 1880, American heavy industry set itself the task of massively investing in new sites of production, such as buildings, plant and equipment. According to Raymond Goldsmith, net capital formation (or the amount of resources devoted to these) rose from 19.2% of net national product in the period 1869–78 to 21.2% in the years 1889-98.[45] Though agriculture and construction accounted for approximately two-thirds of this investment, the expanding sector was producer durables, or machinery, plant and equipment. Table 1 gives an indication of this by comparing the trends in capital formation in construction and producer durables over the period from 1868–98 to 1899–1928.

TABLE 1

Trends in the distribution of capital formation in the USA, 1869-98 to 1899-1928

	Construction	*Producer durables*
1869–98	69.6	20.6
1879–1908	69.5	23.3
1889–1918	66.6	26.9
1899–1928	62.0	30.9

Source:
Simon Kuznets, *Capital in the American Economy*, National Bureau of Economic Research, Princeton University Press, 1961, Table 14, pp. 146-7. The figures are in terms of 1929 prices.

Obviously, in contrast to Britain's earlier industrial revolution, America after 1850 had to devote a large proportion of its investment capital to the creation of an extensive network of factories, warehouses, utilities and railways. By the 1880s, though, this investment appears to have peaked and a period was ushered in when investment in machinery became the leading sector. It was almost as if producer durables were being inserted into the 'construction shell'. It is also important to notice in this period that investment in plant and equipment coincided with a peaking and then subsequent fall in overall capital formation. The years 1889–98 with their average capital formation rates of 21.2% fell to 13.1% in the period 1909–1919.[46] Goldsmith has suggested that this fall in net capital formation was linked to changes in the life-span of investment and how quickly it was used up (or what scholars call an increasing ratio of capital consumption to gross capital expenditure).[47] In other words, up to the 1880s American investment in the construction of new sites of production was an investment in a form of fixed capital whose life-span could be anything from fifty to one hundred years. Its consumption, therefore, occurred at a very slow rate and enterprises had to wait long periods of time before their investment and profit returned to them. After the 1880s, on the other hand, the marked shift of investment into machinery and equipment meant that fixed capital had an economic life-span that was more likely to be between five and twenty-five years. It could be used up more quickly, and hence offered enterprises the possibility of seeing a complete return on their investment within a relatively short space of time. As I am unable to give a precise picture of American depreciation rates on plant and equipment, some British evidence may be illustrative, especially as we shall consider the European experience in more detail in the subsequent chapters.

TABLE 2

Approximate depreciation rates for plant and machinery in Britain, 1914

Plant or Machine	Approximate economical life in years
Brickbuildings and chimneys	40 years
Water turbines	30 "
Lancashire boilers	25 "
Feed water heaters	25 "
Air compressors	20 "
Dynamos and motors	20 "
Switch boards, instruments	20 "
Underground and lead covered cables	20 "
Ordinary machine tools	20 "
Trucks	20 "
Water tube boilers	20 "
Frame and fixed part stokers	20 "
Feed pumps	20 "
Slow speed steam engines	20 "
Steam turbines	18 "
High speed steam engines	15 "
Lead covered cables and aerials	15 "
Turret lathes	15 "
Shafting and millwork	15 "
Steel chimneys	15 "
Small fire tube and locomotive boilers	14 "
Accumulators	10 "
Screw and automatic machines	10 "
Stokers with movable parts	5 "

Source:
D. Smith and P.C.N. Pickworth, *Engineers' Costs and Economical Workshop Production,* Emmott, London, 1914, p. 188, Table XVIII.

N.B. The depreciation rates are only approximate owing to the different types of machinery included under the same headings and the different conditions under which they were used.

Table 2 gives an approximate idea of the economical life of various forms of plant and machinery in 1914. In other words, we are not speaking of the physical life of the machinery, which may go on for many years after the investment on it has been returned to the enterprise, but of its life as a 'cost' on the capitalist. As will be seen, the difference between investing in either brick buildings or turret lathes was quite pronounced, at least as far as capitalist expectations were concerned. Two consequences of this have to be analysed.

First, it was no longer necessary for capitalists to maintain high levels of capital formation when an ever-increasing proportion of it could be turned over and reinvested in shorter periods of time. Second, the costs of 'inefficiency', in terms of capitalist expectations, tended to multiply with every extra dollar invested in a machine tool, as distinct from a building or a warehouse. The first has been well studied by Simon Kuznets; the second provided the basis for the rise of Taylorism and professional management.

Simon Kuznets has performed a very useful service in noting some of the implications in the fall of capital formation proportions in America and Europe. In his view, only 8-13% of gross domestic product in the late nineteenth century or 5% to 9% of net domestic product were devoted to the gross and net accumulation of capital goods which acted as bearers of technological change, i.e., plant, equipment and machinery. His evidence here is directed against the 'savings' theorists, such as Walt Rostow, who suggest that a high rate of capital formation is necessary to generate high levels of technical change and economic growth. On the contrary, Kuznets suggests, only a small proportion of savings, and, therefore, of capital formation were needed to finance capital goods bearing new technologies.[48] Certainly, the 1911-13 Bureau of Labor survey supports his interpretation. From the ports, which fed the steel industry with its raw materials, came new scooping equipment that allowed for fifteen times more ore to be unloaded per worker; at the blast furnace, mechanical charging increased output twelve-fold from 1887 to the mid-1900s; in the steel mills themselves, the new Wellman charger allowed a driver to deposit large amounts of scrap and pig-iron into an open-hearth furnace and provided the possibility for only one man to tend four to six 75-ton furnaces, where previously a crew was required to charge one furnace over several hours; finally, in the Bessemer plants, mechanically-controlled ladles were introduced to carry molten metal from the blast furnace to the Bessemer converters and subsequently increased output four-fold per worker.[49]

Falling capital formation and increasing productivity were, however, only the mirror image of growing threats to enterprise profitability coming from the more direct role that plant and equipment were playing in the immediate process of production. Frederick Winslow Taylor's speech before the American Society of Mechanical Engineers in 1895 was a classic exposition of these pressures. Fixed costs, he argued, such as taxes, insurance, depreciation, rent, salaries, office expenses and power often amounted to as much, if not more than, the wages of the workers. At the same time, these costs remained about the same whether output was high or low, so that any substantial increase in output would reduce the relative weight of these expenses in the overall costs of production.[50] Two English engineers, D. Smith and P.C.N. Pickworth, following Taylor, suggested that in the context of rising fixed costs the only solution was to obtain the 'maximum effort from the operator', so that the utmost work was done on a machine in a given period of time. Yet, it was not only necessary to keep the machine constantly running: 'If possible', it was also necessary for it to be 'constantly producing a maximum output'.[51] One of Britain's leading machine tool industrialists, John Batey, made the point equally succinctly on the eve of World War One: the problem was not just the worker's 'capability to keep the machine at work as long as possible', but also of doing so 'with the shortest intervals of setting and unsetting work'.[52] Batey was referring to the problem that though the specialisation of labour may tend to compel the worker to exert his or her utmost energy and 'skill', and mechanisation may give the pace and flow of a production line a more spatial and temporal unity increasingly independent of the volition of an individual worker, there were invariably jobs or parts of jobs spread throughout the line requiring various levels of skill, strength and attention from workers, if the overall job was to be completed at all. Moreover, there were parts of the working day when workers, through no fault of their own, were not producing and therefore not producing profit. Expensive plant and equipment may lie idle, perhaps for refitting and maintenance; or workers may at times just be waiting for the next job to arrive. These 'interruptions' to the continuous flow of production gave the working day a *porous character*. The labour process literally had holes in its operation, which tended to dilute the *potential profitability* of an enterprise.[53]

3. Labour and 'efficiency'

As a result of these changes, higher management became increasingly anxious about what David Landes calls, 'bottlenecks', 'sloppiness', or 'slack',[54] and increasingly questioned the utility of a fragmented and decentralised managerial structure based on labour intensive methods of production. It was not so much that the idea of intensifying labour in direct production was questioned, rather it was a matter of linking it to a more intensive use of the expensive machinery. Higher management had to *know* what the optimal levels of production were and be *sure* that any intermission in the use of machinery was not causing a loss on investment. Out of such anxieties grew an aggressive programme to streamline and extend higher managerial authority into the workplace in a systematic manner.

First, the desire to make the machine pay meant that workloads had to be increased. Workers had to be 'pushed' harder and work, in general, had to be speeded up. The steel industry provided a graphic example of this. A British observer of the Bessemer steel mills was moved to claim that workers were 'selling their lives'; while one historian has suggested that machinery was becoming the 'measure of output', not the worker. It, rather than a worker's ability, was being used to fix 'the upper limit to operations'.[55] The working day was also increased from eight hours to twelve hours during the 1890s, and this was defended on the basis that labour was now more mechanical and, therefore, easier, rather than more manual and physical. The seven-day week and extensive overtime were also systematically applied.[56]

Added to this, new ideologies and practices were built of what constituted work, the role of the worker and the place of the manager-cum-engineer in industry and society. Between the years 1890–1914, the change was brutalising, not only for contractors, but also for the workforce as a whole. In the first instance, the contractors' presentation of themselves as a self-enclosed association of elite workers with craft attributes forced employers and their consultants to redefine work. In the words of C.B. Thompson, an advocate of scientific management, 'one's everyday work' could no longer be considered as 'a matter of aesthetic satisfaction, an artistic pleasure, and therefore to be pursued only in accordance with the dictates of one's "temperament" '. Work was now 'the conservation of personal effort', and part of a 'broader movement for the conservation of all resources'. It was to be considered as 'economically advantageous, and therefore, a personal and social duty'.[57] The development of this 'efficiency' conception of work also sought to endorse what one historian calls 'an acceptance of the inherent laziness of man', and 'a perception of labour as bestial and/or machine like'.[58] Efficient work was something a worker had to be compelled to do because of the 'natural laziness of man', as Frederick Winslow Taylor noted.[59] He was quick to emphasise that work was intrinsically analogous to the labour of an ox, horse or dog, requiring an occasional managerial 'plum' for the worker to 'climb after', plus 'an occasional touch of the lash'.[60]

It need not be thought that this attack upon populist or producerist images of labour was new. With respect to Europe, it was quite a late development. Many historians have drawn attention to employer attacks on artisanal and craft conceptions of labour dating from the mid-eighteenth century in England and the early nineteenth century on the Continent.[61] What was different about the American experience was that such a crude redefinition of work was associated with an *all-embracing* notion of its compulsive efficiency, where the worker was seen to enjoy no formal rights in industry except those bequeathed by management. The right to form independent trade unions and engage in collective bargaining could no longer be allowed, as they cut across a company's efforts to increase output and efficiency. In Taylor's view, unions personified and legitimised the workers' natural desire to engage in 'systematic soldiering', restrict output and prevent employers from obtaining exact knowledge of, and control over, the labour process.[62]

Finally, in order to ensure a more intensive use of their expensive machinery and guarantee enterprise profitability, leading engineers argued that managers could no longer allow a worker to ' "tinker around" with some idea of improving his own machine. He must produce, "from whistle to whistle", and think of nothing else—or at least do nothing else. . . Every machine must earn a dividend, and the man behind the machine who keeps its production up to the highest figure is the man who, although sure of a steady job, is just as sure of an inexorable detention at that one job'.[63] By the early 1900s such conceptions of workers, their rights and the nature of their labour had provided the large steel and engineering companies, especially those owned by Andrew Carnegie, with the ideological justification to sweep aside all the unions in the industry, including the contractors' unions.[64]

4. Qualification and training

If it can be suggested that these images of work and the worker amounted to an ideology of the de-qualification of labour, then its inversion was the formulation of an ideology of management's intrinsic and integral hyper-qualification. This particularly affected the image of the professional engineers in industry, and the movement was in fact led by them. It was noted earlier that engineers had been assuming practical managerial functions in the French metal industry from the mid-nineteenth century. American engineers had also been assuming such functions, especially from the 1880s. But what was novel about the American phenomenon was the simultaneous development of a complete ideology which sustained and advanced the interests of the engineers—'scientific management'. Led by professionally trained engineers and theorists, such as F.W. Taylor, H.L. Gantt, Frank Gilbreth and C.B. Thompson, the movement found its voice within the pages of the *Engineering Magazine,* and the *Transactions of the American Society of Mechanical Engineers.*[65] Their emphasis was on the formally obtained attributes of 'mental power', with which no worker or contractor could compare their 'rule of thumb' knowledge. Even the boss had to allow them functional 'autonomy' unless he too was trained in the 'science'.[66] They represented the 'one best way' of doing things and their tools were the slide rule, algebra, and formally acquired knowledge of workshop layout, the handling of materials and workers, chemistry, dynamics, and metals; while all this was informed by their 'experimental method'.[67] They saw themselves as the exclusive agents who, on the one hand, mediated the theoretical principles of science and their practical application, and, on the other hand, the conflicting claims of capital and labour in the interests of greater productivity, profitability and efficiency. There was no better justification than this for expropriating the powers of the contractor and abolishing his position. He and his workers were too prone to 'unscientific' practices and 'inefficient' techniques in order to 'bargain' effectively with the employer.[68]

The idea that work and labour had to be organised by professionals, who had the necessary technical intelligence, was part of a larger ideological movement which sought to separate labour from 'intelligence' and associate 'brains' with capital. Whether it took the form of Herbert Spencer's grim picture of industry and society as the 'survival of the fittest' or the prescriptions of the 'New Thought' movement that 'Business success is due to certain qualities of the mind', the essential message was the natural polarisation of society into those who would forever remain 'drones' or workers labouring for a wage and those who, because of their professional intelligence or their capital were 'capable' of assuming the responsibilities of management.[69]

Several studies of this redefinition of work, and the role of the worker and manager, emphasise that the ideology of 'scientific management' was part of a movement aimed at the destruction of the functional autonomy of the craftsmen in the heavy metal industry.[70] At the same time, other students have suggested that this movement was more 'ideological' than 'real', by which they mean that the new managerial and scientific ideology of the engineer had more success in shaping an atmosphere than in taking over American industry or significantly changing management practices.[71] Both interpretations tend to read the evidence too literally. In the former case, it is a question of whether American industry can be considered so 'backward' as to have within the very bowels of its monopolistic and progressive industries a 'corporate' form of labour organisation. We have already seen that in Britain, France and Germany, countries which to varying degrees did have material craft heritages, such questions as craft-based skill compositions and industrial training methods had ceased to play any significant role since the mid-nineteenth century at least. It is just too difficult to sustain an interpretation that seeks to make heavy industry in nineteenth-century America a bastion of a craft system of production. If different conditions did operate in America, then a major hypothesis would be that the influx of millions of immigrants with few industrial skills and little or no experience of factory life created the material basis for the employer's ideology that work was brutal, manual and lacking in intelligence. At the same time, perhaps it is more likely that the formal constraints placed on production by the contractors were used by employers to construct an image of 'labour' failing to accept its real subordination to capital, even though the challenge came from within the ill-defined and contradictory structures of 'management' itself. Perhaps, also, it is only to be expected that employers would seek to construct a unifying idea of management by berating the outrageous interference of 'craftsmen', who would have to learn to work rather than manage, than give ideological recognition to a managerially based counter-regulation of skills, job control and industrial training. The metal industrialists certainly wanted to 'compel the revision of labour organisation', to use a phrase from C.B. Thompson.[72] They wanted a free hand. Yet when one of

Carnegie's men, Charles Schwab, claimed in 1901 that he could train a farm worker to be a steel melter in six to eight weeks his threat had as much, if not more, meaning to the contractors and their organisations as it did to the workforce as a whole; the number one melter was the contractor.[73] As far as the ideological significance of 'scientific management' is concerned, what can be suggested is that a recomposition of skills and industrial training did take place. In other words, the ideology of professional management was put into practice.

The cutting-edge of the attack on contracting, for example, is to be found in the establishment of internal works 'apprenticeship' schools in the large metal enterprises from the heavy and electrical engineering trades, iron and steel, and locomotive building. The schools, which were established in the early 1900s at firms like Westinghouse, General Electric, the National Cash Register Co., Brown and Sharp's, and Baldwin's, were designed to achieve three goals, all directed at one particular section of the workforce. First, the schools were seen to be an ideological arm of management for the inculcation of solid bourgeois values in the students. The virtues, not to say the study of, hard work, thrift, loyalty, respect for authority, patriotism, and citizenship, were lauded in Baldwin's three year courses.[74] Second, the schools sought to provide practical training in new methods of production for specialist workers, as for example in foundries.[75] Finally, and most important of all, the schools aimed to build a stratum of professionally trained, semi-managerial cadres, such as foremen, super-skilled mechanics, and leading hands who would provide a reservoir for internal promotion.[76] As these aims were directly associated with the need for a more intense supervision and training of the workforce, the old contracting foreman could not be allowed to independently participate in any way. He was, in fact, to be 'freed' from the tasks of training and recruiting workers, especially now when he no longer 'had the time'.[77]

The Baldwin's firm, for instance, had three different 'apprenticeship' courses in 1904, and on 'graduation' the apprentices received a diploma from the firm which stated the degree of their theoretical and practical proficiency, as well as their particular qualities as employees.[78] In one course, for the training of mechanics and tool-makers, the maximum age of entrance was seventeen years and three months. The course lasted for four years, while the first three years comprised two nights a week at evening school, where such subjects as algebra, elementary geometry and the principles of machine design were taught. A second course was directed at creating lower-echelon foremen and leading hands. The minimum age of entrance was eighteen and was conditional on the previous attainment of a good secondary education. The course comprised a three year apprenticeship of which the first two years involved evening classes in machine design. The third course was aimed at training No. 1 foremen and management technicians. Here the minimum age of entrance was twenty-one, and generally students had to have either a university or technical college education. The managerial content of the second and third courses was concerned with providing the students with the necessary habits and skills for controlling a job and evaluating the costs involved in the production of articles. The students learnt how to use job tickets, which comprised the number of the order, the shop, the name of the foreman, the number of the machine to be used and the date on which the job was to be started. Below these instructions were details of all the characteristics of the work to be executed, the nature and dimensions of the tools to be used, the various times of production and the type of tool steel to be used. All this had to be accounted for and signed by the 'apprentice'.[79]

David Noble has described the character of such 'corporation graduate training programmes' as being designed to meet the needs of industry and guarantee the technical proficiency of college-trained employees. They were to 'habituate young men into corporate life and prepare them for managerial responsibility'.[80] For a firm like Baldwin's, which had previously relied on contractors to organise production and training,[81] these schools provided not so much a structure to abolish and recompose the craftsman's position and skills, as a structure to by-pass the contractor's position, by professionalising production management and subordinating this to the firm's own management hierarchy. This interpretation is supported by the fact that for a firm which employed approximately 13,000 people in 1900, making it one of the four largest workforces in the country at this time, only 545 'apprentices' had been enrolled in these schools between January 1901 and 1904. Of this number, 352 had been enrolled in the course of hyper-qualified mechanics and tool designers, 124 in the course for leading hands and lower foremen, and 69 in the course for senior foremen and technicians, the latter two requiring at least a high school education.[82] The courses were not designed to form a stratum of skilled manual workers to take the place of previously intractable craftsmen. As a point of comparison the situation should be compared with that in the machine tool trade. According to a survey into apprenticeship in this trade, the proportion of apprentices to workers was 18% in 1906.[83] At Baldwin's, in the early years of this century, the proportion of 'apprentices' was less than 4%, with over a third being directly trained to take up shop-floor management positions.[84] Baldwin's, like the other big enterprises, were creating a new *petite bourgeoisie,* comprising technicians and foremen, and a new stratum of super-skilled workers who would better represent the interests of the enterprise on the shop floor. They were formed to act as the agents of an organised management's technical intelligence.

A similar programme of training was introduced into the Lynn Works of General Electric during the early 1900s. The boys who were enrolled in the company's school were first placed on two months' probation, in which time they had to give proof of their 'native ability' for the trade they wished to learn. The successful demonstration of this meant not only the possibility of becoming one of the company's 'skilled artisans', but also of becoming an 'assistant foreman or foreman at some future time'.[85] For Magnus W. Alexander, one of the company's managers in 1907, the aim of the General Electric Company was:

> To train skilled artisans in the various trades of machinist and tool-maker, carpenter and pattern-maker, iron, steel, and brass moulder, instrument-maker and electrical worker, in such a thorough manner that the leading positions in the factory, such as assistant foreman, master mechanic, and superintendent, may be filled from the ranks of graduated apprentices.[86]

Special emphasis in the G.E. course was given to figuring the amounts of raw materials used in production so that orders could be filled exactly. Classes were also given in mechanical drawing for making up jigs and fixtures, and tool designing. The school rooms were located close to the workshops and were run by the firm's own specialist teachers. As in the Baldwin's case, it was again a question of not involving the foremen in the training of workers, especially given the new economic conditions. They would be just too inclined to rely on traditional techniques of driving and would, therefore, tend to use up a talented boy with single machine work or running errands, while the boy himself would ultimately have to push a foreman for new and higher duties.

As at Baldwin's also, this was an elite course comprising a very few students. By 1907 only 293 boys had been admitted to the programme; 29 had graduated with 24 remaining with the firm. One hundred and seventy-one other students were still coming through, while the balance of 98 boys had been either weeded out, had broken their agreement, or had been dismissed. In such an exclusive atmosphere the phrase 'alma mater' could be frequently heard by boys who joined the list of 'graduates'.[87] This phenomenon spread to many firms and was often complemented by young graduates moving from firm to firm as they moved up the supervisory and managerial hierarchy. According to a National Association of Schools survey conducted in 1914, of the 9,459 company apprentices on probation in 19 firms up to 1914 only 1,585, or 16.7% graduated. Of this number, approximately 42% moved to other firms after the completion of their course, and took up supervisory and executive positions at firms like General Electric, Westinghouse Electrical, American Locomotive Co., Cadillac, and the engineering firm of Yale and Towne.[88]

One last example of the new style apprenticeship courses that sought to bring on men with a 'thorough all-round training' and 'a higher industrial intelligence' can be taken from the 'university' at the Pennsylvania Railroad Company in Altoona.[89] The young men who took their 'special apprenticeships' at these works had to be graduates of either a technical school or college. They were then taken through a four-year workshop course in fourteen shops ranging from two to six months in each. They spent six months in the erecting shop, two months in the clerks' office, two months in the testing department, six months in the machine shop and two months in the drawing room. The positions to be filled from this course by those who had attended technical school were inspector, assistant master mechanic, assistant engineer of motive power, assistant road foreman of engines, master mechanic, and superintendent of motive power. As far as the college men were concerned, Frederic Warren noted that, 'Many bright young men of good parentage, having passed through college and being vouched for by one of the general officers of the company, put on jumpers and spend several years in the shops in order to fit themselves for higher work in railroad service'.[90] Frank Thomson, a former president of the company, was one of those who removed his black coat and put on a jumper, as did the young civil engineers from the principal assistant engineer's department. For this group such training was essential if they were to obtain high positions in the construction division of the firm or in the superintendent's department. A cultural ambience also pervaded training at the 'University' of Altoona. There were clubs for officers from the 'maintenance-of-way', motive power and other departments, as well as for the 'special assistants' which comprised golf courses, tennis courts and indoor games.[91]

Complementing the development of corporate schools at individual enterprises was the rise of trade association schools. The National Foundry-men's Association and the National Metal Trades Association formed trade and technical schools under their control in the 1900s, particularly in Indianapolis and Cincinnati. As shall be seen later, this movement had a strong influence on trade education in France. By 1913, though, many of these trade associations brought their schools into the jurisdiction of the newly-formed National Association of Corporation Schools, whose found-ing members included G.E., Western Electric, Thomas A. Edison (and the Edison subsidiaries), the Consolidated Gas Co. of New York, Burroughs Adding Machine, National Cash Register, American Locomotive, Yale and Towne Manufacturing Co., Packard, Cadillac, Pennsylvania Railroad, Travellers Insurance, and the Curtis Publishing Co.[92]

The Association acted as a 'clearing house' for the exchange of ideas, the gathering and dissemination of information on successful and un-successful schemes and generally sought to promote an interest in the training of corporate employees. The implication of this appears to be that firms were beginning to feel they had common needs and problems when it came to training their supervisors and managerial employees, rather than just plant or enterprise specific problems. In this context, the Association promoted approved methods of vocational training, especially for office workers, technicians, apprentices, machine draughtsmen, tool makers and maintenance men.[93]

Though it is not possible to give a complete listing of the corporate schools in operation by 1913, it is possible to give a listing of forty-three such schools run by leading concerns in the metal and allied trades. The information is presented in Table 3 and includes the year of the school's establishment.

TABLE 3

A list of forty-three corporate schools in operation by 1913 in the United States metal and allied trades.

Year of establishment	Corporation
1871	Pennsylvania Railroad, Altoona
1872	Hoe and Co.
1888	Westinghouse Machine Co., Pittsburgh
1901	Baldwin Locomotive Works
	General Electric, Schenectady and Lynn
1905	Central Railway, N.J.
	Cleveland Twist Drill Co., Cleveland, Ohio
1906	New York Central Railway
	Union Pacific
	Burroughs Adding Machine, Detroit
	Consolidated Gas Co., New York, N.Y.
	Western Electric, Chicago
	Westinghouse Air Brake Co., Wilmerding, Pa.
1907	Atchinson Railway
	Santa Fé Railway
	Delaware Railway
	Hudson Railway
	Luton Sos Co., Philadelphia
	Cadillac Motor Co., Detroit
1908	Browne and Sharpe, Providence, R.I.
	Cincinnata Planer Co., Cincinnati
	R.R. Donnelly and Sons, Chicago
	Fore River Shipbuilding Co., Quincy, Mass.
	Solvay Co., Syracuse, N.Y.
	Yale and Towne Manufacturing Co., Stamford, Conn.
	Chicago Railway
	Great Western Railway
	Eric Railway
1909	Westinghouse Electric and Manufacturing Co., East Pittsburgh
	Leland and Co., Worcester, Mass.
1910	Franklin Manufacturing Co., Syracuse, N.Y.
	General Electric, Pittsburgh
	Leigh Valley Railway
1911	Warner, Swasey and Co., Cleveland
	Baltimore Railway

TABLE 3 *(cont.)*

Year of establishment	Corporation
	Ohio Railway
1912	Royal Typewriter Co., Hartford, Conn.
	Foote and Davis Co., Atlanta
	Illinois Central Railway
1913	Packard Motor Co., Detroit
	Fort Wayne Electrical Works
	Southern Pacific Railway

Sources:
Engineering Review, 1900–1915; *The Machinist*, 1890–1915 (various years).

Against this background of company training for the labour of super-intendence and management, a number of commentators came to believe that it was now unnecessary to even bother with the training of a skilled worker stratum. The extensive application of modern machinery was believed to be placing a low premium on such workers.[94] These beliefs were not without a good deal of exaggerated hope, but they did point towards a general feeling that the new apprenticeship movement was not designed to bring on a stratum of skilled workers to take the place of the contractors. In a number of cities, however, privately endowed Trade Schools did play a role in providing a small supply of traditional and new skilled workers. These were often vociferously opposed by trade unions seeking to prevent a growing supply of workers who could dilute and threaten their position. The New York Trade School, for example, established in 1881 by the 'loving friend of youth' and strike-breaker, Colonel Auchmuty, was designed to provide boys with the opportunity to learn a trade and circumvent union restrictions on training workers. It provided day and evening classes in plumbing, electrical engineering, and tradesmen's courses in sheetmetal, and fitting for household work. By 1913 some 17,598 pupils had been through the school.[95] Charles Pratt's privately endowed Pratt Institute, formed in 1887, performed similar functions and gave classes in many metal activities, including mechanical drawing, the strength of metals, applied electricity, as well as general courses on science and technology. Other schools included New York's Baron de Hirsch Trade School, the Williamson Free School of Mechanical Trades (where incidentally all products made in the school had to be destroyed or given away so as not to overly antagonise the local unions), the California School of Mechanical Arts and San Francisco's Wildmerding School of Industrial Arts.[96] Overall, though, such schools were only turning out 10,000 or so pupils a year by the early 1900s, hardly a ready supply to take the place of recalcitrant 'craftsmen' on a mass scale.[97]

After 1906, a number of cities, such as Philadelphia, Milwaukee, Buffalo and Portland, established publicly administered trade schools in an attempt both to overcome the chronic abuse of child labour by employers and expand the supply of skilled workers. The schools were seen as a means of providing industrial education for youths on a mass scale. Yet they met stiff opposition from the proponents of the new-style apprenticeship movement, who saw them as attempting to imitate the trade school movement in Germany, where compulsory trade education had been introduced for all teenagers of fifteen and over until they were eighteen years of age. The opponents of the movement argued that these schools were a false imitation of their German counterparts. In Germany such schools were designed to provide higher technical training for young workers who would later undertake NCO functions in the factories. In America, by contrast, they merely sought to replicate the archaic apprenticeship system and, even worse, sought to do so on a mass scale. Invariably, only thoroughly trained workmen in Germany, with several years shop experience behind them, gained entry to the proper trade schools, as distinct from the compulsory schools for workers in general. With this reality in mind, Dr George Kirchensteiner, an industrial educationalist from Munich, toured America during 1910-11 and was widely quoted by propagandists for the new apprenticeship movement as saying that, if the American trade schools sought to take over the functions of the bygone apprenticeship system, they would be wasting money and resources; further, they would be failing to address the real issue. They could not supply the skilled labour that was needed on a widespread basis and, if they tried to do so, they would soon find themselves stagnating, as the factory environment itself now provided the atmosphere for the training of the rank and file specialised, skilled workers.[98] As General Electric's Magnus Alexander put it, 'artisan all-round skill' had been 'gradually supplanted by the specialist skilled worker', who was more than likely to be proficient in only 'one particular operation'.[99]

By the 1910s education boards were becoming aware of this and began to redefine what their trade schools should do, especially with regard to industry's need for trained supervisors and foremen. In 1913, for instance, the Massachusetts Board of Education reported to the state legislature that:

Long hours of monotonous employment, and the fact that under present conditions workers are being restricted to the operation of one or a few machines, with little opportunity to gain a general knowledge of the trade or business, make it imperative that part-time schools be established to give to young workers a broader knowledge of the industry than they are now able to secure. Under the present industrial system there is a dearth of capable foremen and superintendents, due to the lack of opportunity to obtain a general knowledge of the industry, a situation which should be met by part-time schools.[100]

Where schools for the sons of rank and file workers did exist (one can forget about those for their daughters), was in the area of preparing them for a life of unskilled and semi-skilled work. Trade Preparatory Schools for children aged fourteen to sixteen were created for this purpose. The schools did not seek to substitute themselves for the old apprenticeship training' for labour itself. No specialised instruction was given. What was studied were the various materials used in industry, the tools employed studied were the various materials used in industry, the tools employed and the nature of the products. The metal trades generally were all taught together, with students gaining some idea of the tools used in plumbing, fitting and machining, and of products manufactured in iron and steel.[101] Apart from these schools, there were also a number of 'industrial schools' where manual training was given to the most marginal children of the working class—those who were deaf, blind, 'feeble-minded', black, or Indian.[102] Thus, as far as children or youths in general were concerned there was literally no change in their position. In 1914, in the metal trades of Hartford, Connecticut, which was the home of firms such as Royal Typewriter, a Government committee found the same situation as before. Young teenagers between fourteen and sixteen were generally confined to 'dead end' jobs, such as errand work, stock boxing, inspecting finished products, sorting, assembling, light grinding, polishing, wiring and unwiring and, finally, drilling.[103]

When Paul Douglas, a leading expert in the field of industrial training, came to assess the significance and direction of these changes to apprentice-ship in 1915, he was struck by the 'sharp differentiation of skill' now required from the workforce:

> A large number of highly trained and competent engineers are needed in the drafting room. For other workers, however, muscle and endurance rather than skill and dexterity are required.[104]

Those involved in the growing field of machine repairing also had to be added to the list of those requiring competence and high training, as well as the 'sub-bosses, foremen and superintendents'. These groups were the 'aristocracy of the labour force' and, in order for them to do their work they required a 'thorough technical and practical training'. They were the 'cream', while the rest, the large majority of workers, were the 'skin milk' *(sic.)*, and it was the training of these 'non-commissioned officers of industry' that was of 'great importance'.[105]

The general displacement of the old contracting *petite bourgeoisie* by a new *petite bourgeoisie* also required a massive expansion of the second-ary education system in the United States. In 1894, only 2% of the population, or 97,000 students, attended secondary school. By 1904, this had risen to 9%, or 730,000 students.[106] When the Educational Commission to the United States arrived from Britain in 1901, the members were struck by the remarkable developments in education. They bore witness to the Americans' deep desire for, and attachment to, instruction, as well as the status accorded the professionally trained engineer.[107] Similarly, when Mosely's Educational Commission to the USA returned to Britain in 1904, it too was impressed by these developments. In their report, the committee members also emphasised the importance that American employers attached to a person's level of instruction and their future salary. From an assessment of the wage levels for four groups of employees (the unskilled, the shop trained, trade school students and technical college students, it was found that though all members of these groups began their working lives at around the same wage level, the speed of wage increases for the higher educated groups was astonishing. Furthermore, whereas the wage level for the unskilled peaked at about twenty-two years of age, at twenty-four for the shop trained, and twenty-five to thirty for workers with a trade school education, the wage levels for the technical college graduates constantly increased with age.[108]

When the Belgian theorist of modern psychological and physical attributes of labour, Omer Buyse, went to America he too praised the education system. He was more concerned with the system as a whole than with just the secondary system, and drew attention to the importance placed on developing technical knowledge and skills in the students from the primary school, which the child entered at the age of six, through to the Institutes of Technology, which the student graduated from at about twenty-two years of age. From practice in design and modelling in primary schools through to the more sophisticated skills obtained in trade schools, such as in woodwork and metalwork, and the study of physics and chemistry in secondary school laboratories, and finally in the courses available at colleges and universities, the students were given a professional and practical outlook on work which would enable them to fill positions in technical work, management and the labour of superintendence in industry.[109]

The growth of technical high schools was a very important part of this movement. Though debate in the early 1900s again centred on whether they should seek to substitute themselves for the traditional apprenticeship system or develop a more refined purpose, they soon settled down to the task of providing technical instruction for the 'different ranks in industry', especially its 'non-commissioned officers'. The curriculum was both academic and technical, and also placed emphasis on the study of history, economics and mathematics. Entrance was from sixteen years of age, and though some advocates thought the schools should be a training ground for the engineering colleges, as the general high schools were, they generally became specialised technical high schools, as at the Lane and Harrison Technical Schools of Chicago, the Stuyvesant High School in

New York and similar institutions in Cleveland, Detroit and Pennsylvania.[110] In Pennsylvania, for example, a technical high school was established in February 1907, at Altoona, in order 'to turn out young men ready to earn a living' at the Pennsylvania Railroad Company, not to say to be better qualified to take advantage of the Company's own training programmes.[111] Fees at these schools were approximately $100 per year and hence the great mass of children from working class families found themselves excluded. Even highly paid workers would have found it difficult to raise such a sum for the education of their sons. As Paul Douglas put it:

> The education is too costly and the poorer pupils cannot afford the time required. . . This type of school, furthermore, does not touch the children who because of poverty must leave school at fourteen. It must recruit its members almost entirely from the upper grades of labour and not from the lower grades. . . it does not afford a ladder by which men may climb from the unskilled to the skilled labour group.[112]

A further indication of the exclusive middle-class character of these schools can be seen in their relations with the corporation schools, which have already been hinted at with regard to the railway high school at Altoona. There was a great deal of cross fertilisation between the two, and this included joint congresses, planning arrangements and generally organising the technical schools as feeders for the corporate schools.[113] At the university level, the training of future engineers was built around four-year courses with an emphasis on the acquisition of manual experience. At the University of Columbia, New York, for instance, first year students had to do one hundred hours of work in the university's mini 'factories', like the machine shop.[114] Once the students had graduated they were immediately called 'engineers' even though they had no real factory work experience behind them. They often began their careers as 'simple' workers at first, but promotion from then on was very rapid.[115] Other universities, such as Cincinnati, intensified their students' practical factory experience by combining academic work with sojourns to the local plants over substantial periods of time. In this way it was hoped that the students would come in contact with the workers they would later supervise and obtain knowledge of worker-employer relations, the role of unions and the social life of the factory. Having gained an all-round training the students could later specialise.[116] When this scheme was started in 1906 twelve enterprises were brought in to support it, largely because of the influence of Herman Schneider. He had been at Leigh University some years before and had coordinated undergraduate technical training there in cooperation with the Bethlehem Steel Company, one of Frederick Winslow Taylor's old hunting grounds.[117] This pattern of 'industrial cooperation' with large enterprises in the training of university students became quite widespread, as other universities, such as Pittsburg, followed the examples set at Cincinnati and Leigh.[118] By the mid 1900s the engineering colleges were being run on a huge scale. Cornell, for instance, had over 1,300 engineering students in 1906; Purdue had over 1,000, while many other universities had between 500 and 1,000.[119]

The technical education system though, did have its critics. In 1906, when F.W. Taylor gave a speech which inaugurated the technical section of the University of Pennsylvania, he spoke of the difficulties faced by young engineers entering factories after graduation. Finding resentment from management at their inexperience in the practical matters of engineering, Taylor suggested that students should obtain substantial practical experience in the factory by doing an 'apprenticeship'.[120] Yet even Taylor would have had difficulties begrudging the success of the movement which was professionalising the labour of production management. When Alex Sahlin made visits to twenty-one blast furnace plants during 1901, he found that eighteen of them were managed by university graduates.[121] After 1880, the ranks of the engineering profession swelled enormously, rising from 7,000 to 136,000 in 1920, an increase of more than 2,000%.[122] The number of engineering schools also rose rapidly, from 85 in 1880 to 126 by 1917. During this time the number of graduate engineers from the colleges rose from approximately 100 per year in 1870 to 4,300 by World War One. By the late nineteenth century, as well, a number of universities had developed research-based graduate studies programmes, particularly at Johns Hopkins, Clark, Harvard, Columbia and Wisconsin. Work in research laboratories was considered to be an essential function of these programmes and was designed to serve the needs of industry.[123]

According to one study, though it deals only with the situation in 1924, the ranks of the engineers were overwhelmingly drawn from the sons of the old and new middle class; owners of small businesses, works supervisors and the low echelon executives. Only a minute proportion came from the ranks of the bourgeoisie or the working class.[124]

It can be seen that the basic impulse behind the new training methods in America's heavy metal industry was to abolish the employer's traditional reliance on a competitive and empiricist system of labour management and put in its place a structure more in tune with the needs of monopolistic and bureaucratic corporations. Where previously production management was organised through a relatively *open and internal factory-based structure,* in which the employer competitively selected an empirically qualified worker to be promoted to the ranks of a contracting foreman and undertake the labour of superintendence, the new system was organised through a relatively *open extra-factory structure,* where entry to the ranks of production management was based on the acquisition of a formal and professional education topped up by company training. Where formerly the ranks of the *petite bourgeoisie* in the factory were filled vertically, they were now filled horizontally. David Noble has described the change in similar terms: 'The integration of formal education into the industrial structure', he suggests, 'weakened the traditional link between work experience and advancement, driving a wedge between managers and managed and separating the two by the college campus'.[125]

How this transformation of industrial training influenced Europe's progressive metal industry managers, industrialists and theorists is the subject to which we now turn. As was pointed out at the beginning of this study, many contemporary advocates of 'scientific management', and many historians since, have argued that metal industrialists in Britain, France and Germany were too cautious, if not actually too flabby, to put into practice what was happening in America. What we must consider then, is whether the American example is to be understood in such a negative way or whether a change in practice did take place.

5. A note on the new skills

A final note of caution is necessary before turning to this question. It should not be thought that our emphasis on the changing organisation of mental labour inside and outside of the factory provided the possibility for reducing the overwhelming number of workers to the condition of mindless automatons, either in America or, as we shall see, in Europe. There were material barriers to the concentration of mental labour in the hands of management—barriers rendered effective by the fact that human labour still remained essential to the execution of the product. Though the quality of their skills and training did undergo relative and absolute division and degradation, direct human labour still had to 'get the swing' of a machine, regulate its speed and take care of it, if just to prevent too many costly breakdowns and maiming 'accidents'. Workers were still required to use their mental and manual faculties to direct the machine, so as to cut and form the required shape. From an employer's point of view, this also had beneficial effects, for it reduced the need for costly maintenance work when a machine had broken down and could no longer produce.[126] However, to assess the actual content of these skills and their methods of training in purely quantitative terms as 'substantial' or 'genuine', is to miss the overall qualitative changes to the design and organisation of production initiated by employers. The rationalisation and fragmentation of industrial training particularly bore witness to the concentration of scientific and technical knowledge amongst ever fewer employees in the American metal industry. As a result, this knowledge literally became inaccessible to the mass of workers. Second, the definition of 'skill' itself was now completely degraded. It no longer meant, even in theory, technical and social mastery over the mental and manual attributes of direct production, but rather 'speed', 'efficiency', and 'dexterity'. The understanding of Karl Marx rings true here; skills were now 'prudently and in homeopathic doses' spread·amongst workers as a result of their *adjustment* to the new needs of capital.[127] As the productiveness of their labour increased with the extensive application of sophisticated and costly machinery, they were compelled to endure a further fragmentation of their tasks and training. They were increasingly forced to demonstrate their skilfulness as 'efficiency'. Theirs was the labour of Sysiphus always to be rolled back every time the rock was pushed up the mountain. In this situation skill not only assumed a bourgeois definition and form; it also assumed a bourgeois content.

When Harry Braverman discussed these issues in his own work he made exactly the same point: 'With the development of the capitalist mode of production, the very concept of skill becomes degraded along with the degradation of labour and the yardstick by which it is measured shrinks to such a point that today the worker is considered to possess a "skill" if his or her job requires a few days' or weeks' training, several months of training is regarded as unusually demanding, and the job that calls for a learning period of six months or a year... inspires a paroxysm of awe'.[128] Braverman was quite right. In this context, the study of proletarian skill and the methods by which it is trained is in reality a study of the adaptation of the labourer to the technical and social conditions of capitalist production. As we have seen, there was nothing ominously conspiratorial, pre-given or teleological about this development. It was an historical *result,* a product of machinery being stamped with the character of fixed *capital* and having to pay a dividend. Hence, 'the more skilful and dextrous' a worker became 'the more surely' he was doomed to the 'continual service in... one narrow rut'. At least this was what George Frederick Stratton thought in 1907. He was no leading Marxist, but a product of the new system of training—a leading engineer.[129]

If the new skill compositions and methods of training did lead to an 'upgrading' of the workforce; if there was a prospect for the workforce *as a whole* to gain 'substantial' skills; if 'average skill' levels did remain constant or decline only slowly, then we must know whether the new abilities associated with the labour of superintendence and management were, as Braverman put it, 'adequate to compensate the loss'.[130] The fact that the new training procedures concentrated many skills in a managerial hierarchy of supervisors, foremen, technicians and engineers is hardly *proof* that the majority were compensated for their loss or that they were left with 'substantial' skills. Workers certainly developed a talent for deciding whether or not to sabotage a machine; they grew to know what a machine's 'quirks' were; but it is not rhetorical to ask: was this the continuity of 'average skill'? If it was not, then such an interpretation merely glosses over the existence of what Braverman calls, a widening social 'chasm'.[131] The fact that Charles Sabel believes he can not only discount this argument but also ask, 'why do workers put up with the possibilities for work', which 'from a middle class point of view [are] often appallingly limited', indicates that training and skill requirements were indeed 'appallingly' degraded. The words 'substantial' or 'genuine' skill, in this context, only register the genteel paternalism of academia. It has invented the words, lives with them, and studies them; only workers have to labour by them. It is nothing less than the commodity talking, dressed in Madison Avenue garb, and proclaiming its 'substantial' and 'genuine' differences from the other brands of soap detergents or lemonades. It is the perverse logic of what Braverman called the mad statistician who, 'with one foot in the fire and the other in ice water, will tell you that, "on average", he is perfectly comfortable'.[132] It is, finally, an approach which rests 'exclusively upon the increase in the number of specialised technical occupations, without recognising that the multiplication of technical specialities is the condition for dispossessing the mass of workers from the realms of science, knowledge and skill'. That Braverman should associate these three is as interesting as the fact that neo-Taylorite scholarship would have us obfuscate the issue by only referring to 'skill'. If new skills did compensate the loss of old ones, then the job of the neo-Taylorite sociologists and historians is to show that the vast majority of *workers* assumed the scientific, design and operational responsibilities of modern engineering. Short of revolution or an equally revolutionary rewriting of history, this would seem to be a tall order.

NOTES

1. On the shortage of skilled labour see Peter Temin, 'Labour Scarcity and the Problem of American Industrial Efficiency in the 1850s', in *Journal of Economic History*, Vol. XXVI, No. 3, September 1966, pp. 227-98, and H.J. Habakkuk, *American and British Technology in the Nineteenth Century*, CUP, Cambridge, 1962. For a general introduction to the restrictions placed on work by skilled workers, see Philip S. Foner, *History of the Labour Movement in the United States, Vol. III, The Policies and Practices of the American Federation of Labour, 1900-09*, International Publishers, New York, 1973, p. 181 ff.

2. See the report of the United States Immigration Commission, 1911-12, an extract of which can be found in Brinley Thomas, *Migration and Economic Growth*, CUP, Cambridge, 1954, pp. 170-1. Thomas' study is the classic and standard reference on the role played by unskilled immigrant labour in spurring on the mechanisation of production and the *adaptation* of machinery to the lower levels of skills present in the American workforce during the nineteenth century. A more recent work, by Jeff Henderson and Robin Cohen, 'Capital and the Work Ethic', *Monthly Review*, Vol. 36, No. 6, November 1979, pp. 11-26, seeks to give added weight to this perspective in the twentieth century. The authors argue that, 'it seems plausible. . . the rapid growth of technology in American industry, relative to Europe, resulted from the need to habituate successive waves of first generation working people throughout the bulk of the twentieth century'. See p. 16. In Thomas' own study, he found that the population of the United States increased by 6,243,000 through migration in the years 1900-1910. See Thomas, *op. cit.*, p. 195.

3. See Paul H. Douglas, *American Apprenticeship and Industrial Education,* Columbia University Studies in History and Economics, New York, 1915, pp. 76-7.

4. See Daniel Nelson, *Workers and Managers: Origins of the New Factory System in the United States, 1880-1920,* University of Wisconsin Press, Wisconsin, 1975, *passim,* especially pp. 79-83.

5. On the steel industry see Katherine Stone, 'The Origin of Job Structures in the Steel Industry', in Root and Branch, eds., *Root and Branch: The Rise of the Workers' Movements,* p. 124 ff. On the engineering industry, see Dan Clawson, *Bureaucracy and the Labour Process: The Transformation of U.S. Industry, 1860-1920,* p. 71 ff, and Nelson, *op. cit.,* pp. 36-7. John Buttrick has made a special study of contracting in the Winchester Repeating Arms Company; see his 'The Inside Contract System', *Journal of Economic History,* Vol. 12, No. 3, Summer 1952, pp. 201-21.

6. Nelson, *op. cit.,* pp. 87-8.

7. *ibid.,* pp. 79-83.

8. *ibid.,* pp. 90-95 and David Brody, *Steelworkers in America and the Non-Union Era,* Harvard University Press, Cambridge, Mass., 1960, pp. 112-24.

9. Brody, *op. cit.,* p. 50 ff. The phrase is Clawson's, *op. cit.,* p. 116.

10. See Jesse S. Robinson, *Amalgamated Association of Iron, Steel and Tin Workers,* Baltimore, 1920, p. 114. See also David Montgomery's, 'Workers Control of Machine Production in the Nineteenth Century', *Labor History,* Vol. 17, No. 4, Fall 1976, p. 488, for a comparable example on iron rollers at the Columbus Iron Works, Ohio, during the 1870s.

11. Brody, *op. cit.,* pp. 53-5, and Stone, *loc. cit.,* p. 127.

12. See Nelson, *op. cit.,* pp. 36-8, and Stone, *loc. cit.,* p. 127 ff.

13. Nelson, *op. cit.,* p. 38, and Clawson, *op. cit.,* pp. 118, 121-2.

14. Clawson, *op. cit.,* p. 113 ff.

15. Brody, *op. cit.,* pp. 53-5.

16. David Schloss, *Methods of Industrial Remuneration,* Williams and Norgate, Oxford, 1898, pp. 118-19.

17. See Gerhard Brandt, *Gewerkschaftliche Interessenvertretung und sozialer Wandel. Eine soziologische Untersuchung über die Entwicklung der Gewerkschaften in der Britischen Eisen und Stahlindustrie, 1886-1917,* E.V.A. Frankfurt, 1975, p. 123.

18. *ibid.,* p. 67. See also *Royal Commission on Labour, Second Report, Précis of Evidence,* Part 2, Iron, Engineering, Hardware, 1892, Cd. 6795-1, *Parliamentary Papers, Evidence of J. Long, Barrow and Workington Association of Iron and Steel Workers,* p. 55. Amongst Barrow's Bessemer steel workers subcontracting was abolished in 1886, but remained prevalent in other branches of the industry.

19. *Royal Commission on Labour, Second Report. Précis of Evidence. . .,* 1892, p. 52. See also the evidence by E. Thomas, Eston, Association of Iron and Steel Workers, p. 56; E. Trow, General Secretary, Association of Iron and Steel Workers, p. 58, and R. Anson, National Association of Steel Smelters, p. 65. See also *Report of an Enquiry by the Board of Trade into Working Class Rents in the United Kingdom, 'Sheffield', Parliamentary Papers,* 1908, CVII, Col. 3869, Vol. 46, p. 409, and *Engineering,* January 1, 1909, p. 16.

20. Duncan Burn, *An Economic History of Steel Making, 1867-1939,* Cambridge University Press, Cambridge, 1940, pp. 142-3, n. 3.

21. Schloss, *op. cit.,* p. 148 ff. See also, Ewart C. Amos, 'Modern Workshop Management', *Fielden's Magazine,* Vol. 4, No. 1, January 1901, p. 138.

22. See *Report of the German Confidential Man, Martin Segitz, Fürth, Bavaria, to the International Congress of Metalworkers, London, 1896,* in *International*

Metal Workers' Federation, compiled by Charles Hobson, Secretary of the British Section, Industrial Training and Internationalism, Hudson and Son, Birmingham, 1915, p. 163.

23. *Report of the German Moulders' Central Society to the International Metalworkers' Congress in London, 1896,* in *International Metalworkers' Federation,* p. 167.

24. See H. Reichelt, *Die Arbeitsverhältnisse in einem Berliner Grossbetrieb der Maschinenindustrie,* Centralverein für das Wohl der arbeitenden Klassen, Leonhard Simion, Berlin, 1907, pp. 43-7, for an excellent description of the situation in Berlin until the end of the 1880s. See also Fritz Schulte, *Die Entlönungsmethoden in der Berliner Maschinenindustrie,* Centralverein. . . Leonhard Simion, Berlin, 1906, pp. 45-6. Ernst Günther, *Die Entlöhnungsmethoden in der Bayrischen Eisen und Maschinenindustrie,* Centralverein. . . Leonhard Simion, Berlin, 1908, pp. 48-61 describes the same situation in Bavaria. On Hanover, see Walter Timmerman, *Die Entlöhnungsmethoden in der Hannoverschen Eisenindustrie,* Centralverein. . ., Leonhard Simion, Berlin, 1906, pp. 46-9. On the Rhine and Siegerland see Otto Jeidels, *Die Methoden der Arbeiterentlöhnung in der rheinischwestfälischen Eisenindustrie,* Centralverein. . ., Leonhard Simion, Berlin, 1907, p. 30 ff, and also Richard Ehrenberg, 'Die Frühzeit der Krupp'schen Arbeiterschaft', *Archiv für exacte Wirtschaftsforschung,* Bd. 3, 1911, pp. 148-50. In the Rhineland, however, it should be noted that contracting never developed in the metal industry to the same extent as in other regions. Many of the firms were built after 1850 in a new era of industrialisation and, therefore, this method of organising the labour process made little headway. See Jeidels, *op. cit.,* p. 33. See also Hans Ehrenberg, *Die Eisenhüttentechnik und der deutsche Hüttenarbeiter,* J.G. Cotta'sche Buchhandlung, Stuttgart and Berlin, 1960, p. 80 ff.

25. See *Royal Commission on Labour, Second Report. . . 1892,* the evidence of R. Anson, National Association of Steel Smelters, p. 65.

26. See Clawson, *op. cit.,* pp. 106, 109.

27. Nelson, for example, suggests that not all operations were placed in the hands of contractors. Rather they were mainly used for components production. In the mass-production gun factories of America, for instance, he argues that the contractors undertook the production of barrels, stocks and screws, but did not put together the finished gun. This was done by the employees of the firm. As the work was of a highly skilled nature, it required the cooperation of skilled craftsmen who resented being driven by foremen, and who preferred to contract and subcontract amongst themselves, supervise each other and generally get the job out by organising themselves. See Nelson, *op. cit.,* p. 36. Brandt's work on the British iron and steel industry has a similar emphasis. He argues that contracting systems were more prone to exist in those technically backward sections of the industry, such as in puddling, unmechanised rolling, and in the Bessemer plants, where skilled workers were essential for the successful operation of plant and equipment, rather than in the Siemens Martin steel plants where only *ouvrier spécialiste* type workers were required. See Brandt, *op. cit.,* p. 38.

28. See Clawson, *op. cit.,* p. 165.

29. See Hans Ehrenberg, *op. cit.,* pp. 46-8, and also Otto Jeidels, *op. cit.,* p. 106.

30. Reichelt, *op. cit.,* pp. 72-81. Similar responses can be seen amongst skilled smith's strikers in Britain in the 1890s and in the smiths' shops of Württemberg. See Schloss, *op. cit.,* p. 154, and Günther, *op. cit.,* p. 61. As well, much of the history of labour relations in the British iron and steel industry in the late nineteenth-century is concerned with the attempt to restrict, regulate and lastly abolish the role of contractors by both skilled and unskilled iron and steel

workers. See Brandt, *op. cit.,* pp. 128-9.

31. The German historian, Gerhard Brandt, in his work on labour relations in the British iron and steel industry, argues for a 'backward' view of the industry in the late nineteenth century. Employers, he suggests, failed to develop any specialisation of their functions and took no part in decisive organisational innovations, especially in the area of the organisation of the labour process and in company administration. The 'contract system', for Brandt, expressed the 'fettered' *(sprengten)* relationship between changing technical conditions of production and the continuation of paternalistic forms of enterprise management. Furthermore, its existence pointed to the absence of an intermediate level of labour management, where 'pre-industrial' relations of production dominated. See Brandt, *op. cit.,* p. 65 ff. Brandt does, however, take his argument concerning British 'backwardness' too far, when he claims that the contract system represented 'a specific form of British development'. *ibid.,* p. 68. As we have already seen the contract system was by no means unique to Britain in the nineteenth century. This error has also been reproduced by a number of British historians and contemporary observers of continental practice. On the alleged absence of contracting in the German metal industry in the late nineteenth century, see J. Carr and W. Taplin, *A History of the British Steel Industry,* Basil Blackwell, Oxford, 1962, p. 175. As we saw in an earlier chapter, Roth and Brockhaus also suggest that the role of skilled labour in the German engineering industry contributed to the industry's 'technical and economic stagnation'. Though not specifically concerned with the contracting system, they are concerned to describe the power of craft workers in controlling the labour process and of the cooperation employers sought from them. See Karl Heinz Roth, *Die 'andere' Arbeiterbewegung,* p. 23 ff, and Eckhard Brockhaus, *Zusammensetzung und Neustrukturierung der Arbeiterklasse von dem ersten Weltkrieg,* 1975, p. 14 ff. From America, Clawson suggests that contracting represented 'the knowledge and skill of people directly involved in the process of production, who both plan and carry out the necessary tasks'. For him, 'Capitalists left the craft system basically intact, but attempted to give selected workers a special incentive to cooperate with capital and management'. See Clawson, *op. cit.,* pp. 133, 194. It must be added though, that Clawson perceives nothing backward, either technically or organisationally, about the contract system.

32. Schloss, *op. cit.,* p. 148.

33. *ibid.,* pp. 147-8.

34. See Clawson, *op. cit.,* p. 102.

35. Patrick McGeown, *Heat the Furnace Seven Times More,* p. 60.

36. Clawson, in his own study of the American engineering industry, touches on this point, but argues from the point of view that incentives to increase output are a general and permanent aspect of capitalism. This, however, fails to realise the specific historical character of the incentive as the basis on which supervisors extracted the maximum amount of labour from time-wage workers. See Clawson, *op. cit.,* pp. 123-4. Nelson, on the other hand, seems to understand the basis of this incentive. See his comments for the iron and steel industry in America, *op. cit.,* pp. 44-5.

37. McGeown, *op. cit.,* p. 60. See also Elaine Glovka Spencer, 'Between Capital and Labour: Supervisory Personnel in Ruhr Heavy Industry Before 1914', *Journal of Social History,* Vol. 9, No. 2, Winter 1975, pp. 178-92.

38. According to Clawson, the average income of a contractor was more than three times that of the average income of a worker in 1874. See Clawson, *op. cit.,* p. 116. See also p. 97 ff.

39. See Gerd Hardach, *Der soziale Status des Arbeiters. . .,* p. 158. Clawson should

have had some inkling of this in his study of contracting in the American engineering industry, for he speaks of the foreman's position in much the same way as he speaks of the contractor's position. 'The foreman', he suggests, 'was a powerful figure not simply in relation to his workers, but also with respect to higher authority. As with contractors, there was essentially only one level of authority above the foreman. In many cases, each foreman operated what was quite literally a plant unto itself. . . What higher authority there was tried to ensure cooperation between foremen, not give them specific orders or directives on how to run their operations. . . When foremen and higher authority did quarrel, it was not necessarily the foreman who lost'. See Clawson, *op. cit.*, p. 128.

40. Hardach, *Der soziale Status des Arbeiters. . .*, pp. 155–60, 160 ff. I am also indebted to Reinhard Bendix for many of the ideas behind this conceptualisation. See his *Work and Authority in Industry: Ideologies of Management in the Course of Industrialisation,* University of California Press, Berkeley, London, 1974, p. 213, n. 24. It is exactly on this point that Harry Braverman is seriously misleading, for he confuses pre-factory forms of contracting, such as 'putting out' systems, with factory contracting. Braverman would have us believe that both 'The early domestic and subcontracting systems represented a transitional form, a phase during which the capitalist had not yet assumed the essential function of management in industrial capitalism, control over the labour process; for this reason it was incompatible with the overall development of capitalist production. . .

'Such methods of dealing with labour bore the marks of the origins of industrial capitalism in mercantile capitalism, which understood the buying and selling of commodities, but not their production, and sought to treat labour like all other commodities. It was bound to prove inadequate. . . The subcontracting and "putting out" systems were plagued by problems of irregularity of production, loss of materials in transit and through embezzlement, slowness of manufacture, lack of uniformity and uncertainty of the quality of the product. But most of all, they were limited by their inability to change the processes of production'. See Braverman, *Labour and Monopoly Capital,* p. 63.

41. See Ewart C. Amos, 'Modern Workshop Practice', *Fielden's Magazine,* Vol. 4, No. 1, January 1901, p. 138.

42. For a description of the ideology of the 'craftsman' in nineteenth-century industry, see David Montgomery, 'Workers' Control of Machine Production in the Nineteenth Century', *loc. cit.*, pp. 485–509. See also Stone, *loc. cit.*, and Mike Davis, 'Why the U.S. Working Class is Different', *New Left Review,* No. 123, September–October, 1980, p. 13.

43. In the colonial period, for instance, apprenticeship in the north-eastern States often served as a means of paying debts, where the sons of the debtor could be 'boundout' to the creditor. It was also used as a means of checking the movements of itinerant 'idle youths', as well as forming a system of poor relief once the children of poor parents were brought under the control of local councils. Overall, this system was more renowned for its exploitation of child labour than for its cultivation of craft relations, especially as poor parents could ill afford not to take the extra income or solvency derived from binding out their children, and rapacious manufacturers sought cheap labour. In the early nineteenth century, for instance, the Philadelphian mechanics' trades were apparently very much under the spell of cheap child labour, as was much of American manufacturing industry in general during the nineteenth and early twentieth centuries. See Douglas, *op. cit.*, pp. 41–8, 50, 60–1, 85–108.

44. David Montgomery, one of the historians of the 'craft mode of production',

points to some of these features of contracting, but for him they were 'individualistic' aberrations from the 'mutualistic ethic', rather than the core of the ethic itself. See David Montgomery, 'Workers' Control of Machine Production in the Nineteenth Century', *loc. cit.*, pp. 492-3.

45. See Raymond Goldsmith, *The Flow of Capital Funds in the Post-War Economy,* National Bureau of Economic Research, Columbia University Press, New York and London, 1965, Table 19, pp. 99-102.

46. *ibid.,* Table 19, pp. 99-102.

47. *ibid.,* pp. 91-102.

48. Simon Kuznets, 'Capital Formation and Economic Growth', in *Population, Capital and Growth,* Heinemann, London, 1973, pp. 127-8. Like Goldsmith, Kuznets also suggests that since the 1870s the consumption of 'durable capital' grew rapidly in terms of a quickening pace of obsolescence, and grew at a faster rate than did capital formation. According to his calculations for the period 1869-1955, capital consumption as a proportion of gross capital formation rose from 40% to approximately 66%, thus demonstrating the speed-up in the turnover time of fixed capital. See Kuznets, *Capital in the American Economy,* pp. 9, 57.

49. See Brody, *op. cit.*, pp. 29-31.

50. See F.W. Taylor, 'A Piece-Rate System' (1895), in *Cassier's Magazine,* Vol. XIII, No. 4, February 1898, pp. 369/4.

51. D. Smith and P.C.N. Pickworth, *Engineers' Costs and Economical Workshop Production,* p. 46.

52. John Batey, *The Science of Works Management,* Scott, Greenwood and Son, London, 1914, p. 67.

53. For a more general discussion on these points, see Karl Marx, *Capital,* Vol. 1, p. 460, and Christian Palloix, 'The Labour Process: from Fordism to neo-Fordism', in *The Labour Process and Class Struggles,* pp. 46-7.

54. See David Landes, *The Unbound Prometheus,* p. 302.

55. See Brody, *op. cit.*, p. 33.

56. *ibid.,* pp. 35-40. The twelve-hour day was not abolished in the steel industry until 1923. See Charles Hill, 'Fighting the Twelve-Hour Day in the American Steel Industry', *Labor History,* Vol. 15, No. 1, Winter 1974, pp. 18-35.

57. C. Bertrand Thompson, 'Scientific Management in Practice', *Quarterly Journal of Economics,* Vol. 29, 1914-1915, p. 307.

58. See Bryan Palmer, 'Class, Conception and Conflict: The Thrust for Efficiency, Managerial Views of Labour and the Working Class Rebellion 1903-22', in *The Review of Radical Political Economics,* Vol. 7, No. 2, Summer 1975, p. 36.

59. Quoted, *ibid.,* p. 37.

60. Quoted, *ibid.,* p. 37.

61. See, for example, E.P. Thompson's, 'The Moral and Political Economy of the English Crowd in the Eighteenth Century', *Past and Present,* Vol. 50, 1971, p. 76 ff; and also by the same author, 'Time, Work-Discipline, and Industrial Capitalism', *Past and Present,* Vol. 38, 1967, pp. 56-97. See also Sidney Pollard, *The Genesis of Modern Management,* Arnold, London, 1956, Ch. 12; Maurice Dobb, *Essays in the Development of Capitalism,* Routledge and Kegan Paul, London, 1972, Ch. 7. On France, see Sewell, *Work and Revolution in France,* for a description of the resistance of artisan lyric poets of the 'mechanical arts' to the new capitalist definitions of work and labour.

62. See F.W. Taylor, 'A Piece-Rate System', *loc. cit.,* p. 369/1 ff.

63. See George Frederick Stratton, 'The Improvement of Opportunity for the Young Workman', *Engineering Magazine,* Vol. XXXIII, No. 5, August 1907,

p. 775.

64. For a description of the destruction of unionism in the steel industry between 1880 and 1914, see Brody, *op. cit., passim;* and Stone, *loc. cit.*

65. The classic exposition of 'scientific management' as an ideology and a movement still remains R.F. Hoxie's report to the American Congress in 1915. See his, *Scientific Management and Labour,* Appleton, New York, London, 1915. See also M.J. Nadworny, *Scientific Management and the Unions, 1900-32: a Historical Analysis,* Harvard University Press, Cambridge, Mass., 1955. On the role of engineers, see David F. Noble, *America by Design. Science Technology and the Rise of Corporate Capitalism,* Alfred A. Knopf, New York, pp. 35 ff, 41.

66. See, for example, the writings of F.W. Taylor, especially, 'A Piece-Rate System', *loc. cit.,* and his *Scientific Management,* Harper, New York, Western Reserve University, Cleveland, 1971, p. 139 ff.

67. Taylor's own writings were a perfect example of this professional acquisition of scientific knowledge and its application. See his *Notes on Belting,* (1893), *Colours in Heated Steel,* with Maunsal White, (1899), and *The Art of Cutting Metals,* (1906). See also, Noble, *op. cit.,* Ch. 5, for a discussion of standardisation movements covering weights and measures.

68. See, for example, Taylor's 'A Piece-Rate System', *loc. cit.*

69. An excellent description of the movements which emphasised the 'power of thought' may be found in Reinhard Bendix, *Work and Authority in Industry,* University of California Press, Berkeley, Los Angeles, London, 1974, Ch. 5, esp. pp. 258-60.

70. The works of Harry Braverman, Katherine Stone, and Dan Clawson have already been noted. The list however, can be extended to include David Montgomery, Jeremy Brecher and David Stark. Brecher's 'Uncovering the Hidden History of the American Workplace', in the *Review of Radical Political Economics,* Vol. 10, No. 4, Winter 1978, pp. 1-23, suggests that America's industrialists at this time were seeking the 'destruction of craft production' and its 'world' of craft organisations (see p. 6). Stark, in his 'Class Struggle and the Transformation of the Labour Process: A Relational Approach', *Theory and Society,* 9, 1980, pp. 89-139, argues that, 'Scientific management was an attempt to smash control of the labour provess and to replace craft forms of supervision with a bureaucratic administration of production' (see pp. 100-1). See also David Montgomery, 'Workers Control of Machine Production in the Nineteenth Century', *loc. cit.,* p. 507.

71. This is certainly the most important aspect of Palmer's work, for his 'hypothesis' is that 'the thrust for efficiency contributed to the attainment of what could be termed bourgeois hegemony'. See Palmer, *loc. cit.,* p. 44. Palmer is also keen to quote from M.A. Calvert's, *The Mechanical Engineer in America, 1830-1910; Professional Cultures in Conflict,* John Hopkins Press, Baltimore, 1967, pp. 278-9, to the effect that 'Scientific management provided a role for the elite engineer; significantly it did not take over American Industry (as a movement) as the engineers planned'.

72. C.B. Thompson, 'Relation of Scientific Management to Labour', *Quarterly Journal of Economics,* Vol. 30, 1915-16, p. 338.

73. See Brody, *op. cit.,* pp. 53-5, 58. See also Craig R. Littler, 'Understanding Taylorism', *British Journal of Sociology,* Vol. XXIX, No. 2, June 1978, pp. 144-5. Littler is also of the view that the rise of new management methods, such as Taylorism, are to be seen, in the first instance, as an attack on contracting.

74. See Nelson, *op. cit.,* pp. 95-100; Douglas, *op. cit.,* p. 213 ff.

75. See H.E. Field, 'Technical Education for the Foundry', *Iron Age,* Vol. LXXVIII,

1906, p. 1687.

76. See O.M. Becker, 'Modern Adaptations of the "Apprenticeship System" ', *The Engineering Magazine*, Vol. XXXII, No. 3, December 1906, pp. 321–38. See also C.W. Cross and W.B. Russell, 'A Railroad Apprentice System on the New York Central Lines', *Engineering Magazine*, Vol. XXXIII, No. 5, August 1907, pp. 786–8.

77. See 'The Education of Apprentices', *The Iron Review*, Vol. XXXVIII, 1905, p. 33.

78. See S.M. Vauclain, 'The Apprenticeship System at the Baldwin Locomotive Works', *The Engineering Magazine*, Vol. XXVII, No. 3, June 1904, pp. 321–33. The following account is based on this study by Vauclain.

79. For a comparable description of the corporate schools in the electrical industry, especially at A.T&T, G.E., and Westinghouse, see David Noble, *op. cit.*, Ch. 8, pp. 167–223, especially his comments on the G.E. Test Course set up in the 1890s, p. 171 ff.

80. *ibid.*, p. 171.

81. Clawson, *op. cit.*, p. 76.

82. See also O.M. Becker, *loc. cit.*, 1906, who reported that Westinghouse, the National Cash Register Co., and Brown and Sharp's also drew on High School graduates for their 'apprentices'.

83. See 'L'apprentissage dans les usines de construction de machines-outils aux Etats-Unis', in *Iron Age*, Vol. LXXVIII, 1906, pp. 1234–6; abstract in *Revue de Métallurgie*, Extraits, Vol. 4, 1907, p. 258.

84. The machine-tool employers were obviously impressed by the new model apprenticeship schools. In their 1906 report they came out in support of cutting down the time required for a youth to obtain a traditional apprenticed training and raising the status of the new forms of apprenticeship by encouraging technical college students to enter the system. See 'L'apprentissage dans les usines de construction de machines-outils aux Etats-Unis', 1906, *loc. cit.*, p. 258.

85. See Magnus W. Alexander, 'A Plan to Provide for a Supply of Skilled Workmen', paper read before the 'American Society of Mechanical Engineers', published in *Engineering*, Vol. LXXXIII, March 8, 1907, p. 328.

86. *ibid.*, p. 328.

87. *ibid.*, pp. 328–30; see also Noble, *op. cit.*, pp. 302–3 for further description of the G.E. apprenticeship schools.

88. See Douglas, *op. cit.*, pp. 225–7.

89. The phrases are from Alexander, 'A Plan to Provide for a Supply of Skilled Workmen', *loc. cit.*, p. 328.

90. See Frederic Blount Warren, 'A Railroad Company. Altoona and its Methods', *Engineering Magazine*, Vol. XXXIII, No. 2, May 1907, pp. 171–83. The quote may be found on pp. 178–9.

91. *ibid., passim.*

92. See Noble, *op. cit.*, pp. 178–9, and Douglas, *op. cit.*, p. 214.

93. Douglas, *op. cit.*, pp. 214–15.

94. See Frederick William Roman, *The Industrial and Commercial Schools of the United States and Germany*, G. Putnam's Sons, N.Y., 1915, pp. 158–9, for examples.

95. *ibid.*, pp. 161–3.

96. See Douglas, *op. cit.*, pp. 187–8.

97. See *ibid.*, pp. 193–4, and Roman, *op. cit.*, pp. 161–99.

98. See Douglas, *op. cit.*, pp. 190–3.

99. Magnus W. Alexander, 'A Plan to Provide for a Supply of Skilled Workmen', *loc. cit.*, p. 328.

100. Quoted in Roman, *op. cit.*, p. 279.
101. See Douglas, *op. cit.*, pp. 205-7.
102. *ibid.*, pp. 208-9.
103. *ibid.*, pp. 97-8.
104. *ibid.*, p. 111.
105. *ibid.*, pp. 119, 122, 130.
106. See Omer Buyse, Directeur de l'Ecole Industrielle supérieure de Charleroi, Conservateur du Musée provincial de l'enseignement technique du Hainaut, 'Les méthodes américaines d'éducation générale technique', in *Revue de Métallurgie*, Vol. 6, 1909, p. 382.
107. See Alice Ravenhill, 'Some Points of Interest in the Schools of the United States', September 1901, in *Education: Special Reports: Special Report on Educational Subjects, Vol. X. Education in the United States of America, Part 1, Cd. 837, Parliamentary Papers*, Vol. XXVIII, 1902, pp. 401-20.
108. *Reports of the Mosely Educational Commission to the United States of America*, London, 1904, p. x. See also 'Reports of the Mosely Educational Commission to the United States of America', analysé par M. Guillet, in *Revue de Métallurgie*, Vol. 3, No. 10, octobre 1906, pp. 579-81.
109. Omer Buyse, *loc. cit.*, 1909, p. 370-407. See also H. Thiselton Mark, 'Education and Industry in the United States', in *Education Special Reports on Educational Subjects, Vol. XI, Education in the United States of America, Pt. 2, Cd. 1156, Parliamentary Papers*, Vol. XXIX, 1902, pp. 101-232. See also 'The Development of Technical Schools in the United States', *Iron Trade Review*, Vol. XXXVIII, 1905, p. 26, for a description of the laboratories and testing rooms at Purdue University.
110. Douglas, *op. cit.*, pp. 202-5.
111. Frederic Blount Warren, 'A Railroad University. Altoona and its Methods', *loc. cit.*, pp. 182-3.
112. Douglas, *op. cit.*, p. 205.
113. *ibid.*, p. 205, esp. n. 1.
114. André Pelletan, 'Les écoles techniques allemandes', *Revue de Métallurgie*, Vol. 3, No. 11, November 1906, p. 607. See also Noble, *op. cit.*, for a discussion of the Massachusetts Institute of Technology's 'Course VI', which provided practical training for electrical engineers with the equipment supplied by Thomas Edison and Westinghouse. See p. 136 ff.
115. Pelletan, 'Les écoles techniques allemandes', *loc. cit.*, p. 608.
116. See Herman Schneider, 'Une expérience unique en matière d'éducation technique', extract translated from *The Iron Trade Review*, Vol. XXXIX, 1906, by Robert Le Chatelier, in *Revue de Métallurgie*, Extraits, Vol. 4, 1907, p. 260.
117. See Douglas, *op. cit.*, pp. 246-8 and ff. for further examples.
118. See 'The Education of Engineers at the University of Pittsburg', *Iron Trade Review*, Vol. XLVI, 1908, p. 1118 ff; see also *Engineering*, Vol. LXXXII, November 6, 1906, p. 672 for a description of the mutual research facilities in the universities and the companies; and also Noble, *op. cit.*, p. 145.
119. See *Engineering*, Vol. LXXXII, 16 November 1906, p. 672; and for a general discussion of the rise of scientific and engineering universities in the U.S.A., see Noble, *op. cit.*, p. 20 ff.
120. See *The Iron Trade Review*, Vol. XXXIV, 1906, pp. 17-18, extract translated in *Revue de Métallurgie*, Vol. 4, No. 5, mai 1907, pp. 511-14. Taylor was also critical of the absence of discipline within the universities, which therefore ill-prepared their students for the disciplined life of the factory. He also argued that many technical courses were too broad and suggested that more specialisation in the subject matter was needed. For further evidence see Noble, *op. cit.*,

pp. 27-9, 184 ff.

121. See Brody, *op. cit.*, p. 23. In a survey of the educational attainments of America's leading businessmen between 1831 and 1920, taken from those to be of interest to the *National Cyclopedia of American Biography*, Reinhard Bendix has found that, though a college education or more remained a minority pursuit for 'entrepreneurs', for company 'bureaucrats' the proportion with a college education or more, rose from 38% in the years 1831-75 to 65% in the period 1876-1920. See Bendix, *op. cit.*, p. 230.

122. See Edwin Layton, *op. cit.*, p. 3.

123. Noble, *op. cit.*, pp. 24, 131.

124. See Layton, *op. cit.*, p. 9. The sons of farmers also provided their quota of engineers. See, for example, William Kent's remarks in 'Technical Education in the United States', *Iron Trade Review*, Vol. XXXVIII, 1905, pp. 20-5. See also Noble, *op. cit.*, p. 39.

125. Noble, *op. cit.*, p. 168.

126. See Douglas, *op. cit.*, pp. 126-8.

127. Karl Marx, *Capital*, Vol. 1 (1867), p. 432.

128. Harry Braverman, *Labour and Monopoly Capital*, p. 444.

129. See George Frederick Stratton, 'The Improvement of Opportunity for the Young Workman', *loc. cit.*, p. 774.

130. Braverman, *op. cit.*, p. 425.

131. *ibid.*, p. 425.

132. *ibid.*, p. 425.

CHAPTER 3: GREAT BRITAIN

By the end of the nineteenth century the free-wheeling pioneer was certainly relying heavily on its inheritance of private and competitive methods of training and regulating skills. To a certain extent this was checked in the engineering industry by the role of unions in determining who could do a particular job, but even here there could be no challenge to the employer determining the actual skills required in production. At the same time, production management could not yet be seen as having 'professional' attributes. A future executive or employer generally continued to come up through the factory ranks to a management position or receive his training in other plants at home or abroad. In the steel industry, for example, Charlotte Erickson has found that the sons of partners, owners or directors continued to be the largest source of managerial cadres in the period 1905-25, accounting for some 36% of her sample. The number of skilled workers making it to the top declined by one third, from 3% in 1865 to 2% in the years 1905-25.[1] Education at the highest levels of the management hierarchy also continued to remain unconnected to professional training. Though the number of future industrialists in the steel industry attending universities or colleges rose from 13% in 1865 to 19% during 1905-25, the overwhelming majority (15 of the 19%) received an Oxbridge education in the liberal arts. At the summits of the management hierarchy an education according to one's 'social status' remained more important than training for an industrial career.[2] Advocates of professional management drew attention to the weaknesses of this relatively open, plant-based internal structure of training and lamented the blockage to horizontal mobility from the university to the office and boardroom. A.P.M. Fleming and R.W. Bailey in their tract, *Engineering as a Profession,* published in 1913, spoke of the fact that while other professions had well-defined standards and regulations, engineering had 'no such regulations'. There was also a 'deplorable lack of appreciation of the scope of this profession, as well as a widespread erroneous notion as to the real work of an engineer'.[3] Engineers, they claimed, had little knowledge of business and needed more training in commercial law, costing, accounting and foreign languages integrated into their courses. On the other hand, the need for a more commercial orientation in the training of engineers had to be complemented by more cooperation between the factory and the colleges so that the future engineer would obtain more practical experience before he took up a leading position in a factory.[4]

1. The rise of professional training for managerial and supervisory labour

If one's only guide in assessing this criticism was the fact that it was not until 1913 that the Institute of Mechanical Engineers introduced examination as a criterion of selection and membership, or that in the chemical and metallurgical trades future scientists often had to obtain their technical training in Germany and Austria,[5] then one would be hard pressed to answer Professor Hobsbawm's judgment that, by 1914 Britain had inherited at all levels, a 'spectacularly ill-educated' workforce. Yet in a period of renewed expansion lasting from 1898 to 1914, Britain's metal industrialists, with the aid of the state, did broaden the basis of production management, introduce horizontal mobility from the college to the factory, and professionalise the ideology of 'technical intelligence'. In the first instance, the upper class ideology surrounding Britain's class structure (of knowing one's place, of contempt for the 'professional' classes and of the outright rejection of working-class mobility), was not immune to the American influence of 'professionalisation'. In the words of Francis Burton, whose treatise on the *Commercial Management of Engineering Works* appeared in 1905, 'We educate by classes, and by the very nature of things are compelled to do so. It is, therefore, false economy to place a member of a more mechanically-trained class (a higher craftsman) to perform the duties of a brain worker, for which he has shown no special aptitude, merely to save a few shillings per week in wages'.[6] Burton was criticising the waste and false saving produced by 'educational experts', local authorities and employers in assuming that the need was for 'advanced schooling and higher technical training for artisans' so that the growing number of scientific and managerial positions could be filled. They assumed that if a fitter was taught 'to produce imperfect drawings, or a journeyman dyer to read a chemical equation without a blunder, great progress will have been made in this country'. But 'much more than this is necessary to maintain our manufacturing and commercial supremacy, or what is left of it. . . [It] is chiefly in the manufacturer's appreciation of the scientific branches of his establishment, and of research work, that the need lies. . .'[7] Quoting from a 'brilliant essay' by Dr Karl Pearson, F.R.S., Burton argued, that the expanding role of science in industry was not aided by promoting a manual worker out of his 'caste or class':

> . . . if we remember how few generations are needful for a special human group to breed true. . . it serves no social purpose, to drag a man of only moderate intellectual power from the hand-working to the brain-working group; yet this seems too often the result of the present system. If there be a moderately capable worker, the State should strive, in the first place, that he should be trained to better

craftsmanship. Do not let us assume that he will turn out a Faraday because he shows some relative capacity. In at least nine cases out of ten, disappointment will be in store for the State if it does. . . The cry for 'an easy ladder' is a most mistaken one, especially as long as any false feeling of gentility attaches to one or another class of workers. . . If national education at the present day be a *sine qua non* of national fitness for success in the world struggle, it must none the less, be a specialised education suited to develop the intelligence of each caste and class. Training is essential to a nation, but it must be specialised to each social activity, if it is to perform its function.[8]

Such attitudes from a 'democratic thinker' and a 'progressive teacher' were often shaped by a mood of Spencerism, which became very popular amongst the middle class during the late 1890s. Professor R.H. Thurston, for example, sought to supply his weight to professionally 'feudalising' education and industrial training by bringing to bear the pseudo-sociological determinism of Spencer's law of the 'survival of the fittest'. Writing in the popular engineering magazine, *Cassier's,* he argued that:

For the simple-minded worker who has no talent, no ability to acquire knowledge through study, and but little power of learning through the senses. . . it is. . . evident that it would be absurd to attempt as someone has expressed it, 'to put a three-storey education into a one-storey brain'. For this class. . . the best education is that which gives its members preparation for its special work in the hewing of wood and the drawing of water, a manual training and a physical education such as will best fit the student for his daily work in the field or the shop.[9]

Through these arguments, educationalists, engineers and popular magazine writers sought to turn employers and the state away from a policy of the internal, plant-based promotion of leading workers to the ranks of lower scientific and semi-managerial cadres towards a more 'economical', specialised and re-vamped class-based policy of extra-factory appointments from the school, college and university. Certainly, since the 1870s, an awareness had been developing of the need for technically trained personnel and commercial employees who could better respond to the competition coming from the U.S.A. and Germany in heavy metal production. When it came to developing concrete policies to meet these demands in the early 1900s, we must turn to the proposals drawn up by the Council of the Institution of Civil Engineers in April, 1906.

The Council represented all the major engineering branches and enterprises from naval through to electrical engineering. It suggested that boys wanting to enter the engineering profession should, before leaving school and specialising, pass the Institution's Scholarship Examination or its equivalent. This would comprise, at a general level, a leaving exam throughout the United Kingdom similar to that in Scotland and Wales. It would include history, geography, essay writing; a little Greek, some Latin, and definitely French and German; instruction in mathematics, especially trigonometry and logarithms; physics and chemistry; and finally technical drawing. Once this was attained, the boy who had left school at about seventeen would undertake a one-year introductory workshop course, during which time he would be treated like an ordinary apprentice with the same wages; he would attend evening classes, and then enter a college or university for two years, in which time the student would take courses that emphasised advanced mathematics. The student would not be allowed to specialise in a particular branch of engineering; rather he would take subjects in common with the other engineering students in order to get a broad training in the field. After college the young engineer would then undertake three years of practical training in a factory, mine or steel mill, specialising in a particular field of engineering. In the Institution's view all students would have to gain a competence in engineering drawing and spend many hours in laboratory and experimental work in order to obtain a degree. Facilities for postgraduate study in engineering would also have to be extended, while all this required sympathetic assistance from employers.[10]

In order to underwrite the success of developing scientific production and training, many observers advocated that this should centre on the best industrial universities and colleges, like those at Birmingham, Manchester, Sheffield, and Glasgow, rather than on the Oxbridge system. They believed, quite rightly, that it was in the industrial areas that were to be found the machines, laboratories, factories, accumulated and practical scientific knowledge, as well as the living organisations, which were so eminently suitable for advancing professional industrial training and research work.[11]

It would be an exaggeration to assume that this new emphasis on formally acquired brain-power, seeping its way from the school to the factory *via* a highly stratified education system, brought about revolutionary changes to the role of science in industry or to the actual training methods of scientific and managerial cadres. The transformation was more evolutionary and drew on fifty years' worth of previous experience in privately-based and factory-orientated engineering training. In Sheffield's steel industry, for example, the production of high quality 'special' steels, such as those made from silicon, tungsten, nickel, chrome and other alloys, by the crucible process or in the electric furnace, had been based on systematic research and development since at least the 1880s. Companies like John Brown's, William Jessop and Sons, Thomas Firth and Sons, Vickers, and Robert Hadfield's Hecla Works had established research laboratories for the development of their products.[12] Mr Trebilcock has shown that in the years between the 1880s and the turn of the century the 'spin-off' effects from armaments production also played an important part in the development of pure and applied science in Sheffield's metal industry. By the 1900s, however, these concerns were very much 'mixed' metal enterprises involved in steel, engineering, vehicle and ship production, apart from their munitions work; and, in order to service these many and varied activities several of them began to plough back 6–12% of their net profits into research and development.[13] Sheffield's industrialists were also unrivalled in promoting university-based scientific research and training. John Brown, for instance, was behind the establishment of a university in Sheffield in the late nineteenth century, which would both promote research into metallurgy and produce highly qualified chemists, engineers and technicians. By the early 1900s the University's Metallurgical Department was world-renowned for its work and the sophisticated array of equipment which inhabited its laboratories for the study of pyrometry, microscopy and geology.[14] The University produced not only graduates in metallurgy who would take up senior scientific and management positions in the factories, but also supplied technical instruction to evening students through the Department of Applied Science for young men seeking promotion to white-collar technical work in their local plants.[15]

Sheffield's employers may have been unrivalled in their commitment to scientific research and training, but they were not alone.[16] As we shall see, there is no need to set them apart from an alleged 'conservative mass of British industrialists', as Mr Trebilcock would have us do, at least as far as the British metal industry is concerned.[17] By the late nineteenth century, the development of the chemical and electrical industries, as well as innovations in general engineering and metallurgy, called for what Michael Sanderson has termed, 'a new higher level of labour educated in scientific theory'.[18] And, metal industrialists, the state and local authorities were not above cooperating in gradually building up an effective higher technical education system.

By 1913 there was an array of universities and technical colleges that prospective engineering students could attend. At the university level, engineering students could attend courses at Oxford, Cambridge and London; but it was more likely that they went to university in either Birmingham, Bristol, Durham, or the City and Guilds Engineering College in London; or to universities in Leeds, Liverpool, Manchester, Sheffield, Edinburgh, Glasgow, Wales University in Cardiff, or to universities in Dublin and Belfast. In London the university training of future engineers was further complemented by the existence of the University of London's King's College, University College and the 'great engineering school of the Metropolis', the Central Technical College.[19] Outside of the University of London's authority until 1906 was also the Royal College of Sciences, which formed part of the Royal School of Mines.[20] As well, by 1907 the Imperial College of Technology had been formed by bringing together under one authority the Royal College of Science, the School of Mines and the Central Technical College.[21]

Apart from these 'civic' universities, students could attend one of the various Technical College institutes in Belfast, Brighton, Dublin, Edinburgh, Glasgow, London, Nottingham, Southampton, or Sunderland.[22] It was the university system, though, which came to produce the bulk of formally-trained higher management engineers rather than the technical institutes. According to the Government's *Statistics of Public Education in England and Wales* for 1912–13, of the 1,999 students attending one of the colleges on a full-time basis, only 584 were studying engineering. Though the number of college students studying engineering full-time rose to over 1,000 in the post-war years they were not a significant source of recruits to the higher echelons of engineering production management.[23] The most important role of the colleges was in the provision of evening tuition for youths and men seeking promotion to the ranks of highly-qualified skilled labour or low-level technical, white-collar work. This is discussed in more detail below when we consider industrial training for the workforce as a whole.

Leading engineering and steel enterprises on the look-out for prospective recruits were by 1913 also providing practical experience for university students during the six months summer vacation. In Scotland, the firms included W. Denny and Sons of Dumbarton, and David Rowan and Co., Glasgow. In England, the Vickers plants of Barrow-in-Furness, Kent, and Sheffield provided not only this type of opportunity, but also allowed their own students to attend day classes at technical college or the four-to-five-year 'sandwich' courses at local universities in Kent and Sheffield.[24] Armstrong-Whitworth maintained a similar facility for their students attending Manchester University or the city's Municipal Technical School. Those who were so privileged attended school or college each Monday for the entire day and were expected to do home-work in the evenings for the rest of the week.[25] At Barr and Stroud, in Glasgow, engineering students were given the winter months off so that they could attend Glasgow University;[26] while Mather and Platt of Salford, and Yarrow and Sons of Poplar, provided their future engineers with the opportunity of first attending a local technical school and then a university college.[27]

When one of the British metal industry's leading magazines, *Engineering,* sought to describe the aims of this higher technical education, it claimed that the goal was 'to supply the commissioned ranks of industry'. It was 'not to recruit the ranks of those whose life is to be spent in the exercise of a *handicraft*'.[28] Complementing this pattern of training were the opportunities provided by the Empire.

The Empire was not just a training ground for the civil service and the military. Young men from the civic and old universities on graduating in engineering would frequently go off to work on the African or Indian railways, water works, and other engineering projects. This could be done through either private companies or state concerns and after a few years of experience the young men would return and work for leading metal enterprises. Glasgow Technical College, now the University of Strathclyde, Imperial College, and the Cambridge Engineering Department, were particularly involved in sponsoring this sort of activity in conjunction with leading firms. The influence of the National Efficiency Movement should also be brought in here, because of its role fostering imperial training so that the requisite talent would be available to maintain and extend all the interests of the Empire, whether they be political, cultural or economic.[29]

Overall, this sort of training and education was a sophisticated extension of the training managers and engineering scientists received in the early nineteenth century, where firms sent their future engineering executives off to the Continent in order to obtain foreign experience. An appreciation of, and a willingness to implement, continental advances in technical education were also evident in the early 1900s. Some leading politicians of the National Efficiency Movement were involved here, especially Joseph Chamberlain, the Webbs and Lord Roseberry. With Chamberlain at Birmingham, the Webbs at the London School of Economics and Lords Roseberry and Haldane at Imperial College, an attempt was made to anglicise aspects of the German higher technical education system, particularly its role in mediating the application of science to industry. All this was to be in the interests of a more efficient Britain and a more efficient Empire. It is well known, for instance, that when Imperial College received its Royal Charter in 1907 Lord Roseberry thought that he had created an 'English Charlottenburg', a version of the Physical Technical Institute founded by Werner von Siemens in Berlin, and so designed as to meet the German challenge at home and abroad.[30]

It will be seen, therefore, that a dialectic was developing between the universities and the metal industry, which was proving to be 'cumulative'. As Michael Sanderson suggests:

> . . . as innovation became more scientific so universities were needed for the production of rank and file scientists to manage the scientific industries. In turn the technologies of those industries were yet further developed by the research carried on by the universities themselves.[31]

It is certainly true that this system of higher education had its critics who emphasised either the need for students to obtain an even greater theoretical training in mathematics, physics, chemistry and modern languages or a more intensive practical training in the factories.[32] Other critics, like the Balfour Committee, when describing the basic principles of technical instruction during the nineteenth and early twentieth centuries, also lamented the 'accidental rather than systematic' relations between the universities and the technical schools'.[33] All these lines of criticism had some merit in them, the latter particularly. Technical schools, such as Junior Day Technical Schools for students up to fourteen years of age and Senior Day Schools for students who were seventeen or older, were not designed to feed the university system. On the contrary, the Junior Schools were basically pre-apprenticeship schools, of which there were about sixty, teaching drawing, mechanics, arithmetic and English, and designed to meet the needs of future manual workers. The Senior Schools were mainly part-time and directed at apprentices already learning a trade. The instruction was mainly theoretical and classes were taken on a part-time basis, either during the day or in the evening.[34] The reason why there was no systematic relationship between these schools and the universities is not hard to discover: even with an expanded clientele drawn from the ranks of the middle class, the universities remained bastions of privilege and monitors of class rank. Unlike America, the technical secondary school system in Britain was exclusively designed to fill the ranks of skilled manual labour, rather than provide a reservoir for promotion to higher managerial and technical positions *via* the university system. Though neither system can be seen as a harbinger of social mobility for the working class, the American system provided more room for the middle class to achieve its ambitions *via* a state secondary system which sought to promote its interests, whereas in Britain a more exclusive private secondary system served this purpose.[35] Yet, irrespective of such criticism, the higher technical education system did turn out many engineers for the staple metal trades. It also produced many future managers and engineers for the youthful automobile industry. As Professor Saul has shown, T.N. Fulton of the Albion Motor Company had been educated in Glasgow and at the West of England Technical College before taking his apprenticeship in a Glasgow engineering works. His partner, T. Blackwood Murray, had studied engineering at Edinburgh before being apprenticed to an electrical engineering company. The Daimler company's Sir Edward Manville studied at University College, London, as did Lucien Alphonse Legros of Iris Motors. After studying, they both did their stint as employer apprentices at several textile, rail, gas, and engineering companies. Professor Saul, though, is not impressed with such training. In his view their technical expertise cast a shadow over the industry, as it was too perfectionist and individualistic. These men were more 'mechanics' than 'production engineers'.[36]

This conclusion, however, is too pessimistic. As Saul himself notes, for an industry tied to an upper-class market, and which had only really got off the ground in 1896, it was only five years behind American mass production methods by 1914. Furthermore, a recent study on the car industry has shown in detail how important was the role of production engineers. Enterprises such as Daimler, Rover and Sunbeam, though not using American flow production techniques (which were only perfected by Henry Ford in 1914), were designing production methods around functional mass production principles. At Rover and Daimler—from the early 1900s the production of components for an entire automobile was organised so that they moved in a consecutive way through the various departments. The experience of cycle production had been an important pointer to such organisation, as Rover's early cycle techniques suggested. The planned introduction of American specialised machine tools also fitted into this strategy, as did the use of jigs and fixtures on general-purpose machinery to standardise component production. Sunbeam was an example of the latter method. Though skilled workers generally remained the largest group in the trade it was not because their work continued to be craft based. They were obliged to undertake specialised semi-skilled labour on a mass scale, while those who were lucky enough to be able to do more varied manual labour generally did so amongst the ranks of the hyper-qualified in the tool rooms. Boy labour, as well, was becoming common. As early as 1899, for instance, half the operations in Daimler Motors turning shop were being undertaken by boys.[37]

As this evidence suggests, formally-trained production engineers rather than employer 'mechanics' were playing the most important role in the trade, especially in the areas of factory lay-out and the uses of plant and equipment. At the end of this chapter I shall consider in more detail the actual skill compositions used in various branches of the metal industry and their relation to methods of industrial training. For the moment, though, it needs to be said that a great deal of professionally-trained employer and managerial talent flowed into the automobile trade from other branches of the metal industry. Daimler Motors, for example, was part of the Birmingham Small Arms group, munitions producers, and provided the automobile concern with managerial and engineering talent, as well as other technical knowledge. It also imposed strict rules of financial accountability. The general manager of Austin, J.F. Ingleback, gained his managerial and engineering skills at Armstrong's.[38] Such migration between the different branches of the metal industry indicated the existence of a well-established pool of professionally-trained managerial and engineering talent.

This interpretation can be supported by referring to two indices. First, the number of members of the Institute of Mechanical Engineers took off after 1897–98. In 1898 the total membership was 2,684. By 1913 it had more than doubled, reaching 6,346 members. What is interesting about this expansion in the ranks of the mechanical engineers is not just the fact that it happened, but that it also marked a major change in the composition of the Institute, as well as in its role in the engineering community. The number of full members, for example, remained fairly stable in the period 1898–1913, rising from 2,000 to 2,694. Full members were elected, had to be 25 years old or more and must have held for a 'sufficient period, a responsible position in connection with the practice or science of Engineering. . .' The Associate Members, by contrast, who

were younger engineers not yet occupying 'positions of sufficient responsibility' in industry to be eligible for full membership, grew from
approximately 500 in 1898 to 2,916 in 1913. The number of engineering
students, known as 'Graduates', also grew from about 150 to 675 during
this time. Graduates had to be 'persons holding subordinate positions'
and undergoing 'training in the principles as well as the practice of
Engineering', and be between the ages of eighteen and twenty-five. What
this change in the numbers and composition of the Institute meant was
that membership of a professional club was increasingly important to the
status of young engineers, even though they could not take up a full role
within the Institution's proceedings. For the Institution's part, the growth
in the membership of young engineers not holding leading positions in
industry enabled it to regulate the professional status of mechanical
engineers in general. The introduction of examinations as a condition of
eligibility for election to Associate Member or Graduate was built around
their equivalence to a degree or diploma in Mechanical Engineering,
offered at the main British universities in the case of Associate Members,
or to the science matriculation exams in the case of student members. The
overall status of the engineer, therefore, was not just reflected in their
formal degree training, but also in their membership of 'clubs', which
reflected and regulated their career lines from students through to full
engineers occupying leading positions in industry. Membership of the
other professional societies, such as the Iron and Steel Institute, the
Institute of Civil Engineers, and the Institution of Electrical Engineers,
had many of the same prestigious and regulatory overtones.[39] New
associations were also formed to regulate the growing specialisation
of engineering training such as the British Foundrymen's Association, the
Institute of Metals (1908), the Concrete Institute (1908), the Illuminating
Engineering Society (1909), the Institution of Railway Signal Engineers
(1912) and the Association of Supervising Electrical Engineers (1914).[40]

A second index of professionalisation was the growth of 'a new and
important field of engineering employment'—special business training for
engineers or scientific management. Managers who were both practical
engineers and also able to control and organise labour, undertake costing
and industrial accounting, plan the use of tools and machines, and organise
efficient production methods were always prized, if also at times resented,
as their skills did not traditionally 'fall within the scope of engineering
proper'.[41] However, by the early 1900s, recognition was beginning to be
given to the fact that engineers required special business training in order
to do their work effectively. From 1901 a number of universities and
university colleges began to draw up and offer courses in business, as in
Birmingham, Liverpool and Manchester. The number of courses expanded
in the post-war years, with universities in Durham, London, Reading and
the University Colleges of Northampton and Southampton also being

drawn in. In Birmingham the curriculum for a Bachelor of Commerce degree was drawn up in 1901-2, after long consultation with members of the Chamber of Commerce. Sir William Ashley, who was spoken about at the beginning of this work in regard to his qualitative conception of skill, was head of the Commerce Department at this time. He liaised with business leaders to set up the Department and develop the content of the courses. Similar ventures were started up at Cambridge in 1903 with the introduction of the undergraduate Economic Tripos, and at the London School of Economics several years before. The LSE, in fact, had been running courses since 1895 where 'training for business administration' was emphasised.[42] This pattern of noticeable business involvement in the establishment of such courses was generally followed by the other universities, though it should be noted that some firms were reluctant to go all the way and provide facilities for their staff to attend day courses, and encouraged evening attendance instead.[43]

It would be a mistake to assume that the traditional system of training future employers and managers by employer apprenticeships was completely overturned in these years. Rather it became an essential aspect of the engineers' practical training, complementing their higher education in much the form envisaged by the Institution of Civil Engineers. Many well-known engineering firms continued to offer 'premium' apprenticeships for their future managers. Middle and upper class youths often paid fees to an enterprise in order to be trained in its 'pupilage' system. These 'apprentices' may have received wages, but as often as not had to support themselves (or their fathers had to), throughout their two to five years training period. Some of the firms which continued to operate a pupilage system were Armstrong, Whitworth of Newcastle; W.H. Allen, Bedford; W.H. Bailey, Salford; Daimler Motor Co., Coventry; Fielding and Platt, Gloucester; General Electric, Birmingham; Alfred Herbert, Coventry; British Westinghouse, Manchester; Mather and Platt, Manchester; and Vickers, Son and Maxim, Erith, Kent.[44]

The state-run Royal Ordnance factories can provide us with a useful example here. When the factories came to reorganise the training of their managers and supervisors in 1905, they sought to combine strong shop experience with formal higher education. The story began in October 1902, when the Secretary of State for War set up an enquiry to investigate the training of managers and foremen in state ordnance plants. The committee came to the view that training should be divided into four main streams: for managers, assistant managers, shop managers, and supervisors. This 'upper-managerial staff' had to possess 'business capacity', 'commercial knowledge' and the 'widest possible technical and theoretical training', plus 'extensive practical knowledge' of the trades over which they were to 'exercise control'. The inclusion of supervisors within the category of upper managerial personnel was considered to be a new departure and associated with raising the standards of shop floor management. All the streams were to be based on the acquisition of an approved university education and three years' workshop training, which would be the equivalent of the Associate Member class at the Institution of Civil Engineers. As it would take some time before these reforms could filter through the managerial ranks, it was proposed that competent foremen who possessed a 'fair general education', elementary scientific knowledge, 'practical knowledge of all the branches of trade under [their] control', and a capacity to 'organise' and 'control the work of men' should be brought on to fill higher supervisory and managerial positions. They would become 'supervisors' and assist managers, assistant managers and shop managers, as well as undertake the three-year workshop course. Their pay would also increase to £150 per year, and would rise by £10 a year to a maximum of £250; no mean salary at the time.[45]

This form of training for supervisory and managerial positions irritated proletarian apprentices no end, as they could neither expect to benefit nor hope to obtain its privileges. As the recalcitrant worker, 'No Class', wrote to *Engineering* in March 1907:

> I know what 'premiums' are, and so does everybody who is not one. There are three sorts. The first find the shops are not clean and genteel, and so they go away and become bank clerks, after a few months of it; they do not matter much. The second sort are allowed to break all the rules they like, and have days off when they get a nasty job. Whenever they do try to do anything, it has to be made right by somebody else or scrapped. They are often rather good at football or cricket, and if they did not get all the best jobs, and make messes of them, the other apprentices would not mind them much. The third sort are the worst of all. They come from technical schools, and have eye-glasses and slide-rules. They wonder whenever engineers will appreciate science and use the metric system, till everyone is sick of them. If they would only shut up about science and learn how to file flat and tap a hole straight, it would be better. They think they are going to be great men some day, and do everything much more scientifically than is done now; but they will have to find out that they are born first. All they do now is grumble and spoil jobs, smash their fingers. . .[46]

What 'No Class' failed to realise, however, was that these young men were not being trained for a life of manual toil, as he was; and, if Professor Saul's information is correct, the attitude was mutual. American observers of the machine tool trade, for instance, believed that employers cared little for workers' attitudes or advice with regard to production methods and training. 'You are paid for working, not thinking', was the alleged reproof for any such 'help'.[47]

From a managerial point of view, then, engineering had become a 'profession' by 1913.[48] The metal industry's bourgeoisie were certainly not ill-educated amateurs with little sensitivity to the pulse of change occurring in their own factories and educational institutions or on the other side of the Atlantic. Though they professionalised themselves within the segmented world of exclusivist class cultures and maintained their connection with apprenticeships, this had less to do with any regressive 'peculiarities of the English' and more to do with their ability to synthesise the older internal factory-based structure of training with the newer extra-factory structure of higher education. In achieving this they successfully 'cocooned' the class basis of their increasingly professionalised production management.[49] By turning to developments within the workforce as a whole, some further features of this can be seen.

2. The changing characteristics of the workforce

By any measure the expansion of the British metal industry's workforce in the years between 1890 and 1914 was truly remarkable. According to the *Censuses of Population* for England and Wales undertaken in 1891 and 1911, those employed in the 'manufacture of metals, implements and conveyances' grew from 1,095,000 to 1,779,000, an increase of 62.5%.[50] Unfortunately, these figures do not allow for a breakdown of the people employed in the two main branches of the industry, iron and steel, and engineering,[51] but it can be noted that in the period 1891–1901, the metal industry had become the largest employer of industrial labour, overtaking the textile industry.[52] If we concentrate on the main branches of the metal industry, it will be seen from Table 4 that engineering proper was by far the largest employer in 1907, comprising some 461,700 workers, followed by the iron and steel trades, railway building and shipbuilding. These five branches alone accounted for 71.8% of persons employed in the twenty-three branches listed.

TABLE 4

The number of persons employed in the various branches of the British metal Industry, 1907

Branch	Persons employed (thousands)
Blast Furnace Rolling, Smelting and Founding	261.66
Wrought Iron and Steel Tube	20.22
Tinplate	20.63
Wire	18.32
Blacksmithing	20.89
Engineering	461.70
Railway Carriage	28.85
Motors and Cycles	54.04
Railway Works (of Railway Companies)	241.80
Needle, Fish hooks, etc.	13.25
Tools and Implements	23.71
Cutlery	14.83
Small Arms	4.85
Typewriters	6.50

TABLE 4 *(cont)*

Branch	Persons employed (thousands)
Shipbuilding	188.31
Hardware, Holloware and Bedsteeds	82.70
Anchor, Chain, Nail, Nut, Bolt, Screw and Rivet	28.02
Copper and Brass (Smelting, Rolling and Casting)	21.45
Other Non-Ferrous Metals (Rolling and Casting)	11.42
Finished Brass	38.92
Watch and Clockmaking	5.30
Jewellery, Gold, Silver and Electroplate	38.39
TOTAL	1605.76

Source:
Constructed from the *Third Census of Production,* Vol. 3, HMSO, London, 1933.

Several aspects of this expansion require attention, as they provide an essential context for assessing the development of new methods of training and the new compositions of skills: the concentration of the workforce into fewer enterprises and larger establishments; the growing importance of the Sheffield–Leeds or West Yorkshire region for the location and expansion of progressive metal enterprises; the position of women in the industry; and, finally, the investment boom in fixed capital which began in the late 1890s.

As far as the concentration of the workforce is concerned, Table 5 may be consulted. It is a survey of fifty-one metal enterprises listed in the top one hundred manufacturing concerns *by employment* during the period 1900–14.*

Eight groups can be seen, ranging from employment in the 'mixed' metal enterprises to those employed by the leading shipbuilding and marine engineering firms. The data covers only the very largest enterprises with 3,000 or more employees. Therefore, it is not a completely accurate profile of how concentrated the workforce was at this time. If this was to be done, we would need to know how many firms employed 1,000 or more personnel. Even so, these fifty-one firms alone employed more than 24% of the entire industry's workforce by 1907. This can be deduced by comparing the total workforce in the metal industry as given in Table 4 with the totals presented in Table 5. The figure is approximate, of course, for some 27% of the citations relate to employment levels after 1907; but it is a good indicator. When we come to study the concentration of the workforce in Germany, it will be seen that fifty-three firms employed

---

*I would like to thank Mrs Christine Shaw for making this data available to me. Only another historian can really appreciate the time-consuming chore such an endeavour requires. A full citing of Mrs Shaw's work may be found at the end of Table 5.

approximately 30% of the industry's workforce, and their numbers comprised many firms with 1,000 to 3,000 employees. In the fifty-one British firms, though, the average number of employees per enterprise was much larger than 3,000. In fact, they averaged approximately 7,672 employees per firm and 2,223 per plant or establishment. Many of these firms we are already familiar with in regard to the training of their management personnel. More of them will become familiar as we consider the training of their workforce.

If at least a quarter of the workforce were labouring in very large establishments, with the Singer Sewing Machine Co. and the Great Eastern Railway Co. leading the way, then the overall expansion of the metal industry was characterised by the growing dominance of the Sheffield-Leeds area, at least for the heavy iron and steel trade. Employment grew

TABLE 5

The number of people employed by fifty-one metal enterprises listed in the top one hundred firms by employment in the United Kingdom, 1900-14

Rank*	Year	Firm	No. of work-people employed	No. of establish-ments	Average No. of employees per establish-ment
*Group I—The Mixed Metal Enterprises** *					
1.(3)	1906	Sir W.G. Armstrong Whitworth & Co.	25,000	4	6,250
2.(4)	1907	Vickers, Sons & Maxim	22,500	8	2,812
3.(7)	1907	John Brown & Co.	16,205	3	5,402
4.(12)	1903	Guest, Keen & Nettlefolds	12,451	7	1,779
5.(26)	1907	G. Kynoch & Co.	8,000	11	727
6.(56)	1903	William Beardmore & Co.	4,500	2	2,250
7.(63)	1905	Hawthorn, Leslie & Co.	4,127	3	1,376
8.(75)	1910	Cammell, Laird & Co.	3,950	5	790
9.(77)	1903	Dick, Kerr & Co.	3,850	2	1,925
10.(84)	1911	Richardsons, Westgarth & Co.	3,500	3	1,167
		TOTALS GROUP I	104,083	48	2,168
Group II—The Iron and Steel Enterprises					
1.(15)	1910	Stewart & Lloyds	10,600	11	964
2.(39)	1907	Steel Company of Scotland	5,694	2	2,847
3.(40)	1910	Bolckow, Vaughan & Co.	5,487	6	914
4.(58)	1907	Dorman, Long & Co.	4,361	6	727
5.(70)	1905	Hadfield's Steel Foundry Co.	4,000	2	2,000
6.(93)	1903	John Lysaght	3,070	3	1,023
		TOTALS GROUP II	33,212	30	1,107

TABLE 5 *(Cont)*

Rank*	Year	Firm	No. of work-people employed	No. of establish-ments	Average No. of employees per establish-ment
Group III—The Mechanical Engineering Enterprises					
1.(14)	1907	Platt Brothers	10,708	5	2,142
2.(31)	1900	Singer Sewing Maching Co.	7,000	1	7,000
3.(41)	1910	Fairbairn, Lawson, Coombe, Barbour	5,050	3	1,683
4.(45)	1907	Howard & Bullough	5,000	1	5,000
5.(54)	1907	Dobson & Barlow	4,500	2	2,250
6.(60)	1907	John Hetherington	4,200	3	1,400
7.(69)	1907	Mather & Platt	4,000	1	4,000
8.(82)	1911	Richard Hornsby & Sons	3,500	2	1,750
9.(83)	1903	Marshall, Sons & Co.	3,500	2	1,750
10.(97)	1907	Asa Lees	3,000	1	3,000
11.(98)	1912	Tangyes	3,000	—	—
		TOTALS GROUP III	53,458	21	2,546
Group IV—The Electrical Engineering Enterprises					
1.(36)	1907	General Electric	6,000	6	1,000
2.(47)	1907	British Westinghouse Electrical Co.	5,000	1	5,000
3.(61)	1911	Siemens Brothers & Co.	4,150	3	1,383
		TOTALS GROUP IV	15,150	10	1,515
Group V—The Arms and Munitions Enterprises (Private and State)					
1.(2)	1907	Royal Dockyards	25,580	5	5,116
2.(8)	1907	Royal Ordnance Factories	15,651	5	3,130
3.(62)	1907	Birmingham Small Arms Co.	4,150	4	1,037
		TOTALS GROUP V	45,381	14	3,241
Group VI—The Railway Engineering Enterprises					
1.(6)	1913	Great Western Railway Co.	17,770	4	4,442
2.(9)	1907	Metropolitan Amalgamated Railway Carriage and Wagon Co.	13,868	6	2,311
3.(10)	1910	London and North Western Railway Co.	13,500	3	4,500
4.(17)	1900	North Eastern Railway Co.	10,000	7	1,429
5.(21)	1901	Midland Railway Co.	8,500	4	2,125
6.(25)	1907	North British Locomotive Co.	8,000	1	8,000
7.(29)	1907	Lancashire and Yorkshire Railway Co.	7,250	3	2,417
8.(32)	1914	Great Eastern Railway Co.	7,000	1	7,000

TABLE 5 *(Cont)*

Rank*	Year	Firm	No. of work-people employed	No. of establish-ments	Average No. of employees per establish-ment
Group VI—The Railway Engineering Enterprises (cont)					
9.(66)	1914	Great Northern Railway Co.	4,000	1	4,000
		TOTALS GROUP VI	89,888	30	2,996
Group VII—The Precision Instrument Engineering Enterprises					
1.(100)	1907	W. & T. Avery	3,000	1	3,000
		TOTALS GROUP VII	3,000	1	3,000
Group VIII—The Shipbuilding and Marine Engineering Enterprises					
1.(22)	1907	Harland & Wolff	8,500	2	4,250
2.(23)	1907	Workman, Clark & Co.	8,000	4	2,000
3.(27)	1908	Palmers' Shipbuilding & Iron Co.	7,500	7	1,071
4.(38)	1903	Fairfield Shipbuilding & Engineering Co.	6,000	1	6,000
5.(43)	1907	Scotts' Shipbuilding & Engineering Co.	5,000	1	5,000
6.(52)	1903	Swan, Hunter & Wigham Richardson	4,600	3	1,533
7.(68)	1907	Thames Ironworks, Ship-building & Engineering Co.	4,000	1	4,000
8.(86)	1913	North Eastern Marine Engineering Co.	3,500	3	1,167
		TOTALS GROUP VIII	47,100	22	2,141
TOTALS GROUPS I to VIII		51 Enterprises	391,272	176	2,223

Average number of employees per enterprise: 7,672

Source:
Derived and calculated from: Christine Shaw, 'One Hundred Large Firms of 1907', *Business History,* Vol. XXV, No. 1, March 1983, pp. 52-3.

* Numbers listed in brackets refer to the enterprise's position in the top one hundred firms engaged in manufacturing industry by employment.
** By 'mixed metal enterprises' I mean a company engaged in two or more activities listed in Groups II to VIII.

from some 24% of the workforce in 1907 to 30% by 1917 (see Table 6). Though other regions, such as the North East Coast, Wales and Scotland experienced increases in their workforces, the proportions of the national workforce that they employed either stagnated or, in the cases of the Midlands and the North West Coast, actually declined. After considering general developments in the training of the workforce we shall, therefore, turn to the situation in the Sheffield area because of its growing prominence in the industry.

The role of women in the heavy metal industry is important to consider for it remained so marginal until World War One. As Table 7 shows, though the number of females employed grew from 43,000 in 1891 to 101,000 in 1911, they worked mainly in the lighter sections of the industry: the cutlery and tool trades, typewriter making, the small ammunition trades, fuse and cartridge making, gun-engraving, gun-belt making and in the production of electrical appliances, such as telephones.[53] Where they made their entrance into the heavier sections of the industry, like automobiles and aircraft production, they were generally relegated to jobs requiring 'female' skills, like lining and upholstering, where they weaved and worked with a needle and thread.[54] In this sense, they bore more resemblance to textile and clothing workers than they did to metal workers. Of the explanations advanced to account for this, one put forward by Adelaide Anderson in 1918 cuts across the direction of this study. She argued, against the background of the widespread introduction of women into the engineering industry during the War that in the pre-war period women were excluded from the engineering and metal trades because of 'the demands made by these trades on great muscular strength and endurance. . . heavy work, special skill, and the extremes of heat and exposure'.[55] A similar interpretation has been advanced more recently by Charles More. He also argues that the war-time dilution of engineering work can be taken as evidence of the earlier commitment of engineering employers to a male workforce that required 'considerable' skills for production to be effectively undertaken.[56]

Another explanation, however, put forward by Barbara Drake for the Labour Research Department in 1917, emphasised that the *technical* possibilities for widespread female employment in the metal industry were already present in the pre-war period, especially in the engineering trades. The destruction of the millwright's craft by the mid-nineteenth century, the development of more intensive and less varied skills for fitters and turners etc., combined with the growth of intensively trained, skilled tool-setters, machine maintenance workers and managerial NCOs, like foremen and examiners, meant that little stood in the way of the widespread use of female 'machine-minders'. Certainly, the 'two-pence half-penny' and technically progressive mass-production trades, such as the typewriter, small ammunition, sewing-machine and telephone trades,

TABLE 6

Employment by region in the British iron and steel industry, 1907–1917

	North-East Coast	North-West Coast	Sheffield/Leeds	Midlands	Wales	Scotland	Total
1907	20,684	10,391	23,811	15,660	10,544	18,349	99,439
1912	20,986	10,206	26,038	14,743	13,699	19,738	105,410
1917	25,635	9,573	35,713	14,109	14,200	20,398	119,627
			By Percentage				
1907	21	10	24	16	11	18	100
1912	20	9	25	14	13	19	100
1917	21	8	30	12	12	17	100

Source:
Gerhard Brandt, *Gewerkschaftliche Interessenvertretung und sozialer Wandel. Eine soziologische Untersuchung über die Entwicklung der Gewerkschaften in der Britischen Eisen und Stahlindustrie, 1886–1917*, E.V.A., Frankfurt, 1975, Table 12, p. 50.

TABLE 7

The number of females employed in the various branches of the metal industry in England and Wales, 1891-1911

	1891	1901	1911
The total occupied in the manufacture of metals (not precious), machines, implements and conveyances etc.	43,000	56,000	101,000
Including:			
Iron and Steel (including Tubes)	–	–	1,000
Brass Founding and Finishing	–	–	6,000
Forging	–	–	2,000
Tinplate and Galvanised Sheet	–	–	3,000
Wire, Wire Netting, Wire Rope	1,000	2,000	3,000
Ironfounding, Engineering, Boilermaking and Shipbuilding	–	–	8,000
Electrical Appliances and Instruments	*	2,000	11,000
Vehicles	1,000	3,000	11,000
Cutlery and Tools (including Pins and Needles)	7,000	7,000	10,000

Source:
Censuses of Population, 1891, 1901, 1911, in Committee on Industry and Trade (Balfour Committee), *Survey of Industrial Relations,* pp. 424–5.

*   Less than fifty engaged.

highlighted this development. What stood in the way of their widespread introduction though was the well-organised ASE, which saw the prospect of its members being reduced to the status of those in the 'sweated trades'; trades where women earned less than half the men's rate and where the men themselves were sweated. Not to be underestimated either was this union's fear that females were a new source of 'blackleg' labour for the employers, as conflicts in the fuse and cartridge trades of Birmingham, Coventry and Newcastle during the pre-war years seemed to illustrate. For employers, females, whether girls or women, were as cheap and docile as boy labour; for 'skilled' engineering unionists, their absence of a trade monopoly, their less effective trade union organisation, the 'meantime' character of their work, and their desire just for 'pocket-money' meant that they were not only easily exploited, but also unable to be organised, let alone deserving of membership to the ASE. Hence, in Drake's view the issue was not so much the technical problem of employing women, but rather the ability of male engineering workers to prevent their managements from introducing females onto work that was already integrally diluted. Where the opposition was weak or eroded, as in Birmingham's and Coventry's munitions plants, female labour was introduced; where the opposition was strong and effective, as in Sheffield and the Woolwich Arsenal in the pre-war years, their introduction was prevented.[57] It is this explanation which bears a closer resemblance to the situation in the British heavy metal industry, as the following discussion hopefully shows, especially when considered in the context of the large investment boom in fixed capital at the turn of the century.

3. Capital consumption and the consumption of labour

The boom began in 1896 and did not fully exhaust itself until 1905, though it did include a short depression during 1902 and 1903. Firms filled up their order books with projects that would take some time to execute and refitted themselves with the latest machinery, tools and appliances. Ewart C. Amos, writing in a leading engineering journal, Fielden's Magazine, in August 1899, believed that the engineering industry 'has probably never been in such a prosperous condition as it is today'.[58] This state of affairs, of course, was not just limited to Britain. It was an international wave of expansion.

If we concentrate our attention on the Sheffield area some of the important contours of this boom can be drawn out. All the major firms attempted in various ways to raise and invest enormous amounts of capital for refitting and extension programmes. Vickers, for instance, during the five years 1898-1902 issued £950,000 worth of new shares at a premium and ploughed back £1.4 million from profits, so as to build new or extend old works at Sheffield, Barrow and Erith.[59] Between 1900 and 1905, John Brown and Company, which had shipyards and engineering works on the Clyde in Scotland and collieries and heavy metal plants in Sheffield and Rotherham, doubled its producing capacity. Large modern armour plate machine shops were built in Sheffield, and the machine tools installed were all electrically driven.[60] At Hadfield's Steel Foundry Co., a new works was constructed after 1897. The original works, known as the old Hecla Works, had been constructed in 1872 and was exclusively devoted to munitions work, such as the production of shells and projectiles. The newer East Hecla Works, by contrast, was designed to take advantage of the general engineering boom and to extend the company's activities. A modern foundry was established and considered to be one of the most extensive in the world. Occupying a space of six acres, it was equipped with modern appliances like electric overhead travelling cranes, pneumatic machinery and annealing furnaces. In the machine shops, the machine tools were modern and electrically driven, while the works as a whole was supplied with electric power from a central power station.

It was certainly not the case that only traditional arms producers, such as Vickers, John Brown and Hadfields took advantage of the boom to extend their activities into general engineering through expensive investment programmes. Traditional general engineering firms in Sheffield were also at the forefront of activity. Edgar Allen and Co., located in Tinsley and producers of everything from tramway equipment, conveyors, separators, crushing equipment and special steels for tools and dynamos, invested heavily in 1903 in order to acquire the modern general engineering works of Messrs Askram Bros. and Wilson Ltd., and the Yorkshire Steel and Engineering Works located in Sheffield. Messrs Davy Bros., involved in engineering and boiler work, completely remodelled their Park Iron Works during the years 1900–1905. All the machine tools were replaced by up-to-date models, which would be suitable for using high speed steel. Vertical and horizontal reversing rolling mill engines, forging presses and gas-fired metal mixers suitable for acid and basic steel production methods were introduced into the steel mills; while the boiler branch was completely rebuilt so as to take in the construction of big Lancashire boilers.

A final example of how general engineering firms invested heavily in new plant and equipment during these years can be taken from the experience of Samuel Osborn and Company's Clyde Steel and Iron Works. The Sheffield plants included the Wicker Works, the Rutland Works and the Brookhill Works. The company produced a variety of products ranging from crucible steel, forgings, railway and wagon springs, tools and files. At the beginning of the 1900s, the Brookhill Works were completely remodelled. New plant was put down embodying the latest American technologies for producing high-speed tool steel, twist drills and milling cutters. New hammers, gas-producing plant and electrically generated power were also laid in so as to expand file production.

As can be seen, the electrification of producing equipment was an important aspect of the Sheffield employers' investment strategies. This was also noted in the reports of Sheffield's factory inspector, Mr Arbuckle in 1909, especially with regard to the powering of rolling mill equipment and other machinery.[61] Sheffield, however, was neither alone in this matter nor in the investment boom. As far as the former is concerned, one historian estimates that by 1907 as much as a half of the machinery in use in the British engineering and shipbuilding trades was electrically driven, whereas in industry as a whole only perhaps one-ninth of machinery was electrically driven, though this did rise to approximately a quarter by 1912.[62] Metal producers were, then, investing heavily in modern equipment, which would both rid them of that clumsy and now inefficient labyrinth of steam-powered shafting that traditionally drove plant and equipment, and would generally allow them to reorganise workshop practice and production methods.

A clear appreciation of this general investment boom in fixed capital may be gained from data compiled by C. Feinstein. According to his series, capital formation on a gross basis in the UK peaked in 1903, as can be seen from Table 8. The figure of 11.1% registered in this year was the highest recorded for the period 1870–1936. After 1903, gross capital formation rapidly declined to 6.1% by 1912. Associated with this was a rise in the share of capital devoted to plant and equipment or producer goods, as may be seen in Table 9. As in America, this took place in the context of a declining share of capital devoted to non-residential construction, such as factories and warehouses. Though this shift in the composition of capital can be seen to have started in the 1880s, the process was greatly speeded up at the turn of the century, when the share of capital devoted to producer goods rose to approximately 47%. By 1913, it had risen even higher—to 55% of gross capital formation.[63] If producer durables were eating up an absolutely and relatively larger proportion of capital formation until 1903 and thereafter consolidated their relative position, then, the overwhelming proportion of this investment flowed into industry rather than agriculture. Unlike America or, as we shall see, Germany, agriculture's share of capital formation was negligible at this time. Though I have not been able to find comparable figures, it can be noted that in America as late as 1909, agricultural investment still accounted for 18.32% of gross national product, while in Britain this share was down to 6.3% by 1907.[64] A reflection of this was that in America investment in agricultural capital stock still accounted for between 22.8% and 25.5% of total capital stock in 1900. Again, I have not been able to discover strictly comparable figures for Britain at this time; however, by 1922 Britain's share of capital stock invested in agriculture was only 5.14%, while in the USA it was still running at approximately 18.6%.[65]

TABLE 8

Fixed capital cycles in the United Kingdom, 1900–1913.

(1) Gross capital formation as a proportion of gross national product; (2) capital consumption as a proportion of gross domestic fixed capital; (3) net fixed capital formation as a proportion of net national product; (4) capital consumption as a proportion of gross domestic product, 1900-1913

Year	(1) %	(2) %	(3) %	(4) %
1900	10.4	44.2	6.1	4.9
1901	10.4	43.0	6.2	4.7
1902	10.9	43.3	6.5	5.0
1903	11.1	43.2	6.6	5.1
1904	10.4	46.2	5.9	5.1
1905	9.8	49.5	5.2	5.2
1906	9.2	52.6	4.6	5.1
1907	7.7	61.1	3.1	5.0
1908	6.8	74.6	1.8	5.5
1909	6.8	73.3	1.9	5.4
1910	6.7	73.0	1.9	5.3
1911	6.3	77.3	1.5	5.2
1912	6.1	80.4	1.3	5.3
1913	6.6	72.6	1.8	5.2

Source:
C. Feinstein, *National Income, Expenditure and Output of the United Kingdom, 1856-1965,* CUP, Cambridge, 1972, Table 19, pp. T48-9, Table 5, pp. T15-16. (1900 constant prices.)

TABLE 9

Trends in the distribution of capital formation in the United Kingdom, 1856-1938

	Dwellings	*Other new buildings and works*	*Producer durables*
1856–1888	18.1	40.8	39.8
1865–1898	19.0	40.4	40.3
1875–1908	18.9	40.0	40.3
1879–1908	18.6	39.6	41.4
1889–1912	16.0	36.7	47.0
1899–1928	17.3	33.6	49.0
1909–1938	21.9	29.3	49.0

Source:
C. Feinstein, *National Income, Expenditure and Output of the United Kingdom, 1856-1965*, CUP, Cambridge, 1972, Table 90, pp. T88-90 (calculated). The figures are calculated in terms of 1900 and 1938 prices.

What this evidence suggests is that British industry, much more so than American, was able to take advantage of its already well-established infrastructure of roads, factories, buildings and agriculture, and devote a relatively much larger proportion of its investment capital to expanding and filling this infrastructure with increasingly elaborate machinery.[66] It just did not require either a relatively large share of its capital formation to be devoted to investment in order to actually build a capital goods industry, nor a high level of capital formation in order to make this sector effective. This was reflected in the relatively slow growth of overall capital stock since the 1870s. In the period 1876-1893, for example, this grew at 0.9% per annum and rose to 1.66% between the years 1894-1913. This latter figure, though, was quite substantial for it represented a cumulative growth in the nation's capital stock of approximately 33.2%.[67]

Another feature of this boom is very much comparable to the experience of America. It will be remembered that by the late 1890s investment in plant and machinery in the USA had peaked and moved rapidly into decline. In Britain, as we have seen, this decline in investment began in 1903. But common to both countries was a rapid rise in the rate of consumption of fixed capital. It will be seen from Table 8, column 2, that capital consumption as a proportion of gross domestic fixed capital rose rapidly after 1903, from approximately 43.2% to 80.4% in 1912. The graph in Diagram 1 very clearly shows this: as capital formation peaked on a gross and net basis (lines (1) and (3) respectively), the consumption of fixed capital, or the rate at which it was used up, began to rise—line (2), read off B axis. In fact, their movements mirrored each other: as capital formation moved into decline the consumption of capital rose; and when capital formation temporarily picked up, as it did unevenly in the period

1908-1913, capital consumption also unevenly declined. The key to understanding this diagram is line (4), which is tabulated in Table 8, column (4). Here it will be seen that in contrast to the inverted relationship between capital formation and capital consumption, the movement of capital consumption as a proportion of gross domestic product remained remarkably stable, oscillating between 4.7% of GDP in 1901 and 5.5% in 1908. In other words, the respective rise and fall in capital consumption and capital formation did not substantially affect the *relative* amount of capital consumed as a proportion of *how much was produced*. The conclusion to be drawn, therefore, is that as the composition of capital shifted from infrastructure to producer durables, the plant and machinery were beginning to be used up much more intensively, allowing for a rise in output irrespective of the fall in capital formation.

Certainly, the indices for industrial production bear out this hypothesis. Industrial output rose from 80.1 in 1900 to 100.0 in 1913, as Table 10 shows. Furthermore, the substantial growth in industrial output did not begin until 1903, which was the exact time when investment in plant and machinery reached its peak in these pre-war years. In terms of 1913 prices, investment in plant and machinery rose from approximately £32 million in 1895 to £64 million in 1903. Thereafter, it declined to £41 million by 1908 and unevenly rose to £53 million by 1913.[68] By turning to Table 11 we can return to see how the metal industry fitted into these developments.

TABLE 10

Indices of industrial production in the United Kingdom, 1900-1913. (1913 = 100)

Year	Indice
1900	80.1
1901	80.3
1902	81.7
1903	80.0
1904	81.0
1905	85.7
1906	89.3
1907	91.0
1908	83.7
1909	84.3
1910	85.5
1911	91.5
1912	93.0
1913	100.0

Source:
C. Feinstein, *National Income, Expenditure and Output of the United Kingdom, 1856-1965*, CUP, Cambridge, 1972, Table 51, p. T112.

Diagram 1: Fixed capital cycles in the United Kingdom, 1900–1913

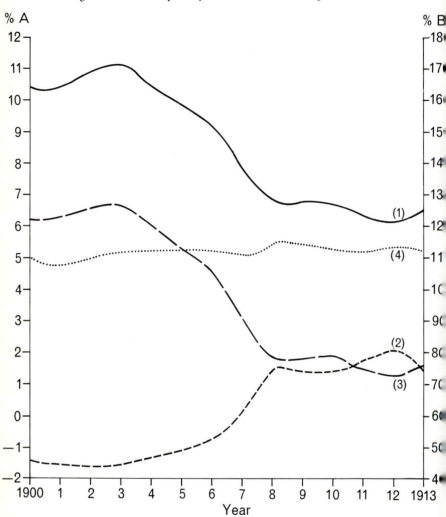

Source:
Calculated and graphed from C. Feinstein, *National Income, Expenditure and Output of the United Kingdom, 1856-1965*, CUP, Cambridge, 1972, Table 5, pp. T15-16, Table 19, pp. T48-9.

1. Gross capital formation as a proportion of gross national product.
2. Capital consumption as a proportion of gross domestic fixed capital.
3. Net fixed capital formation as a proportion of net national product.
4. Capital consumption as a proportion of gross domestic product.

In all the major branches of metal production output does not begin to grow until the very end of the investment boom in 1904. The situation in Sheffield also bears this out. According to Mitchell and Deane's figures, which cover the regions of Sheffield and West Yorkshire, the production of pig iron and ferro-alloys stagnated at levels between 247,000 and 263,000 tons during the years 1901-1904. These were the peak years of refitting and expansion for the Sheffield firms. After 1904, however, pig iron and ferro-alloys output climbed substantially: to 293,000 tons in 1905 and to 336,000 tons by 1906.[69] Enterprises were obviously beginning to gain some benefits from their previous investment strategy. Yet, if it were possible to imagine these production figures superimposed on Graph 1, we would see how closely related the pace of industrial production in the metal trades was to the increasing pace at which fixed capital was being consumed in the production process. It would also be possible to see that when output began to falter, as it did during 1908-1910, so too did the rate of fixed capital consumption begin to stagnate at rates of between 70% and 80% of gross domestic fixed capital formation.

TABLE 11

Output indices in the British metal industry, 1900-1913 (1913 = 100).

Year	Metal manufacture	Engineering and allied	Ferrous	Mechanical engineering	Vehicles
1900	80.4	67.0	75.3	69.5	—
1901	80.7	67.2	75.6	69.1	—
1902	77.4	66.0	74.0	67.4	—
1903	79.7	62.9	75.6	67.4	—
1904	77.8	65.6	74.5	67.3	—
1905	86.9	74.1	84.1	77.0	—
1906	93.8	81.5	91.0	84.9	—
1907	94.3	81.6	91.5	85.7	27.0
1908	82.2	66.0	78.0	72.0	24.0
1909	87.9	70.2	84.9	78.2	25.0
1910	93.3	69.3	90.0	72.8	32.0
1911	91.4	85.3	88.5	84.9	43.0
1912	89.2	86.3	86.8	86.8	50.0
1913	100.0	100.0	100.0	100.0	100.0

Source:
C. Feinstein, *National Income, Expenditure and Output of the United Kingdom, 1856-1965*, CUP, Cambridge, 1972, Tables 51-52, pp. T112, 114-15.

Though it has not been possible to obtain quantitative evidence on rates of capital consumption for a number of Sheffield firms, it is possible to show what occurred in practice. In the words of the two English engineers, Smith and Pickworth, referred to in the last chapter, it meant obtaining 'maximum effort from the operator' and keeping the machinery 'constantly producing a maximum output'.

The situation at Vickers' Sheffield plant in 1907, can be taken as an example. As has been shown, 1907 represented the peak of the output boom in metal production, which was not advanced upon until 1913 (see Table 11). This also was the year when the increasing consumption of fixed capital was in full swing (see Graph 1). The Vickers' plant at the time was working twenty-four hours a day, in two twelve-hour shifts—from 6 a.m. to 5 p.m. and from 5 p.m. to 6 a.m. The only breaks during each shift were half-hour pauses for breakfast and dinner. It does not appear that the company worked systematic overtime at this time, but this did not prevent one of the leading managers of the firm, William Marshall, in his testimony to the Royal Commission on the Poor Laws, from proclaiming that at the end of each shift a worker's 'physical powers are pretty well exhausted'.[70] With the smell of prestige in his nostrils, he told the commissioners: 'Certainly, we speed [production] . . . up as far as lathes, planing machines and other engineering tools are concerned'.[71] For Marshall, this represented nothing more than the fact that the standard of efficiency required from each worker was rising. For the workers, by contrast, speed-up meant ever more accidents and injuries in production, and growing pressure on the older workers who were weeded out if they could not stand the frantic pace. The factory was becoming less and less of a safe place to work. In comparison with the period 1887-1897, when the number of accidents requiring surgical attendance averaged 6.15% of the total number of men and boys employed, the period 1898-1906 witnessed a more than 100% increase. It was averaging 14.55%, and, as Table 12 shows, with every passing year the average number of accidents was increasing with the speed at which the machinery was being paced. One can only speculate what the injury rate was in 1907, during the peak year of capital consumption in the industry, but it is very interesting to note in passing that if this data could be graphed over the diagram on fixed capital cycles in the United Kingdom, they would bear a remarkable resemblance to the pattern of increasing capital consumption.

At the time, though, and perhaps only in public forums like the Poor Law Commission, managers such as Marshall put the increasing injury rate down to the effects of the new Workers' Compensation Act, which came onto the statute books during 1897. For employers in the metal industry especially, accidents at work could now be easily explained away because of their workers' too comfortable feeling of security if they ever lost a finger, arm or leg through their own 'negligence'. 'Compensation', rather than an intact body, was allegedly all workers thought about when they wilfully put their head or leg into a machine trying to keep pace with death.[72]

If the Compensation Act explained the rising injury rate at Vickers, then so too did it provide a rationalisation of why the company no longer

TABLE 12

Accident rates at the Vickers' plant, Sheffield, 1898–1906

Year	Number of accidents requiring surgical attendance	Average number of employees	Proportion of employees involved
1898	289	2,449	11.80
1899	470	3,292	14.27
1900	598	3,868	15.46
1901	650	4,612	14.09
1902	535	4,080	13.11
1903	387	3,204	12.08
1904	467	3,152	14.81
1905	637	3,805	16.74
1906	739	4,338	17.03

Source:
William Marshall's evidence to the *Royal Commission on the Poor Laws and Relief of Distress, Appendix Vol. VIII, Minutes of Evidence*, Cd. 5066, 1910, *Parliamentary Papers*, Vol. XLVIII, 1910, p. 452.

sought to 'burden' itself with workers reaching or having passed middle age. From the 'employer's point of view', Marshall told the Commissioners, the 'physical powers of the old men are less than those of the young men, and consequently their earning powers. . . are reduced. Employers are averse to start new men over middle age after other companies have had the benefit of the best years of their lives'.[73] Moreover, older men were more liable to accidents and had lower recouperative powers. Hence new men over middle age were not taken on at the plant. Hiring was concentrated on boys and men aged between twenty and forty.[74] As far as men past middle age who had worked at the plant all their lives were concerned, if they had not been struck down by injury then they were given lighter duties or pensioned off, though a pension was 'considered on its merits'. It was not a right. It was a gratuity.[75]

If, as in America, higher rates of labour and capital utilisation were inextricably related to falling capital formation and increasing output, it could be argued that as the metal industry had been a 'capital intensive' industry since the 1850s, then none of this was new or exceptional. Certainly, as Keith Burgess has shown for the engineering branch, the industry was capital intensive from the mid-nineteenth century.[76] From this time until the end of the century however, the metal industry was only learning to stand on its own feet, as it were. Only at the turn of the century did it develop a coherent strategy for *using up* this capital and labour force;[77] and an outstanding feature of this strategy was the new patterns of industrial training brought in to shore up the more intensive forms of labour and capital utilisation. We shall first consider the situation in general and then turn our attention back to Sheffield.

4. The factory: 'Apprenticeship is dead'

It will be remembered that the Engineering Employers' Federation still considered 60% of its workforce as skilled in 1914, so we should begin by examining what sort of skills these workers required at this time and what sort of instruction they received, first, from the point of view of their experience in the factory and, second, from their experience in the schools.

In their manual, *Principles of Apprenticeship Training,* published in 1916, A.P.M. Fleming and J.G. Pearce, the well-known popularisers of progressive management, argued that skilled workers in the engineering industry needed the following characteristics of mental and manual labour, in order to do their work effectively.

'1. Specific artisan characteristics.
2. Physical Fitness.
3. General Intelligence, the ability to 'see' things, i.e. Judgment.
4. Manual Dexterity.
5. Mechanical Instinct.
6. Delicacy of Touch.
7. Adaptability.
8. Cooperative Faculty.
9. Pride of Achievement.
10. Capacity for Spontaneous Attention.
11. Instinct for Appraising a Number of Conditions Conjointly.
12. Rapidity of Thought and Action.
13. Memory.
14. Capacity for Learning by Experience.
15. Observation.
16. Neatness.
17. Economical Working.
18. Miscellaneous.'[78]

Obviously skilled engineering workers needed everything, even that somewhat intangible capacity to be 'miscellaneous'. Charles More has put forward a similar litany of attributes required for a skilled turner. A 'considerable number of techniques' had to be 'master[ed]'. Eleven to be exact; and these ranged from 'knowledge of the drawing office and the machine tool store' to the use of planing machines and the manifold aspects of lathe work. In More's view, these constituted the 'average skill level' for the majority of workers in the industry.[79]

For the overwhelming majority, however, the reality was both more differentiated and degraded. In the view of the London County Council's 1909 'Report on the Apprenticeship Question':

At the present time, at the age of eighteen, after four years' course of employment, whose chief characteristics are the long hours, the lack of supervision, and
the total lack of any educational influence, the lad is a distinctly less valuable
article in the labour market than he was when he left school four years previously.
His only asset is represented by greater physical strength, accompanied probably
by a marked decrease in general health and vigour. He has lost the intelligence and
aptitude of the boy, and remains a clumsy and unintelligent man, fitted for
nothing but unskilled labour, and likely to become sooner or later one of the
unemployed.[80]

The employers' information and technical magazine, *Engineering,* also
held this opinion. The 'business' of training, it lamented in February 1907,
'has become so subdivided that it needs a good deal of shifting from
department to department to enable a general working knowledge to be
obtained; and when an apprentice has acquired sufficient skill to be useful
in one branch, or in one operation of one branch, the management, from
foreman upwards, do their best to keep him at this one operation. In fact,
apprenticeship is dead; employees are no longer taught a trade, they
simply learn an operation'. The boys, of course, would 'not mind' in the
least being under 'the orders of a foreman'; they would 'cheerfully hold
the candle and fetch tools for a fitter'; they would come in at six, and,
generally, 'be the fags of the whole establishment—as they may have been
at school—if they can but learn their business'.[81]

These general indictments of industrial training by the apprenticeship
system may be challenged on certain points, but their overall emphasis was
well placed. By the turn of the century the apprenticeship system was
effectively dead as a form of training in the skills allegedly required by a
modern engineering worker. What forms of 'apprenticeship' did exist
merely hid an entire world of useless training. R.H. Tawney, in his 1909
study of training in 100 engineering firms in Glasgow, was struck by the
specialisation of production which made the integral skills of the type
advocated by Fleming and Pearce no longer necessary for the majority
of engineering workers.

On entering the works the lad who is going to be a fitter goes straight to the
fitting shop and learns nothing else; a lad who is going to be a turner goes straight
to the machine shop and does not learn fitting.[82]

Moreover, in Glasgow's machine shops, youths were systematically kept
on a single machine, such as a drilling, milling, slotting, punching, screwing
or band-sawing machine after only a few days of training. For one leading
employer describing what occurred at his works: 'Boys are kept, as a rule,
in their own departments. They are not taught; they are made to work',[83]
and for one district secretary of the ASE in Glasgow, describing the
practice of one large firm, an engineering enterprise was now nothing more

than 'a reception home for young bakers and grocers'. Boys go to it from other occupations to do one small part of the machine. . . When they leave they are not competent engineers, and find it difficult to get work elsewhere.[84]

Such impressions cannot be dismissed as 'emotive' or 'non-rational', as Dr More believes they may. The observations were hardly made by 'scaremongers'.[85] Quite the contrary, a wide spectrum of opinion, comprising employers, engineers, workers and independent commentators were agreed that quite fundamental changes were occurring to the apprenticeship system. If the indentured apprenticeship of the craft sort was dead or obsolete then the main form of training was 'picking up a trade'. This meant that a boy entered a shop, and took his chance of learning the trade from watching and assisting the men around him. The employer, generally, was under no obligation to train the boy in all aspects of a trade, and the boy himself, in the view of one observer, acquired only a dexterity in the performance of one or two operations. Thus, 'however proficient he may become in that operation his general intelligence and skill suffer from a narrow and exclusive specialisation'.[86] This was the state of affairs at G. & J. Weir Ltd., Glasgow. The management considered the traditional apprenticeship system obsolete and no longer attuned to the new skills of accuracy and precision work required from engineering workers. Workers, therefore, entered the company as 'learners' and were 'instructed' and 'examined' in the particular *spécialité* they acquired.[87]

'Picking up a trade' generally took three forms and depended on what a firm expected from a worker and what skill requirements needed to be filled. These forms were factory promotion and migration for the semi-skilled and verbal agreements for the new skilled workers. By 1914, factory promotion took the form of a boy leaving school at the age of fourteen and entering a large works as an 'apprentice' or boy labourer. After a probationary period of floor-sweeping or fetching and carrying he would be promoted to working some of the simpler processes carried on in the factory. The boy then rose step by step receiving his instruction along the way.

There was little regular teaching in this method, as skills were acquired over short and disjointed periods of time. Spurred on by the opportunity of earning more money or bettering himself, the boy strove to get on a new process and 'pick up that'. The system was not just limited to boys. Adult labourers too, seeking better jobs and more money, sought promotion to semi-skilled vacancies as they occurred.[88] For Sir Benjamin Browne, who described the situation in the North East of England in his evidence to the Poor Law Commission during November 1907:

> In our trade, the semi-skilled man is the man who was on the floor, that is, a shop labourer. If he is any good at all, he is taken to a small machine, say a drilling

machine; then if he is any good at that, he goes to a planing machine, and so on to a slotting machine, and other things, but not to lathe work usually; planing, drilling, and slotting are generally worked by semi-skilled men who get higher and higher wages. . ., they get very good wages, not so good as the engineers, though better than the labourers get.[89]

Another form of the promotion system, a form more orientated to the maintenance of the formalities of a craft hierarchy, occurred in those branches of a trade reliant on gang work, for example in plumbing, smithing and boilermaking. Here, as with the glass workers of Carmaux, skilled mechanics and their assistants often formed their own self-contained squads, i.e. plumbers and their 'mates', smiths and their hammermen, and rivet boys with the boilermakers. Such squads would look for jobs together and a foreman would have to take on all of them if he was to take on any. In a boilermaker's squad, for instance, usually made up of five members—two riveters, one holder-up, and two boys (a heater and a carrier)—the riveters would drive in the rivets to boilers and ships' hulls brought to them by the boys, while the holder-up held the plates in position during the job. A rivet boy completed five years' continuous 'training' in this work before promotion was granted to a holder-up, and he could begin this training no later than the age of sixteen.[90] The difference between these two forms of training by promotion was, of course, who regulated them and not the intrinsic difficulties of learning a trade over a protracted period of time.

The method of migratory training was more common in those trades less reliant on the need to maintain a highly trained and geographically stable skilled workforce. The light electrical machinery trade with its extensive division of labour and specialisation of products was an example of this. Here the need was for competent semi-skilled machinists who had a history of working three or four machines. As in the promotion system a boy would start at fourteen and learn an easy machine, say a punch-press. Later he would move onto a drilling machine, a machine which required little skill. After about three years on this work he would be promoted to the status of an 'improver' at a wage rate of threepence half-penny per hour, and undertake more elaborate jobs. At the same time, he may apply for or be offered an 'improvership' elsewhere and take it. In this way the youth would pick up skills useful in several different firms. Dearle described this 'learning by moving' as a form of training which lay in an 'intermediate state between that of the beginner and that of the competent workman'. It carried 'the learner a further stage on his journey'. Yet, if this journey was to be completed, the youth would probably have to move to other firms and so gradually perfect himself'.[91]

Though indentured apprenticeships still remained common in pattern-making, smithing, to some extent in founding, and in boilerwork,[92] verbal agreements had become dominant in the main engineering branches where skilled workers were required, especially in fitting and turning. The verbal agreement, if strictly adhered to by an employer, was meant to ensure that an apprenticed youth received an all-round training in a specialised branch of the trade, if he maintained 'regular service'. The absence of formal articles of indentureship, though, meant that in slack periods boys could be sacked and those with little aptitude could be treated badly by an employer failing to train them in anything else but simple tasks. On the other hand, though employers in theory did not recognise any union rules about the number of apprentices that could be under the charge of a skilled tradesman, in practice they lived with the ASE's ruling that only one-third of the skilled workforce in a plant could be apprenticed labour.[93] We will describe below how this system operated at the Vickers plant in Sheffield, but for the moment we can take an example from optical and scientific instrument making, a trade renowned during the nineteenth century for the craft training of its skilled workforce.

In lens and instrument making the 'journeymen' were known as glass and metal workers respectively. The latter were divided into framers and turners, the equivalents of the more orthodox fitters and turners in the engineering machine shops. The trade combined a very high degree of skill in its workers with a very marked division of labour by the early twentieth century. Like the early nineteenth century Boulton and Watt Soho works, the labour was delicate, and the specialised skills acquired made it difficult for workers to take up more than one branch of the trade. Though the teaching was narrow and not supported by any legally binding or definite agreements as to what would be taught, it was thorough and easily lent itself to 'regular service' training. It was unusual for workers to migrate to other firms to broaden their training as firms were very strict that an apprentice must stay in his place of employ for at least three years.[94] The system certainly produced 'skilled' workers, but they were generally so specialised that they found it very difficult to transfer their skills to other enterprises.[95]

As with the promotion method, the verbal agreement had a proletarian version, especially in the shipbuilding industry. The shipwrights in the north and those working on the Thames and in the ship-repairing firms of London imposed seven-year apprenticeships on their trade, while the engineering and boilermaking sections had five-year apprenticeships. Yet as in the case of the rivet boys, unions were more interested that the verbal agreement be strung out as long as possible in order to restrict the labour supply, the educational value of which had more to do with imparting a quasi-religious belief in the status of the 'craft' while the apprentice lit fires, carried rivets, swept floors, did a little drawing, spent a year or two in a fitting shop and, if lucky, received some sympathetic advice from a fore-man or a skilled tradesman. If he was not so lucky, he would have to learn by his own observations and 'practice as best he could'.[96]

What both these examples show is that the traditional five years of training was no longer technically necessary for the future, 'average', skilled engineering worker, as Charles More argues. Where serving such an amount of time did continue to exist, it represented more the success with which workers could establish customary 'rights' of access to their trade, than employers bowing to the technical obstacles of training their workforce. It is stretching the historical imagination a bit too far for Dr More to contend that within the 'customary' five years of training, it was only by the third year that the apprentice became moderately productive, while the last two made him properly productive.[97] It is not just the above evidence that suggests a very different picture, it is also the fact that in Germany, as we shall see, a full learning period in engineering comprised only three years, even for the most skilled or hyper-qualified workers; and within the genuine meaning of the terms 'training' and 'productiveness', German engineering workers can hardly be considered badly trained, too quickly brought on, or less productive. More important- ly, though, as we shall see in a moment, employers were turning to three- year training programmes for their most 'qualified' employees, especially their foremen, who had a crucial role to play in the direction of the labour process.[98]

The degradation of formal plant-based apprenticeships as the method of training a skilled, specialised workforce and the generalisation of various picking-up systems was conditioned not just by an extension of managerial technical intelligence in the factory. Although enterprises were less dependent on formally imparting specialised skills and dexterities to their workforce in general, let alone reliant on the artisanal skills of a craft workforce, they were reliant on the existence of a stratum of well- qualified machine-setters, maintenance men, tool-makers, foremen and white-collar workers who had formally acquired an all-round technical knowledge of production methods. Yet it was not until 1902 that the state came to their rescue with the Education Act, which laid the basis for the establishment of day continuation, technical secondary schools and the extension of evening instruction.

5. *The School: 'Training up a higher class. . . for responsible positions'*
Before the passage of the Act, technical secondary education was largely private and voluntary. Since 1824, young apprentices could attend one of the Mechanics Institutes which by 1860 numbered some 750, to obtain formal instruction in the principles of their trade. About 300 of these Institutes were located in Yorkshire and Lancashire and one estimate put the number of students attending courses in these two counties at about 20,000 in 1860.[99] Part-time and evening instruction lay at the heart of the Mechanics Institute's structure. By 1879 the City and Guilds of

London Institute, in conjunction with the Science and Art Department, were extending this work by encouraging local classes throughout the country in technological subjects. Some employers, especially in railway engineering, also established or sponsored the creation of Mechanics Institutes. The Lancashire and Yorkshire Railway Works founded one in Horwich in 1887. The tuition was mainly given in the evenings and the subjects taught included the use of steam, applied mechanics, machine drawing and mathematics. Though the institute generally instructed pupils with a view to meeting the needs of the Railway Works, pupils from other firms could also attend by paying a slightly higher fee. Private schools like these, furthermore, could better assure their future if they linked themselves to local Boards of Education, especially in the matter of supervising their courses.[100] Yet no amount of private encouragement and tuition could provide the necessary sustenance to feed the growing need for formal and state-based extra-factory technical education. By the end of the century, the wide range of materials, tools, machine and production processes in use, combined with the increasing subdivision and specialisation of labour, meant that employers in the factory could no longer rely on their own technical intelligence for the creation, transmission and preservation of skills in the workforce. They could, of course, still breed the main grades of labour-power, generation after generation, by the industrial 'atmosphere' they created in their factories (fitters, turners, machinists, furnacemen, cranemen, lifters and carriers, etc.); but the new grades of skilled labour, the new *ouvriers d'art,* such as drawing room workers, examiners, testers, tool designers, materials analysts, machine-tool setters, maintenance men, electrical furnace workers, all required theoretical instruction in the principles of the new machines, materials and processes.

Some firms sought to solve this problem privately by phasing in 'new' apprenticeship programmes, which were generally much shorter and more intensive than the traditional trade apprenticeships. The system devised by the engineering firm Clayton and Shuttleworth of Lincoln can be taken as an example. The firm saw itself as grafting 'the advantages of the bygone system upon the so-called factory system of modern times'. This meant that both works' apprenticeships and newly formed works' schools had to be brought into a close relationship with one another. At Clayton and Shuttleworth, approximately fifty boys were selected to take on the firm's apprenticeship courses and be instructed in the company's school run by trained specialist teachers. Eight trades were taught comprising: (1) general machining and turning; (2) fitting and erecting; (3) toolmaking; (4) patternmaking; (5) joinery, wheelwrighting and woodworking; (6) moulding; (7) smiths' work; and (8) boilermaking. Apprentices were expected to remain in one branch for their entire training, but for periods of time they were also to be taken to the other branches to see the connections of their work with the larger production process and generally gain experience. The scheme was directed at 'training up a higher class of well-educated artisans', who 'by their efforts and natural ability. . . are likely to become fitted for responsible positions. . . in the higher branches of works management and administration'. It was also to be expected that many college graduates would apply to the firm so as to do their practical training in these courses.[101] Unlike America, however, this system of formal factory apprenticeship schools never became popular amongst metal enterprises. It was considered to be too expensive and called for the mobilisation of too many of a firm's material and intellectual resources. Only by the systematic provision of extra-factory higher education for these new grades of labour could management see itself underwriting its own necessary hyper-qualification and the dequalification of the traditional grades of labour-power. As Table 13 shows, technical and commercial education for those who were sixteen years or older had attained a widespread basis by 1913. In the academic year 1912–13, according to the Public Education statistics, there were 798,881 boys and girls, men and women attending either Senior Day Technical Schools or one of the evening technical colleges in England and Wales on a part-time basis. As can be seen, tuition in the various branches of metal manufacture were well provided for, with 14,958 classes in operation.

TABLE 13

The state of continuation, technical and commercial education in England and Wales, 1912-13, part-time, comprising evening instruction and Senior Day Technical Schools for those sixteen years and over

	1912–1913
Boys and Men	467,240
Girls and Women	331,641
Number of Classes in Engineering (all)	3,081
Number of Classes in Mathematics	10,785
Number of Classes in Electrical Production	785
Number of Classes in Metal Mining and Metallurgy	206
Number of Classes in Iron and Steel Manufacture	34
Number of Classes in Gas Engineering	67

Source:
Statistics of Public Education in England and Wales, Pt. 1, 1912-13, Cd. 7674, 1914, in Committee on Industry and Trade (Balfour Committee), *Industrial and Commercial Efficiency, Pt. 1*, pp. 175-6.

Several examples should be given of how this instruction operated at the grass roots, particularly in relation to the needs of the individual enterprise. As far as state enterprises are concerned, the Royal Arsenal at Woolwich, London, provides a useful example. Here, after 1905, apprenticeship was no longer allowed to be organised around picking-up systems in the works in order to bring on boys 'for the position of foremen or assistant foremen'.[102] Such methods were satisfactory for the traditional grades of skilled and semi-skilled labour, but for men who could potentially organise and direct all the operations conducted in their branch it was considered best to send them off to the Woolwich Polytechnic. There, through a combination of evening classes and one paid afternoon class per week, comprising in all no less than ten hours per week, they would undertake a three-year course and study workshop mathematics, drawing, elementary experimental science, mechanics, heat, magnetism and electricity. The second-year heat and electricity course can be taken as a good example of the technical intelligence they were being instructed into. The students studied 'combustion, production of heat, elementary thermodynamics, chemical action [and] —its effects in developing heat and electrical action, the general connection with currents of electricity, permanent magnets, [and] the basis of electrical measurements as applied to currents'.[103] The practical workshop course also lasted for three years, and the boy or young man was to be attached to a 'competent workman'. If great progress was shown the youth would then be given the opportunity to work in other departments under other trained men.[104] Under such circumstances the Woolwich Arsenal abolished all class teaching inside the plant.[105]

Similarly styled training schemes were also established during these years at the Great Western Railway Works in Swindon, at Andrew Barclay, Sons and Co., Kilmarnock, and Barr and Stroud. At Great Western, courses for future hyper-qualified employees were run in association with Swindon's Technical School, and also included courses for the company's clerks who studied modern business methods.[106] The Barclay firm had their boys under the supervision of the local school board, and similarly provided opportunities for their 'apprenticed' clerks to receive extra-factory instruction.[106] The system in operation at the British Westinghouse Company, though similar to these, had a distinctly American colouring owing to its lineages. In fact, it was a combination of American methods with British extra-factory training.

The scheme at Westinghouse was essentially three-tiered. A college course was organised for those over eighteen who had passed an intermediate examination for the Bachelor of Science degree, or had obtained an equivalent qualification such as a certificate of honours from the City and Guilds. The course was to last for three years. A school course was also offered for those who were fourteen or older and who had obtained certificates and a technical training equivalent to the second stage of the Science and Arts Department courses, particularly in magnetism and physics. Finally, there was the Trade Apprenticeship course, which adapted itself to the customary five to seven-year training periods insisted upon by unions for boys fourteen and over who would become skilled workers. Interestingly, *none* of these apprentices was taken through all the aspects of the theory and practice of their trade either in the works or outside throughout all the years of their training. Rather, they were confined to only one department, such as the machine shop manufacturing A.C. and continuous generators and motors or the transformer department. By contrast, the three-year college and school 'apprentices' were expected not only to gain knowledge and experience of all aspects of production in their section, but also further specialise in areas of their section that were common to several other sections of the works, especially pattern-making and founding. Trade apprentices were excluded from such general knowledge and were also not expected to participate in the several clubs and societies run by British Westinghouse for the benefit of the supervisory and technical employees. The company's billiard rooms, sports activities, reading-rooms and informal lectures on technical subjects were reserved for the exclusivist world of the *petite bourgeoisie* and higher management and sought to inspire an *alma mater* feeling among the staff.[107]

To a certain extent, however, British employers in the metal industry were anticipating by a good ten years American training methods, especially when it came to seeking the introduction of standardised programmes relevant to a number of firms in a region. In 1903, for instance, the Educational Committee of the North-East Coast Institute of Engineers and Shipbuilders sought to encourage member firms to accept its recommendations for the handling of apprentices, either as 'tradesmen' or as college and university-trained 'pupils'. This was a good ten years before the American National Association of Corporation Schools was founded to standardise company and public training for employees. For the 'pupils', the Institute wished to introduce three schemes: one for those who had completed a full-time engineering course at a university, had obtained their degrees and now needed practical experience in a management pupillage course, which would last for three years; another for those who wished to combine workshop training and college at the same time, where a six-year training period would be in order; and finally, a scheme for those 'exceptional' trade apprentices who could be brought into the combined workshop and college programme if they passed a relevant examination. By early 1908, two firms on the North East Coast, Swan, Hunter and Wigham Richardson, and Richardson's Westgarth and Co., had introduced such a programme of training at their Walker and Hartlepool works respectively. I have not been able, however, to find out how many other firms in the region had introduced such standardised training programmes by 1913.[108]

In any case, the force of this evidence suggests two conclusions at this time. First, firms were actively involved in public and private training programmes designed to bring on a stratum of employees who could undertake more stringent and scientifically-based supervisory duties. In this way, they sought to adapt to the new economics of fixed capital investment and to the need for a more intensive utilisation of labour-power in direct production. Second, against the background of these changes, it is difficult to substantiate the claims made either by historians or contemporaries like the London County Council that, 'continuing education in England still follows the plan of *laissez faire*, or go as you please'.[109] It is equally difficult to substantiate the claim made by Professor Hobsbawm concerning the 'feebleness of formal technological training' on the eve of World War One. Though the system continued to be voluntary and part-time, therefore drawing on the experience of the past, it did represent a serious and successful attempt to provide wide-spread middle and lower level technical instruction for the future skilled workforce. Looked at from an overall point of view, the training of both higher echelon managers and the new skilled employees also represented a concerted effort to integrate and develop the private and public dimensions of the capitalist regulation of skill required at the time. It should also be noted that the weaknesses detected by some British contemporaries and historians were seen as the system's overall strengths on the Continent. Where British observers and historians have lamented the voluntary, gruelling, part-time and socially polarised structures of the system, continental observers, such as the *Revue de Métallurgie,* out to reform its own system, spoke of the English system as theoretically the 'more perfect', requiring as it did that future engineers and managers periodically enter the mines and factories during their courses and that future skilled workers had no other option but to attend part-time day or evening classes. The *Revue* probably would not have been disconcerted to find out, as Pollard and Robertson are, that on the North-East Coast 'only about 20% of [shipbuilding and engineering apprentices] . . . passed any evening examinations' in the pre-war years or that 'In Sunderland in 1913-14 only 38% of the engineering apprentices and 12% of the shipbuilding apprentices attended evening classes'.[110] In the *Revue's* opinion, the great will and dedication required of students to undertake these courses successfully meant that 'elite' managers, employees and workers were being formed, while the mediocre were forced to fall by the wayside. In comparing their own system with the English, the *Revue* argued that in France practical training was only obtained after a student had left school or college and, therefore, the student did not profit as much as the English student did from the theoretical training received. The *Revue* was in fact in two minds about the 'relative superiority of these different methods', which in its view 'experience has not yet pronounced on'.[111] However, leading British engineers and industrialists were in little doubt about the issue. When Sir William White opened the Poplar Municipal School of Marine Engineering in London, in 1906, he emphasised to the assembled audience that this school was established in a working class district so as to bring up 'from the ranks' a few men of high scientific attainment and practical knowledge. Only a few were expected to be able to stand the 'strenuous application and much self denial' required and go onto feed the commissioned ranks of the Institution of Naval Architects.[112] Others saw voluntary attendance at technical schools and evening classes as necessary 'stepping stones to raise the better boys above the crowd', or as a means of 'enabling a few to raise themselves above the average [and] pass onto further advancement.'[113]

It can also be noted that if the commitment by Belgium in the pre-war period to this English method is anything to go by, then it would seem that the English system was not only popular, but also one of the most viable and successful models available at the time for the professional training of the workforce. Germany, as well, introduced part-time courses along English lines into her elite engineering schools during the post-war period.[114]

In his own research Charles More also attempts to show how firms encouraged formal technical instruction for the higher grades of labour power. However, his quantitative approach to skill and training leads him astray in his conclusions. He is certainly correct to suggest that 'there was undoubtedly a steady erosion of the manual skill needed by some groups of workers', but he is much in error, as we have seen in some detail, when he argues that 'there would seem to be a case for saying that the amount of knowledge and intelligence needed for *most groups* was increasing'.[115] The whole tenor and substance of the evidence presented here suggests quite the opposite. Knowledge and higher forms of training were not being ever more quantitatively dispersed in lumps throughout the workforce, rather they were, on the one hand, being specialised and fragmented, and, on the other, recomposed and subordinated to a managerial hierarchy inside and outside of the workplace. The creation of a new petty bourgeoisie who could coordinate these activities was an essential part of this process. A small stratum of hyper-qualified workers, such as tool makers, maintenance men and machine setters, also had to be brought on; but these cannot in any way be defined as 'most groups' of the workforce. This is not to suggest in the least that these new 'aristocrats' of the labour process were themselves not subjected to managerial hierarchies and a managerial division of labour, or that they were immune to conflicts with higher management. On the Clyde, for example, the growth of staff foremen tended to reduce the status of the under-foremen to little more than glorified charge hands. Many of these men felt little compunction about joining the ASE, as they watched their old 'empire' being subjected to a division of labour and capitalist regulation of skill: this time the regulation of skills and training involved in supervisory labour.[116] Yet, in no meaningful sense should the possibilities for discontent amongst this stratum be seen as a threat to an enterprise's overall regulation of training and skill. More so than workers, these NCOs and commissioned technical employees were dependent for their positions and status on the say-so of higher management. The very nature of their tasks and their access to such positions required daily subservience to the factory bourgeoisie and their instructions.

We again turn now to the situation in Sheffield.

6. Sheffield

Table 14 presents an overview of the main branches of the metal industry in Sheffield in 1901, and the number of males and females emloyed. As can be seen, the cutlery and scissor, engineering, and iron and steel branches accounted for over three-fifths of employment in the city's metal industry, with the light metal trade heading the list. The metal trades overall employed 54.4% of the city's workforce in 1901, with the cutlery and scissor trades employing 14.7%, the engineering trade 12.2%, and the iron and steel branch, 10.9%.[117] It will also be noticed that the heavy metal trades, iron and steel, engineering, and railway coach and wagon making were uniformly male occupations, whereas women played a much more important role in the lighter trades, accounting for some 21% of file makers, 14.4% of cutlers and scissors makers, and 34% of white-metal workers.

TABLE 14

The metal industry workforce in Sheffield, 1901

	Males	*Females*
	(Over 10 years)	*(Over 10 years)*
Iron and Steel	10,736	
Engineering and Machine Making	12,419	
File Makers	5,266	1,399
Saw Makers	1,173	125
Cutlers and Scissors Makers	14,436	2,423
Bolt, Nut, Rivet, Screw and Staple Makers	353	106
Stove, Grate, Range, Fire-Iron Makers	347	
Wire Drawers	840	
White Metal and Electro-Plate Ware	6,934	3,576
Iron Workers (undefined or indeterminable)	1,503	
Railway Coach and Wagon Makers	894	
Gold and Silver Smiths and Jewellers	1,479	113
Electrical Apparatus Makers	649	
Surgical Instrument Makers	254	62
TOTAL	57,283	7,804

Source:
Report of an Enquiry by the Board of Trade into Working Class Rents in the United Kingdom, 'Sheffield', Accounts and Papers, 46, 1906, CVII, Cd. 3864, pp. 408-9.

It would be an exaggeration to assume that the large role played by female labour in the lighter trades meant that 'dilution' or the decomposition and recomposition of skills was only taking place here. Though several employers in their evidence to the Royal Commission on the Poor Laws in 1907 considered the mass of employment in Sheffield's heavy metal industry as 'skilled' work, both branches were in fact undergoing major changes to methods of training and skill compositions.[118] In the Vickers' plant, for instance, where some 4,400 men and boys were employed in 1907, indentured apprenticeship had died out. In its place had come a private 'contract' or verbal agreement between the boy and the firm, but no legal responsibilities for either party flowed from this. In the absence of any female labour employed at the plant, boy labour played a large role.[119]

According to William Marshall, boys generally started as unskilled workers at the age of fourteen, and if they applied themselves they had the chance of having 'something useful' put into their hands, i.e., a semi-skilled job.[120] For the higher grades of boy labour, a more formal verbal agreement allowed a youth to be taken on at thirteen or fourteen for a seven-year period. Here the training was aimed at filling higher technical and skilled labour positions. The boys were encouraged to attend evening classes in order to complement their practical factory training. The classes were given at the technical school connected to the University of Sheffield and they were administered by the City Council. The theoretical courses given on metallurgical and engineering subjects, machine construction and drawing, etc. were considered a very effective method of training by the Vickers' managers.[121] One defect with this theoretical training, however, was that managers thought it would be better if boys remained at school longer before they entered the factory. Marshall suggested to the Poor Law Royal Commissioners that the school leaving age be raised so that boys could obtain a deeper technical instruction.[122] Implicit in this was the view that the technical, theoretical knowledge expected from young teenage boys was becoming quite demanding and if higher echelon managers and engineers were not entering the factory full-time until they were twenty-one, then the future technical and skilled workers should also have their full-time entrance to the factory postponed until they were better prepared to undertake practical training. In early 1905 a similar scheme was introduced into the Vickers' plant at Barrow, and, if anything, the programme was even more demanding. Apprentices from the engineering and ordnance departments were required to pass exams in algebra, geometry, reading, writing and arithmetic before they took up their training. The pupils were also advised to attend the local technical college, while for those who sought promotion to the drawing office, such attendance was compulsory.[123]

The only part of the plant where more traditional apprenticeships remained was in the foundry. Yet this was more a trade union variation of the 'picking-up' method. Foundry workers regulated the number of apprentices at $33\frac{1}{3}\%$ of the skilled men employed and insisted on seven to eight-year apprenticeships. There were no limits on the number of apprentices that the firm could take on in the other parts of the plant. At the same time, the Vickers' management loudly applauded that this did not lead to any ill-treatment of their apprentices or to sackings once they were qualified and therefore more expensive. Apparently apprentices stayed with the firm after finishing their training, often for their entire working lives. As a rule the Vickers' management relied on generation after generation of their apprentices coming from families which stayed with the firm.[124]

In the years spanning the turn of the century and World War One, Sheffield's light trades were undergoing changes similar in character to that which heavy industry experienced after 1850: the degradation of formal apprenticeship, the introduction of the principles of manufacture into a factory-based division of labour and the creation of an industrial reserve army based on the capitalist regulation of skill. A number of observers bore witness to the collapse of legal and corporately regulated apprenticeships, in place of which came large numbers of boys and females working 'informally' under another workman, known as a 'little master'.[125] Historically, apprenticeships had been regulated by home-working journeymen, especially in the metal smithing, grinding and cutlery trades. Generally, seven-year indentureships were required and in the normal course of events followed an hereditary succession from father to son.[126] The quality of a trade's products, like cutlery, was regulated by an association of 'middlemen' who bought the journeyman's product and increasingly provided him with a place of work (a 'tenement'), some machines, and tools, the costs of which were deducted from the journeyman's price; in this case, by the members of the Master Cutlers' Association.[127] In the scissors section of the cutlery trade (which also comprised pen-knives, pocket or jacket knives, razors and table cutlery), Sheffield maintained an internationally pre-eminent position until the mid-1870s. It was a period when scissors were hand-forged from a rod of steel. Output was therefore limited to the amount of work that could be done by hand-forgers working in a cooperative manner. Following the introduction in Germany of casting scissors and then a stamping press which cut them out, scissors were cheapened dramatically and Sheffield producers found their trade under threat, especially in the colonies. The middlemen sought to reduce the journeymen's prices and introduce the new techniques of production.[128] These pressures on the journeymen's position brought about a two-fold response. In the first instance, their position as sub-contractors forced them to dilute the work of their 'underlings' and introduce sweating as a way of maintaining, if not improving, their profits.[129] In the table-cutlery section, for example, a section subject to the same pressures as the scissors branch, an all-round handicraft cutler with an order for six dozen table knives found he could better maintain his position if he did all the difficult operations himself, specialising in them, and if his underlings specialised in the more simple operations, such as boring handles and polishing.[130] In this situation, even if a boy was an apprentice it generally meant that his master would keep him on one or two operations for the entire period of his training. In Albert Hobson's view, it was in the contractor's 'interest not to give him an all-round training'.[131] This situation deteriorated even further as the light trades fell into German hands and became subject to increased competitive pressures. At the turn of the century traditional middlemen like Alfred Beckett and Sons built up large factories. Beckett's Brooklyn Works produced steel saws, machine knives, hammers and shears. The management not only maintained the principle of deductions for *their* workers' use of power, such as gas and a working space, but also appropriated the benefits of journeymen's manufacturing division of labour.[132] As Albert Hobson observed, the larger manufacturing employers continued to train boys and young men 'imperfectly'. They also swelled the ranks of the reserve army of labour by introducing girls and women to the work. Apprenticed boys working for cheap wages, no matter how 'ill-trained', had a tendency to grow up and demand a journeyman's wage and act in an 'independent' manner. From an employer's point of view:

> . . . a girl who is polishing a handle can in six months, be nearly as good at that work as a man will be when he has served his apprenticeship, and is worth £2 a week, and as to polishing handles [the employer] may as well get somebody at, say 7s. a week to do that work. . .[133]

In this situation, he continued, 'badly trained men swell the numbers of unemployed, whenever trade is not at its very best'.[134]

A second response from these increasingly proletarianised journeymen flowed more directly from the decomposition of their skills and the introduction of female labour. This was to restrict the supply of labour by the introduction of formal trade union regulations on apprenticeship training.[135] In the early 1900s, grinders attempted to enforce a rule that a tradesman could not take on an apprentice until he himself was twenty-eight years old and the apprentice was the son of a grinder.[136] The Britannia-Metal Smiths went even further. Not only were apprenticeships restricted to the sons of journeymen (in this case the journeyman had to be twenty-five years old to take one on), but no journeyman could have more than one apprentice at any one time. In the case of partnerships, the number of apprentices was one for each partner; and for limited companies, one for every ten men, two for every eleven to twenty-five men, and thereafter, one boy for every fifteen men. In 1892, the union attempted to strengthen this rule by suspending apprenticeships altogether for a period of five years, which was renewed again in 1897 for a further five years.[137]

These attempts to regulate industrial training from an anachronistic craft-base did little to prevent employers from enlarging their labour supply. The combination of factory and home-based production in the light trades meant that trade union organisations remained fragmented and exclusive restrictions redundant. Moreover, the gradual transition from handicraft to machine methods of production continued to widen the ambit of the reserve army of labour.[138]

File making was a classical example of this. Already by the late nineteenth century it was a trade carried on in both the home and the factory. Married women working at home played a large role in this trade due to the fineness of their work and their accumulated dexterity, not to say the cheapness of their labour-power.[139] As was noted above, females accounted for 21% of the workforce in this trade by 1901. With the introduction of new forging and grinding processes, as well as cutting machines, the position of qualified male hand-workers continued to deteriorate. They were gradually replaced by machinists whose work was not recognised by the traditional forgers and grinders. File cutters, too, because they were less organised, could do even less in the face of the introduction of new machining processes. In any case, the trade as a whole was opened to non-union and unrecognised labour on a widespread basis. With the passing of over eighty years an historian can not afford to mock cynically the hand-forgers of Sheffield who carried their guild restrictions to the dole queue, while the machine cutters formed their own broadly-based union in 1897.[140] For the likes of hand-forgers and others the situation was anything but funny. Councillor Holmshaw, President of the Sheffield Trades Council and a Member of the Distress Committee, in his evidence to the Poor Laws Royal Commission, described the effects of the bad years of 1903–5. It was a time of government cut-backs for munitions and military equipment, as well as of a cyclical downturn in trade.

Light metal employers were forced to rationalise production and mechanise work processes to cut costs, with the effect that:

> Machinery has displaced men. . . everywhere; this is especially noticeable in the file trade, also in the forging of blades for knives, scissors, and razors.[141]

The plight of traditionally skilled workers in the light trades did not exhaust the problem of rising unemployment or the threat of it. Mr Thomas Shaw, J.P., Vice-Chairman of the Sheffield Distress Committee, when explaining the situation in the metal trades as a whole, claimed:

I think it can be very clearly shown that the improvements in machinery and their substitution for hand labour has much to do with the large number of men who are to be found unemployed. It reduces and in some cases destroys the market value of the special skilled workmen and enables the owner of the machine to acquire wealth very rapidly.[142]

William Marshall spoke of the developing surplus of unskilled labour in Sheffield, which was increasingly threatened by industrial and technical change.[143] In his evidence, Marshall was ambiguous, perhaps intentionally so, about whether the unskilled were being wiped out by technical change and replaced by specialised semi-skilled workers, or whether the ranks of the unskilled were being swelled by the more intensive methods of training and the new skill compositions. Most observers, however, were clearly struck by the ease and readiness of heavy metal industry employers to throw their workers temporarily and regularly out of work as trade fluctuated, with little fear that these displaced workers and their skills would be easily replaced once trade improved. This was particularly seen to be the case in the iron and steel branch.[144]

It certainly appears to be the case, then, that all the major branches of Sheffield's metal industry, heavy and light, were developing permanent surplus labour populations. Whether this was caused by changes to industrial training methods and new skill compositions resulting from either the more intensive role of fixed capital in the heavy trades or the more conventional uses of sub-contracting and specialisation in the lighter trades, the sum effect appears to have been a quite widespread de-qualification of proletarian labour. Neither the newer emphasis given to public technical education nor the more traditional emphasis on the private regulation of skill and training can be seen as generating a *uniform* tendency where the working class 'moved up from the bottom all along the line'. The 'congested surplus of unemployed non-skilled labour' did not disappear. When the Sheffield cutler, Charles Hobson, in his role as secretary of the British Section of the International Metalworkers' Federation, made these claims about the social advantages of technical education in 1915, he was speaking about what had allegedly happened on the Continent. If he was correct one could expect that it would have happened in Britain as well. Yet his judgment was far too simplistic. It is not so much that Britain was in this respect different or unique. As we shall see, Hobson's claims did not apply to the Continent either. Rather, the very structure of technical education and training was itself very differentiated, diverse in its effects and socially polarised in its origins. Hobson was certainly correct when he detected that the new methods of training had produced a 'well-employed and numerous set of skilled workmen. . . busy at work' at the top of the non-managerial workforce. Yet they comprised a new stratum of highly specialised *ouvriers d'art* whose skills were at the apex of a pyramid which descended and extended its way down *via* the other well-crafted and easily reproducible blocks of specialised skills and dexterities. As an ensemble, it was a pyramid of work designed, constructed and directed by the new architects and stone-masons versed in the exclusive skills of a professional-managerial technical intelligence.[145]

The non-managerial workforce in the British iron and steel trade had long been modelled on this pyramid in both its older and more modern branches. In the tinplate branch, renowned during the pre-war years for its inability to mechanise production methods, a boy started as a 'cold roll', 'list' or grease boy and was later promoted to the mill or tin house. In the mill, promotion was from behinder to furnaceman and then to doubler and rollerman, and finally shearer, who was also generally the foreman. As one historian of the industry has noted, 'Workers learnt their next job by watching those with whom they were working and then by practice'.[146] Unions in the industry sought to regulate this promotion system as best they could by insisting that job progression be determined by seniority and length of service. The unions went so far as to oppose all forms of apprenticeship, except for maintenance men. Apprentices, they believed, offered an employer too much of an opportunity to debase wages, as they could be paid lower rates than non-apprenticed youths and men doing the same work. Apprentices, also, generally gained quicker promotion once they were qualified, thus threatening the positions of more senior men who had already 'mastered' higher skilled processes. Finally, apprentices could be easily sacked in bad times and therefore were considered a destabilising influence on job security.[147] Union regula-ted progression, on the other hand, offered all workers an equal opportunity to gain higher positions in a job hierarchy composed of highly specialised and fragmented skills. Hence, if a worker transferred from one plant to another he would not be able to obtain the position that he had at his former plant. He would have to start again at the bottom and 'progress' in the same way as the others.

In the more mechanised steel smelting branch, a similar method of progression was in operation by the pre-war years. Of the three grades of smelters who had charge of a Bessemer or open-hearth furnace, each had varying degrees of responsibility for the production process. When a vacancy occurred at the third or lowest level, then one of the 'charge-wheeling' men who brought to the furnace heavy loads of pig iron and scrap, etc. for charging would be offered the vacancy on the basis of seniority. Vacancies at the higher levels were filled by smelters occupying positions directly below. If workers in the factory were not available to fill a position, then it would be filled by an unemployed man who had the necessary seniority; and if all this failed then the employer himself could select a man to fill the position.[148] Lower grades of labour in the steel mills were equally involved in the system of job progression. Plant labourers who lifted and carried heavy weights like pig iron around the plant in Sheffield's steel mills acquired an 'extra skill' which would enable them to gain promotion and higher wages, especially if it was in connection with furnace work, the uses of cranes, motive machinery or auxiliary equipment.[149] In contrast, then, to the many workers in the engineering and light metal trades who felt extremely threatened by the new methods of training and more fragmented skill compositions, the workers in the iron and steel branch quickly and readily adapted to the realities of both the capitalist regulation of skill and the professionalisation of production management. They also successfully and formally counter-regulated if not the skills of work then at least promotion within the hierarchy, which workers in other branches of the industry could only sometimes achieve after prolonged and bitter skirmishes with their employers.

7. *Technology and skill*

The pioneer of free-wheeling competitive capitalism, therefore, was certainly no laggardly lay-about at the beginning of this century. The British metal industry in its own way did seek to adapt, and adapt successfully, the existing institutions of industrial training to the new needs of the industry. Bound by an exclusive and highly segmented class structure, the training of leading managers and engineers was structured by modern forms of factory and university education. Part-time day and evening courses at technical institutes and colleges provided the basis for bringing on the rank and file engineers, technicians and supervisory personnel; while, for the mass of workers, training was becoming both more specialised and dequalified by the extension of essentially factory-based picking-up methods of training. The upgrading of management's technical intelligence against the background of a rapid expansion of the workforce, increasing concentration and more intense work-rhythms did, however, require that a new stratum of highly qualified workers be brought on to maintain, design and set machinery. Sheffield's heavy metal industry was probably the exemplary representative of all this, though it was by no means alone. But, if all this added up to a widespread recomposition of training and skills used in production, and to a growing displacement of instruction from the factory to the school, then for both an older and younger generation of historians all this is either completely inexplicable or has remained unseen. The problem is even more apparent when it is suggested that these changes are in fact and substance comparable to developments taking place in America at this time.

For historians firmly committed to the belief that only with the extensive application of technically integrated, American, mass-production techniques could any of these changes to skill compositions and training come about, all this must seem impossible. However, even within the alleged confines of the less mass-production orientated technologies evolving in the British metal industry, it was possible to bring about a recomposition of the skills of the workforce and how people learned to work. Charles More's views, which have been closely observed in the course of this chapter, can again be highlighted here. It will be remembered that in the case of the engineering industry More believed, like a number of other historians, that because of the varied nature of the output of the branch and its heterogeneous markets, all-round production methods were required.[150] The term *general engineering* is perhaps a good working definition of the character of the industry here, as it draws attention to the commitment of enterprises to maintain *flexibility* both in the area of their techniques of production and in their markets. This obvious character of the industry is not in doubt. What can be doubted, however, is the leap of imagination required to make the next proposition that, as a result of the many and varied markets and production processes, the industry tended to be 'skill maximizing', in the sense that all-round, trained, skilled workers were required to use the all-round production processes.[151] In other words, there were technical and market obstacles to a major recomposition of skills in the workforce, the proof of which is to be found in the legacy of the 1897–98 lock-out in the engineering industry: for though employers won the right to place whomsoever they liked on any job, this could not be done in practice given the nature of the technologies in use and the varied products being made.[152] There is no need to go over the 1897–98 dispute again and haggle about whether trade union obstacles were more important than technical ones in determining who could work a particular machine. What must be considered instead is the underlying character of general technologies, how they evolved and how they were organised.

To my knowledge, such a task has never been undertaken by an historian for this period. My own research, however, has begun to reveal that the underlying impulse of technical change in the engineering industry was to break down general or 'standard' machine tools, such as lathes, into their individual components or 'cells', so that they could be composed and recomposed into either specialised or multi-purpose machines: in the former case, vertical, radial and horizontal milling machines, boring machines, and drills; and, in the latter case, 'universal machines' which could undertake several consecutive functions semi-automatically, such as multi-purpose turret lathes that could tap, stock, drill, bore and face; and other machines which could saw, mill, plane and finish. These were machines no longer defined by their fixed place or general function, as the more traditional lathes and planing machines were. They were *multi-purpose mechanisms* and their use allowed for a *decomposition* or simplification of the *mental and manual faculties applied in direct production.*[153]

In the first instance, the need for skilled attendance at a machine was greatly reduced, especially in the area of setting a machine. No longer was it necessary constantly to set and reset a machine for every operation, and no longer was it necessary for many workers to undertake such tasks. This was made possible by the extended use of jigs, stops, templates and gauges, especially on multi-purpose machine-tools like turret lathes, where the movement of the various tools either in succession or broken sequence was made possible by a wide use of stops, which increasingly automated an entire work process. Each tool was limited and arrested by a stopper, as a result of which the machine could function with little attention from an operative. In the turret instead of one stop doing duty for all tools, which involved the careful resetting of every tool in relation to the stopper, each tool now had its own independent stop adjusted to accommodate the tool. Such changes made a number of traditional machine-shop skills redundant. As one correspondent for the *Engineering Review* wrote in 1911, though a skilled worker previously did have to work to within one to two thousandths of an inch, this was done by trial and error, involving the fine (but indeterminate) use of a file, rule and shifting caliper. With the new methods these instruments were discarded for precision-fixed calipers, i.e. plugs and rings, gauges and micrometers. Though in both old and new methods, sight and touch were used by the worker, in the latter method the ultimate standard was not the worker's judgment of divisions on a rule, but rather the *precise dimensions crystallised in pre-given gauges, jigs, rings and fixtures, etc.*[154]

As far as more specialised tools were concerned, these were so designed as to take over an activity from the general tools of the same class, which would later make possible a further decomposition of the special tools themselves. Gear-cutting machines were an excellent example of this dual process of specialisation. Firstly, they appropriated many functions from the less specialised milling machine. In turn, these functions were further decomposed and then embodied in separate machines: for example, machines which could only produce either spur wheels, bevels, worms, or worm wheels.[155] The milling machine, which had previously usurped a number of functions from general lathes and planers, also found a number of its activities being decomposed and newly composed in various sorts of grinding machines.

All these changes allowed for an increasing systematisation of workshop knowledge and its centralisation in a managerial hierarchy. Furthermore, the standards of works organisation and production techniques could become both more *flexible* and *precise*. Thus, whether a firm was wholly committed to the specialised mass production of one or two products and another to producing large numbers of varied products, both could benefit. Moreover, this underlying principle of the decomposition of machinery and skill into their elementary forms affected all sectors of the labour process to varying degrees, and this made their impact on the entire engineering industry potentially wide ranging. A discussion of diagram 2 will show this quite clearly.

Diagram 2. The Principal Labour Processes of Engineering Production 1890–1914

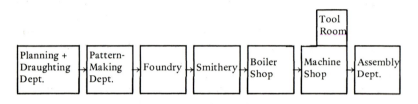

The diagram shows the principal labour processes of engineering and the direction in which they moved, from the planning department and draughting room through to assembling. The planning department and draughting room increasingly became the 'brains' of an enterprise, fixing nearly every detail and dimension of the production, as well as the processes to be used *before* being sent out for manufacture. It was the site of exclusively mental labour, centralising and accumulating knowledge from other departments. In the pattern-making, founding and smithing departments, manual skill remained very important, but it was increasingly prefigured by managerial knowledge of design and metallurgy, which allowed for the possibility of management-set standards of work, rather than rules and standards set by workers. Where possible, manual skill was decomposed, as in pattern-making with the introduction of metal patterns, and in founding with the introduction of mechanical rammers and forgers, and in the smithery with die forging. In the machine shop the process of technical specialisation and the recomposition of manual and mental labour went furthest. The introduction of specialised and multi-purpose ('universal') machine tools, as well as developments in transmission and motive machinery was reflected in the elemental decomposition and recomposition of skills, increasingly crystallised in machinery or hived off to workers in other departments, as in the tool room. Rules of scientific accuracy, precipitated by accumulating knowledge of the operation of the individual components of machinery, found their way into the hands of management. Where older manual skills remained, or even if given over to new groups of machine shop workers, such as machine setters, this was on the basis of increasingly pre-given management rules and standards.

These changes gave general-purpose engineering a new meaning. All the advantages of serial and repetitive production were potentially, at least, the same advantages of a multi-product enterprise using specialised and multi-purpose equipment. This is not to argue, as one historian has, that there was any 'convergence' of industrial processes and technologies, i.e. 'common processes'.[156] All that was common between serial and general-purpose engineering were the *technical elements* and *industrial components* on which both came to be based. To be sure, by 1900 'there existed an extensive accumulation of technological and engineering experience in the production of machine tools and a highly developed sophistication in designing and adapting basic types of machine tools for special production purposes'.[157] However, general-purpose engineering independently developed this in a novel manner. Staying clear of the limitations of flow production and maintaining its traditional flexibility, a general-purpose engineering firm could absorb the basic impulses of specialised innovation and 'be able to thrive' on them.[158]

Two other technical innovations also advanced the cause of general engineering. The first was the adoption of the American traveller crane. Able to move freely up and down a workshop by being connected to a 'bridge' spanning both sides of the shop, operated by hand or levers it could carry heavy items or hot metals. Its main significance was that it brought work to the labourer, rather than *vice versa* and tended both to extend and intensify the production line, subordinating it to the direction and rhythms of ever more interlocking machinery.[159]

However, the greatest handicap to the extension of an organised system of specialised and multi-purpose machinery was the problem of motive power. Steam or gas engines had been, since the middle of the nineteenth century, the prime movers that drove the labyrinth-line system of belts, pulleys and shafting that in turn drove the machine tools. Where the work was dispersed and desynchronised, or where machines had to run at different speeds to do different jobs, which was very common in engineering practice, the amount of shafting, belts and pulleys increased almost *ad infinitum*.[160] Furthermore, the farther a job was away from the source of power, the weaker and slower was the belt speed, with consequent effects on the rate of production.[161] At the same time, some detached tools could not be conveniently placed to be driven from main line shafts.

The introduction of electrically powered motors rapidly overcame this problem, freeing the machine and the tool, as one historian has suggestively argued, 'from the bondage of place'.[162] Though at first very expensive, the use of electricity as a source of motive power gradually did away with the long lines of shafting, pulleys and belts which lined the ceilings, floors and walls of engineering enterprises. Even if only used to complement the weaknesses of the traditional system, the use of electricity enabled the concentration of formerly dispersed sources of power in one place under one roof. Auxiliary machinery was therefore reduced and the wasteful use of steam coming through the long lines of piping was cut down.[163] It

also intensified the process of mechanisation by extending the use of
mechanical lifting appliances such as cranes, formerly held in check by
the obstacle course of shafting and pulleys, and by allowing machine tools
to be brought to the job at hand, rather than *unnecessarily* compelling
the job to be brought to the machine tools.[164] Finally, by fitting an
electric motor to a machine tool, it was possible to obtain a more flexible
determination of the rates at which individual tools and machines could be
driven—a situation not possible under the inflexible dictatorship of the
long shaft.[165] As was noted in 1898, 'belting made each tool, down to
the smallest, a fixed and immovable unit to which all work had to be
brought. . . electricity will restore to these smaller tools their portability,
so that the tool may be brought to the work, and not the work to the
tool'.[166]

The changes wrought to transmission and power machinery formed
the basis for a new and more intensive organisation of the space and
time of the machine shop. Overall, the production line, as an organised
system of interlocking machinery, was temporally more unified and
interdependent, even though the individual components of the line were
physically more independent. Feeds and gearing were now embodied in
machine tools rather than external to them. Electrical motors were fitted
separately to each machine, so that each element of the line, though more
independent, could be decomposed and recomposed into different 'lines'
by a mere reshuffling of elements. Finally, the interdependence of the
whole line was held together by the travelling crane, which spatially
linked one machine to another at different points of the shop. In a
temporal and physical sense, therefore, an enterprise could interlock,
interchange, compose and recompose machinery, skills, industrial processes and production lines.

How far these potentialities became realities in the British engineering
industry may be judged against our description of the investment boom
in Sheffield during the late 1890s and early 1900s. Both the mass-
production armaments manufacturers, like Vickers, John Brown and
Hadfield's, and the more general engineering firms, such as Edgar Allen and
Samuel Osborne, took the opportunity to lay in modern machine tools,
travelling cranes, pneumatic machinery, semi-automatic reversing rolling
mill engines, new hammers and presses, as well as to remodel and electrify
their works. The Mather and Platt works in Manchester may be taken as
another example. The Old Salford Works, which produced textile
machinery, could not in the early 1900s sustain a major extension and
modernisation programme once electric power became available. The
storied nature of the factory, with the machines ranked in solid banks by
their particular function, and the interminable lines of shafting, meant that
a new plant was necessary. The new Park plant, which was in operation by
1913, by contrast, transformed all this. This plant also produced textile

machinery, as well as an array of motors, pipes, and brass and iron castings. Though there was no 'flow' production, the plant had many interlocking features. The power house was situated between the machine shops and the foundry. There were no stories except in the plating and paint shops. All the rest were single storey. Electrification meant that power arrangements were very flexible, making it unnecessary to concentrate machinery together, and therefore able to be composed and recomposed around the work if that was necessary. Each shop was served by powerful electric cranes and hand-motivated hydraulic cranes. The shops were illuminated by filament lamps and the energy for the entire works was supplied by the Manchester Corporation Electric Supply.[167]

In no way can Mather and Platt's be considered a specialised firm based on mass production techniques. Yet, like its general engineering counterparts in Sheffield, the firm was able to take full advantage of the boom years and the technical innovations present at that time. It will also be seen that all these innovations were perfectly compatible with British engineering's commitment to varied products and heterogeneous markets. In fact, it was more than likely the case that the more precise and flexible production arrangements became the more competitively these markets were supplied.

As far as qualitative changes to skill compositions are concerned, these innovations, in conjunction with the new patterns of industrial training, tended to extend and intensify the technical intelligence of management, while at the same time deepen the specialisation and dequalification of labour. Even where manual and mental skills were recomposed for hyperqualified workers, as they were in the tool room and in the maintenance of machinery, or remained largely intact, as in pattern-making, founding and smithing, these faculties were ever more prefigured by managerial knowledge and training programmes. All workers now could be better trained, checked, paced and subjected to closer surveillance.

Only once does Charles More address himself to these consequences of technical innovation and new training methods in the engineering industry, and that is at the very end of his story. Unintentionally, however, he is forced to undermine his entire thesis. For, after writing so much on the 'considerable' and 'genuine' skills of skilled workers, he is driven to admit that they were not 'significantly better off' than the 'unskilled or semiskilled. . . in terms of control over aspects of working life such as hours, [the] pace of work and working regulations'. They could not exercise control over their work as the 'old-fashioned craftsman' could.[168] So much for skilled workers holding a dominant position in the division of labour. However, the very reference to the 'pace of work and working regulations' is indicative of the problems an exclusively quantitative approach to skill is bound to come up against, deluding both the researcher and the reader as to what are the real and qualitative dimensions of the capitalist regulation of skill.

NOTES

1. Charlotte Erickson, *British Industrialists: Steel and Hosiery, 1850-1950*, Table 2, p. 12.
2. *ibid.*, pp. 37–8.
3. A.P.M. Fleming and R.W. Bailey, *Engineering as a Profession: scope, training and opportunities for advancement*, John Long, London, 1913, p. 13.
4. *ibid.*, pp. 272–4. For a discussion of similar criticisms made during the 1870s and 1880s, see Michael Sanderson, *The Universities and British Industry, 1850-1970*, Routledge and Kegan Paul, London, 1972, pp. 14–18.
5. See M. Sanderson, *The Universities and British Industries, 1850-1970*, pp. 18-19. Sanderson's citing of critics of British chemical and metallurgical science relates explicitly to the 1870s and 1880s, and, therefore, one should be careful not to carry these criticisms forward to the 1900s where they may not apply.
6. F.G. Burton, *The Commercial Management of Engineering Works*, Second Edition, The Scientific Publishing Company, Manchester, 1905, pp. 52–4.
7. *ibid.*, pp. 52–4.
8. *ibid.*, pp. 52–4.
9. See *Cassier's Magazine*, Vol. IX, No. 5, March 1896, p. 473.
10. See 'Report of a Committee Appointed by the Institution of Civil Engineers on November 24, 1903, adopted on April 24, 1906', in *Journal of the Iron and Steel Institute*, Pt. 1, 1906, pp. 262–8. See also 'Education and Training of Engineers', *Engineering*, Vol. LXXXI, April 27, 1906, pp. 556–7, and 'The Technical Training of Engineers', *Engineering*, Vol. LXXXI, May 4, 1906, pp. 587–8, and also 'Education and Training of Engineers', *The Engineer*, Vol. 101-2, April 27, 1906, pp. 421–2, 425.
11. See M. Appleyard, in *The Times*, 5 June, 1907.
12. See J. Carr and W. Taplin, *A History of the British Steel Industry*, pp. 132–5, 220–2.
13. Clive Trebilcock, ' "Spin-off" in British Economic History: Armaments and Industry, 1760-1914', *Economic History Review*, Second Series, Vol. 22, No. 3, December 1969, pp. 481, 483, 487.
14. See F.W. Harbord and E.F. Low, 'British Iron and Steel Industry', in *Empire Mining and Metallurgical Congress, 3-6 June, 1924*, Cleveland House, London, 1925, p. 187, and 'Visits to Works, Sheffield', *Journal of the Iron and Steel Institute*, Pt. II, 1905, p. 460. See also M. Sanderson, *The Universities and British Industry, 1850-1970*, pp. 88–9.
15. See Committee on Industry and Trade (Balfour Committee), *Industrial and Commercial Efficiency*, Vol. I, HMSO, London, 1927, p. 180 ff. For a general discussion of the role of the laboratory in the university and in industry, see Professor Betrem Hopkinson (University of Cambridge), 'The Organisation of Technical Laboratories in the Universities', *Engineering*, 7 July, 1911, p. 40.
16. See Sanderson, *The Universities and British Industry, 1850-1970*, pp. 21–2.
17. See Clive Trebilcock, ' "Spin-off" in British Economic History: Armaments and Industry, 1760-1914', *loc. cit.*, p. 481.
18. Michael Sanderson, ed., *The Universities in the Nineteenth Century*, Routledge and Kegan Paul, London, 1975, p. 11.
19. See 'The Control of Technical Education', *Engineering*, Vol. LXXXI, 9 March 1906, pp. 314–16.
20. *ibid.*, pp. 314–16.

21. See 'Science and Manufacturing Industry', *Engineering,* Vol. LXXXI, 16 March 1906, p. 347.
22. See Fleming and Bailey, *op. cit.,* pp. 36-93; see also M. Sanderson, *The Universities and British Industry,* Chs. 2, 4, esp. pp. 43-4, 61-70, and also by the same author, *The Universities in the Nineteenth Century,* pp. 11-12. For a description of the creation of a Technological High School in South Kensington, London, see 'The Application of Science to Industry', *Engineering,* Vol. LXXXI, 9 February 1906, pp. 189-90.
23. *Statistics of Public Education in England and Wales, Part 1, 1912-13,* Cd. 7674, HMSO, London, 1914, quoted in Committee on Industry and Trade (Balfour Committee), *Industrial and Commercial Efficiency,* Vol. 1, pp. 174-6.
24. Fleming and Bailey, *op. cit.,* pp. 117-18.
25. See 'Technical Education', being a report of the meeting of the Association of Technical Institutions, *Engineering,* Vol. LXXXI, 2 February 1906, p. 157.
26. N.J. Maclean, B.Sc., Works Manager, Barr and Stroud, Glasgow, Letter to the Editor, *Engineering,* Vol. LXIII, 14 June 1907, p. 772.
27. See 'The Training of Engineering Apprentices—No. VI', *The Engineer,* Vol. 105-6, March 20, 1908, p. 286.
28. 'Technical Education', *Engineering,* Vol. LXXXI, 2 February 1906, p. 158. (My emphasis, C. McG.)
29. See M. Sanderson, *The Universities and British Industry,* p. 113, and by the same author, *The Universities in the Nineteenth Century,* pp. 14-15.
30. See M. Sanderson, *The Universities and British Industry,* pp. 22-3.
31. *ibid.,* p. 13.
32. Fleming and Bailey, *op. cit.,* pp. 36-93. See also W. Bardill, 'The Education of the Commercial Engineer', *The Engineer,* Vol. 101-2, March 16, 1906.
33. Committee on Industry and Trade (Balfour Committee), *Industrial and Commercial Efficiency,* Vol. 1, p. 180.
34. *ibid.,* pp. 192-3.
35. See for example, W.J. Reader, *Professional Men: The Rise of the Professional Classes in Nineteenth-Century England,* Weidenfeld and Nicolson, London, 1966, Ch. 7 and esp. p. 196.
36. S.B. Saul, 'The Motor Industry in Britain to 1914', *Business History,* Vol. V, No. 1, December 1962, pp. 27 ff, 41-3. Michael Sanderson blemishes his own valuable study by reproducing this opinion. See *The Universities and British Industry,* p. 25.
37. See Wayne Lewchuck, *The Economics of Technical Change: A Case Study of the British Motor Industry, 1896-1932,* Ph.D., Cambridge University, 1982, pp. 227 ff, 235, 237, 242, 244.
38. See Clive Trebilcock, ' "Spin-off" in British Economic History: Armaments and Industry, 1760-1914', *loc. cit.,* pp. 488, 489.
39. For the figures on the membership of the Institution of Mechanical Engineers, see 'Annual Report of the Council', *Institution of Mechanical Engineers, Proceedings,* Pts. 1-2, 1899, p. 6, and Pts. 1-2, 1914, p. 99. The conditions of elections to Member, Associate Member and Graduate before the introduction of examinations may be found in 'By-Laws, Last Revision, February 1894', in *ibid.,* Pts. 1-2, 1898, pp. xix-xxiii. For details of the examinations introduced in 1913, see 'By-Laws, Last Revision, February 13, 1913', *ibid.,* pp. xix-xxxii. It does not appear to be possible to determine the membership of the Institute of Civil Engineers and the Iron and Steel Institute from their *Proceedings.* The Institution of Electrical Engineers, by contrast, published total membership figures from 1905. In the year 1904, the Institution had 5,410 members and by 1913 this had grown to 7,084 members, an increase of 23.6%. See 'Report of

the Council', *The Institution of Electrical Engineers,* Vol. XXXV, 1905, p. 545 and Vol. 52, 1914, p. 632.

40. See for further details, W.H.G. Armytage, *A Social History of Engineering,* Faber and Faber, London, 1976, pp. 246-7.

41. See Fleming and Bailey, *op. cit.,* p. 278.

42. See W.A.S. Hewins, *The Apologia of an Imperialist,* document 74 in Michael Sanderson, ed., *The Universities in the Nineteenth Century,* pp. 201-2; and by the same author, *The Universities of British Industry,* Ch. 7, esp. p. 190 ff. Roy Hay's, 'The British Business Community, Social Insurance and the German Example', in W.J. Mommsen, ed., *The Emergence of the Welfare State in Britain and Germany,* Croom Helm, London, 1981, pp. 107-32, should also be consulted for further information on the Birmingham situation and Ashley's activities. See especially p. 115 ff.

43. See W.G. Cass, 'Training in Industrial Administration', *Cassier's Magazine,* Vol. LIV, No. 2, August 1918, pp. 97-102, and Committee on Industry and Trade (Balfour Committee), *Industrial and Commercial Efficiency,* Vol. 1, p. 233 ff. See also M. Sanderson, *The Universities and British Industry,* pp. 197 and 205 ff.

44. See Fleming and Bailey, *op. cit.,* pp. 101-9. For a description of the W.H. Allen scheme see *The Engineer,* Vol. 105-106, February 28, 1908, pp. 222-3. See also M. Sanderson, *The Universities and British Industry,* p. 14.

45. See *The Engineer,* Vol. 99-100, March 31, 1905, p. 326.

46. See Letters to the Editor, *Engineering,* Vol. LXXXIII, 15 March 1907, p. 347.

47. S.B. Saul, 'The American Impact on British Industry', *Business History,* Vol. III, No. 1, December 1960, p. 28.

48. See Dr W. Cathorne Unwin, Vice-President of the Institution of Mechanical Engineers, speech on the 'Alteration of By-Laws', in *Institution of Mechanical Engineers, Proceedings,* 1913, Pts. 1-2, p. 168. See also Donald A. Metheson, President of the Institution of Civil Engineers and Engineer in Chief at the Caledonian Railway Company, 'The Training of Civil Engineers', being a speech to the Glasgow Association of Students of the Institution of Civil Engineers, 20 December 1905, in *The Engineer,* Vol. 99-100, December 22, 1905, p. 515.

49. According to Pollard and Robertson, the professionalisation of production management and the growing exclusivism associated with this can be detected in the shipbuilding industry as well by 1914. Though the industry was dependent on scientific developments and technical innovations made in other trades, such as steel making, and electrical and general engineering, it required university and other higher education for its potential naval architects and engineers at such places as the Royal Naval College, Greenwich, and the Armstrong College, in Newcastle. The barriers to apprentices from working-class families making it to the ranks of engineering or naval architecture were formidable. Evening classes were their only hope and even here a youth faced the gruelling prospect of having to work eleven hours a day before going to school in the evening. Full-time education during the day was only available for the well-to-do, though by 1914, a number of firms had begun to introduce 'sandwich' courses. See Sidney Pollard and Paul Robertson, *The British Shipbuilding Industry, 1870-1914,* pp. 140-8.

50. See Committee on Industry and Trade (Balfour Committee), *Survey of Industrial Relations,* HMSO, London, 1926, pp. 416-17. Until 1901, the census figures excluded those occupations in a branch which were common to all industries, such as maintenance staff, clerks, carmen, etc., but after this they were included in the census for the particular branch.

51. The breakdown of the figures for those employed in the various branches of

the industry was undertaken only for England and Wales. We have to rely on the various *Censuses of Production* in order to obtain information on the employment composition of the industry for the entire country.

52. In the census period 1891-1901, the workforce in the textile industry fell from 1,253,000 to 1,169,000, while those engaged in the 'manufacture of metals, implements and conveyances' grew from 1,095,000 to 1,447,000. See Committee on Industry and Trade (Balfour Committee), *Survey of Industrial Relations,* pp. 416-17.

53. See Barbara Drake, *Women in the Engineering Trades,* pp. 11-13, and Adelaide Anderson's article in S.J. Chapman, ed., *Labour and Capital After the War,* John Murray, London, 1918, p. 73. Drake calculated that for Britain as a whole (including Scotland), the number of females engaged in the engineering and allied trades rose from 58,000 in 1891 to 170,000 in July 1914, a rate of growth twice that of male employment in the engineering industry. See Drake, *op. cit.,* p. 8.

54. Anderson, *loc. cit.,* 1918, p. 74.

55. *ibid.,* p. 74.

56. Charles More, *Skill and the English Working Class,* Preface and Ch. 1. See also Lewchuck, *op. cit.,* p. 51.

57. Drake, *op. cit.,* pp. 11-13. It should be noted also that where male engineering workers had no vested interest or craft heritage to defend, as those organised in the Workers' Union and the National Union of General Workers, there was little opposition to the recruitment of women. Women themselves, however, preferred to be organised in the National Federation of Women Workers, especially in the volatile munitions trade. See *ibid.,* pp. 11-13.

58. Ewart C. Amos,'Machine Tools', *Fielden's Magazine,* Vol. 1, No. 1, August, 1899, p. 74.

59. See Carr and Taplin, *op. cit.,* p. 270.

60. This evidence and all the following relating to Sheffield is derived from a very wide span of sources and it would be clumsy to cite them all individually in many footnotes. I will, therefore, list some of them here. See *Iron and Coal Trades Review,* Vol. LXXXI, No. 1961, 1905; *Ironmonger,* Vol. CXII, September 30, 1905; *The Engineer,* Vol. C, October 13, 1905, pp. 356-7; *Engineering,* Vol. LXXX, Nos. 2074-2075, September 29 and October 6, 1905, pp. 402-7, 453-4; *Page's Weekly,* Vol. VII, Nos. 55-56, September 29, 1905, pp. 679-96, 709-12; *Stahl und Eisen,* Vol. XXV, Nos. 20-21, 1905. See also the September through October, 1905, issues of the *Sheffield and Rotherham Independent, Sheffield Daily Telegraph,* and the *Yorkshire Post.*

61. See *Annual Report of the Chief Inspector of Factories and Workshops,* 1909, *Parliamentary Papers,* Vol. XXVIII, Cd. 5191, 1910, p. 57.

62. See I.C. Byatt, 'Electrical Products', in D.H. Aldcroft, ed., *The Development of British Industry and Foreign Competition, 1875-1914,* George Allen and Unwin, London, 1968, p. 243.

63. C. Feinstein, *National Income, Expenditure and Output of the United Kingdom, 1856-1965,* CUP, Cambridge, 1972, Table 90, pp. T88-90 (calculated).

64. In terms of net domestic product, agriculture accounted for only 6%. See B.R. Mitchell, *European Historical Statistics, 1750-1970,* Macmillan, London, 1975, p. 799 ff.

65. See Simon Kuznets, *Capital in the American Economy,* pp. 198-9; Feinstein, *op. cit.,* Table 44, p. T98 (calculated); and W.P. Kennedy, *Economic Growth and Structural Change in the United Kingdom, 1870-1914,* Tables 2a and 2b, pp. 18-21.

66. Kuznets, in his *Capital in the American Economy,* makes many of these same

points in regard to the American economy during the nineteenth century, and I have adapted his ideas to the British economy. See especially pp. 133 ff and 257-8.

67. See Feinstein, *op. cit.,* Table 43, pp. T96-7.

68. *ibid.,* Table 90, pp. T88-9.

69. See B.R. Mitchell and P. Deane, *Abstract of British Historical Statistics,* CUP, Cambridge, 1962, pp. 132-3.

70. See *Royal Commission on the Poor Laws and Relief of Distress, Appendix Vol. VIII, Minutes of Evidence,* Cd. 5066, 1910, *Parliamentary Papers,* Vol. XLVIII, 1910, p. 456.

71. *ibid.,* p. 453.

72. *ibid.,* pp. 451-2.

73. *ibid.,* p. 452.

74. *ibid.,* p. 457.

75. *ibid.,* p. 452.

76. See Keith Burgess, 'Technological Change and the 1852 Lock-Out', *International Review of Social History,* 1979, Pt. 2, p. 227.

77. Even the much lamented tinplate branch of the iron and steel trades adapted itself to this situation. It too underwent a major investment boom during the pre-war years, with the number of mills rising from 396 in 1905 to 550 by 1914, though, as the historian of the industry has found, 'all these works were small and in no case was there technical integration with the preceding processes'. In any case, firms were successful in not only expanding their activities into new fields, such as the canning and petrol industry, they also modernised their mills and intensified labour accordingly. In 1892 unions had been forced to give up their restriction on output to 36 boxes of tinplate per shift and output was forced up to an average of 750 boxes per week by 1913. By 1913 also the unions were forced to concede the introduction of the American 'helper' system, which allowed for the use of relay teams to keep production going at all times. As well, women and girls were making their way in numbers to the mills and could be seen lifting and carrying 60 to 70-pound weights for a pittance of a wage, most no older than sixteen or eighteen years of age. See W. Minchinton, *The British Tinplate Industry, A History,* Clarendon Press, Oxford, 1956, pp. 82-3, 133-4.

78. A.P.M. Fleming and J.G. Pearce, *Principles of Apprenticeship Training: with special reference to the Engineering Industry,* pp. 28-34.

79. See More, *op. cit.,* pp. 140-1.

80. See London County Council, *Report on the Apprenticeship Question, Minutes of the Education Committee of the London County Council,* February 24, 1909, p. 424. For a similar view of the state of apprenticeship, especially in London, see Ronald A. Bray, 'The Apprenticeship Question', *Economic Journal,* Vol. 19, September 1909, pp. 404-15, particularly pp. 413-14.

81. See *Engineering,* 'An Apprenticeship Question', Vol. LXXXIII, February 22, 1907, p. 243.

82. R.W. Tawney, 'The Economics of Boy Labour', *Economic Journal,* Vol. XIX, December, 1909, p. 521.

83. *ibid.,* pp. 521-2.

84. *ibid.,* p. 532. See also Lord Askwith, *Industrial Problems and Disputes,* Murray, London, 1920, pp. 18-21.

85. See More, *op. cit.,* pp. 19, 71.

86. See R.A. Bray, *Boy Labour and Apprenticeship,* 1911, p. 136.

87. See *Engineering Review,* Vol. XXIV, No. 9, September 15, 1911, p. 142.

88. See Bray, *op. cit.,* p. 136; H.E. Morgan, *Munitions of Peace: Our Preparedness*

for the Trade War, Nisbet and Co., London, 1916, pp. 55-6; and N.B. Dearle, *Industrial Training,* 1914, p. 145.

89. *Royal Commission on the Poor Laws and the Relief of Distress, Appendix, Vol. VIII, Minutes of Evidence,* Cd. 5066, 1910, *Parliamentary Papers,* Vol. XLVIII, 1910: Evidence of Sir Benjamin Browne, November 26, 1907, Q. 86334, p. 399. These conditions did not apply to the same degree in London, where the ship repairing and machine maintenance shops required workers with a larger range of skills even though semi-skilled workers were as efficient in the use of a particular machine as the skilled workmen. See Dearle, *op. cit.,* p. 148.

90. Dearle, *op. cit.,* pp. 117, 130-1.

91. *ibid.,* pp. 65-6, 110-11.

92. See *ibid.,* pp. 62-3, and Pollard and Robertson, *op. cit.,* p. 155.

93. *ibid.,* p. 66. Where the ASE was weak however, as in many sections of the ship-building industry, firms such as Reads of Portsmouth, Waterman Brothers, and Caird and Co., became 'notorious' for the large number of apprentices they employed. See Pollard and Robertson, *op. cit.,* p. 154. The Boilermakers' Union was a little more successful, though equally under threat from its ranks being flooded with apprenticed labour. In 1891 the union sought a national agreement to formalise its claims that only one apprentice could be employed per five journey-men, but when a National Shipyard Agreement was reached in 1893, they settled for a proportion of two apprentices for every seven journeymen. See *ibid.,* p. 155. In this context it should be noted that Charles More is quite wrong to suggest 'there is no evidence that there was widespread exploitation of apprentices, in the sense of using them as cheap labour to do elementary work'. See More, *op. cit.,* p. 84.

94. Dearle, *op. cit.,* pp. 68-9, 102.

95. For a contrary interpretation of the verbal agreement system see More, *op. cit.,* p. 48. More suggests that verbal agreements, to all extent and purposes, can be placed on the same level as indentured apprenticeships and involved similar forms of training and held comparable status.

96. See 'Rules of the Boilermakers' Society on the Admission of Apprentices, Manning and the Use of Machines', in E.A. Pratt, *Trade Unionism and British Industry,* 1904, pp. 55-8; see also p. 53, and Pollard and Robertson, *op. cit.,* pp. 155-6.

97. More, *op. cit.,* p. 141.

98. Dr More's theoretical tools also let him down here. His argument for the technical basis of five-year training programmes for skilled workers is derived from modern-day Taylorist job evaluation studies. Within the terms of such a quantitative picture of skill, he refers to the 'Experienced Worker Standard', 'defined by the British Standards Institution' as ' "the rate of output which qualified workers will *naturally* achieve without *over-exertion* in an *average* working day" '. Such an average 'standard', as we have already shown, is neither meaningful, nor does it have any concrete basis in reality. It is merely a defini-tion of skill in terms of efficiency and a predetermined rate of output. More to the point, it would not be pressing the issue to suggest that even Messrs Taylor and Thompson would find something cock-eyed here. Where they were trying to train smelters, pig-iron carriers and machinists in a matter of months, weeks and days, Dr More would prefer to carry out his own historical experiments concern-ing the technical efficiency of five-year training programmes for turners. More has also confused himself here, for in referring to present-day job evaluation studies, he draws attention to their rationale, which is to cut down the time required for setting and maintaining semi-automatic machinery from as little as eighteen months to fifteen months. It is surely not rhetorical to suggest that this

was exactly the direction British management in the engineering trades sought to follow at the beginning of this century. See *ibid.*, pp. 55 ff. 151. (The emphases are all mine, C. McG.)

99. See Committee on Industry and Trade (Balfour Committee), *Industrial and Commercial Efficiency,* Vol. 1, p. 178 ff.

100. See 'The Training of Engineering Apprentices', V, *The Engineer*, Vol. 105-6, March 13, 1908, pp. 264-5. The Great Western Railway Works also set up a Mechanics Institute at Swindon during the late nineteenth century, while the London and North Western Railway Co. did the same at Crewe as early as 1846. See 'The Training of Engineering Apprentices', *The Engineer*, Vol. 105-6, May 8, 1908, p. 471.

101. See 'An Apprenticeship System', *Engineering,* Vol. LXXXIII, February 27, 1907, p. 243. See also 'The Training of Engineering Apprentices', *The Engineer,* Vol. 105-6, January 17, 1908, pp. 52-3.

102. See 'The Training of Managers and Foremen: Memorandum with Regard to the Report by the Foremen's Qualification Committee, on matters relating to the Royal Ordnance Factories', *The Engineer*, Vol. 99-100, March 31, 1905, p. 326.

103. 'Entry and Training of Trade Lads, Royal Ordnance Factories, Woolwich Arsenal', *The Engineer*, Vol. 99-100, June 23, 1905, pp. 634-5.

104. *ibid.*

105. 'The Training of Managers and Foremen: Memorandum with Regard to the Report by the Foremen's Qualification Committee, on matters relating to the Royal Ordinance Factories', *loc. cit.,* p. 326.

106. See 'The Training of Engineering Apprentices', VII, *The Engineer*, Vol. 105-6, April 10, 1908, pp. 377-8; and 'The Training of Engineering Apprentices', *ibid.*, July 10, 1908, p. 35. For further information on similar schemes in operation at W.H. Allen, Son and Co., Bedford; Cochran and Co., Annan, Scotland; Robert Stephenson and Co., Darlington; Thomas Robinson and Sons Ltd., Rochdale; and Dobson and Barlow, Bolton, see 'The Training of Engineering Apprentices', IV, *The Engineer*, Vol. 105-6, February 28, 1908, pp. 222-3; *ibid.,* January 31, 1908, p. 106; and *ibid.,* January 17, 1908, pp. 52-4. The scheme at W.H. Allen was run in conjunction with the City and Guild College, Finsbury for the training of graduate engineers, and the Bedford Evening Institute for the training of supervisory and technical employees. The Cochran and Robert Stephenson schemes were run in conjunction with the Darlington Technical School, which provided day-time classes; while Dobson and Barlow organised their training schemes in conjunction with the Bolton Municipal Technical School.

107. See 'The Training of Engineering Apprentices', II, *The Engineer*, Vol. 105-6. January 31, 1908, p. 106.

108. 'The Training of Engineering Apprentices', III, *The Engineer*, Vol.. 105-6, February 14, 1908, pp. 155-6.

109. See *Report of the London County Council on Trade and Technical Education in Germany and France,* London County Council, London, 1914, p. 2. Michael Sanderson is of a similar opinion here. He suggests that the notion of a lack of state involvement as a 'condition of *laissez faire*', particularly in the area of higher education, is a 'mythical view'. See *Universities in the Nineteenth Century,* p. 13.

110. See Pollard and Robertson, *op. cit.,* p. 146.

111. See editorial in *Revue de Métallurgie,* Vol. 3, No. 5, mai 1906, pp. 230-1, and also M. Vogt, 'L'enseignement technique', *Revue de Métallurgie,* Vol. 4, No. 5, mai 1907, pp. 473-4.

112. See 'A Municipal School of Marine Engineering', *Engineering*, Vol. LXXXII, January 26, 1906, pp. 123-4.

113. See Harold Thomson, Letter to the Editor, *Engineering*, Vol. LXXXII, December, 1906, p. 797; and the views of W.G. Spence of Swan, Hunter and Wigham Richardson, in 'The Training of Engineering Apprentices', III, *The Engineer*, Vol. 105-6, February 14, 1908, p. 155.

114. On Germany, see Committee on Industry and Trade (Balfour Committee), *Industrial and Commercial Efficiency*, Vol. 1, p. 257. The system of technical education in Belgium is interesting, for it combined many of the features of the American and British systems. As in America, an extensive system of primary and secondary schools provided courses in manual work and gave emphasis to the ideology of professional manual and mental labour. In 1879, for example, courses in manual work started at the No. 12 Primary School for Boys in Brussels, where children did joinery, wood-work and modelling. This was meant to provide them with a 'taste for handicrafts' and educate the children of the working class. In 1887, the *Normal Schools* and all the other primary schools of Brussels began to provide courses in manual work, where the aim was to develop 'general ability, quickness, dexterity of both hands, prompt and firm movement, a taste for, and a love of work, and to inculcate habits of order and correctness, to develop the faculties of attention and perception, to supply a more complete and a deeper intuition of geometric ideas and forms of calculation. . . [not to say cultivate a] sense of beauty through the harmony of form and colour of the objects made. . .' The teaching, of course, was of the pedagogic rather than of the theoretical kind. When the child left primary school at the age of 12 or 13, he or she entered a secondary school, known as the Fourth Primary Standard School. As in England, these schools were aimed at the children of the working class, especially those who would join the ranks of new skilled workers. As distinct from Britain, though, the children made a permanent transition from primary to secondary school at the age of twelve or thirteen, whereas in England boys left school at about fourteen and could not enter a technical school or college until they were sixteen and had started an apprenticeship. In Belgium a boy who was fifteen years old could enter a technical school part-time and begin his apprenticeship. In the district of Charleroi, the technical schools comprised Industrial Day Schools, Industrial Evening and Sunday Schools, Upper Industrial Schools and Upper Finishing Schools for about six thousand pupils in 1913. The schools were highly stratified with regard to course work and the destiny of the pupils. The Industrial Evening and Sunday Schools concentrated on training apprentices in printing, tailoring and traditional metal skills, such as moulding and founding, while at the other extreme the Upper Finishing Schools were 'intended for all the young men of the wealthy classes destined to form a staff of specialists for the great national industries of the country', and led to a Technician's Diploma. See Dr Josefa Ioteyko, *The Science of Labour and its Organisation*, 1919, pp. 155-99 and by the same author, 'Les méthodes belges d'éducation technique', *Revue générale de Sciences*, 30 May 1917. For further information on the Belgian technical school system see H. Verney, 'Notes sur deux Ecoles techniques en Belgique', *Bulletin de la Société de l'Industrie Minérale*, Vol. LI, 1907, p. 255 ff. Verney presented a description of the industrial schools for Mons and Liège for Diploma training. See also by the same author a report on the Higher Technical Education Congress held in Mons during September, 1905, 'L'enseignement technique supérieur en Belgique', *Bulletin de la Société de l'Industrie Minérale*, Vol. LI, 1907, pp. 223-292.

115. See More, *op. cit.*, pp. 216, 220. The quote may be found on p. 187. (My

emphasis, C. McG.)

116. An interesting discussion along these lines may be found in Joseph Melling's, ' "Non-Commissioned Officers": British Employers and their Supervisory Workers, 1880-1920', *Social History*, Vol. 5, No. 2, May 1980, pp. 183-221. Sable, in his *Work and Politics*, p. 86 ff, makes many similar points.

117. Calculated from *Report of an Enquiry by the Board of Trade into Working Class Rents in the United Kingdom*, 'Sheffield', *Accounts and Papers*, 46, 1906, CVII, Cd. 3864, pp. 408-9.

118. See *Royal Commission on the Poor Laws. . ., Appendix, Vol. VIII, Minutes of Evidence*, Cd. 5066, 1919 *Parliamentary Papers*, Vol. XLVIII, 1910: Evidence by William Marshall, a manager at the Vickers plant, p. 474; and Albert Hobson, a cutlery employer and partner in T. Turner and Co., p. 452.

119. *ibid.*, Evidence by William Marshall, p. 451 and p. 455.

120. *ibid.*, p. 456.

121. *ibid.*, pp. 455-6. After 1908 the steel works of Sheffield's Thomas Firth and Sons also began to encourage their junior workers to attend evening school and offered advances in wages and prizes for regular attendance, and for passing exams. See 'Welfare at an English Steel Works', *Engineering and Industrial Management*, Vol. 4, No. 8, 19 August, 1920, p. 236. This was the common practice for most engineering firms at this time. For a description of the various incentives offered at Mather and Platt's Salford Works, Andrew Barclay's Caledonia Works, Kilmarnock, and Barr and Stroud, see Thos. Thurner, Managing Director of Andrew Barclay and Sons and Co., Letter to the Editor, *Engineering*, Vol. LXXXII, December 28, 1906, p. 865; 'Technical Education', *Engineering*, Vol. LXXXI, February 2, 1906, p. 157; and N.J. Maclean, B.Sc., Works Manager at Barr and Stroud, Letter to the Editor, *Engineering*, Vol. LXXXIII, June 14, 1907, p. 772.

122. *Royal Commission on the Poor Laws. . ., Appendix, Vol. VIII, Minutes of Evidence*, Cd. 5066, 1910, *Parliamentary Papers*, Vol. XLVIII, 1910: Evidence by William Marshall, p. 455.

123. See *The Engineer*, Vol. 99-100, March 31, 1905, p. 317.

124. See *Royal Commission on the Poor Laws. . ., Appendix, Vol. VIII, Minutes of Evidence*, Cd. 5066, 1910, *Parliamentary Papers*, Vol. XLVIII, 1910: Evidence by William Marshall, pp. 454-5.

125. *ibid.*, Evidence from Albert Hobson, p. 474; E.A. Pratt, *Trade Unionism and British Industry*, 1904, pp. 126-7; and *Report of an Enquiry by the Board of Trade into Working Class Rents in the United Kingdom*, 1906, *loc. cit.*, p. 408.

126. See Sidney and Beatrice Webb, *Industrial Democracy*, pp. 457-9.

127. See *Annual Report of the Chief Inspector of Factories and Workshops, 1908*, Cd. 4664. *Parliamentary Papers*, Vol. XXI, 1909, p. 75; and *Report of Minutes of Evidence Taken Before the Truck Committee, 1908-9*, Cd. 4444, *Parliamentary Papers*, Vol. XLIX, 1908, p. 72 ff.

128. See Pratt, *op. cit.*, pp. 135-7.

129. As Sheffield's Past-Master Cutler, Albert Hobson, put it: 'There is no question about it that the man who most hustles is a workman who is going to get a profit out of other workmen'. See his evidence to the *Royal Commission on the Poor Laws. . ., Appendix, Vol. VIII, Minutes of Evidence*, Cd. 5066, 1910, *Parliamentary Papers*, Vol. XLVIII, 1910, p. 476.

130. *ibid.*, p. 476.

131. *ibid.*, p. 476.

132. At Beckett's in 1907, the rates for gas ranged from threepence to sixpence per week. See *Report of Minutes of Evidence. . . Truck Committee, loc. cit.* Evidence from William Beckett, representing his firm and the Sheffield Chamber of

Commerce, May 30, 1907, Q. 12595-12607, p. 95.

133. *Royal Commission on the Poor Laws. . ., Appendix, Vol. VIII, Minutes of Evidence,* Cd. 5066, 1910, *Parliamentary Papers,* Vol. XLVIII, 1910: Evidence from Albert Hobson, p. 474 and p. 476.

134. *ibid.,* p. 474.

135. Pratt, *op. cit.,* pp. 126-7.

136. *ibid.,* pp. 135-7.

137. *ibid.,* pp. 131-4. Also, in the edge-tool trade, the grinders' union proclaimed during the early 1900s that polishing could not be done by unskilled labour. Though grinding was done by skilled labour, the union demanded that the two processes be done by the same skilled worker. See *ibid.,* pp. 139-40.

138. *Royal Commission on the Poor Laws. . ., Appendix, Vol. VIII, Minutes of Evidence,* Cd. 5066, 1910, *Parliamentary Papers,* Vol. XLVIII, 1910, Evidence from Albert Hobson, p. 474.

139. See *Report of an Enquiry by the Board of Trade into Working Class Rents in the United Kingdom,* 'Sheffield', *Accounts and Papers,* Vol. 46, CVII, Cd. 3864, 1906, p. 409.

140. See Sidney Pollard, 'Wages and Earnings in the Sheffield Trades, 1851-1914', *Yorkshire Bulletin of Economic and Social Research,* Vol. VI, 1954, p. 54.

141. *Royal Commission on the Poor Laws. . ., Appendix, Vol. VIII, Minutes of Evidence,* Cd. 5066, 1910, *Parliamentary Papers,* Vol. XLVIII, 1910, Evidence from Councillor Holmshaw, p. 533.

142. *ibid.,* Evidence from Mr Thomas Shaw, J.P., p. 562.

143. *ibid.,* Evidence from William Marshall, p. 453.

144. *ibid.,* See the evidence from Councillor Holmshaw, p. 453.

145. It could be the case that Hobson's attitudes to the continental systems of technical education and their 'progressive' effects on the working classes were shaped by his own experience of the cutlery trades in Sheffield and Solingen in Germany's Rhineland. Hobson was a journeyman cutler by training, and the degradation of his trade in Sheffield was a striking contrast to the situation in the cutlery centre of Solingen. In this town the move towards manufactory principles of production and factories was very uneven, and was especially held in check by the widespread use of cheap and efficient electric motors in small workshops. Workers, too, were able to maintain control over access to their trade by effective labour organisation, and, at the same time, sought to adapt professional industrial education to their own ends. The old craft school, for instance, was converted into a modern *Fachschule,* which was exclusively devoted to the training of those in the cutlery handicrafts. The state Industrial Code also enforced compulsory written indentureships for apprentices usually for four years. However, the situation in Solingen was very unusual; as we shall see, the *Fachschulen* in Germany were much more orientated to the training of professional employees and a new stratum of hyper-qualified workers and, in fact, ratified the dispossession of various forms of knowledge and skill from the overwhelming majority of workers. An interesting contemporary account of the Solingen cutlery trades may be found in G.I.H. Lloyd's, 'Labour Organisation in the Cutlery Trades of Solingen', *Economic Journal,* Vol. 18, September 1908, pp. 373-91. The most substantial historical account of labour organisation in Solingen (in comparison with nearby Remscheid) during the early years of this century is E. Lucas's *Zwei Formen von Radikalismus in der deutschen Arbeiterbewegung,* Verlag Roter Stern, Frankfurt, 1976.

146. See W.E. Minchinton, *op. cit.,* p. 111.

147. *ibid.,* p. 111.

148. See Sidney and Beatrice Webb, *Industrial Democracy,* p. 490.

149. See *Royal Commission on the Poor Laws. . ., Appendix, Vol. VIII, Minutes of Evidence*, Cd. 5066, 1910, *Parliamentary Papers*, Vol. XLVIII, Evidence from Albert Hobson, p. 475.

150. See Charles More, *op. cit.*, pp. 154-5.

151. *ibid.*, p. 157.

152. Jonathan Zeitlin has put forward a more market-orientated interpretation of the legacy of the lock-out which leads to a similar conclusion. In his opinion, employers did not press home their victory of 1898 because of the boom which began to sweep the industry. Trade conditions became buoyant as order books were filled by Third World countries, and colonies requested engineering products. Not wishing to penalise themselves by dramatically changing customary work practices, employers left things as they were and thought it better to fill orders rather than precipitate costly conflicts with workers. See Jonathan Zeitlin, 'Craft Control and the Division of Labour', *Cambridge Journal of Economics*, Vol. 3, No. 3, September 1979, p. 271.

153. The following discussion is based on: Joseph Horner, 'Recent Developments in Machine Tool Design', *Engineering Review*, Vol. XVIII, No. 5, May 1908, p. 288 ff; Joseph Horner, 'The Modern Machine Shop', *Cassier's Magazine*, Vol. XVIII, No. 5, March 1900, p. 390 ff; Anonymous, 'Interchangeability', *Engineering Review*, Vol. XXIV, No. 5, May 1911, pp. 302-3; and Joseph Horner, 'The Trend of Modern Machine Tool Design', *Cassier's Magazine*, Vol. XXIII, No. 1, November 1902, pp. 211-32. Within the limits of this volume only a quite introductory description can be given of the nature of technical change in the engineering industry. At a later time I will present a more detailed picture of the process of technical change in the European metal industry, for as will be appreciated such a topic requires separate study.

154. See Joseph Horner, 'The Modern Machine Shop', *loc. cit.*, March 1900, p. 396 and Anonymous, 'Interchangeability', *loc. cit.*, pp. 302-3.

155. See Joseph Horner, 'The Modern Machine Shop', *Cassier's Magazine*, Vol. XXXI, No. 2, December 1906, pp. 150-66.

156. See Nathan Rosenberg, 'Technological Change in the Machine Tool Industry' 1840-1910', *Journal of Economic History*, Vol. 33, 1963, pp. 414-43.

157. *ibid.*, p. 437.

158. Anonymous, 'Interchangeability', *loc. cit.*, May 1911, p. 303.

159. See Henry Suplee, 'Typical American Cranes—II', *Cassier's Magazine*, Vol. II, 1892, p. 17 ff.

160. See David Landes, *The Unbound Prometheus*, p. 281 ff.

161. This was noted by A.R. Bellamy before the Manchester Society of Engineers in 1900. See *Fielden's Magazine*, Vol. 2, No. 7, February 1900, pp. 205-6.

162. Landes, *op. cit.*, p. 282, and also R.E.B. Crompton, 'Electrically Operated Factories', *Cassier's Magazine*, Vol. IX, No. 3, January 1896, p. 291 ff; and Anonymous, 'Electric Power in the Machine Shop', *Cassier's Magazine*, Vol. XIII, No. 3, January 1898, pp. 240-56.

163. Anonymous, 'Electric Power in the Machine Shop', *loc. cit.*, January 1898, pp. 243-5.

164. Crompton, 'Electrically Operated Factories', *loc. cit.*, pp. 296-7.

165. R.T.E. Lozier, 'Direct Electric Driving in Machine Shops', *Cassier's Magazine*, Vol. XVII, No. 3, December 1899, pp. 158-65.

166. Anonymous, 'Electric Power in the Machine Shop', *loc. cit.*, January 1898, p. 256. W.D. Wansbourgh, 'The Evolution of the Portable Engine', *Cassier's Magazine*, Vol. IX, No. 2, December 1895, p. 83 ff; T.W. Sheffield, 'The Application of Electric Motors', *Fielden's Magazine*, Vol. 5, No. 6, December 1901, pp. 519-25; W.M. MacFarland, 'Electric Power in the Machine Shop', *Cassier's*

Magazine, Vol. XXIII, No. 1, November 1902, pp. 60–92. The introduction of pneumatically-driven tools and appliances had a similar, though less extensive, impact, especially in founding and shipbuilding. The tools became lighter, more portable and dispensed with the necessity of the expensive and cumbersome piping characteristic of steam and hydraulically-motivated tools. Their introduction facilitated a major transformation of riveting and boilermaking. See Ewert C. Amos, 'Pneumatic Tools and Appliances', *Fielden's Magazine,* Vol. 1, No. 5, December 1899.
167. Anonymous, 'A Modern Engineering Factory', *Engineering Review,* Vol. XXVI, No. 10, April 15, 1913, pp. 384–6.
168. More, *op. cit.,* p. 237.

CHAPTER 4: FRANCE

1. *The radical Taylorite critique*

It will be remembered that a broad spectrum of historical opinion suggests that French industry at the beginning of this century, including the metal trades, was neither given sufficient attention in the matter of professionally training up a managerial cadre force, nor adequately supplied with an apparatus of research and development. The training of the workforce is also believed to have been amateurish and dominated by a too-ready acceptance of aristocratic and craftsmanly values. Much of this opinion, as the reader will be aware, is derived from arguments advanced by the *Revue de Métallurgie* and its editor, Henry Le Chatelier, in the very early 1900s.

Le Chatelier himself seemingly never tired in his struggle against the existing system, whether it was in the pages of the *Revue,* in the *Bulletin de la Société d'Encouragement pour l'Industrie Nationale,* or at public forums like the *Faculté des Sciences.* His leadership of what can only be considered a campaign began to assume influential proportions from 1904 with the publication of 'On the Role of Science in Industry', in the *Revue.*[1] In his view, 'The unheard-of development of industry during the second half of the nineteenth century' had been 'the direct consequence of the progress of experimental science'.[2] The work of Carnot on the law of definite proportions in chemistry made possible the introduction of the dephosphoration of steel and the production of special steels. Experimental science had also produced thermodynamics and led to the introduction of steam and gas-driven engines. Yet the benefits to be gained from the systematic application of experimental science to industry often remained unconscious and tardy, while in the latter part of the nineteenth century science itself broke its *de facto* relationship with industry and made its way into the world of high theory. Theoreticians interested in practical questions were becoming rare.[3] Unconsciously, many scientists thought that a true scientific education was contrary to *'l'esprit pratique'* that ran through industry, while from industry's point of view the use of scientific methods was too onerous and expensive to be put into practice.[4] Le Chatelier lambasted the confusion that resulted from this separation of science from industry. When scientists condemned 'practice' they really meant 'empiricism'—'the collaborator of honourable mediocrity in the factory', and when industrialists condemned 'science' they really meant

171

'theory'—a deviation from the scientific spirit, uninformed by experimental practice. This theoretical deviation, he argued, informed the entire structure of secondary and higher education and had to be renounced. University training was too tied to preparing young men for government administration and the doctoral thesis, which did not favour real scientific development. It had to be reformed, as it was completely out of step with the need for the systematic application of science to industry.[5] In 1912, in a speech to the Students' Association at the Special Schools of the University of Liège, Belgium, Le Chatelier was still hard at work propagandising for educational reform. He called for the teaching of not just pure science—geometry, physics, chemistry, etc.—but also of what he termed 'industrial science', which involved the practical and precise application of science to industry. Students, therefore, would of necessity have to come into contact with the actual methods and procedures of production used in industry.[6]

A second aspect of Le Chatelier's critique of the higher education system was aimed at weaknesses in industry. In the 1904 article, he spoke of industry's principal concern to use science to reduce costs of production. Yet this could only be achieved if industry itself appreciated that scientific development, especially in well-equipped works' laboratories, cost money, the returns on which would not show up for some time.[7] Industry also had to commit itself to science in order to ensure the regularity and quality of production, especially at a time when industrial processes relied less and less for their success on the initiative of the worker and more on the direct intervention of the engineer. It was essential, therefore, that the engineer not only receive a methodical and 'really scientific' education, but also have at hand the necessary equipment and support of management in his place of work in order to undertake his duties effectively.[8]

Over the years 1904–12, Le Chatelier believed that the greatest obstacle to overcome in the reform of scientific education and in uniting it with industry was the 'general indifference of the French public' to this important factor in the 'power' of any 'modern people'.[9] Other countries had made great progress, even turning technical education into a 'veritable cult'.[10] In Britain, for example, the work of Sir Henry White, President of the Society of Civil Engineers, in instigating an enquiry into higher education for engineers and drawing up a plan in 1906 for its reform, demonstrated how public opinion in one advanced country was attuned to the advances being made in modern technical education.[11] A report at the time by André Pelletan, from the Ministry of Public Works in France, was similarly impressed with the manner in which this rich industrial country took the initiative and profoundly reformed its education structure.[12] Germany, too, under the presidency of Dr Th. Peters' twenty thousand-strong German Engineers' Association (VDI) had been waging a twenty-years old 'incessant campaign for the improvement of technical education'.[13] In collaboration with leading enterprises like Krupp, model technical schools were established, such as the one at Aix-la-Chapelle. In America the work of F.W. Taylor and the industrialist, Andrew Carnegie, inspired widespread reform of the university system. Taylor's campaign against too much student freedom and the over-emphasis on the teaching of theory in the universities, and Carnegie's endowments of technical libraries to local communities were seen as classic examples of the mood sweeping both sides of the Atlantic.[14] Similar educational reforms in Belgium also impressed the *Société d'Encouragement pour l'Industrie Nationale.*[15]

For Le Chatelier and his colleagues, the American system of higher education and the work of Taylor provided the model of reform, as well as the guidance of a 'unifying idea' *(idée d'ensemble).*[16] Taylor's work was 'an extremely remarkable example of the rigorous application of the scientific method to a very complex technical problem, the organisation of labour in the factory', and could only succeed if engineers were 'profoundly imbued with the scientific method' and taught in reformed colleges and universities.[17]

In order to substantiate their general criticism of the French educational system, these 'metallurgical Taylorites' focused their attack on the School of Mines *(École des Mines)* and the *Polytechnique.* Pelletan was actually one of the directors of the *École des Mines* when he drew up his 1906 report for the Ministry of Public Works and therefore automatically created controversy. The *École des Mines,* in the first instance, was not to be compared with the German *Bergakademie.* The French school was not exclusively given over to the study of minerals and metallurgy as in Germany; it was in fact more comparable to the German *Hochschule* and produced an array of engineers for both private industry and the state.[18] But this is where the comparison ended. Whereas in other countries engineers completed their formal training between the ages of twenty-two and twenty-four, French students were just starting the final stages of their studies in engineering. After arriving as graduates of the *Polytechnique* at about twenty-five, a further three years at the *Mines* was required. If a student began his studies at the *Polytechnique* at eighteen, he was at least twenty-eight before he finished at the *Mines,* and this included two years' military service at the *Polytechnique* and a further year while attending the *Mines.*[19] In Pelletan's opinion, a German engineer had already left school and was using his training, while his French counterpart was still studying, and absurdly 'still has an apprenticeship to do'.[20] The plight of the future engineer was even worse when the actual nature of the courses was taken into account. Throughout these many years the aspiring French engineer did an estimated ten times more mathematical work than his German, American or English counterpart, which was 'absolutely aberrant'.[21] In Germany, for instance, the amount of time given over to mathematics in the five to six years course was very restrained, and placed less of an emphasis on theoretical mathematics and more on the mathematics required only for the particular branch of engineering in which the student was specialising. In France, by contrast, the maths courses were repetitive, theoretical and unnecessary, defended purely as an 'intellectual exercise' or as useful in creating a disciplined and abstract mentality.[22] The courses were also encyclopaedic rather than specialised, as in Germany or America. For Pelletan, very few could digest such huge amounts of information and even if they could, it was only useful to those small numbers of engineers who entered the banks or became commercial engineers.[23] Finally, education at the *Mines* was not practical enough. A German engineering student, by the time he completed his course, would have undertaken both factory and laboratory work especially designed for his speciality and be capable of directing a shop. He would have the know-how to demonstrate, make repairs and direct the use of men and machinery, while the French graduate at twenty-eight still had to undertake practical training by occupying a lowly and humble position in the factory. Furthermore, even when practical and experimental work was provided for at the *Mines* the laboratories were primitive by German standards.[24]

Pelletan's conclusions were particularly stinging, as they came from a man who was an eminent member of the *Mines*. Surely, he argued, such a school, and the system in general, should be turning out technicians and not intellectual boffins *(savants)* trained and skilled in the speculative sciences and only eligible to be members of the *Institut*.[25] The training of French engineers in sum was behind developments in the rest of the world and there was a need for an injection of a 'practical spirit', not to say initiative and reform. The training was too intense, too long and geared to producing an intellectual elite.[26] He made four major recommendations, which included reducing the theoretical training to only what was necessary for a particular specialism, developing specialised course work itself by encouraging students to select an area they would like to form a career in, and building an appropriate course of study around this;[27] developing programmes of practical study and training involving both the factories and laboratories; and, finally, forming a committee to study foreign developments and to recommend practical ways for further reforming the system, as the Institute of Civil Engineers in Britain had done.[28]

Following the appearance of Pelletan's report, the *Revue* asked its readers for their views on the problems and future of industrial training in France. No industrialist replied to the request and this only reinforced the *Revue*'s belief about the indifference of the public and the depth of the problem.[29] Some leading intellectuals and students did, however, come forward with their criticisms and suggestions. Baclé, a former president of *L'Association des anciens élèves de l'École des Mines de Paris*, made similar, but less polemical recommendations. Against the tide of Pelletan's criticisms, however, Baclé suggested that the *Mines* was already 'disposed to accept the new reforms', as was evident in the school's laboratory work and the students' sojourns into the factories during vacations.[30] A group of students from the *Mines,* though, were not so impressed with this reformist disposition. Following Pelletan's criticisms to the letter, they presented another stinging indictment of overwork, long courses, and the encyclopaedic education. They called for the introduction of faculties to facilitate the specialisation of instruction, shorter courses and practical training which would enable them to apply their knowledge and shape their futures. This would also have to include visits to factories.[31]

Unlike their American counterparts, the French Taylorites did not think that their education system lacked the necessary discipline to prepare the young engineer for the future monotony of factory life. For Chalres de Fréminville, one of the leading Taylorite radicals, discipline was 'severe', courses were 'assiduously followed' and examinations were 'serious'.[32] Yet discipline was not the only characteristic required in the future engineer. He also needed a 'tenacious will', 'intellectual activism' and a 'spirit of observation'. Yet the rigidities in the higher education system did not encourage such characteristics. Young engineers who were just out of school tended to rely too much on the habits of their theoretical research and training, rather than develop a more flexible and practical spirit of observation.[33] Like Pelletan, de Freminville advocated 'that such students be allowed to choose subjects, courses and teachers so that they would develop into interested and flexible specialists'.[34]

Some reformers went off the deep end with their programmes. Appell, the president of *L'Association pour l'Avancement des Sciences* in 1908, called for an end to the teaching of all sciences outside the universities, especially an end to those first year subjects taught at the *Mines, Ponts et Chaussées* and the *École Centrale*.[35] Le Chatelier thanked the president for being very polemical and for sparking off debate, but what was required was the rationalisation of the higher education system, not its demolition.[36] It was left to Le Chatelier, in fact, to produce the most ideologically coherent programme of reform. The programme appeared in the *Revue* in June 1911, under the title 'Higher Technical Education: Its Aim and Methods'.

Le Chatelier's own main interest concerned the highest forms of training for future managers and directors. Over the years he had become very critical of the 'anarchy' and 'multiplicity of aims' present in the schools, which led to overlapping courses and a failure to give an appropriate training to the various strata of managers and hyper-qualified workers.[37] In this context, he argued for the planned specialisation and stratification of higher educational training. At the top would be schools for the *supérieurs* or future directors of enterprises. Below this would be schools for the middle engineers or the 'captains' of plants, and at the bottom would be schools for professional and manual workers who would later take up hyper-qualified positions in the factories.[38] In his opinion the preparation of the future heads of industry was the most pressing problem, though in time this system could produce the cadres necessary to direct enterprises at all levels.[39] When he spoke of the qualities required in the *supérieurs* he referred to 'character'; 'intelligence'; scientific knowledge, i.e., the precise understanding of the properties of matter and natural phenomena and their application to industry; psychological knowledge, i.e., the knowledge of how to get the best out of colleagues and subordinates, and finally, 'professional' or managerial knowledge.[40] These were the characteristics of not just a business engineer, but of a technocratic engineer—an engineer who could not only take charge of the commercial aspects of a business, but who could also direct and administer the bureaucracy of an enterprise. For Le Chatelier, such characteristics could only be taught in highly specialised schools informed by the 'democratic spirit' of equality of opportunity. They could not be taught in the closed, rigid, and theoretical world of the existing system.[41]

As was noted at the beginning of this study, many of these criticisms have flowed straight into the standard historical texts on this period. Cameron, after speaking highly of the education system during the early part of the nineteenth century, suggests that by the end of the century its exclusive bourgeois base was an obstacle to further advancement and, in fact, as the technical needs of society expanded the clientele of the schools continued to come from this narrow social class. Hence, as the demand for engineers rose dramatically at the turn of the century, the higher school system could not keep up and produce enough of them. This historian, though, remains tentative about his judgment.[42] Yves Lequin, on the other hand, has no such hesitancy. He contends that the quality and quantity of higher education actually declined in the late nineteenth and early twentieth centuries. Not only did the ruling classes fail to appreciate the needs of the economy and of technical education, but the system of education itself was also thrown out of gear. He does point out that there was a growth of schools of commerce, and chemical and technical institutes, such as at Nancy in 1890, and at Grenoble in 1892, but like Cameron, he emphasises that the supply of trained cadres could not keep up with the demand. The proportion of the population attending secondary schools, and who could therefore feed the *grandes écoles,* also remained stagnant over the years spanning the 1890s and the Great War, totalling only 3.8% by 1914.[43] According also to Lequin, the number of science matriculation students doing their *baccalauréat* probably declined from about 3,000 in 1880 to approximately 2,500 by 1913.[44] When it comes to explanations of this allegedly parlous situation, Aimée Moutet believes, just as Le Chatelier did, that the theoretical training of French engineers ill-prepared them for an appreciation of Taylorist movements and the new methods of industrial training. They were actually more impressed by Taylor's mathematical skills than they were with him and his international followers' *savoir-faire technique*.[45] Moutet goes so far as to suggest that it was only with the campaign led by Le Chatelier and de Fréminville that French science began to appreciate and serve the needs of French industry. That this was a protracted and uneven match is illustrated by the fate of Le Chatelier, who lost his editorship of the *Revue* in 1912 during the controversy over industrial higher education.[46] The implication of this is that the very tentative attempts to reform the education system and to advance the professional role of the engineers in industry and society were partly stifled, at least in public, when Le Chatelier lost his position and the *Revue* became more of a mouthpiece for technical and theoretical engineering and metallurgy.[47]

2. Myths and realities

It is necessary to be very cautious when assessing the validity of these criticisms. The judgments of such eminently qualified gentlemen from inside the system, who apparently had no vested interests to advance, may be proof enough for some students and scholars, but this overlooks the equally strong case made for the defence of the system and the possibility that structural changes were in fact occurring. The radical Taylorites certainly did not have a monopoly of wisdom on the 'one best method' of industrial training and education at the highest levels. When Aguillon, the *inspecteur général des mines* and a professor at *l'Ecole des Mines,* replied to Pelletan's report, he was sympathetic towards the specialisation of schools and courses, but not towards turning the *Mines* into a school like *Arts et Manufactures,* which Pelletan seemed to be suggesting. In the *inspecteur's* view it was best to have a variety of different schools which specialised in the various disciplines and promoted differing levels of expertise.[48] This point had a lot of validity, for one of the biases of the Taylorites was their exclusive concentration on the *Mines* and the *Polytechnique,* and their failure to address the growing network of schools, like the *Arts et Manufactures* and the various technical institutes in Paris and the provinces. When it is remembered that the *Mines* and the *Polytechnique* were already the training grounds for the future *heads* of enterprises and ministries of state, like the Oxbridge system in Britain, then the Taylorite criticism about the need for further specialisation here lost a lot of its force. Le Chatelier's highly stratified education for the *supérieurs* was already a fact of life, though the nature of the education may have differed from his dream. Moreover, the defenders of the *supérieurs* education put great store by the encyclopaedic training. It was intentionally designed to give future leaders of industry and state the necessary knowledge and skills to be directors. They were not turning out specialist engineers, but men who could practically direct and administer the 'totality' of affairs in industry and the state. In this work, they believed, France had a marked *supériorité* over other countries and specialisation would defeat this purpose.[49] In this context, Pelletan was quite wrong to draw a parallel between the German *Hochschule* and the *Mines.* If there was anything to compare with the *Hochschule* it would have been either the *École Centrale des Arts et Manufactures,* the various schools of *Arts et Métiers,* the *Ecole de Physique et de Chimie industrielle,* Paris, or the provincial, industrial and commercial institutes, which began to proliferate from the 1890s. Apart from the *Arts et Manufactures,* which tended towards the production of hyper-qualified, upper-managerial engineers, all these schools had four to five-year courses. The courses were neither encyclopaedic, exclusively theoretical, nor unspecialised. They were generally aimed at generating a cadre force for technical, middle-management positions, such as future works managers, laboratory analysts, chemists, and civil and mechanical engineers. They were also generally based on hard academic research, with specialisation taking place in the third or fourth year of the course.[50] At the School of Industrial Physics and Chemistry, the students graduated in chemical engineering and physics, and had close contact with industry. In the words of Professor Féry, one of the school's teachers, the school had 'really practical courses on industrial electricity and applied chemistry', with its graduates making a marked contribution to the growth of the automobile industry, especially in the area of gas engines, itself derived from research into the use of gas engines at the blast furnace. Pelletan's criticisms were, in this case, 'unfortunately based'. There was no emphasis on 'speculative science' here.[51] From the provinces, the director of the *Institut de chimie de Nancy,* Arth, described how his college was turning out 'neither men who were empiricists nor theorists'. An encyclopaedic education was not provided and an important emphasis was given to laboratory work. Nancy was, in fact, 'animated by the spirit' that Pelletan discovered in Germany's Rhineland.[52] This was a view supported by Rolland and Dreux, the president and administrative director of the steel company, *La Société des Aciéries de Longwy,* from the same region: specialisation and shorter courses were a fact, not a dream.[53] By 1912, the *Institut* also had attached to the college a commercial institute, formed with the cooperation of the Meurthe and Moselle Chamber of Commerce, to provide practical instruction to young employers wishing to complete their 'professional training' in modern methods of internal factory organisation, management and commercial organisation.[54]

Another aspect of Pelletan's and Le Chatelier's critique which did not go unchallenged was their advocacy of factory training for students before they had finished their courses and allowing students themselves to select their particular specialisation. In the former case, Vogt had his doubts about allowing students to begin their practical training before starting their courses, as in Germany. They would only be 'amateur workers' and there only for a short period of time, while their instruction most likely would be mediocre, consisting of 'helping' rather than working in their own right. For Vogt, it was much better if the students concentrated their formal and practical instruction in the schools, measuring the resistance of metals, testing materials, undertaking chemical and physical experiments and assembling machinery, etc.[55] In the case of allowing students to select their own subjects and specialise, a number of defenders of the existing system believed that this could not be allowed to occur too early. The young men, they believed, perhaps quite rightly, did not have any real notion of the diverse trades and industries which would best suit their talents until quite late in their formal training. One or two years in a particular branch of the metal industry or in a particular factory was surely a slim basis on which to encourage the specialisation of training. In the early years it was best to encourage general and overlapping studies and leave specialisation until later.[56]

As far as the alleged separation of science from industry was concerned, this brought forth not so much howls of revolt as a deadly silence. More exactly, it was ignored, while the pages of the *Revue* itself bore testimony to the close and structural relationship between the two. Since the mid-nineteenth century, as we have seen, developments in the science of metallurgy and in the scientific control of iron and steel production were extended and intensified. In blast furnace practice, such as at *Le Creusot,* laboratories were formed which employed a large number of engineers and chemists to control the heats, study the composition of metals and ensure that the pig iron produced was of a rigidly uniform quality.[57] This had been going on at *Le Creusot* since the 1860s, and with the development of special steels at the end of the century, other firms like, *La Société Commentry-Fourchambault-Imphy,* equipped their plants with extensive scientific laboratories.[58] In the foundries of modern engineering plants, such as *Cail à Denain,* it was essential to have chemical laboratories so that the quality of the iron used could be determined and controlled, especially at the point of fusion when various materials used in moulding could act in a volatile and unpredictable manner. This required extensive micrographic work from chemists and engineers, testing materials and the use of scientific apparatus such as microscopes.[59] By the 1900s, the education system was playing a direct role in this area. The *Conservatoire National des Arts et Métiers* performed some 1,755 tests for government and private enterprises in 1908 on the uses and application of metals, materials, machines, and chemicals. The *Conservatoire* also played an important role in the development of scientific instruments of measurement for testing humidity, water pressure, the strength and composition of metals, and of electrical apparatus for testing dynamos.[60] In 1912 the *Association Technique de Fonderie* was established and took a lot of inspiration from its US counterpart. It sought to perfect the science of founding from technical, economic and commercial points of view. The Association promoted congresses, subventions, research and scientific publications, and was particularly interested in sponsoring research prizes for technical advances in foundry practice.[61] Similar advances were made at the designing end of metal enterprises. The drafting department at the *Cail à Denain* locomotive works employed about one hundred engineers and designers in scientific precision work tracing out not only the dimensions of every piece to be used on a job, but also designing how the work itself was to be executed.[62] It would certainly prove fruitful to study these developments in the light of Mr Trebilcock's work on the spin-offs from the British armaments industry, as Professor Crouzet has suggested. With the exception of the firm of *Cail á Denain,* all the firms we have referred to were engaged in one form or another with armament contracts, and their shell and big gun work required research into the nature of metals, particularly their strengths and resistance to heat and friction. Professor Crouzet, though, is pessimistic that the arms industry produced noticeable spin-offs in France, especially as its producers were a very select and self-enclosed group of firms subject to tight government regulations.[63] But whatever the influence of the arms trade on the relationship between science and industry in French metal production, the overall picture is fairly clear.

All these developments reflected the form of specialisation taking place in the French metal industry at the turn of the century. As the industry was unable for various reasons to advance on the American and German pattern of mass production output, emphasis was given to its quality, whether it was in the fabrication of special steels for the munitions and automobile industry, or in the production of special machine tools, the export of ferrous alloys and steels from electrical furnaces, or finally in the growth of the automobile industry itself. The names of the men associated with this quality specialisation became renowned around the world—Le Chatelier, Osmond, Guillet, Charpy, Dumas, Revol, de Fréminville and Ram. All were products of the allegedly encyclopaedic, theoretical and unscientific French education system, and the special products of the *Polytechnique,* the *Mines* and *Arts et Manufactures.* Finally, all of them were either editors of, or contributors to, the *Revue de Métallurgie.* The *Revue* itself played a special role in this, giving itself over to the study of the composition of metals, alloys and special steels; the nature of stress, shock and elasticity in metals; while all this was underpinned by that allegedly useless mathematics—advanced calculus and algebra.[64]

Many key features then of the Taylorite critique were ill-founded. The system was neither out of step with the basic trajectory of specialisation taking place in the industry nor a complete obstacle to the professionalisation of production management. These failures of judgment can be partly explained by the impact on these intellectuals of American Taylorist ideology, which gave their criticisms a certain anachronistic character. When the situation in the American metal industry was considered, we drew attention to the employers' attempts to replace the old contracting *petite bourgeoisie* with a new *petite bourgeoisie* of employee-technicians, including engineers, foremen and a small, new stratum of specialist skilled workers. Upper management, as well, was forced to develop its own technical intelligence in order to direct the entire labour process through its shop-floor representatives. An essential aspect of this transformation was the development of a new ideology of work based on the image of its compulsive and efficient character and the importance of the role of the professionally trained engineer in the efficient functioning of industry. Since at least the 1850s, these problems had been nowhere near as pressing in the French metal industry. Contracting had ceased to play an important role and upper management had already gained a long experience in technically controlling and directing the labour process. By failing to appreciate the unique situation faced by American employers or the advances made by the French metal employers in the field of professional instruction for managers, the radical Taylorite criticism was many years out of date. On the other hand, the Taylorite emphasis on the need for an *idée d'ensemble* in higher education highlighted a major weakness in the French education system; the absence of an extensive network of schools for training of lower technical and managerial cadres, as Le Chatelier suggested. The system as a whole was geared more to producing upper-managerial cadres who could *run* the industry rather than *administer* it.

This posed serious problems, especially at a time of expansion when an array of petty bourgeois technocrats and technicians were required. As the social basis of the bourgeoisie's professional, technical intelligence remained exclusive, shortages developed in the ranks of technical and lower managerial cadres. Though schools for these administrators were in existence, there were neither enough of them nor enough students in attendance. In this case, Lequin has made a very useful observation; where in America 9% of the population attended secondary school in 1904, 3.8% did so in France in 1914. This was a very slim basis indeed for the development of a new technical *petite bourgeoisie* who could administer the day-to-day functioning of the industry. In this context, the focus of the Taylorite critique on the *Polytechnique* and the *Mines* had some merit. It was not enough just to produce rulers, it was also essential to produce the rulers' administrators. With the hegemony of *Poly-*

technique and the *Mines* underpinning the exclusive basis of bourgeois rule in the factory this was unlikely to occur. At least one French historian would probably sympathise with this overall perspective: M. Lévy-Leboyer. He also feels that the vociferous critique of French employers, especially of their apparently poor adaptability to the needs of a modern capitalist economy, is out of step with the realities. He also perceives an 'immobility' in the training and recruitment of upper management which, though very professional, was cut off from adequate mechanisms of renewal and expansion. The managers and industrialists who went through the *Polytechnique* or *Ecole Centrale* needed an 'encyclopaedic' and mathematical education to prepare them to rule their fathers' enterprises in heavy industry. Neither were they immune to the development of 'new talents in the world of affairs' which contributed to a 'diffusion of advanced technologies'.[65] They were, however, lacking when it came to providing for those below them. By turning to developments within the workforce as a whole this problem can be seen quite clearly, as well as how it was partially solved.

3. The crisis of apprenticeship

Between 1896 and 1913, the number of those engaged in the French metal industry expanded from 736,000 to 1,120,000.[66] This was a 52% increase in the size of the workforce and with the exception of the clothing industry the metal trades had become the largest source of industrial employment by 1906, overtaking the two historically most important sectors of industry, construction and textiles.[67] The size of the expansion was particularly noticeable in the primary production of metals, which grew by 125%, or from 56,000 people in 1896 to 125,000 in 1913. Yet the most important source of the expansion took place in the transformation of metals, or in the engineering and allied trades, where the workforce increased from 680,000 to 995,000 over the same period, or by 46%. Due to the slow, almost imperceptible growth in the birth rate up to World War One, much of this expansion could only be sustained by a large increase in immigrant labour.

From Italy, Belgium, Spain, and French North Africa came thousands of untrained workers to fill Lorraine's iron, steel, and engineering plants.[68] Iron and steel industrialists set up recruiting agencies on the borders, and in 1911, for example, one agency negotiated the placement of 7,000 Italians for the north-eastern metal region, especially for the steel plants of Briey and Longwy.[69] In Briey (French Lorraine) by 1914 foreigners outnumbered the French population. Out of a population of approximately 125,000 some 72,000 were foreigners, with the Italian community comprising 46,000 people.[70] Slightly further east, in Luxembourg, where several large French metal establishments were located, the canton of Esch comprised 16,263 workers in 1900. Of this number, 10,198 were foreigners—5,678 Italians, 3,010 Germans, 683 Belgians, 664 French workers and 185 from other nationalities.[71] The increasing role of immigrant labour in the heavy metal industry at a time of rapid expansion served to highlight many new problems for employers seeking to form, maintain and train a workforce. In many ways the problems were comparable to those experienced by American employers. The larger workforce tended to be more unstable, as immigrant workers went home after saving enough money to support their families. Job turnover, therefore, became a growing problem.[72] Also, by being not only unskilled but untrained, these workers were particularly vulnerable to injuries. Employers were themselves generally reluctant to do much about safety at work, but the problem became particularly pressing during the boom years 1895–1900. Employers sought to take advantage of the improved trade conditions by speeding up existing plant and introducing more modern, productive machinery. This tended to force up the injury rate, especially amongst unskilled Italian workers who had come from mining or construction and who had little knowledge or experience of the ways, means and dangers of heavy metal production.[73] Both these problems drew attention to a growing crisis in industrial training, particularly in the provision of highly qualified cadres and new skilled workers who could safely and efficiently direct the production process at a time of expansion and rapid technical change.

In July 1901, for instance, a report was given to the *Chambre syndicale* and described at length the shortages of technically trained personnel in the fields of the various applications of electricity to industry.[74] By 1905, M. Alfassa, Secretary-General of the *Société de protection des apprentis,* was moved to exclaim that France was 'no longer training apprentices' when technically qualified personnel were desperately needed.[75] Whether the cause was the growth of *precision* production, which tended to reduce the need for all-round ability and increase the need for a more 'professional ability in a given speciality'; or workers possessing a craft refusing to train apprentices properly for fear of creating substitutes for their own jobs; or employers seeking to exploit boys as cheap specialised labour; or, finally, parents wishing to get an extra income from their children and therefore not encouraging their sons to take up an apprenticeship at very low wages, the problem was both pressing and widespread.[76]

Such 'cries of alarm', according to M. de Ribes-Christofle from the *Fédération des industriels et commerçants français,* appeared to 'gush forth' each day from the newspapers, magazines and the National Assembly,[77] and in one instance they were all brought together under one roof when the National Congress on Apprenticeship met in Roubaix in 1911. The Congress comprised delegates from business, trade unions and government, and gave voice to the problems faced by all the main branches of industry. According to Paul Jannettaz, the secretary-general of the

Congress, the problem was most marked in the technically advanced industries, such as in chemicals and engineering, where there was an 'alarming' shortage of foremen and technical personnel 'knowing the whole production process'.[78] A.M. Lambert reported that the number of apprentices needed to fill such positions in the *Nord* engineering trades had to be doubled, in order for the trades to work efficiently; while M. Wauquier, president of the *Syndicat des constructeurs mécaniciens et chaudronniers du Nord de la France,* called for the introduction of obligatory apprenticeships in the industry.[79] Though this problem was not seen to be as pressing in mining and metallurgy, many observers believed that it had national dimensions and required national solutions.[80]

Until 1911, the Third Republic had witnessed many *ad hoc* public and private schemes for the formation and training of new *ouvriers d'art.* Though the Republic was meant to guarantee a public education system that was free, compulsory and secular, the French section of the International Metalworkers' Federation claimed that only its 'gratuitousness is everywhere assured'.[81] At the elementary level the religious impulse of Catholicism still remained strong, while compulsory attendance was rarely enforced. Illiteracy, too, continued to maintain its grip on a large section of the population, especially in the countryside, as attested by the Annual Levy of Recruits to the army. Every year the Levy found some ten to eleven thousand recruits unable to read or write.[82] For those who did attend primary school, nothing prevented them from leaving once they had reached the age of thirteen, in which case they went to the factories or mines ill-prepared to take up the skilled positions becoming available and had no further formal education required of them. There were, of course, the *grandes écoles,* but the training they provided was far in advance of the needs of even the most skilled workers. Evening classes, as well, after a long day's work taxed the stamina of even the fittest boys and youths.[83] At a time when 'the idea of *[traditional]* apprenticeship seemed to have been abandoned' to the private and factory-based capitalist regulation of skill, the remedies that came forth tended to highlight the need for systematic state intervention, rather than provide a substitute for it.[84] During the 1880s, for instance, public schools of apprenticeship were established, particularly in the Paris area, and provided practical and specialist instruction for metalworkers, such as future fitters. These developed largely under the influence of the proletarian senators, Tolain and Corban. The schools were run by local authorities and governed by the Ministry of Commerce. They were considered to be the equal of state primary schools. At the same time, the Ministry of Public Instruction established Higher Primary Schools to prepare pupils for a 'professional' manual education.[85] At the level of a secondary education, there was also the Paris-based Diderot Technical School *(Ecole Municipale Professionnelle Diderot),* which was established in 1873 by the Municipal Council of Paris. When the

International Metalworkers' Federation (IMF) met in Paris in 1900 for their congress and visited the school, they saw its aim as training students who, after leaving elementary school, did three years' training at the Diderot so that they could take up a position as a journeyman worker in their particular trade.[86] Though the instruction certainly could be seen as equivalent to a traditional apprenticeship, 'in reality it [was] very much more':

> for the student receives for three years the most up-to-date instruction that the City of Paris can command, and when at the end of three years, he receives his 'certificate' (granted after examination), he is naturally better equipped for life's battle than the youth whose means of education in his trade has been nothing beyond the usual term of apprenticeship.[87]

Tuition was free and the students were allowed to enter the school between the ages of thirteen and sixteen after having passed an entrance examination. The branches of metal work covered in the instruction included forging, metal-turning, fitting, instrument making, electricity, modelling, copper-smithing, carpentry, locksmithing and sanitary plumbing. The professional and hyper-qualified nature of the instruction, which led to supervisory positions in industry, may be gleaned from the training received by a youthful smith, a hitherto craft orientated vocation:

> In the first year he is taught the handling of tools, how to manage his hearth and the elements of the trade. In the second year he learns the use of the various tools and makes small things; while in the third year he makes responsible work, such as machine parts. So much for the technical side of the education. The theoretical is not neglected, for while 'in class' he receives instruction in French, geography, arithmetic, algebra, geometry, mechanics, drawing, hygiene, economy, etc., these subjects increasing in depth as the end of the three years' period draws nearer.[88]

As the Diderot Technical School could hold only three hundred students, no amount of professional instruction could render it anything more than an island of enlightenment in a sea of technical darkness and poor facilities for widespread industrial training. By 1892, however, the first inklings of a solution were becoming apparent. New Model apprenticeship schools, such as the Practical Schools of Commerce and Industry, were established.[89] About 1,717 pupils were in attendance in 1893, for the training of foremen, highly qualified workers and some craftsmen. This figure had risen to 14,766 by 1912.[90] By the late 1900s, the Paris region had seven schools for boys and eight schools for girls, comprising some 5,000 students.[91] Yet as Lequin has suggested, if it is remembered that over five million pupils were receiving a primary education in the 1880s, such paltry numbers at the secondary level only further highlighted the serious blockage to higher technical instruction.[92] The training too, left a lot to be desired, as it was largely empirical, in complete contrast to the Diderot school. As the French section of the IMF reported, the law which governed the schools and the training of apprentices 'nowhere. . . mentioned' theoretical instruction. The only article which could be seen to raise the question of formal theoretical training was: if the apprentice was less than sixteen and could 'neither read, write, nor reckon, or if he had not finished his religious instruction', then 'the master is obliged to allow him during the working day the necessary time and liberty for his education'.[93] In other words, not only were the numbers of schools and pupils small, but the training was poor and completely voluntary. In the view of the French section of the IMF, these conditions made it 'impossible for the great mass of the young workmen and workwomen of Paris, and of the whole of France, to acquire even the rudiments of the theory of their profession'.[94]

The entire responsibility for this problem cannot be laid solely at the feet of the central government. Employers as well must share part of the blame. A good example of this was their response to the passage of two laws through the National Assembly designed to improve the apprenticeship situation. On 30th March 1900, the Assembly offered premiums to industrialists to take on apprentices if they did not have any. At the same time, the legal working day was reduced to ten hours. The offer of premiums, however, seemed to fall on deaf ears. The *Conseil supérieur du Travail* noted that by 1902 there was still no improvement in the numbers of apprentices, especially in the large towns.[95] As far as legal regulation of the working day went, a move designed to make it more expensive to hire adult labour and cheaper for apprenticed labour, employers responded by dismissing many apprentices from engineering works in order to demonstrate their disapproval with such 'unwarranted interference' in the running of their works. It was not for them, they claimed, to carry the 'burden' or costs involved in solving the shortage of technically trained personnel.[96]

These responses were quite symptomatic of more general reluctance to abandon full control over their company-based training programmes; but it also pointed to the poisonous atmosphere that all too often surrounded relations between enterprises and their workers, in much the same way as the insufferable heat of the furnace encloaked the toil of those who worked in the mill or the foundry. The hallmark of French industrial training for the workforce during the nineteenth century was the extensive network of factory training programmes, which were developed in response to the shortages of trained labour power in the metal industry.

By the turn of the century, these programmes had not only been continued, they had also been 'professionalised'. At the *Cail à Denain* locomotive shops, by 1909 there were 750 apprentices between the ages of thirteen and eighteen in a workforce of 2,750. About three-quarters of the apprentices were the sons of local adult workers working at the plant. In order to maintain harmonious relations with their adult workforce the enterprise limited the hours of work for apprentices to ten hours a day. Even so, this was still a long working day for the youths.[97] The courses were devised by foremen and engineers and the instruction was highly specialised in mechanics and machine design, assembling, forging, founding, modelling and pattern-making. Over the three years' course students had to do five hundred hours of theoretical work and 250 hours of practical instruction under supervision. The success of the programme was reflected in the fact that the firm only needed half of its *élèves*, while the remainder went off to other plants once they had completed their training.[98] Yet by this period the *Cail à Denain* firm was exceptional in being able not only to fill its own needs but also service other firms with its highly qualified workers. However, this did not stop many employers from believing that state intervention and the formation of schools of commerce and industry were largely a waste of time and too costly. Moreover, they were concerned that such schools did not 'habituate' the adolescent to the 'intensive mode of work' which he would obtain by a factory-based training.[99] In these cases the provision of labour discipline had as much educational value as formal technical instruction, if not more.

If heavy metal industry employers, and employers generally, did not overwhelmingly welcome state intervention in the training of their workers, they were wholeheartedly in support of state intervention to crush labour agitation and to regulate trade unionism. Following the fright of the civil war and the massacre of thousands of Parisian workers in 1871, the 'slave-holders' Third Republic in 1884 obliged all reconstituted unions to register their constitutions, by-laws, and the names of their officials. The Republic's Interior Minister, Waldeck-Rousseau, hoped to sponsor trade unions of an innocuous sort, which would be peaceful, non-revolutionary, and non-socialist. He also gave support to employer blacklists, the sacking of unionists, lock-outs, the use of *agents provocateurs* and spies, and straight out suppression.[100] By the late 1890s however, many unions had re-formed on an independent basis and were ready to enter into battle again for better wages, conditions and safety at work, particularly on a local level. In 1900, for instance, the members of the Federal Union of Metalworkers went on strike at Schneider's *Le Creusot* iron and steel works. With the complicity of the 'Government of Republican Defence' the enterprise ruthlessly crushed the strike, sacked 3,000 'subversives , turned the union from 'red' to 'yellow', and by 'adroit selection' engaged only those workers 'who were without conscience and devoted to the cause of the masters'.[101] When workers undertook similar actions in Lorraine during 1905 and in areas of the Loire, the metal enterprises responded with lock-outs, blacklists, yellow unions, the formation of employer syndicates for mutual defence and the use of police repression to dig out 'dissidents'.[102] In 1902, a national federation of yellow unions was formed in the steel industry and claimed a membership of 200,000 workers, while by 1910, some 63 employer anti-strike syndicates had been formed with assets of 20 million francs.[103] The employers' fear of and antagonism towards independent labour organisation in their factories was coloured not just by the political legacies of 1871, but also by its social legacy—the experience of workers' control and the prospect of a revolutionary democratisation of factory management. In some ways it was comparable to American employer fears of the contractors, as the ideology was based on producerist images of work and skill; but in this case it was not the employer who could be drawn into the net of productive labour—only the workers. It was a legacy which continued to maintain a strong grip over the thought and practice of many workers and was at complete loggerheads with the employers' vision of the capitalist regulation of skill and their control over the professionalisation of production management.[104]

The anonymous 'G' articulated the thought with great clarity within the pages of the *Mouvement socialiste* on February 1, 1899;

> A widely held view today is that mechanical systems no longer call for the application of manual skill and that training must become purely theoretical. Such an illusion only springs from the minds of people who have never had to manage workers. Never has a worker had more need of skilfulness than since the day when machinery took a leading role in production. Machines are precision instruments which have to be carefully maintained, used with intelligence and constantly monitored, if methods are to be found of perfecting them.[105]

The feelings expressed by 'G' that manual labour was in reality a combination of the *'sentiment artistique',* intelligence and precision work were meant to counter the growing middle-class view that in a world of machines only an 'abstract education' was required, while manual labour was itself only an *'accessoire de luxe'.*[106] In response to these views, and the reality that an 'abstract education' was increasingly synonymous with a hyper-qualified and professional training for managers, while the large majority of workers had to settle for a purely factory-based training, a number of unions autonomously sought to counter-regulate industrial training and bring theoretical and practical training together. In the first instance, it took the form of unions agitating for the return of the *'compagnonnage'* system, or the master-journeyman-apprentice relation, as the basis of training.[107] But the movement quickly developed into an extensive system where trade unions themselves established trade schools, which revolved around the technical value of 'workmanship'. By 1905 some four hundred and eight unions and some small employers were servicing the training of approximately 95,000 students.[108]

In the metal industry, the Association of Engineers from the late 1880s instituted in Paris courses of instruction in geometry, drawing, wire-drawing, electricity, and also organised lectures on current technical questions. In other towns unions did much the same work, at times with the cooperation of municipal councils, which as we have seen were also playing an important role in the local trade school movement.[109] The prominent French historian, Yves Lequin, however, has argued that this movement was not an adequate response to the training problem, as too much emphasis was placed on the 'harmonious and creative thought' of the artisan-producer, when in fact mechanisation and the new forms of training applicable in industry had killed off this form of instruction and apprenticeship. Different and higher sorts of qualification were now needed, he suggests, which the union movement and its producerist images of labour were ill-suited for.[110] Though there is some truth in this, as can be seen from 'G's' sentiments, it will also be seen that there was an equally strong emphasis on machinery as 'instruments of precision' requiring 'intelligent' and highly-skilled workers to run them; an emphasis which was itself the hallmark of the new production management and of its need for new *ouvriers d'art.* To be sure, many of the courses taught by the Association of Engineers in Paris may have represented an attempt to preserve archaic and now useless skills, but the courses on geometry, drawing and the uses of electricity were exactly the courses required for the new *ouvriers d'art.* Though they may not have met the demand, the courses represented a viable basis for the counter-regulation of industrial training and provided many workers with an opportunity to acquire the new skills, especially when employers were caught in a bind, largely of their own making. As the state was not providing an extensive system of higher education, which would have for its clientele a *petite bourgeoisie* capable of administering the professional-technical intelligence of the bourgeoisie, then enterprises found themselves faced with the prospect of either having to train *extensively* their own 'subversive' workers in the new technical intelligence or adapting to a trade union-based based movement, which both counter-regulated industrial training and provided some of its own members with the new skills.

One historian has noted an added dimension of this in the changing emphasis employers began to give to factory regulations. More of their rules demanded from workers a respect for the technical needs of production, so as to speed up production, avoid accidents and encourage a better use of machinery through stricter penalties. It was not so much that factory rules based on the maintenance of discipline were abandoned, rather they were broadened to include technical regulations that would hopefully ensure that the machinery used by workers would pay a higher dividend.[111] Yet without a changing respect *for* workers, rather than demanding it from them, the dilemmas would continue. It may be that Yves Lequin found in this *impasse* the basis for his judgment that no real solutions presented themselves for the training of the new *ouvriers d'art* and lower echelon managers before World War One. In his view the crisis continued.[112] Lequin however, makes no mention of the National Apprenticeship Congress which met in Roubaix in 1911, where government, employers and workers hammered out a political and social compromise, which not only had a bearing on the future of industrial training for the workforce as a whole, but also represented one of the first sustained attempts to bury the violent and poisonous legacy of the *Commune de Paris*. Neither does he analyse the growing importance of the new apprenticeship movements that sought to professionalise the training of the workforce and, in fact, laid the foundations for a substantial reform of industrial training during the three years before World War One.

4. *The new 'apprenticeship' movement*

A new apprenticeship movement was gaining strength during the early 1900s, and it was led by the *Commission permanente du Conseil supérieur de l'Enseignement technique.* This body advanced a more cooperative form of state intervention for the training of the workforce, and its guiding principle was obligatory attendance at trade schools for all youths below the age of eighteen. The state's role in this was to work in cooperation with local municipalities, employers and workers' organisations.[113] Between 1905 and 1910 similar proposals were developed within the employers' organisation, the *Fédération des industriels et commerçants français.* It especially wanted to see a return to written contracts between employers and their trainees and the abolition of verbal agreements. These contracts, it was suggested, should be supervised by the state-inspired *Conseil des prud'hommes,* which would also grant formal diplomas on completion of courses.[114] Beside the work of the *Commission* and the *Fédération,* various government bodies, like the *Conseil supérieur du Travail,* made reports and posed possible reforms, including free and compulsory practical and theoretical instruction for all those engaged in industry under eighteen years of age.[115] Conferences were also held under the aegis of the *Ligue de l'Enseignement* and brought together employers, state bodies and municipal education authorities to hammer out plans and, more particularly, specify for how long these courses should run: three years was coming to be the commonly held view.[116]

If these proposals were designed to do anything, they were to lay the basis for employers and the state to develop a new orientation towards the training of manual labour and produce for the future, what M. Jully, the Inspector of Manual Education for Paris Schools, called, 'the cadres of our industrial army'.[117] M. Villemin was a leading architect of this new orientation, both through his work with the *Bulletin de l'Association pour le développement de l'Enseignement technique* and at the important Bourges Conference held a year before the Roubaix National Conference. At Bourges, on 13 February 1910, he spoke of the need for the development of two forms of apprenticeship if industry was to survive and progress, and these had to be seen as 'absolutely distinct'. One had to be for manual apprentices and the other for the new skilled workers and technical personnel. Yet for the latter to even come into existence, let alone be systematically trained in the new production and supervisory positions, a pool of reasonably well-trained workers would first have to be created, for without such a supply of young workers ready to be trained to the higher levels, industry would deteriorate.

Employers, then, had to overcome their brutal condescension and paternalism towards manual labour, while society in general had to give it a 'place of honour'.[118] A practical and pioneering example of this had been the work of the Diderot Technical School controlled by the Paris Municipal Council. By the early 1900s, however, similar but more modest schools were also being created, especially through the cooperation of Paris' leading firms, the municipal authorities and educational organisations like the Society for the Protection of Apprentices *(Société de protection des apprentis)*. In 1904–5 the *Société* began to provide afternoon courses twice a week for future *mécaniciens* in the 14th and 15th Paris arrondissements. Its plans were modestly supported by the *Société d'Encouragement pour l'Industrie Nationale* and by local employers. By 1908 it had received municipal recognition and became one of Paris's municipal schools, and though its apprentice intake was only tiny—80 apprentices in 1910—the pupils came from the leading companies, such as the *Société Industrielle des Téléphones, Dard, Carpentier, Thomas-Houston, Grouvelle-Arquembour, Ponthus et Therods, Sizzare et Naudin, Coirard et Richard,* and *Hollebecke.*[119] Furthermore, two tinplate trade schools had been established in Paris by November 1909 for the training of super-skilled supervisory employees. They studied modern plating processes, especially the application of electricity in tin plating, which the French became famous for, as well as geometry, applied mathematics, technical design and practical experimentation.[120] Though these examples were just that (examples and nothing more), they did create a new atmosphere within which Villemin's ideas and the programmes of other progressive organisations could receive sympathetic attention. Employers were becoming used to the idea of dealing with local state institutions, either through their chambers of commerce or privately, and they were not unsympathetic to the idea of the central state providing some sort of *framework* within which these developments could obtain a national impact, as long as the central state was made aware that it must confine its *direct* intervention to the policing of strikes and trade unionism.[121] Against this background employers grudgingly came to accept the need for change and the Roubaix National Congress on industrial training took place.

5. *Providing a framework: the Roubaix Congress*

The Congress was held during October 1911, and comprised delegates from business, trade unions, chambers of commerce, local and central government and a number of technical education experts. P. Coupat represented the Association of Engineers which, as we have seen, had a large stake in the question of industrial training. The meetings and debates that took place were not just important because of the recommendations and solutions which ensued, but also because of the atmosphere in which they were debated. The majority of delegates sought, in the words of the Secretary-General, a 'new orientation towards manual labour' for the younger generation. They saw themselves as having to counter 'the thrust towards *petit fonctionnarisme'*, which had developed as a by-product of the generalised de-qualification of manual labour and the hyper-qualification of higher management.[122]

In the context of a slowing down in the rate of population increase and a growing need for maximum national productivity, it was counter-productive to degrade the value of manual labour and only highlight the value of the functionary. It was often argued that, if this continued, then not only would the shortages of new skilled manual and technical employees remain, but also the classes which composed French society would develop a cultural bias against them, as was already apparent in the middle class and in the sons of workers being encouraged to seek out a vocation as functionaries, rather than as skilled manual workers.[123] The aim, therefore, of the new orientation towards manual labour had to be 'the formation of youths who would become skilled workers, machine setters, fitters, *chefs d'équipes,* and in general form the elements of the officer corps *(cadres)* in the workers' army'.[124] This emphasis integrated a great deal of the producerist images of labour propounded by socialists, trade unions and workers at the time, but as can be seen it was given an efficiency rather than workerist cutting-edge, which better suited the needs of a professionalised management. It was an emphasis that did not seem to worry trade unionists very much, as long as it was complemented by the implementation of practical proposals which would overcome the 'bad conditions' of 'trade instruction'.[125] From the point of view of all the parties concerned this was the precise role of the Congress. Its Organizing Commission was made up of twelve sections and produced twenty-three reports in all concerning the reform of industrial training in the main branches of industry. There were eleven main recommendations, summarised below, which proposed:

    1. Fixing the school leaving age at thirteen.[126]

2. Abolishing the ten hours working day for apprentices under the age of eighteen in order to encourage employers to take on more youths for training.

3. Encouraging apprentices under the age of eighteen to attend compulsory professional apprenticeship courses during the legal working day. This would hopefully put an end to night school and was supported in principle by the Paris Chamber of Commerce.

4. Forming local committees made up of employers, workers, former students, state and communal representatives to manage and supervise the training of apprentices. Each committee was to be known as a *comité local d'apprentissage* and was to take the place of organisations which had been established in the wake of the trade school law of 2 November 1892. These earlier organisations had merely been designed to protect children and apprentices in industry.

5. Recognising the major role to be played by employers and trade unions in the training of apprentices, the costs of which were to be divided between the employers, the state and the communes.

6. Utilising existing professional schools and schools of commerce and industry for apprenticeship training, such as those at Armentières, Nantes, Vierzon, and Voiron, with the aim of educating workers to be foremen and shop-floor managers. Overall, there were sixty-four schools of commerce and industry in existence for boys and thirteen for girls, while in Paris there were, as we have seen, seven municipal professional schools for boys and eight for girls. All of these were to be drawn into the new apprenticeship programme.

7. Establishing reciprocal obligations for employers and apprentices in industrial training, which each party would have to guarantee.

8. Binding these guarantees would be a contract.

9. Handing out certificates after youths had completed their training, which would free both parties from any further obligations to one another.

10. That this certificate be based on an examination for a diploma; and finally,

11. Forming departmental, regional and local committees to take charge, in a cooperative manner, of the overall direction of the schools. These committees would have the status of corporate bodies and be financed by the state.[127]

Following the Congress, the Minister of Commerce, Couyba, decided to be the 'artisan' and implement several of the recommendations in a decree on 24 October, 1911. Canton committees were formed to create state schools of technical instruction for each department and to request state aid for those schools privately formed in a department, such as those run by enterprises or trade unions. These committees were designed to encourage not only apprenticeship, but also technical education in general. In the same decree the Minister instituted the granting of professional certificates to the *élèves*, who had completed their courses, Certificate of Professional Aptitude [CAP] ; but it was noted at the time that their success would depend a lot on whether employers recognised their value for boys and girls under eighteen.[128] The CAP, it should be noted, was not designed for all boys and girls under eighteen. Only a minority were meant to undertake successfully the three-year course in the theory and practice of their trade, and pass the examination so as to be able to obtain highly qualified positions in the factory's officer corps.

At a more general level, the Ministry of Education set up compulsory education schools for those who could neither read nor write and for young people of both sexes between the ages of thirteen and eighteen who had not completed their elementary education. In every town with a population of 10,000 people or more, trade and commercial schools were to be established which would provide courses of training for apprentices, other young workers and for clerks who were under eighteen years of age. Attendance at these schools was to be compulsory with the approval of the municipal council. Employers also were requested to allow all those under eighteen who had not obtained their elementary certificates or were undertaking an apprenticeship to attend courses during the working day at least three times a week and for at least two hours each time, a minimum of six hours per week. The teachers for the courses all had to be approved by the local canton committees.[129]

Though it would take some time for these reforms and recommendations to make their way through the system, France had finally begun to establish a national and state-based technical education system for the formation of the new skilled workforce.[130] Even in the absence of an extensive apparatus for the training of *petit bourgeois* lower echelon engineers and technicians, the overall system bore a close resemblance to the successful English model, with the exception that training for higher managerial positions was far more proficient. It was in the middle that the French system broke down, but this is a far cry from the wailing of contemporary managerial critics and some historians that the entire educational structure was in a 'crisis'. In fact, in comparison with the English system, the role of the state in providing a public dimension to the capitalist regulation of skill and training was both more formal and centralised.

At this juncture, it is not yet possible to suggest whether the French system as a whole was more elitist or guided than its other European counterparts, as Messrs. Maurice, Sellier and Silvestre would have us believe. What is incontestable, however, is that a less hostile atmosphere was being formed around relations between the state, employers and organised labour for the provision of industrial training. For the state and the metal employers particularly, it was realised that emphasis had to be given to forms of training which would lead to recognised certificates, diplomas, and degrees in order to fill the minority of hyper-qualified positions in the factory's division of labour. Furthermore, this was to be built around the needs of quality specialisation in the French metal industry. French metal employers at this time may have had to pull certain employees out of lowly positions and place them in jobs with higher technical and supervisory responsibilities without having them first obtain any recognised training or diploma. But hardly being satisfied with this state of affairs or unable to do anything about it, they gradually, if at times reluctantly, sought a 'new orientation' to the training of their workforce that was no longer exclusively dominated by the atmosphere of their factories. In conjunction with other public and private organisations, they fashioned a new apprenticeship movement, which provided both an ideology and a practical basis for a structural reform of the educational system, especially for the provision of new supervisory employees and skilled workers. Certainly, one should not completely dismiss the criticisms advanced by that impressive array of radical bourgeois critics influenced by 'Americanism' and the ideas of Frederick Winslow Taylor, grouped around the *Revue de Métallurgie*. But the sting of their general criticism was blunted by being limited to a particular point in time and relevant for only one stratum of the workforce. Ultimately, their contribution to the professionalisation of industrial training in France was to help create a climate for change and forge a unifying approach. It was left to a more diverse grouping of intellectuals, employers and state officials, who appreciated that progress was being made, actually to orchestrate the details of reform.[131]

NOTES

1. See Henry Le Chatelier, 'Du rôle des sciences dans l'industrie', *Revue de Métallurgie*, Vol. 1, 1904, Mémoires, pp. 1-10. Le Chatelier was also at this time the president of the influential *Société d'Encouragement pour l'Industrie Nationale* and his presidential address of 1904 bore witness to the several fronts on which he fought his campaign. See, 'Discours du Président, Séance Générale du 23 décembre 1904', in *Bulletin de la Société d'Encouragement pour l'Industrie Nationale*, janvier, 1905, Vol. 107, pp. 12-22. Unfortunately, this chapter cannot be developed to the same extent as the chapters which flank it. In the cases of Britain and America, and even more so for Germany, there are extensive public and private sources which show in great detail how the composition and structure of the workforce changed and what effects fixed capital investment had on how labour-power was used and trained. In the case of France, though, neither the compilations of historians nor the enterprise archives consulted for this work allow for a ready presentation of these changes. Recent historical research on fixed capital formation in France, particularly Lévy-Leboyer's work, has not yet revealed a series of data on rates of capital consumption for industry, in the manner of Feinstein's findings for the United Kingdom. Also the records of several southern French metal enterprises located in the *Archives Nationales*, Paris, for example, are extremely fragmentary for this period and are mainly of use in describing their commercial activities. Other contemporary records, such as trade journals and reports, are also not of much help here, though they are very rich on the matter of training methods and how these were transformed. There is one untapped source, however, which holds this French study together: a report by the French section of the International Metalworkers' Federation, published in 1915, and entitled 'Elementary Education in France'. This was only one of several reports undertaken by the International Metalworkers' Federation at this time and brought together by the Federation's Secretary, Charles Hobson. Unfortunately, this source is also much

richer for other continental countries, especially Germany, than for France, but it does provide a fairly full picture. For M. Lévy-Leboyer's recent work see, 'Capital Investment and Economic Growth in France, 1820-1930', in Peter Mathias and M.M. Postan, eds., *The Cambridge Economic History of Europe*, Vol. VII, *The Industrial Economies: Capital, Labour and Enterprise*, Pt. 1, pp. 231-95. Lévy-Leboyer also provides a bibliography of recent research on fixed capital formation in France in the same article (see pp. 752-4).

2. Le Chatelier, 'Du rôle des sciences dans l'industrie', *loc. cit.*, p.1.

3. *ibid.*, p. 3.

4. *ibid.*, p. 2.

5. *ibid.*, pp. 2-5. For a survey of similar criticisms made by other educational radicals, see E. Leduc, 'L'organisation syndicale et technique en Allemagne', *Bulletin de la Société d'Encouragement pour l'Industrie Nationale*, Vol. 108, octobre, 1909, p. 221.

6. See Henry Le Chatelier, 'La science pure orienté vers les applications et la science industrielle', *Revue de Métallurgie*, Vol. 9, 1912, pp. 509-12; Speech to *L'Association des élèves des écoles spéciales de l'Université de Liège*, 24 April, 1912.

7. See also the editorial in *Revue de Métallurgie*, Vol. 5, 1908, Mémoires, pp. 562-4, for a discussion of the necessity of a closer cooperation between the sciences and industry, and the need for industry to recognise the high costs of scientific laboratories and the immediately poor short-term results obtainable.

8. Henry Le Chatelier, 'Du rôle des sciences dans l'industrie', *Revue de Métallurgie*, Vol. 1, 1904, Mémoires, p. 6.

9. Henry Le Chatelier, 'L'enseignement technique supérieur: son but et ses méthodes', *Revue de Métallurgie*, Vol. 8, No. 6, juin 1911, p. 398.

10. *ibid.*, p. 398.

11. *ibid.*, p. 398.

12. See André Pelletan, 'Les écoles techniques allemandes', *Revue de Métallurgie*, Vol. 3, No. 11, novembre 1906, p. 608.

13. Henry Le Chatelier, 'L'enseignement technique supérieur: son but et ses méthodes', *Revue de Métallurgie*, Vol. 8, No. 6, juin 1911, p. 398. See also E. Leduc's review, 'L'organisation syndicale et technique en Allemagne', *loc. cit.*, p. 214 ff. Leduc during 1907-1908 was charged with studying developments in Germany by the *Conservatoire nationale des Arts et Métiers*.

14. Henry Le Chatelier, 'L'enseignement supérieur: son but et ses méthodes', *loc. cit.*, p. 399 ff. For a description of Carnegie's endowments to libraries, see 'The Carnegie Institute of Pittsburg', *Iron Age*, Vol. LXXVII, 1906, p. 616.

15. See 'Procès-Verbaux des Séances de la Société d'Encouragement', *Bulletin de la Société d'Encouragement pour l'Industrie Nationale*, 24 novembre 1905, Vol. 107, 1905, pp. 1528-31.

16. See Editorial, *Revue de Métallurgie*, Vol. 4, No. 7, juillet 1907, Mémoires, p. 608. See also, Pelletan, *loc. cit.*, novembre 1906, p. 608.

17. See Henry Le Chatelier's preface to the translation of F.W. Taylor's, *Principles of Scientific Management*, in 'Notes Bibliographiques', *Revue de Métallurgie*, Vol. 9, 1912, pp. 500-1.

18. Pelletan, *loc. cit.*, novembre 1906, pp. 589, 609. Pelletan's report was constructed around a systematic comparison with the training of engineers in Germany.

19. *ibid.*, pp. 609-10.

20. *ibid.*, pp. 616-17.

21. *ibid.*, p. 612.

22. *ibid.*, pp. 611-12.

23. *ibid.*, pp. 614–15. See also Henry Le Chatelier, 'L'enseignement technique supérieur: son but et ses méthodes', *loc. cit.*, p. 401.

24. Pelletan, *loc. cit.*, novembre 1906, pp. 616, 618.

25. *ibid.*, p. 613. A few months before, the university's teaching professors also came under attack. In the *Revue*'s June editorial, it was suggested that the teaching staff at the universities in technical courses should have practical experience in industry in order for them to obtain a position. See Editorial, *Revue de Métallurgie*, Vol. 3, No. 6, juin 1906, pp. 318–19.

26. Pelletan, *loc. cit.*, novembre 1906, p. 619.

27. The idea of encouraging students to select their own subjects and develop a 'spirit of initiative' was based on the German experience of cultivating in students an ability to rely on themselves, be treated as young men and not as children, while at the same time, maintaining rigid selection procedures. See *ibid.*, p. 606.

28. See *ibid.*, pp. 619-20. See also Le Fèvre, 'L'education des ingénieurs en France', *Bulletin de l'Association des anciens élèves de l'Ecole des Mines de Paris*, décembre 1905, pp. 133-40, for similar, though less stinging criticisms.

29. See *Revue de Métallurgie*, Vol. 4, No. 5, mai 1907, p. 470.

30. See M. Baclé, 'L'enseignement des grandes écoles techniques et son influence sur la carrière des élèves', *ibid.*, mai 1907, pp. 487-90.

31. See 'Quelques réflexions d'un groupe d'élèves de l'École des Mines de Paris sur l'enseignement de leur école, *ibid.*, mai 1907, pp. 505-10.

32. See Charles de Freminville, 'Le jeune ingénieur', *ibid.*, Vol. 8, 1911, p. 787.

33. *ibid.*, pp. 787-9.

34. *ibid.*, p. 789. For Mathis, a professor of German at the *Polytechnique* and the *Ecole des Mines*, flexibility would be further encouraged by all students having to become proficient in two foreign languages, especially German and English. This study would also be complemented by trips to Germany and England with visits to factories, so that the students would acquire practical knowledge of foreign techniques. See M. Mathis, 'L'enseignement des langues vivantes dans les écoles techniques supérieures', *Revue de Métallurgie*, Vol. 4, No. 5, mai 1907, pp. 493-97.

35. See *Revue de Métallurgie*, Vol. 5, 1908, Mémoires, pp. 647-8.

36. *ibid.*, pp. 791-6.

37. See Henry Le Chatelier, 'L'enseignement technique supérieur: son but et méthodes', *loc. cit.*, pp. 400-1.

38. *ibid.*, pp. 400-1.

39. *ibid.*, p. 403.

40. *ibid.*, p. 404 ff.

41. *ibid.*, p. 403.

42. Rondo Cameron, *France and the Economic Development of Europe*, pp. 61-3. See also Moody, *French Education Since Napoleon*, pp. 100-1.

43. Yves Lequin, 'Labour in the French Economy since the Revolution', *Cambridge Economic History of Europe*, Vol. VII, pp. 317-18.

44. *ibid.*, p. 318.

45. See Aimée Moutet, 'Les origines du systéme de Taylor en France. Le point de vue patronal (1907-1914)', *Le mouvement social*, No. 93, octobre/décembre, 1975, pp. 20, 22, 25.

46. *ibid.*, pp. 20, n. 15; 26.

47. *ibid.*, p. 23.

48. See M. Aguillon, 'Observations au sujet de la note de M. André Pelletan, sur les écoles techniques allemandes', *Revue de Métallurgie*, Vol. 4, No. 5, mai 1907, pp. 480-3.

49. See M. Vogt, 'L'enseignement technique', *ibid.*, mai 1907, p. 474.
50. *ibid.*, p. 474.
51. M. Féry, 'L'enseignement technique', *ibid.*, mai 1907, pp. 484-6. (The quotes can be found on p. 584.)
52. M. Arth, 'L'enseignement technique', *ibid.*, mai 1907, pp. 477-9. See also Antoine Prost, *L'Enseignement en France, 1800-1967*, pp. 303-4.
53. *ibid.*, pp. 491-2.
54. See *Revue de Métallurgie*, Vol. 9, 1912, p. 207.
55. Vogt, *loc. cit.*, mai 1907, p. 475.
56. *Revue de Métallurgie*, Vol. 3, No. 5, mai 1906, pp. 230-1, and Vogt, *loc. cit.*, mai 1907, pp. 473-4.
57. See Duncan Burn, *An Economic History of Steel Making, 1867-1939*, CUP, Cambridge, 1940, p. 5, n. 2, for observations on the role of engineers and chemists at the furnaces of *Le Creusot*.
58. See L. Guillet, 'Aciers au molybdène', *Revue de Métallurgie*, Vol. 1, Mémoires, 1904, pp. 390-401.
59. See Louis Le Chatelier (a manager at *Cail à Denain*), 'Les Ateliers Cail à Denain', *Revue de Métallurgie*, Vol. 6, 1909, p. 577, and Max Orthey 'La chimie en fonderie', *Revue de Métallurgie*, Vol. 4, 1907, pp. 78-84.
60. L. Guillet, 'Conservatoire National des Arts et Métiers, Laboratoire d'Essais: Rapport sur le fonctionnement pendant l'année 1908', *Revue de Métallurgie*, Vol. 6, 1909, pp. 1005-12, and A. Boyer-Guillon, 'Quelques appareils de mesures employés au laboratoire d'essais du conservatoire national des arts et métiers', *Revue de Métallurgie*, Vol. 8, No. 3, mars 1911, pp. 181-223.
61. *Revue de Métallurgie*, Vol. 9, 1912, pp. 203-7.
62. Louis Le Chatelier, *loc. cit.*, 1909, p. 581.
63. See François Crouzet, 'Remarques sur l'industrie d'armements en France (du milieu du XIXe siècle à 1914)', *Revue historique*, Vol. 231, avril-juin 1974, esp. pp. 420-2.
64. See *Revue de Métallurgie*, Vol. 3, No. 7, juillet 1907, editorial, p. 361. See also, for example, G. Revol, 'Influence de l'emploi des outils en acier à coupe rapide sur la construction de quelques machines-outils', *Revue de Métallurgie*, Vol. 11, No. 4, avril 1914, pp. 357-432, and P. Massot, 'La taille économique des métaux par les aciers à coupe rapide. D'après les expériences de F.W. Taylor', *ibid.*, avril, 1914, pp. 433-63.
65. M. Lévy-Leboyer, 'Le patronat français a-t-il été malthusien?', *Le mouvement social*, No. 88, juillet-septembre, 1974, pp. 6, 21-24. See also Moody, *op. cit.*, p. 100-1.
66. See L.A. Vincent, 'Evolution de la production intérieure brute en France, de 1896 à 1938: Méthode et premiers résultats', *Etudes et Conjoncture*, Vol. XVII, No. 2, 1962, p. 929.
67. *ibid.*, p. 929. According to Vincent, the clothing industry in 1913 employed 1.3 million people. The two traditional sectors of employment, the construction and textile industries, comprised some 789,000 people in the construction sector and 904,000 in the textile sector in 1906. The metal industry, by contrast, was then employing approximately 917,000 people, comprising 70,000 in the primary production of metals and 847,000 in the transformation of metals. *ibid.*, p. 929.
68. See Val. R. Lorwin, *The French Labour Movement*, Cambridge, Harvard University Press, 1954, p. 17, and O. Bosselman, 'Erzbergbau und Eisenindustrie in Lothringen-Luxembourg', *Schriften des Vereins für Socialpolitik*, Bd. 105-106, 1903, p. 6 ff.
69. Yves Lequin, 'Labour in the French Economy since the Revolution', *loc. cit.*, p. 301.

70. See R.P. Serge Bonnet, 'Political Alignments and Religious Attitudes within Italian Immigration to the Metallurgical Districts of Lorraine', *Journal of Social History,* Vol. 2, No. 2, Winter 1968, p. 148.
71. O. Bosselman, 'Erzbergbau und Eisenindustrie in Lothringen-Luxembourg', *loc. cit.,* p. 8.
72. *ibid.,* p. 6 ff.
73. *ibid.,* pp. 33-4.
74. See M. Briat, *L'Enseignement professionel: rapport fait au nom de la Commission permanente du Conseil supérieur du travail,* Imprimerie Nationale, Paris, 1905, pp. 9-10.
75. M. Alfassa, 'Notes économiques: L'enseignement professionnel et la question de l'apprentissage, *Bulletin de la Société d'Encouragement pour l'Industrie Nationale,* Vol. 107, novembre 1905, p. 1324.
76. See *ibid.,* pp. 1324-5; and A. Jully, Inspector of Manual Education for Paris Schools, 'Cours technique d'apprentis et cour de réapprentissage', *Bulletin de la Société d'Encouragement pour l'Industrie Nationale,* Vol. 114, novembre 1910, pp. 405-9 for similar observations.
77. M. de Ribes-Christofle, 'La crise de l'apprentissage', *Bulletin de la Société d'Encouragement pour l'Industrie Nationale,* Vol. 110, juin 1910, p. 823.
78. See Paul Jannettaz, 'Le Congrès de l'Apprentissage de Roubaix', *Revue de Métallurgie,* Vol. 9, No. 6, juin 1912, p. 410.
79. *ibid.,* p. 410.
80. In mining, M. Wauthy claimed that this industry had largely 'escaped the crisis', as ancient traditions had been preserved which allowed a child to follow in his father's footsteps, successively undertaking different jobs and acquiring practical knowledge, which was the basis of a miner's training. By contrast, in the iron and steel trades, the number of skilled craft workers required was very small. Most of the labour was of a *manoeuvres* character, with the noticeable exception of foundry work, where there was an apparent shortage of *métiers bourgeois,* or *bourgeois craftsmen,* such as nail smiths, tin smiths and founders. See *ibid.,* p. 410.
81. See 'Elementary Education in France', Report of the French Section of the International Metalworkers' Federation (1915), in *Industrial Training also Internationalism from 1883 to 1913,* compiled by Charles Hobson, Secretary of the British Section, p. 69.
82. *ibid.,* p. 69.
83. *ibid.,* pp. 69-70 and Yves Lequin, 'Labour in the French Economy since the Revolution', *loc. cit.,* p. 315. The French section of the International Metalworkers' Federation reported that though the city of Paris provided schools for the manual instruction of adults during the day, evening and on Sunday mornings, the courses were 'very insufficient': 'For these young people, who work ten hours a day, and have sometimes to walk a long way from their lodgings to their place of work, have no longer the necessary free time and often not even the required physical strength to really profit by this instruction; thus the results obtained cannot be compared with the efforts of the teachers'. See 'Elementary Education in France', Report of the French Section of the International Metalworkers' Federation, *loc. cit.,* p. 70.
84. The quote is from Lequin, 'Labour in the French Economy since the Revolution', *loc. cit.,* p. 317. See also Antoine Prost, *op. cit.,* p. 306 ff.
85. *ibid.,* pp. 311 and 316. See also Prost, *op. cit.,* p. 308.
86. See *International Congress of Metalworkers, Paris, 1900. The Diderot Technical School,* in *Industrial Training also Internationalism from 1883 to 1913,* p. 249.
87. *ibid.,* p. 249.

88. *ibid.*, p. 249. For further information on the Diderot Technical School see Prost, *op. cit.*, p. 308.

89. 'Elementary Education in France', Report of the French Section of the International Metalworkers' Federation, *loc. cit.*, pp. 69-70. Prost, *op. cit.*, pp. 310-11.

90. Lequin, 'Labour in the French Economy since the Revolution', *loc. cit.*, pp. 311, 316. Over one hundred of these schools were in existence by 1914 and were run by the Ministry of Commerce. The enrolment at this time was approximately 28,000 pupils. See Moody, *op. cit.*, p. 104.

91. 'Elementary Education in France', Report of the French Section of the International Metalworkers' Federation, *loc. cit.*, p. 70.

92. Lequin, 'Labour in the French Economy since the Revolution', *loc. cit.*, p. 316; see also M. Alfassa, 'Notes économiques', *loc. cit.*, p. 1333.

93. 'Elementary Education in France', Report of the French Section of the International Metalworkers' Federation, *loc. cit.*, pp. 69-70.

94. *ibid.*, p. 70.

95. See M. Alfassa, 'Notes économiques', *loc. cit.*, p. 1325.

96. *ibid.*, p. 1327.

97. See Louis Le Chatelier (Manager), 'Les Ateliers Cail à Denain. Conférence faite aux élèves de l'École des Mines, le 24 avril 1909', in *Revue de Métallurgie*, Vol. 6, 1909, pp. 582-3.

98. *ibid.*, pp. 582-3.

99. See Paul Jannettaz, 'Le Congrès de l'Apprentissage de Roubaix', *loc. cit.*, p. 411.

100. See Lorwin, *op. cit.*, pp. 18-19.

101. See 'Report of the Federal Union of the Metalworkers of France', International Metallurgists' Congress, Amsterdam, 1904, in *Industrial Training also Internationalism from 1883 to 1913*, p. 311. For a description of earlier strike movements of a comparable scale and intensity in the French heavy metal industry, see Gerd Hardach, *Der soziale Status. . .*, p. 166 ff and especially p. 180, Table III (2), for the number of times police and troops were used in the period 1818-70 to crush worker resistance. The pinnacle of this repressive state action came in 1870 with a strike at *Le Creusot* when 3,000 troops were used to break a strike, while 2,000 were used to do the same at the Fourchambault steel works in the same year.

102. See P.N. Stearns, 'Against the Strike Threat: Employer Policy toward Labour Agitation in France, 1900-1914', *Journal of Modern History*, Vol. 40, December 1968, pp. 485, 490-1.

103. *ibid.*, pp. 490-1 and Lorwin, *op. cit.*, p. 19.

104. See Sewell, *Work and Revolution in France*, p. 22 ff; and for an interesting analysis of employer ideology at this time, particularly on the question of their seeing themselves as 'masters' exercising absolute power and regarding their workers with complete suspicion, see Albert Melluci, 'Action patronale, pouvoir, organisation. Réglements d'usine et controle de la main-d'oeuvre au XIXe siècle', *Le mouvement social*, No. 97, octobre-décembre 1976, pp. 139-59. Many of Melluci's examples are taken from firms such as *Decazeville, Le Creusot*, and the *Société de Commentry-Fourchambault*.

105. G, 'L'enseignement manuel', *Mouvement socialiste*, No. 2, 1 February 1899, p. 105.

106. *ibid.*, pp. 104-5.

107. Lequin, 'Labour in the French Economy since the Revolution', *loc. cit.*, p. 316.

108. *ibid.*, p. 316, and 'Elementary Education in France', Report of the French Section of the International Metalworkers' Federation, *loc. cit.*, p. 70.

109. 'Elementary Education in France', Report of the French Section of the Inter-

national Metalworkers' Federation, *loc. cit.,* p. 70.

110. Lequin, 'Labour in the French Economy since the Revolution', *loc. cit.,* p. 317.
111. See Melluci, *loc. cit.,* pp. 147-50, 153.
112. Yves Lequin, 'Labour in the French Economy since the Revolution', *loc. cit.,* p. 316.
113. See M. Alfassa, 'Notes économiques', *loc. cit.,* p. 1333.
114. See M. de Ribes-Christofle, 'La crise de l'apprentissage', *loc. cit.,* pp. 825-7. See also, 'The Apprenticeship Question', *The Engineer,* Vol. 99-100, December 29, 1905, p. 641, for a contemporary British view of France's training problems and how they were being overcome.
115. See M. Alfassa, 'Notes économiques', *loc. cit.,* p. 1330 ff.
116. *ibid.,* pp. 1333, 1337-9.
117. See A. Jully, 'Cours technique d'apprentis et cour de réapprentissage', *loc. cit.,* p. 410.
118. See M. Villemin, 'L'apprentissage: Conférence faite devant la Chambre de commerce de Bourges, le 13 février, 1910', *Bulletin de l'Association pour le développement de l'Enseignement technique,* Vol. VIII, 1910, p. 514 ff.
119. See M. Alfassa, 'Notes économiques', *loc. cit.,* pp. 1335-6.
120. A. Jully, 'Cours technique d'apprentis et cour de réapprentissage', *loc. cit.,* pp. 1335-6.
121. See M. Villemin, 'L'apprentissage', *loc. cit.,* p. 514.
122. See Paul Jannettaz, 'Le Congrès de l'Apprentissage de Roubaix', *loc. cit.,* pp. 411-12.
123. *ibid.,* pp. 411-12.
124. *ibid.,* p. 411.
125. See 'Elementary Education in France', Report of the French Section of the International Metalworkers' Federation, *loc. cit.,* p. 71.
126. There was some working class opposition to this proposal, which was originally meant to include a school leaving age of fourteen. Many unionists felt that the higher age limit would deny proletarian families the extra income that came from having their adolescent children at work. As a compromise the age of leaving was fixed to be thirteen. See Paul Jannettaz, 'Le Congrès de l'Apprentissage de Roubaix', *loc. cit.,* p. 401.
127. *ibid.,* pp. 401-8.
128. *ibid.,* p. 409. See also 'Elementary Education in France', Report of the French Section of the International Metalworkers' Federation, *loc. cit.,* pp. 71-2. See also F. Ponteil, *Histoire de l'enseignement en France, les grandes étapes, 1789-1964,* pp. 330-1.
129. See 'Elementary Education in France', Report of the French Section of the International Metalworkers' Federation, *loc. cit.,* pp. 71-2.
130. Another historian also offers cautious optimism in this regard. See Moody, *op. cit.,* p. 104.
131. After the loss of millions of young French citizens during World War One, the French government and employers found their industries to be again under pressure as a result of a general shortage of skilled and trained labour power. Of the measures designed to overcome this problem the 1919 Astier Law stands out. This law tightened up the 1911 decrees and made compulsory those re- commendations of the Roubaix Congress which were expected to be introduced voluntarily. Grants to private schools, whether run by employers, unions or associations, were expanded and formalised. Municipal authorities were com- pelled to establish free trade schools in their localities; while all those under eighteen were compelled to undertake trade instruction courses during working hours. Employers were also forced to abide by these instructions for the training

of their workers. By 1925, Trade Chambers *(chambres de métiers)* were given powers to regulate and enforce apprenticeship contracts and employers were required to pay an apprenticeship tax if they were not directly encouraging the training of skilled labour in their own factories. Finally, in 1928, written contracts became compulsory between an employer and an apprentice which specified the conditions and provisions for the training of skilled labour inside and outside of the factory. See Lequin, 'Labour in the French Economy Since the Revolution', *loc. cit.,* pp. 339–40; Joseph N. Moody, *op. cit.,* p. 140 ff; F. Ponteil, *op. cit.,* p. 346 ff; and Committee on Industry and Trade (Balfour Committee), *Industrial and Commercial Efficiency,* Part 1, HMSO, London, 1927, p. 259.

CHAPTER 5: GERMANY

By the late nineteenth century the facilities for training Germany's heavy metal industry workforce had been extensively developed. The pressures of uneven development with respect to Britain and France had forced employers and the state to adopt the best methods available for the public training of an employer class (the French influence), and for the private, factory-based training of a working class (the British influence). Out of its early backwardness, therefore, the German heavy metal industry developed advanced methods of industrial training, which not only combined the best features of current European practice, but also rapidly overtook French and British training methods by the very synthesis of them.

By the late 1890s, however, the heavy metal industry began a new and massive wave of expansion, which was marked by the growth of huge monopolistic concerns, a staggering increase in the size of the workforce, the introduction of new and sophisticated technologies and an upsurge in the numbers of office personnel and technicians. In order to meet the needs of this expansion the institutions of public and private industrial training had to develop a new orientation which would aim for the systematic and public creation of a professionally-trained labour force from the unskilled workers who would occupy lowly positions in the factories, through to the managers, engineers and employers who would run them. According to a report of the London County Council in 1914, this was exactly what happened with the cooperation of the states, municipalities, unions and employers, who all believed that not only was compulsory and continuous education necessary for the workforce as a whole until at least the age of eighteen, but also that this training would have to be rigidly demarcated, technically specialised and socially stratified.[1] The implication of this is that, by 1914, the technical education system was producing the necessary technical cadre force for the direction of the heavy metal industry, as well as aiding the reproduction and development of the basic class structure of the Wilhelmian Reich. If this assessment is correct then Germany can be considered as the first European country to make the complete transition from an open and internal factory-based system of industrial training to one which was externally based in a public education system, where the students were directed from the school to the factory along well-defined class lines. In other words, it may be the case that Germany led the way in making a complete transition from a private, competitive and empiricist system of industrial training to one which serviced the new and expanding administrative, technical and labour requirements of large monopolistic and bureaucratically organised firms.

1. The contours of expansion

According to the German Metalworkers' Union (Deutsche Metallarbeiter Verband, DMV), the metal industry's workforce grew dramatically in the period 1900-1911. Drawing on a survey of twelve metal trade associations, the Union found that in 1900 almost 1.3 million people were employed in 41,216 establishments, as Table 15 shows. By 1911 this workforce had grown by nearly 700,000 to approximately 2.0 million people, an increase of 52.8%. These figures do not allow for an accurate breakdown of the numbers employed in the two main branches—engineering, and iron and steel, but it will be seen that though all the associations registered large increases in their respective workforces, the largest absolute increases were registered in the technically sophisticated areas of precision instrument making and electrical engineering, whose workforce more than doubled, rising from 143,733 to 308,223, while the Rhineland's engineering workforce increased by 87,358. In order to obtain a perspective on the overall size of this expansion, it can be noted that in 1895 the engineering industry proper (excluding the allied trades), employed only 268,654 people. In 1907, by contrast, employment had grown to 700,184, or had more than doubled.[2]

This expansion of the metal industry's workforce was synonymous with the growing regional dominance of the Rhineland metal trades, whose two main trade associations, the Rhenish-Westphalian Smelting and Rolling Works Association and the Rhenish-Westphalian Engineering and Hardware Manufacturers Association, comprised 435,448 people in 1911, or 22.1% of the nation's metal workforce. It should be noted that this proportion is a very conservative estimate, as a large number of precision and electrical engineering firms were located in this region, yet their employees were included in the returns for the Precision Instrument and Electrical Engineering Association. In the region's capital, Düsseldorf, a similarly large expansion of the metal industry workforce can be detected. As Table 16 demonstrates, the iron, steel and engineering workforce grew from 18,129 to 23,648, an increase of 30.4% in the period 1900-1913. Though the capital's iron and steel workforce expanded by only 6.3% over this time, in contrast to the regional growth of 36.1% during 1900-1911, the engineering branch grew by 65.1%, well in advance of the growth of the region's engineering workforce, which expanded by 53%, according to the Rhenish-Westphalian Engineering and Hardware Association. Throughout the pre-war period, the metal industry in

TABLE 15

Employment per establishment in the German metal industry, 1900-1911

Trade Association	Number of establishments			Number of persons employed			Number of persons per establishment		
	1900	1910	1911	1900	1910	1911	1900	1910	1911
Precision Instrument Making and Electrical Engineering	4,032	6,931	7,287	143,733	247,173	308,223	35.6	35.7	42.3
South German Iron and Steel	10,689	13,302	13,479	177,918	219,361	232,399	16.6	16.5	17.2
South West German Iron and Steel	491	739	767	55,719	61,647	64,478	113.5	83.4	84.1
Rhenish-Westphalian Smelting and Rolling Works	234	218	218	134,717	177,836	183,403	575.7	815.8	841.3
Rhenish-Westphalian Engineering and Hardware Manufacture	7,368	8,419	8,651	164,696	233,906	252,045	22.3	27.8	29.1
Saxo-Thuringian Iron and Steel	4,257	6,259	6,371	123,903	168,184	179,610	29.1	26.9	28.2
North Eastern Iron and Steel	3,297	7,111	7,776	99,405	131,384	138,298	30.1	18.5	17.8
Silesian Iron and Steel	1,459	2,167	2,225	100,539	113,743	117,572	68.9	52.5	52.8
North Western Iron and Steel	4,624	6,320	6,463	132,383	151,431	170,102	28.6	24.0	26.4
South German Precious and Base Metals	2,068	2,553	2,673	56,006	84,370	91,108	27.1	33.0	34.1
North German Metal	2,697	3,850	3,968	99,846	144,811	146,663	37.0	37.6	37.0
Smiths	—	55,700	57,234	—	81,968	85,378	—	1.5	1.5
TOTAL	41,216	113,642	117,113	1,288,945	1,842,814	1,969,279	—	—	—

Source:
Derived and calculated from Deutsche Metallarbeiter Verband, *Report on the General Condition of Trade in Germany, delivered to the Sixth Congress of the International Metalworkers' Federation, Berlin, August 6-7, 1913, in Industrial Training and Internationalism from 1883 to 1913*, compiled by Charles Hobson, Hudson and Sons, London, 1913, p. 528.

Düsseldorf employed approximately 40% of the city's workforce, reaching exactly that figure in 1913,[3] with the iron and steel branch employing 19.2% of the city's workforce, while the engineering trades employed 20.8%.[4] Only the mining industry could compare with the metal trades, employing as it did 17.8% of the workforce in 1913.[5] As far as Düsseldorf is concerned, then, it was its engineering branch which shared, if not led, the regional and national expansion of the metal industry.

TABLE 16

The metal industry workforce in Düsseldorf, 1900 and 1913

	1900	*1913*	*Percent Increase*
Iron and Steel	10,686	11,358	6.3
Engineering	7,443	12,290	65.1

Source:
Calculated from *Bericht über den Stand und die Verwaltung der Gemeinde-Angelegenheiten für die Stadt Düsseldorf, 1900/1913, Stadtarchiv*, Düsseldorf.

A further important aspect of this expansion was the phenomenal increase in the number of metal-working establishments. If Table 15 is considered again, it will be seen that the number of establishments grew from 41,216 in 1900 to 117,113 in 1911, an increase of 184%, whereas the workforce increased by 52.8% over these years. Düsseldorf experienced a similar development. In the iron and steel branch, the number of establishments grew from 64 in 1900 to 186 in 1913, an increase of 190.6%; while in the engineering branch the number of establishments over the same period grew from 41 to 178, a rise of 334.1%.[6] As can be seen from Table 16 these proportional increases in the number of working establishments far outstripped the proportional increases in the iron and steel and engineering workforces, which grew by 6.3% and 65.1% respectively. It has recently been suggested that this over-proportional growth in the number of establishments, especially in the engineering industry, reflected a relative technical and economic stagnation in the pre-war years, as the expansion was not complemented by a growing concentration of the workforce into fewer factories, which would allow for economies of scale, an increase in productivity and technical improvements.[7] On the basis of this assumption, it is argued that the high levels of technical development and industrial organisation reached at firms like Borsig in Berlin, Klett in Nürnberg, Kessler in Esslingen and Hartmann in Chemnitz, were 'not an exemplary expression of the whole branch', rather they were the 'exception' and 'remained on the periphery'.[8]

It is certainly correct to suggest, as Table 15 shows, that the expansion of the workforce did not represent a substantial average increase in the number of persons per establishment. Amongst the twelve trade associations only the Rhenish-Westphalian Smelting and Rolling Works Association registered a substantial increase in the number of persons per establishment, rising from 575.7 in 1900 to 841.3 in 1911. On the other hand, a number of trade associations, such as the South West German Iron and Steel Association and the Silesian Iron and Steel Association witnessed a fall in the number of persons employed in their members' establishments: in the case of the former, a drop from 113.5 to 84.1; and for the latter, a fall from 30.1 to 17.8. The Düsseldorf trades again went through a similar experience. In the steel branch, the average number of persons per establishment dropped from 166.97 in 1900 to 61.06 in 1913; while in the engineering branch the drop was from 181.5 in 1900 to 69.04 in 1913.[9] It is a major error, however, to equate average factory sizes mechanically with a certain level of technical progress and industrial organisation. It is not possible here to enter into a substantial study of the political economy of the German metal industry. This will have to be left for another time. Yet it must be emphasised that a stagnation or fall in the average number of persons per establishment is perfectly consistent with an *overwhelming tendency* towards the concentration of the workforce into fewer and larger establishments. In this case a few large enterprises can not only come to dominate the character of an entire industry, but also give rise to a large tail of smaller enterprises, who ride the crest of the expansion, and are singularly subordinated to the policies, leadership, technical advances and forms of industrial organisation of the great monopolistic concerns. As a comparison between Tables 15 and 17 shows, this is in fact what happened.

Table 17 is a survey of the number of workpeople employed by 53 leading joint-stock companies according to their trade group in the year 1911-12. If a comparison is made between Groups V and VII, of this table (which comprise seven establishments from electrical engineering and six establishments from the precision instruments sector), and the Precision

TABLE 17

The numbers of people employed in fifty-three leading joint-stock companies in the German metal industry, 1911-1912

Names of firms classified by trade groups	Number of Workpeople employed
GROUP I—Iron and Steel Trades (15 establishments)	
1. Gelsenkirchener Bergwerks AG	47,656
2. AG Phönix, Hoerde	38,041
3. Vereinigte Königs-und Laurahütte	26,235
4. Gutehoffnungshütte, Oberhausen	25,251
5. Deutsch-Lux. Bergwerks-und Hütten AG Bochum	22,574

TABLE 17 (Cont)

Names of firms classified by trade groups	Number of Workpeople employed
GROUP I—Iron and Steel Trades (15 establishments) (cont)	
6. Eschweiler Bergwerksverein	14,275
7. Bochumer Verein für Bergbau und Gusstahlfabrik	14,048
8. Oberschlesian Eisenbahnnbedarfs AG Friedenshütte	11,500
9. Rheinische Stahlwerk, Duisberg-Meiderich	10,533
10. Eisen-und Stahlwerk Heosch, Dortmund	10,434
11. Lothringer Hüttenverein, Aumetz-Friede	10,390
12. Rombücher Hüttenwerke	6,813
13. AG Ilseder Hütte und Peiner Walzwerk	5,400
14. Vereinigte Stahlwerke van der Zypgen & Wissener, Cologne	3,224
15. Hasper Eisen-und Stahlwerke	1,778
TOTAL GROUP I	248,152
GROUP II—Shipbuilding (4 establishments)	
1. Vulcanwerke, Hamburg and Stettin	12,000
2. Blohm & Voss, Kommandit-Gesellschaft a. Aktien, Hamburg	8,202
3. Reiherstieg, Schiffswerft und Maschinenfabrik, Hamburg	1,677
4. Stettiner Oderwerke	990
TOTAL GROUP II	22,869
GROUP III—Engineering (13 establishments)	
1. Maschinenfabrik Augsburg-Nürnberg, AG	16,180
2. Bielefelder Maschinenfabrik von Dürkopp & Co.	5,000
3. Maschinenbauanstalt "Humbold", Kalk, Cologne	4,500
4. Adlerwerke, Frankfurt-on-Main	4,500
5. Berlin Anhalt Maschinenbau AG	4,256
6. Hannoversche Maschinenbau AG	3,500
7. Berliner Maschinenbau AG v Schwartzkopff	3,300
8. Gasmoterenfabrik Deutz-Cologne	3,300
9. Maschinenfabrik Kappel, Chemnitz	1,700
10. Vereinigte Fabriken landwirtschaftsliche Maschinen, Augsburg	1,400
11. Kirchener & Co., AG, Leipzig	1,250
12. Lokomotivfabrik Kraus & Co., Munich	1,102
13. Maschinenfabrik Moenus, AG Frankfurt-on-Main	800
TOTAL GROUP III	50,788
GROUP IV—Arms & Ammunition (3 establishments)	
1. Friedrich Krupp, AG Essen	73,405
2. Deutsche Waffen-und Munitionsfabriken, Berlin	8,000
3. Waffenfabrik Mauser, AG, Oberndorf	1,800
TOTAL GROUP IV	83,205

TABLE 17 (Cont)

Names of firms classified by trade groups	Number of Workpeople employed
GROUP V—Electrical Engineering (7 establishments)	
1. Siemens & Halske, Berlin	
2. Siemens-Schuckertwerke, GmbH	77,000
3. Allgemeine Elektrizitätsgesellschaft, Berlin	70,162
4. Bergmann, Elektrizitätswerke, Berlin	10,000
5. Akkumulatorenfabrik AG, Berlin	2,400
6. Telephonfabrik, AG, J. Berliner, Hanover	1,500
7. Hartmann & Braun, Frankfurt-on-Main	766
TOTAL GROUP V	161,828
GROUP VI—Precious and other Metalworking (3 establishments)	
1. Württembergische Metallwarenfabrik, Geislingen	4,500
2. Kollmar & Jourdan, AG, Pforzheim	1,510
3. Rodi & Wienenberger, Pforzheim	800
TOTAL GROUP VI	6,810
GROUP VII—Precision Instruments, Bicycles etc. (6 establishments)	
1. AG Seidel & Naumann, Dresden	2,500
2. Wandererwerke, AG Schönau-Chemnitz	2,500
3. Optische Anstalt C.P. Goertz, Berlin	1,500
4. Eisenbahnsignalbauanstalt, Brunswick	1,000
5. Reiniger, Gebbert & Schall, AG, Erlangen	1,000
6. Exzelsiorfahrradwerke, Branden	650
TOTAL GROUP VII	9,150
GROUP VIII—Watches and Clocks (2 establishments)	
1. Gebr, Junghans, AG, Schramberg	3,700
2. Vereinigte Freiburger Uhrenfabrik AG	2,350
TOTAL GROUP VIII	6,050
GROUPS I to VIII	
TOTAL	588,852
Average number of employees per establishment	11,110

Source:
Derived and calculated from: Deutsche Metallarbeiter Verband, *'Report on the General Condition of Trade in Germany'*, *International Metalworkers' Federation Congress, Berlin, 1913*, in *Industrial Training also Internationalism*, compiled by Charles Hobson, Secretary of the British Section, Hudson and Son, Birmingham, 1915, pp. 532-4.

Instrument Making and Electrical Engineering Association, in Table 15, then it will be seen that: of the 308,223 workpeople represented by the Associations' 7,287 establishments in 1911, 170,978 or 55.5% were employed by only thirteen of these firms. Furthermore, of this 170,978 at least 147,162 workpeople were employed by only three electrical engineering firms—*Siemens & Halske,* Berlin; *Siemens-Schuckertwerke, GmbH;* and *Allgemeine Elektrizitätsgesellschaft,* Berlin; the first two firms were also corporately integrated within the Siemens' empire.[10] Overall, these three establishments employed 47.7% of the entire Trade Association's workforce. Though it is not possible to compare rigorously the other trade groups from Table 17 with the Trade Associations set out in Table 15, as there was a tendency for a number of large mixed metal enterprises like Krupp's to be members of the various iron and steel associations, it is possible to compare the place occupied by these fifty-three leading establishments within the metal industry as a whole. It will be seen that these firms alone employed 588,852 people in 1911-12, with an average of 11,110 people per establishment. They thus employed approximately 30% of the nation's entire metal industry, and this does not account for the fact that a number of other large joint-stock companies and privately-owned firms were not included in this survey: *Thyssen—* 14,124 workpeople in 1909; the *Benrather Maschinenfabrik—*1,000 people in 1900; and another twenty-three heavy metal enterprises, comprising iron, steel and engineering activities, with approximately 219,804 people in 1910.[11] It is difficult to obtain accurate information on the concentration of people per working establishment for German manufacturing industry, as a whole, at this time; however, Jürgen Kocka has calculated from Walter Hoffman's work that, in 1907 only 4.9% of the total manufacturing and handicraft labour force worked in establishments of 1,000 or more people.[12] The metal industry, then, was exceptional in bringing together many thousands of workers in such a concentrated fashion.

Experiencing this process of concentration and expansion first-hand, the *Deutsche Metallarbeiter Verband* was moved in 1913 to explain to its comrades in the International Metalworkers' Federation that:

> Never before was the number of amalgamations and fusions of establishments so large as during the last three or four years. In accordance with the trend of development in all capitalist countries, the number of establishments is decreasing while the number of industrially dependent persons increases.[13]

The change went hand in hand with some enormous increases in productivity. Pig iron output increased by 73% in the years 1900-10, with only a 33% increase in the number of employees. According to the DMV, this was due to 'technical improvements of all kinds and increased exploitation of labours'.[14] As Table 18 shows, the enormous increase in output was spread across all the main branches of metal production. Steel output led the way, rising from an index of 33.4 to 100 in 1913. Carr and Taplin have described this in more quantitative terms. In 1896 steel output was 4.6 million tons. By 1913 it was 17.3 million tons.[15] Engineering output was not far behind, rising from an index of 47.5 in 1900 to 100 by 1913.

On the basis of this evidence one can *begin* to characterise the evolving structure of the German heavy metal industry. It was an industry fractured right down the middle. On the one hand, there were the dominant, technically advanced, highly profitable and largely mixed metal enterprises, which employed almost the majority of the metal workforce in very few factories. They produced iron, steel, arms and munitions, locomotives, railway parts, power machines and tool machines. Aligned politically and economically in a number of cartels, trusts and syndicates that sought to advance their often conflicting interests, these enterprises stood on top of

TABLE 18

Indices of industrial production for the German metal industry, 1900–1913 (1913 = 100)

Year	Pig Iron	Steel	Iron & Steel Castings	Rolling Mill Products	Iron & Steel Output (Total)	Engineering
1900	43.6	33.4	50.6	40.1	42.4	47.5
1901	40.3	32.0	42.7	37.5	38.9	45.3
1902	43.5	38.4	44.2	40.8	42.3	45.5
1903	52.2	42.6	48.4	45.6	47.2	48.1
1904	52.3	42.2	57.4	47.4	50.0	52.2
1905	56.9	47.0	62.3	52.4	54.8	56.8
1906	64.6	53.4	69.7	60.8	62.2	63.1
1907	67.4	55.4	73.1	64.3	65.2	70.6
1908	61.2	64.7	71.8	59.8	64.2	68.9
1909	66.9	68.4	71.8	63.4	67.3	69.1
1910	76.6	75.8	81.4	72.7	75.9	77.8
1911	80.7	83.0	88.0	76.9	81.2	85.2
1912	92.5	95.1	101.3	90.6	94.2	94.8
1913	100.0	100.0	100.0	100.0	100.0	100.0

Source:
Walter G. Hoffman (and Franz Grumbach and Helmut Hesse), *Das Wachstum der Deutsche Wirtschaft seit der Mitte des 19. Jahrhundert,* Springer Verlag, Berlin, 1965, pp. 353–4, 392, 501.

a less advanced, less monopolistic sector, where the other half of the workforce laboured in tens of thousands of medium to small estalishments, producing anything from cutlery and agricultural equipment to rolled plate, textile equipment and agricultural machinery. Kurt

Wiedenfeld's 1916 study of the Rhineland metal industry provides many examples of this fracture. He described a hierarchy of concentration, at the top of which stood the modern Bessemer steel enterprises, which were highly centralised and geared to the fabrication of railway products, internally and for export. Then came the technically advanced, though economically subordinate, Siemens-Martin section, which supplied the indigenous engineering industry, especially its high quality trades. As this branch was often conducted by small enterprises with very 'independent' masters, the firms often found themselves victims of the trade and production policies of the larger Bessemer producers. Below the Siemens-Martin section were a huge number of independent firms, which varied in size, who rolled the products coming from the Siemens-Martin plants. Finally, there was a large tail of often very backward and small enterprises carrying out specialised work, such as cutlery and tool manufacture, the efficiency of which depended on the availability of small electric motors.[16]

2. *From boom to slump: the contradictions of fixed capital investment*

As in America and Britain, the motor force of this expansion and concentration was investment in plant, machines and equipment. Though overall capital formation in Germany had been *relatively* higher than in Britain or France since the mid-nineteenth century, it assumed huge proportions by the century's end. According to Simon Kuznets' calculations, capital formation in Germany as a proportion of gross national product had reached an average of 14.1% during the years 1851-70, and continued to rise, reaching an average of 19.9% in the period 1871-90.[17] From this base, the late 1890s boom took capital formation to 23.7% of gross national product during the years 1891-1913.[18] As in America, agriculture consumed a large share of this investment. During the years 1895-99, for example, its share of capital formation was still running at an average of 27.1%, while industry's share was 26.9%.[19] Industrial investment, however, was increasing at a much faster rate and came to assume a dominant position over agriculture.

Investment in total capital stock, comprising factories, buildings, plant and equipment, etc. grew at a rate of 2.67% per annum in the period 1875-92 and 3.32% during the years 1893-1913. The latter figure represented an overall increase in capital stock of approximately 69.7%.[20] Such massive investment substantially altered the composition of the nation's net domestic product, particularly the shares of agriculture and industry. Over the years 1895-99 the share of net domestic product coming from agriculture, forestry and fisheries was 30.8%, with industry and handwork contributing 35.6%. By 1905-09, the share from agriculture, etc. had fallen to 26%, while that from industry had risen to 38.4%.[21]

Though it is not possible to disaggregate this evidence to find out whether investment in plant, machinery and equipment was becoming more significant than investment in infrastructure, such as roads, buildings and housing, other evidence does suggest that the composition of fixed capital was shifting towards producer durables, particularly within the manufacturing industry. Table 19 allows us to compare total net investment in net national product with the share of this devoted to manufacture from the mid-1880s until 1913. It will be seen that net capital formation peaked during the boom of 1895-99, as did manufacturing's share: 15% and 54.5% respectively. However, where manufacturing's share secularly declined from its peak, net investment overall had recovered by 1905-09 and began to move up again in the years just before World War One. What is very interesting, though, is that industrial production began to secularly increase just at the time manufacturing's share of capital

TABLE 19

Net investment in Germany as a proportion of net national product and the share devoted to manufacture, 1893-1913, in terms of 1913 constant prices

Period	Net investments as a proportion of net national product	Manufacturing's share
1885–89	11.8	45.3
1890–94	12.7	34.0
1895–99	15.0	54.5
1900–04	13.5	36.1
1905–09	15.0	43.2
1910–13	15.5	42.9

Source:
W.G. Hoffman (with Franz Grumbach and Helmut Hesse), *Das Wachstum der Deutschen Wirtschaft seit der Mitte des 19. Jahrhundert*, Springer Verlag, Berlin, 1965, Table 36, pp. 104-5.

formation began to secularly decline, as Table 20 shows. It will also be noticed that the critical period when these cycles moved off in contrary directions was during 1900-1905. The metal industry not only shared in this experience, it was also the leader. The rate of increase in output amongst its various branches after 1902 far outstripped that for industrial production as a whole.

The hypothesis that can be drawn from this evidence is that, though Germany, unlike Britain, continued to devote a large share of its investment in capital stock to infrastructure right up to 1913,[22] its manufacturing sector, like Britain's, was no longer participating to the same extent after 1900. Furthermore, it is reasonable to deduce that the increase in industrial output in the metal industry, and in manufacturing as a whole, can be accounted for by an increase in the rate at which

TABLE 20

Indices of industrial production for Germany, 1900-13 (1913 = 100)

Year	Production Index
1900	61.4
1901	58.7
1902	60.2
1903	64.8
1904	67.5
1905	70.0
1906	73.0
1907	78.7
1908	78.0
1909	81.4
1910	85.5
1911	90.7
1912	97.8
1913	100.0

Source:
W.G. Hoffman, *Das Wachstum der Deutschen Wirtschaft seit der Mitte des 19. Jahrhundert,* Springer Verlag, Berlin, **1965, p. 502.**

existing capital was being consumed, particularly capital invested in producer goods. As no data have been compiled on the rates of capital consumption in Germany at this time, the proof of this hypothesis must rely on a more careful analysis of the boom-bust decade 1895-1905, and the role of the metal industry in all of this.

The economic heart of this decade was the metal industry. When the boom began in 1895 it turned on railway, factory and machine building, which greatly improved the market for the steel branch. Basic metal production doubled during the years 1895-1900, as the steel producers sought to supply not only the engineering sector, but also meet the increasing demands of the army and navy for rearmament programmes.[23] The extension of gas and water utilities and the introduction of electric street cars also pressed the steel trade to increase output, particularly of good quality plating and track.[24] Iron and steel plants began to re-equip. Bigger open-hearth furnaces were being constructed, as were heavier cogging and finishing mills. This in turn pulled in the engineering branch, which supplied steel producers with boilers, pig casting machinery and blast furnace gas engines.[25] Within this tightly woven circle of reciprocal supply and demand, exports and imports played a relatively minor role in either stimulating output or meeting demand. The respective exceptions to this were the pig iron and machine tool trades.

During the years 1896-1899 the amount of pig iron exported rose from 138,000 tons to 179,000 tons, while other iron and steel exports fell from 1,357,000 tons to 1,307,000 tons.[26] Increasing domestic demand for iron and steel products accounts for the fall in exports. As far as the machine tool branch is concerned, a huge number of American products were imported for use in the heavy and electrical engineering trades, though it should be noted that at the height of the boom in 1900 German machine tool-makers were exporting 2 Marks for every 1 Mark of machines and components that were being imported.[27] This branch expanded considerably during the boom, not only at the export level and in supplying domestic users, but also in furnishing its own needs. Extensions to plant and equipment, and the installation of new machine tools to build machine tools, became the order of the day, especially with a view to meeting what was seen to be a heavy future demand. By 1900 this branch of the industry had become important enough to gain a separate entry in the nation's accounts, the *Zolltarif* statistics.[28] The other engineering trades, such as steam engines, boilers, locomotive and gas engines, textile and agricultural machinery, sewing machines and bicycles, all to a varying extent shared in this interlocking pattern of growth.[29] It was the electrical engineering sector, however, which best articulated this experience.

If in the mid-nineteenth century, engineering was a new industry with little pre-history and, therefore, proved capable of taking up the most advanced methods of production and organisation, then the rise of the electrical branch considerably intensified this process at the end of the nineteenth century. Traditional forms of factory organisation were largely absent and the techniques of production were quite new. What this branch did adopt from the previous history of the metal industry, though, was a high level of concentration. Giant enterprises grew up, like *Siemens & Halske, AG.* This firm developed an interconnected divisional structure, so that its various activities could be effectively concentrated in particular geographical areas and branch divisions, yet still be accountable to head office. Like an octopus spreading its tentacles, these companies formed trusts, *Filialbüros,* sister companies and foreign branches.[30] By the end of the century, the electrical engineering branch dominated the world market and held a pre-eminent position at home.[31]

It was in this context that the late 1890s boom sparked off a mass conversion to electrically-powered motors amongst the leading metal producers, as well as amongst smaller producers desperately in need of an economic form of motive power which the steam or gas engine could no longer provide. Electrically-driven motors, large and small, tended to economise on the use of raw materials, lower energy costs and generally reduce the burden of fixed costs. The main reason for this was its flexibility. With a motive power based on steam or gas, the power generated to drive a lathe or a crane could not be turned off when not in use. The need continuously to generate huge amounts of power over and above the needs of an individual machine was a product of one central power station having to drive all the tools and machines. The introduction of electric motors fitted to individual machines, by contrast, meant that power could be now turned off when necessary and generally used more economically.[32] Yet, it was not the case that the traditional forms of motive power were completely by-passed in these years. Gas motors, especially, became more efficient in the generation of power and light, and, according to one commentator, became cheaper than electrically-generated power, though of course it remained less flexible.[33] With metal producers, then, able to refit with either electrical or more efficient, but traditional forms of motive power, the electrical engineering companies invested heavily in modern plant and equipment to reduce costs of production and increase productivity. The fixed capital value of the *Siemens & Halske* concern rose from 30.1 million Marks in 1896 to 55.5 million Marks in 1900. A.E.G. almost doubled its fixed capital assets in this period, rising from 19.7 million Marks to 38.4 million Marks. The *Schuckertwerke* more than doubled its fixed capital assets, bringing them to a value of 42.3 million Marks by 1900, while in 1896 they stood at 16.9 million Marks.[34] Such an expansion brought forth large increases in productivity, and in turn provided the other engineering branches with the opportunity of carrying out their own plans of expansion. Iron and steel producers were also impressed with the possibility of getting equipment which would electrify transport and handling within a mill.[35]

Nevertheless, by the latter half of 1900 it was becoming clear that this boom had run its course. Duncan Burn has provided one of the most accurate commentaries on what happened:

> . . . the prodigious advance had in many directions been unhealthy and mis-judged; capital equipment had been augmented far more rapidly than the effective demand for industrial products. Abounding stocks and empty order books brought prices tumbling, stopped factory building, destroyed credit, broke banks and ruined speculators in shares and commodities.[36]

It can also be added that many metal enterprises now found themselves stuck with overflowing supplies of raw materials and components, which had been bought at higher prices in the boom period. The prices of their own products, on the other hand, fell and when this combined with short-time working and falling output, enterprises were lumbered with rising fixed costs that appeared to be incompressable.[37] Profit rates not only seemed to be under threat or falling, but in fact appeared to be being punished for the major investment boom on which they had been based. Amongst the Rhineland's iron and steel producers, for instance, a general crisis of capacity utilisation developed. The major expansion programmes of Krupp and Thyssen, which had been completed during the boom or in the early months of the depression, were at the heart of this. The enormous increases in their fixed capital meant that they could not shut down for the duration of the depression. If they did, they would be ruined. They had to keep producing at relatively high levels just to break even on their previous commitments.[38] To capitalists long committed to raising productivity through investment in machinery, it all must have seemed that there was now too much productivity. At least, this was what some observers put the problems of the industry down to.[39] Within a chaotically organised capitalist system, productivity increases of 25% to 33% in the space of five years were just indigestible, especially when teased out of the producer-goods industries.[40]

The profitability of fixed capital investment was also eroded by a more long-term phenomenon: the decline of an advantageous wage differential with Great Britain. In 1865, for example, average nominal day wages in Germany were approximately 30% to 40% below those in Britain. By the turn of the century this had fallen to 17%. Also, in continental Europe, as a whole, nominal wages were rising fastest in Germany.[41] If it proved to be the case that it was too hard for firms to contain fixed costs, temporarily at least here there was something to be compressed. And, no grade of manual labour was immune to compression, either through wage cuts or short-time working. Skilled and semi-skilled workers in Halle, Chemnitz and Leipzig were culled from the factories to make as great a saving as possible on wages, whether they were fitters, turners or boilersmiths.[42] Amongst German steel producers in the Luxemburg–Lorraine region sackings and wage reductions were again common during 1900-1, particularly in the non-integrated plants where, for instance, only pig iron was produced. Wage reductions of the order of 5% to 7% for skilled workers, and as much as 20% for the less skilled were quite general, especially if the workers were 'foreign', i.e. Italian.[43] The more integrated steel plants in Lorraine, by contrast, sought to weather the storm either by falling back on or developing their export markets, especially if dumping wares below cost price was possible on international markets.[44]

This at least offered the prospect of keeping expensive plant and equipment going. If we turn to Table 21, some insight into this can be given. It provides a comparative perspective on the exports of the major capitalist countries, with respect to their producer and consumer trades. As will be seen, the USA heads the list in both branches, but had a negligible export trade up to 1880. Developments in Germany and Britain are much more important. For the latter, the export of producer goods represented a sustained attempt to overcome the blockages becoming apparent on the home market in the latter half of the nineteenth century. By the 1900s, Germany had also joined Britain's ranks, constantly seeking new markets for wares which represented overproduction at home. And it was during the depression of 1900-2, i.e. when an absolute fall in production hit the metal industry, that exports rose vigorously. Iron and steel exports doubled between 1900 and 1901, and in 1902 they stood at twice the level of 1898.[45]

TABLE 21

Export indices of producer and consumer goods in Great Britain, the USA and Germany, 1880-1913. (1880 = 100)

	Producer Goods		Consumer Goods	
Country	1880	1913	1880	1913
Great Britain	100	300	100	189
USA	100	2,100	100	600
Germany	100	850	100	275

Source:
Dr Rudolf Wagenführ, 'Die industriewirtschaftlichen. . .', *Sonderhefte des Instituts für Konjunkturforschung,* Vol. 31, Berlin, 1933, p. 17.

If after 1900 dumping offered the large, integrated, steel concerns the temporary alleviation of keeping production going, then this was only possible given their inflexible pricing policy on the domestic market. This policy, however, only brought to a head the need for the metal industry, as a whole, to search out better methods of management which would not only restore profit rates, but also ensure a better or more intensive use of fixed capital.

Throughout the years 1895-1900 iron and steel cartels pushed up their prices to take advantage of the high demand for their products. Between June 1895 and June 1900 the price of foundry pig iron rose from 63 Marks per *tonne* to 102 Marks per tonne. The price of Thomas pig iron also rose dramatically, from 38.2 Marks to 90.2 Marks per tonne.[46] Such price administration by steel producers continued to a lesser extent during the depression. For the non-integrated steel firms, who were reliant on supplies of pig iron for their rolling mills, and for those sections of the engineering industry not caught up in the network of the steel cartels (and there were many of both sorts of firms in the Rhineland), this had a pernicious effect on their fixed costs. The Rhineland's association of boiler producers, *Rhein-Westfälen Kesselfabriken,* lamented in October 1902 that high domestic prices for their raw materials were undermining the industry. It was cheaper for boiler-makers to buy back the German boiler plate sold to foreigners than it was to buy it in Germany.[47] This antagonism spread throughout the entire engineering industry and led to demands for the reduction of tariffs on raw material imports in order to offset high iron and steel prices at home.[48] Machine tool producers were equally in trouble and this was made all the worse by their previous commitment to fixed capital investment. Like the boiler producers, they too found themselves hit by the burden of fixed costs from all directions and wished to export more intensively as their home markets dried up.[49] It must have appeared that a pair of pincers were at work, with one point forcing down the prices for their finished goods and the other forcing up their fixed costs of production.[50]

The only pricing mechanism that engineers had to offset this situation was through the formation of their own buyers associations or, if they were strong enough, to introduce their own price administration. The latter course was chosen by the electrical engineering firms. As the price for Mansfelder copper rose from 98.8 Marks per 100 kilos in 1895 to 160 Marks in 1900, the electrical companies came together to introduce their own uniform price lists. This took place under the leadership of the *Siemens & Halske* concern and was phased in from April 1899.[51] The Rhine-Westphalian Pig Iron Association, *Rheinische-Westfälischen Roheisenvereinigung*, was an example of individually weak producers coming together to form a buyers association. It was founded in the winter of 1901-2 and was composed of twenty-three firms, many of them independent wire and rolling mill producers wishing to overcome the cartel prices for their raw materials. Eight firms came from Düsseldorf: *Düsseldorfer Eisen und Drahtindustrie*, Düsseldorf-Oberbilk; *Düsseldorfer Eisenhütten-Gesellschaft; Düsseldorfer Rohren und Eisenwalzwerk*, Düsseldorf-Oberbilk; *Hannsche Werke, AG.*, Düsseldorf-Oberbilk; *Oberbilker Stahlwerke, AG.*, Düsseldorf-Oberbilk; *Oberbilker Blechwalzwerk, G.m.b.H.*, Düsseldorf-Oberbilk; *Decking & Co. Gussstahlwerk*, Düsseldorf-Lierenfeld; and the *Rheinische Metallwaren und Maschinenfabrik*, Düsseldorf-Derendorf. This consortium set itself the task of supplying pig iron to member firms either through foreign sources or from the cartels at home at better prices. In this way, it sought to become as independent as possible from the iron and steel cartels.

The activities of many of the firms involved in the Rhine-Westphalian Pig Iron Association also have to be considered in another context, and this concerns what they did to improve efficiency in their own plants. It required no major insight to see that such reciprocal beggar thy neighbour pricing and buying policies could only be a short-term solution, if even that. Whether a firm was caught with surplus capacity, as in the steel industry, or high raw material prices and falling orders, as in the finishing branches, all firms had to become more 'cost conscious'. How to bring down 'cost prices' (*Selbstkosten*), became the major issue for heavy metal firms after 1900.[52] As we have already seen with the various output indices, some sort of solution was found after 1902. Output took off again and, with the exception of the staggered recession of 1907-9, continued unabated until 1913. The question that must be answered, therefore, is what force underwrote these years of prosperity? In answering this question we may also provide the much needed material basis for our appreciation of the new methods of training introduced into the metal industry during this period.

3. Towards a new prosperity: 'The labour force is today much more used up'

The solution found did not differ much from its British variation, with the exception that it was perhaps followed more strictly and more intensively. 'Efficiency' and 'prosperity' in this context turned on the same two problems that American metal industrialists had also concerned themselves with since the 1880s: extending the working day and getting more labour out of it. Dieter Groh has attempted to provide a theoretical overview of this, though, as has been mentioned, it lacks hard data. In his view, the lesson of the boom and bust was how it drew out the tendency for the average rate of profit to fall once the organic composition of capital began to rise; in other words, once the value of plant, machinery and equipment began to grow faster than the capital invested in hiring workers. Once this began to occur, and depression made it a necessity, enterprises turned to techniques of management which would not so much improve the productivity of labour through the introduction of new technologies, as cause a more intensive use of existing technologies. In this sense, and Groh does not see this point, one is not speaking of attempts to increase the productivity of labour *per se* (for this would require less input of average effort to obtain the same output, or the same average effort to get a larger output); rather, one can only speak of attempts to obtain a larger input of effort within the same time period, the sum total of which produces a strictly proportionate sum of extra output. Put more simply, we are concerned not so much with the productiveness of labour-power, as with its more intensive use of plant and equipment. Groh implicitly appreciates this, for he refers to attempts to increase the intensity of labour through tighter administration and accounting procedures, such as job cards, new methods of pay and workers having to adapt to the speed of a machine.[53] However, all this remains an imaginative hypothesis. Let us now turn to the reality.

In the first instance, the hypothesis appears to be quite wrong, for one of the primary actions of metal industrialists after the depression was to extend the working day for the manual workforce. Most of this took the form of overtime, which was systematically extended through the threat of dismissal. As the legal working day was ten hours, it usually meant that a metal worker would have to put in twelve hours or more, either during the day or night. In one government district of Düsseldorf during 1912 approximately 24.6 million hours of overtime were worked by the 220,000 workers. That came down to 150 hours per worker, while in individual cases it could mean that a worker may have had as much as twenty-four hours of overtime in a week.[54] The steel industry provided the worst examples of this extension to the working day, in order to keep the machines running for as long as possible.

Between March and November 1911, for instance, Friedrich Syrup conducted a survey of the amounts of overtime worked by different groups of steel workers in the Düsseldorf government district. The furnace workers were the ones hardest hit because of their direct relationship with the expensive plant and equipment. They included converter workers, ladle operators, slag drivers, heaters and rollers, and they could work anything from four to five hours' overtime during the week, plus a six to eighteen hours shift on Sundays to keep the furnaces in operation.[55] In the case of labourers in the steel and rolling mills, he found that during July 1911 a twelve to thirteen hour day was the norm, with overtime taking two forms. This could be either a six hour Sunday shift and/or one to five hours' overtime worked two or three times a week. For the maintenance workers in the steel mills, a key group who had to keep the machines operational, the average working day during March 1911 was 13.5 hours. However, these were the most overworked workers. A twelve to fourteen hour Sunday shift was almost uniform for them, as well as three hours of overtime several nights a week.[56]

Groh's hypothesis, though, is correct, for within the bounds of this rather old-style, English textile manufacturing technique of using an automaton to determine the length of the working day, was the attempt to extract every possible ounce of labour from workers using the costly machinery. Production breaks or 'pauses' were to be kept to a minimum and, if they had to occur, then this would be for 'technical' rather than 'artificial' reasons. The controversy surrounding the introduction of uniform lunch breaks in the metal industry, is a good example of this.

On 19 December 1908, the *Bundesrat* passed legislation for the introduction of rest pauses or lunch breaks in heavy industry. The new law required that at least one hour's rest be given to workers between the fifth and ninth hour of any shift, whether this was at night or during the day. This would generally coincide with either a break at midday or midnight. 'Exceptions', on the other hand, could be applied for under the general heading of the 'nature of establishment or with regard to the worker'.[57] The majority of heavy metal producers, large and small, either opposed outright the introduction of this law or sought 'exceptional' status. The *Regierungspräsident* in Düsseldorf was literally inundated with demands for exceptions because of the 'continuous' nature of establishments.[58] It was also a well-orchestrated campaign, with firms from all over the Rhineland stating their claims in exactly the same way, word for word, and then asking for exceptional status to be granted.

At the *Gutehoffnungshütte*, in Oberhausen, for instance, a one hour general break was seen as 'scarcely implementable', particularly for production workers, such as smelters, oven workers, casting pit workers and power generators. In this case, the firm sought permission to operate a half-hour break for these workers and grant the one hour break only to those who were not required to keep the machinery running continuously.[59] A similar appeal was made by the *Düsseldorfer Rohren und Eisen Walzwerke* in February 1909. In the steel shops, it was agreed that an hour's break could be given to the non-production workers like furnace bricklayers, fitters, smiths, moulders, apprentices, joiners and cast cleaners. Similar grades of workers in the puddling and rolling shops could also be given an hour's break, as could fitters, turners, boilersmiths, moulders, and painters from the machine shops and the electrical division. This firm was adamant, though, that machinists, boiler heaters, No. 1 smelters, gas stockers and puddlers could only have a half-hour break, if 'dangerous situations in the factory are to be avoided'. It was also noted, however, that these workers could not be allowed to leave their posts, for they had to be ready at any time to relieve other workers during their stint and who were too tired to continue.[60] This was exactly the rationale used by *E. Böcking & Co.*, a Mülheim enterprise specialising in rolling mill work, to obtain its exceptions. Here each gang of rollers, generally made up of five workers, was provided with a 'reliever' *(Ablöser)*, who could take over from one of the rollers when he was exhausted. The member of the gang would then come back and later another member would be 'relieved'. For *E. Böcking & Co.*, such a relief system more than compensated for the absence of an unbroken lunch-hour break.[61] It also kept the machines going, so that the company's fixed capital costs could be kept to a minimum.

E. Böcking & Co. were not alone in using the rationale that technically-based production pauses more than compensated for the absence of an uninterrupted lunch break. The *Düsseldorfer Rohren und Eisen Walzwerke* went to the trouble of actually timing the duration of production-based pauses for different grades of workers in making its appeal for exceptions before the *Regierungspräsident*. The management calculated that an average of two hours per shift was taken up with technically-based pauses for the groups of workers for which it sought exceptions.[62]

It is necessary to consider the significance of these timing operations in some detail because of the importance they had for the development of a *management consciousness* of the need to intensify labour in a 'technical' and 'scientific' manner.[63] When *Friedrich Krupp AG.*, the largest employer of metalworkers in the country, applied to the *Regierungspräsident* in September 1909 for its exemptions, the management argued from time studies that in the Siemens-Martin plants production workers already received a *cumulative* three-quarters-of-an-hour break, irrespective of the Government's intention to establish an hour's midday or midnight break. For those working with small rolling equipment in the mills, a three-quarters-of-an-hour cumulative break was also calculated, while in the machine shops it was found to be half an hour. As far as the other sections of the steel works were concerned, it was found that in the Thomas plants the tappers, casting pit workers, oven workers, mixers, machinists, heaters and smelters all averaged a cumulative half-hour break, as did the rollers, oven workers and heaters in the rolling mills. The locomotive leading hands, heaters, switchmen and shunters in the locomotive plants equally received breaks totalling half an hour. Production-based pauses, in fact, were calculated as high as one and a half hours amongst various groups of workers at the blast furnaces and at the Thomas and Siemens-Martin steel plants. At blast furnaces, this included cokery workers, ore loaders, by-product recovery oven workers, machinists, gas producers, heaters and fitters. In the Thomas plants a one and a half hour break was calculated for dolomite liners, fitters, turners and handymen, while for Siemens-Martin workers one could include, smiths, cast cleaners, handymen, bricklayers and fitters. As far as the Krupp management were concerned, there was no need for an hour's uniform production break. An extra half hour, or at most three quarters of an hour, was all that needed to be found. That Krupp actually conducted their survey between the fifth and ninth hour of each shift, i.e. in the period in which the Government stated an hour's break had to be taken, meant that they considered that production pauses either side of these hours would add up to a full 'lunch break'. Such was the magnetic attraction of making fixed capital profitable.

Another example may be taken from *Balcke, Tellering & Co., AG*. Benrath and Hilden, located in Düsseldorf's outer suburbs, and a producer of gas engines and boilers for iron and steel plants. This enterprise also argued against general and uninterrupted lunch breaks. Production-determined pauses were enough. The evidence for such a claim came from a survey of oven stoking where the stokers served two furnaces. At least twenty to thirty minutes separated the times when the stoker tended to one furnace and then the other. As this occurred several times in a shift, the firm believed that these production-determined interruptions should be classed as rest periods. The same argument was put forward for gas stokers and heaters, while in the rolling mills the rollers got their breaks when the fitters and maintenance crews came in to attend to the rolls, either when they were damaged or in need of changing.[64]

In the case of rolling, there were also the 'regular' breaks associated with rolling each ingot or plate. The *Hannsche Werke AG.*, located in Duisberg and Düsseldorf presented tabulated time studies for their universal rolling mill situated in Oberbilk, another Düsseldorf suburb. The data is presented in Table 22 and was taken from a survey conducted over 22 and 23 March 1909.

Hannsche's management presented similar time studies for steel oven workers, pit workers, stokers, and puddlers working large ovens. In these cases, they calculated average production pauses ranging over 175 and 245 minutes per shift.[65] In an earlier letter to the *Regierungspräsident* it was claimed that in the case of the oven workers the twelve-hour shift between 6 a.m. and 6 p.m. gave them plenty of time in which they had

TABLE 22

Production pauses at the universal rolling mill of the Hannsche Werke AG., *Düsseldorf, 22-23 March 1909.*

Day 1		Day 2	
Time of break	*Duration*	*Time of break*	*Duration*
6.00 am– 6.40	40 min.	6.00 am– 6.40	40 min.
8.35 am– 9.05	30 min.	8.15 am– 8.45	30 min.
10.40 am–11.05	25 min.	10.25 am–10.50	25 min.
12.40 pm– 1.05	25 min.	12.15 pm–12.50	35 min.
2.40 pm– 3.00	20 min.	2.15 pm– 2.45	30 min.
4.10 pm– 4.30	20 min.	4.15 pm– 4.40	25 min.
TOTALS	160 min.		180 min.

Source:
Hannsche Werke AG., to the Royal Factory Inspector, Düsseldorf *(Königlichen Gewerbe-Inspektor),* D.H.St.A. *Arbeitsschutz in der Grosseisenindustrie,* 33389, 31 March, 1909.

'very little to do'. This was especially so during smelting times, which occurred twice in each shift. To impose an hour's midday break on top of this would lead to difficulties in keeping the furnaces fully operational and, therefore, cause output to fall. For gas generator stokers, it was argued that if the eleven men on the twelve-hour shift 'take unjustified breaks, then the charging remains uncompleted; in which case the composition of the gas becomes uneconomical'. Their whole appeal had the flavour of technical determinism, with machinists, crane drivers and founders all having their jobs cross-referenced against each other, illustrating the degrees of mutual dependency and what would happen to production if a uniform break was introduced.[66]

Other firms, such as the *Rheinische Stahlwerke,* located in the Duisburg suburb of Meiderich, sought to add another reason why this law should not be introduced. It was just not in the interests of the workers, for it would effectively reduce their working day to nine hours (excluding overtime), and lead to a fall in their wages.[67] But, whatever the argument put forward, there can be no doubt what the basis of enterprise prosperity was in the pre-war years: it was work, and how to make it longer, more intensive and profitable.

Public awareness was also growing of the employers' factory strategies, especially through the work of the *Centralverein für das Wohl der Arbeitenden Klassen* (the Association for the Wellbeing of the Working Classes). One of its leading academic writers, H. Reichelt, informed the public of what such strategies for prosperity were having on Berlin's metalworkers. Moulders could not expect to continue working much past the age of fifty, if they did not die or find themselves maimed from injury and exhaustion. Even worse conditions applied to smiths, who day by day came into contact with blazing heat, which affected their nerves and tested their physical endurance over long and intensive working days. Their productive life, their contribution to the new prosperity, was also complete by the time they were fifty. Their death rate was also high.[68] Associated with this quite 'normal package' of working life was the more hypocritical stance of the State itself. It legislated these laws in 1908, but did not provide an adequate inspectorate to supervise their implementation in the factories. In the entire Rhineland, for instance, the various trade association figures for 1910 (to be found in Table 15), show that there were 8,869 establishments. When the non-associated establishments are taken into consideration the number leaps to 33,580. Many of these, of course, would have been small workshops. However, there were only fifty-eight works inspectors appointed to supervise all these establishments.[69]

In searching through the published and unpublished records for a contemporary appreciation of employer strategy and practice at this time, there is no better summation than Hans Ehrenberg's: 'The labour force is today much more used up.'[70] This intensification of work, though, was only the *result* or product of several other changes to the organisation of the labour of management and direct production. The quasi-autonomous powers of foremen and contractors were to be curtailed and new forms of supervision for the workforce introduced. As Otto Jeidels noted for the Rhineland's metal trades, that foremen, and to a lesser extent contractors, stood between management and the intensification of the labour process. Their role in determining the calculation of a job, how it was to be done and what the wage arrangements were to be, meant that upper management's knowledge of the use of fixed capital was seriously curtailed. These men were 'too independent from management'. They 'mediated' too much power in the supervision and organisation of the labour process. Jeidels went so far as to suggest that, as far as management were concerned, these men were actually 'dangers' to the ongoing profitability of an enterprise.[71] Another commentator, Dora Landé, observed that, as far as Berlin was concerned, the *Meister*'s 'powers of co-determination over the totality of wage relations' increasingly fused together a whole series of unstable, unpredictable and contradictory relations with both employers and workers.[72]

As Tables 23 and 24 show, large metal employers in the engineering, iron and steel branches tightened up the supervision of their workforces by employing many trained office and technical personnel who would be more accountable to them. Apart from exceptions in the engineering branch, where factories comprising 11 to 200 personnel appeared to need relatively more *office* personnel than the larger establishments; and, in the steel branch, where relatively more technicians were required in factories of 1,000 or more personnel, the most important features to emerge are: first, the relative fall in the number of factory managers required by the larger establishments; and, second, the growing relative weight and importance of white-collar and technical workers (*Beamten* and *Fachmänner*) in directing the labour process of these large factories. According to this 1907 industrial census, in engineering factories of up to fifty people there were approximately two white-collar and technical workers for every manager, while in engineering factories with more than 1,000 people there were 107 technical and office workers for every manager. A staggering ratio by any calculation. In other words, though the need for these workers was relatively the same in both small and large enterprises, the need was absolutely greater in the bigger factories. As the process of concentration became more pronounced, the need for thousands of these specialists in mental labour became critical for the successful and efficient operation of the larger enterprises.

TABLE 23

Percentage share of factory managers, office personnel, technicians and workers in the German engineering industry, 1907

		Factories with				
People		*M*	*O*	*T*	*W*	
11–	50	5.4	7.3	5.3	82.0	M = Factory Managers
51–	200	1.5	6.2	5.5	86.8	O = Office Personnel
201–	1000	0.4	4.9	5.7	89.0	T = Technicians
1000+		0.1	4.6	6.1	89.2	W = Workers

TABLE 24

Percentage share of factory managers, office personnel, technicians and workers in the German iron and steel industry, 1907

		Factories with				
People		*M*	*O*	*T*	*W*	
11–	50	5.6	4.7	2.4	87.3	M = Factory Managers
51–	200	1.6	5.2	2.5	90.7	O = Office Personnel
201–	1000	0.5	4.4	2.8	92.3	T = Technicians
1000+		0.1	4.5	4.7	90.7	W = Workers

Source:
F. Passow, 'Die Aufbau der grössern industriellen Betriebe nach den Ergebnissen der gewerblichen Betriebsstatistik von 1907', *Archiv für exacte Wirtschaftsforschung*, Vol. 2, Heft 2, 1912, Table 1, pp. 314-5.

The importance attached by enterprises to greater efficiency is important to appreciate, for it was precisely at this time that the larger firms required not only technical and office workers with an all-round knowledge of the new technical processes, such as draughtsmen, tool and machine designers, laboratory technicians and chemists, but also technical and office employees who could administer and supervise the introduction of new systems of wage payment, such as premium bonuses, as well as calculate and control the costs of every work process undertaken through the use of centralised calculation and rate-fixing offices. The introduction of job-cards, which set out the various rates for particular parts of a job, how the job was to be done, and which tools, machines and materials were to be used, required supervisory employees who had both an all-round technical knowledge of the work processes and of the methods used by workers to get round the more intensive forms of supervision and job organisation.[73]

Elaine Glovka Spencer also touches on some of these issues in her work on supervisory personnel in the Ruhr. However, she views their growing importance and functions purely in terms of 'the needs of modern, large scale industry' and its apparently natural impulse to 'bureaucratise' and 'rationalise' production management.[74] Yet, as we have shown, such a Weberian conception of the changes taking place at this time can hardly come to grips with the strictly bourgeois rationalisation of production management and the economics of fixed capital that impelled it along.

One final aspect of this period of expansion, which perhaps crystallised all the underlying changes taking place, was the contraction in the number of apprentices in the medium to large enterprises where the overwhelming majority of the workforce laboured. According to the 1907 industrial census, as shown in Table 25, the proportion of male apprentices to male metalworkers fell from 17.0% in engineering plants of 11 to 50 workers, to 4.3% in factories with more than 1,000 workers. The medium sized plants as well experienced a similar contraction: down to 10.6% in plants of 51 to 200 workers and to 6.1% in establishments of 201 to 1,000 workers. As will also be noted, the process was even more pronounced in the steel branch and for female apprentices in both branches. Obviously, the larger enterprises required relatively fewer apprentices than the smaller firms, and we shall discuss some of the reasons for this below. For the moment, the strong connection between the decline of plant-based apprenticeships and the growing importance of technical and white-collar workers most probably indicated a quite extensive decomposition and recomposition of skills for both skilled manual workers and the new supervisory staff.

TABLE 25

Percentage share of male apprentices to male workforce and female apprentices to female workforce in the German metal industry, 1907

	Percentage of Male Apprentices to Male Workers			Percentage of Female Apprentices to Female Workers		
	11–50	*51–200*	*201–1000*	*1000+*	*11–50*	*51–200*	*201–1000*	*1000+*
Iron and Steel	15.6	7.1	5.0	2.3	6.3	3.5	1.7	0
Engineering (Machinery, Instruments and Apparatuses)	17.0	10.6	6.1	4.3	1.9	0.5	0.1	0.3

Source:
Richard Passow, 'Der Aufbau der grössern industriellen Betriebe nach den Ergebnissen der gewerblichen Betriebsstatistik von 1907', *Archiv für exacte Wirtschaftsforschung*, Bd. 4, Heft 4, 1912, Table 6, p. 643.

4. Adapting the institutions of training

As a result of these changes to the size and composition of the workforce, and of the growing need to intensify labour in direct production, the institutions of public and private industrial training were expanded, systematised and given a new direction towards the requirements of an increasingly professionalised production management. If we begin at the pinnacle of the training system, i.e. with the universities and colleges, we may see how this was achieved.

(i) The Hochschulen for management engineers

According to a French education mission which visited Germany under the aegis of the French Ministry of Public Works, there were ten technical colleges (Hochschulen) and three mining academies (Bergakademien) in existence in Germany by 1906. All the schools were located in major industrial centres, with the Bergakademien located in Freiburg, Berlin and Clausthal, comprising 923 students. The Hochschulen were located in Munich, Darmstadt, Karlsruhe, Hanover, Stuttgart, Dresden, Aix-la-Chapelle, Danzig, Brunswick, and Charlottenburg in Berlin. The total number of students in these schools was some 16,303 in 1906, and both the Hochschulen and the three mining academies were producing three to four thousand graduates every year.[75] When the mission made its report to the Ministry of Public Works it was claimed that this number of students was 'excessive', reflecting the absence of entrance examinations, which were common in France. It was also argued that too many students encouraged an extremely broad range of ability, spanning those who were excellent and those who were only mediocre.[76] It is not possible to judge the validity of this assessment of German technical college students, but as it was informed by Pelletan's comparison between the Ecole des Mines in Paris and the Hochschule it bore all the resemblance of comparing apples and pears. Only the Bergakademien and the Royal United Engineers' schools in Elberfeld-Barmen could be compared with the quality of students and courses available at the Ecole des Mines.

The three mining schools produced an elite stratum of future managers and engineers for the mining and metallurgical industries on the same exclusive basis as the Ecole des Mines de Paris.[77] The small number of students bore testimony to that. The two Royal Engineers' Schools, located in the sister towns of Elberfeld and Barmen, by contrast, concentrated on educating an elite group of engineers and managers for the heavy electrical and general engineering trades. The schools were under the direct management of the state and belonged to the Ministry of Trade and Commerce. Comprising instruction and drawing rooms, extensive laboratories for electrical engineering, reading rooms for students and a special machine house with experimental workrooms containing power machines, tools, materials, etc. for general engineering instruction, the students undertook strictly scientific courses in mathematics, mechanics, physics, chemistry, technology, electrical engineering, machine construction and drawing over five-year courses.[78] In contrast to these elite schools for upper echelon managers and engineers, the *Hochschulen* were orientated to the production of rank and file engineers and technicians for the state mines, construction trades, and the iron, steel and engineering industries. The colleges generally specialised their instruction in one of these branches. The *Hochschule* in Aix-la-Chapelle, for instance, concentrated on instructing future engineers for the state mines and civil engineers for the mines and steel plants. On the other hand, the *Hochschulen* in Stuttgart and Charlottenburg specialised in the training of future engineers for the metallurgical trades.[79] If we turn to Table 26, some further aspects of this specialisation can be appreciated. The data presented concern the core areas of education at several of the *Hochschulen* in 1908. Electrical engineering, it will be noticed, held an important place at the Hanover, Karlsruhe and Munich *Hochschulen,* while Charlottenburg added naval and marine engineering to its civil and mechanical engineering courses. Since 1899 all the colleges had the right to issue recognised diplomas for their graduates, as well as to direct postgraduate study for doctorates in the various engineering disciplines by an original dissertation.[80]

At the undergraduate level, all students gave over the first two years of their four-year courses to the study of mathematics and theoretical sciences.[81] In the case of students at Hanover's college, it was possible

TABLE 26

The specialisation of higher engineering education in Germany, 1908

Core area of Training	Charlottenburg	Danzig	Hanover	Karlsruhe	Munich
Architecture	+	+	+	+	+
Civil Engineering	+	+	+	+	+
Machinery	+	+	+	+	+
Electricity	/	/	+	+	+
General Sciences	+	+	+	/	+
Mathematics	/	/	+	+	+
(pure and applied)			(general culture)		
Agriculture	/	/	/	/	+
Water and Forests	/	/	/	+	/
Naval Construction and Marine Engineering	+	+	/	/	/
Chemistry, Mines and and Metallurgy	+	/	chemistry only	chemistry only	natural sciences

+   Indicates core area taught at this school.
/   Indicates core area not taught at this school.

Source:
'The Formation of Engineers in Germany', *The Engineering Times,* Vol. 4, 1908, p. 161 ff.

to carry forward exclusively mathematical courses into later years, as Table 26 shows. Far from mathematical and theoretical training being held in contempt, as it was amongst radical Taylorites in France, a German 'encyclopaedic' education in the early years of training was held in high regard. Students also received practical instruction in the college laboratories, which were extremely well equipped with the various sorts of machines and testing instruments that were to be found in machine shops, foundries and laboratories in industry.[82] In the final two years of their course the students undertook exclusively technical subjects in the area of their speciality.[83] The French education mission noted at the time that, in contrast to the *enseignement encyclopédique* received by French students at the elite colleges, the German students had well-marked career and instruction patterns laid out before them, whether the instruction was received at a *Hochschule* or an elite *Bergakademie*. The specialities fed into construction engineering, mechanical engineering, electrical engineering, mining, mineral geography, and metallurgy. In France diplomas were not given in these last three fields, whereas in Germany they were issued for all of the special areas.[84] Also, depending on the diploma taken, students would undertake more instruction in various core subjects. For example, students who were to become mechanical engineers received more mathematical training than students who were going to become metallurgists of iron.[85]

Two further novel features of the *Hochschule* system were that students on completing their courses had to present a number of projects as part of their examination. At Darmstadt's technical college, mechanical engineering students had to present five projects for examination in various sorts of machine design and laboratory work; at the same time, in order to complete a course a student had to undertake an 'apprenticeship', generally for twelve months, in a factory, mine or mill.[86]

Some employer pressure groups and technical associations wished to specialise and rationalise the system even further. In 1907, the VDI, in a report on the higher technical education system, called for more attention to be given to the mathematical and scientific instruction of future engineers and that this be done, not only at the technical colleges, but also in the general education system as a whole. As well, less emphasis should be given to education in the gymnasiums and to the teaching of 'dead' languages, such as Latin and Ancient Greek. Finally, any unnecessary prolongation of technical courses should be discouraged, as they were already 'too long' and 'seriously prejudice the wellbeing and ability to work of young men'.[87] It may have been correct that the quality of the students and the encyclopaedic nature of the instruction received at the elite Parsian colleges highlighted certain 'mediocre' aspects of the *Hochschule* system, but it must be remembered that even after the 1911 technical education reforms France was still without a national system for the training of middle-ranking engineers, technicians and managers. Furthermore, by the late 1900s in Germany middle and upper echelon management training was growing rapidly, as big industrial manufacturers sought to secure a greater number of qualified managers. The Cologne Commercial College, for instance, was established in 1912–13 and started out with 535 matriculated students, with many hundreds attending public and open lectures.[88] All this was certainly no mean feat. Though Britain had also begun to establish commercial and management schools, its technical colleges were more directed towards filling the ranks of lower supervisory personnel, black-coated technicians and a minority of highly qualified workers, rather than towards building up a cadre force of rank and file management engineers, which was the province of the civic and traditional universities. The system bore a closer resemblance to that evolving in America, where entry to the ranks of professional production management was dominated by an increasingly professional *petite bour-geoisie,* whose career lines flowed horizontally from the technical college to the factory.

Yet, in two respects, America had to take second place to the 'unifying idea' developing in Germany. First, as Jürgen Kocka has shown, by 1900 the German universities and technical colleges were producing some 30,000 engineers per year, while at the same time the USA was producing approximately 21,000. As the USA's population was about twenty million larger than Germany's (seventy-six million compared with fifty-six million), the proportion of qualified engineers per head of population was much higher.[89] Second, in the provision of compulsory part-time technical education for the workforce as a whole, until the age of eighteen, Germany stood unequalled.

(ii) Continuation schools for stratifying the workforce
According to the Imperial Trade Law of 1891, employers in any trade were bound to allow all their workmen and workwomen under the age of eighteen to attend trade continuation schools *(Gewerbeschulen)* for a set number of hours, if one was established in a municipality or a state. Whether they were apprentices or not, all male and female workers were obliged to attend them.[90] Trade continuation schools formed the second tier of the German public school system. The first tier of elementary schools was already well established by 1900. Some 8.9 million children aged between six and fourteen attended these schools, which was approximately 90.8% of this age group. The balance of 9.2% attended either middle, higher or private schools.[91]

By 1911, about half of the twenty-six states within the Empire had introduced laws for the systematic formation of trade continuation schools; while the leading industrial state, Prussia, joined these ranks in 1912, obliging communities with 10,000 or more inhabitants to found at least one.[92] In the majority of industrial towns, according to a 1911 DMV report, the students attended these schools for a minimum of six hours a week after they had left elementary school at fifteen. The instruction generally took place during the day and lasted for three years.[93] As the Imperial Trade Law only obliged employers and workpeople to fulfil their duties if a trade continuation school was in existence, there was great scope for variation in the number of students in attendance and the type of schools in existence in a particular region.[94] The DMV report does not mention how many obligatory trade schools were in existence during the 1900s, or where they were located, but it does produce figures on the numbers of students in attendance for thirteen states between the years 1905 to 1908, as Table 27 shows. It will be seen that Bavaria had the largest number of students attending trade continuation schools, 45,202, and this number was calculated some two to three years before the other states, with the exception of Baden which only had 2,515 students in attendance in 1906. Behind Bavaria came the industrial states of Prussia, Saxony and Württemberg. The lead of these four industrial states over the others is partly explained by the encouragement these states had given to advancing their industries since the early nineteenth century. In Bavaria, a law of 1803, which stemmed back to Elector times, provided for the establishment of Sunday schools in all parishes, except during harvest times. The schools were intended for the training of journeymen, apprentices, and every under-aged male and female. Only journeymen were given the right not to attend these schools. These schools continued throughout the nineteenth century under the supervision of local clergymen and inspectors, who issued certificates stating that an apprentice or male or female worker had attended the school for a set number of years. This varied during the course of the century, but was generally for six years, from when the pupil was twelve until he or she was eighteen. By 1870 trade continuation schools had been attached to the Sunday schools for those unable to attend them during the working week. Since 1873, the state of Saxony had made it compulsory for all boys to attend a trade continuation school for at least three years after elementary school, while Württemberg brought in a similar law in March 1895, which built onto its parish school system trade continuation schools and technical Sunday schools. The smaller states, as well, built on the heritage of their parish and Sunday schools, and introduced trade continuation schools, though as the figures show not to the same extent as the larger states. Baden and Saxe-Weimar did so early as 1874, while the others introduced them later, with Saxe-Meiningen introducing a general and obligatory trade school law in January 1908.[95]

These trade continuation schools have to be distinguished from the *general* continuation schools created for the overwhelming majority of youth. As Table 27 shows, only a minority attended trade schools. In the

TABLE 27

The number of students attending obligatory trade continuation schools in thirteen German states, 1905–1908

	Year	Pupils
Prussia	1907	28,427
Bavaria	1905	45,202
Kingdom of Saxony	1906	22,000
Württemberg	1907	20,873
Baden	1906	2,515
Hesse	1908	2,320
Mecklenburg-Schwerin	1908	5,661
Mecklenburg-Strelitz	1908	779
Oldenburg	1908	2,869
Saxe-Weimar	1908	2,645
Saxe-Meiningen	1908	1,622
Anhalt	1908	3,248
Brunswick	1908	1,500

Source:
'Schools for Adults in Germany', presented by Alexander Schlicke for the *Deutsche Metallarbeiter Verband,* December 1911, in *Industrial Training also Internationalism,* 1915, International Metalworkers' Federation, compiled by Charles Hobson, Secretary of the British Section, p. 19.

case of general schools there was less emphasis given to trade or vocational training and more to basic arithmetic, German language, reading, writing, composition and drawing.[96] Württemberg, for instance, in 1908, had 1,967 general continuation schools for boys and 156 for both boys and girls, apart from the 153 trade schools comprising 20,873 pupils already referred to in Table 27.[97] During 1905–06 Prussia had 226,574 pupils in 1,395 continuation schools, while Saxony had 1,966 covering 88,583 pupils. Baden had 5,000 pupils attending several general continuation schools. The construction of these schools happened quite rapidly during the years 1893–1902. As well, the Baden state provided fifty-two other trade schools comprising 10,168 boys and 50 girls, apart from those referred to in Table 27.[98]

It would certainly be correct to suggest, in the absence of central state control of technical education, that there would be a tendency for the richer and industrially more advanced states to be able to provide more schools of better quality than the smaller states. In reality, this did tend to occur, as the DMV noted in 1911, and gave rise to trade union and employer movements 'striving for the unification of these schools all over Germany'.[99] This emphasis, however, can also be used to highlight the fact that in the more advanced states, where the majority of the metal industry's workforce was located, the existence of general continuation schools did not exhaust the public facilities becoming available; nor was their regional basis an obstacle to the systematisation and stratification of industrial training. The general continuation schools, particularly in their relation to the metal industry, were only the bottom rung of a rigidly stratified system of training for the workforce and were generally aimed at familiarising unskilled and semi-skilled metal workers with the type of labour that would be found in a metal factory. The semi-skilled also had the option of attending one of the *Technikum*(s). An American observer, W.H. Dooley, characterised them as 'low grade school(s) of practical technology', as the minimum age of entry was only fifteen and required the American equivalent of one to two years of a high school education, or in Germany, the completion of elementary school.[100] Apprentices, who would later take up hyper-qualified positions, generally went to trade continuation schools. In order to attend these schools, the apprentice was generally allowed ten hours off per week at no loss of pay, and was trained in the theory and practice of trade calculation, book-keeping, mechanical drawing, physics and machinery, the use of materials, and shop work. For skilled workers seeking promotion there were the *Industrieschulen.* The minimum age of entrance was sixteen, plus two or three years' practical experience in the trade. This was a full-time course, which stemmed back to the days when apprenticed journeymen sought further formal training to become master workmen. Above the *Industrieschulen* were the *Werk-meisterschulen* and the *Mittlere Fachschulen.* The *Werkmeisterschulen* or Foremen Schools were, as their name suggests, directed towards the teaching of foremen, and were generally attended by metal workers with long shop experience seeking promotion. They were older workers who may have started off in smaller shops and wished to move into the bigger plants, which provided more opportunity for advancement. These schools were generally run on an evening basis.[101] Future supervisory personnel could also attend one of the *Mittlere Fachschulen,* which also trained employers and higher office personnel for smaller factories so that they could obtain an appreciation of the latest technical advances in the industry. The entrance requirement was a year's military service and the completion of six years' secondary education at either a *Gymnasium* or *Realschüle.* Such schools complemented the activities of the *Neidere Fachschulen,* which trained future works managers for large plants and managers for smaller concerns. It has not been possible to discover how many *Fachschulen* of these types existed in Germany during the 1900s, but in Prussia there were nine already in existence as early as 1891, while four of them were run by private employers.[102]

The most advanced form of technical secondary instruction took place within the *Höhereschulen,* or Higher Trade Schools. To gain entrance to one of these schools a worker had to have a reasonable degree of know-ledge of elementary mathematics, the physical sciences, as well as already have highly-developed workshop skills. The schools were intended for men seeking supervisors' positions in large machine shops where an all-round theoretical knowledge of modern production processes and practical experience were both required.[103] This entire structure of lower managerial and manual technical education was well established by 1911 and suggested the existence of a pyramid of training divided into three exclusive segments: one for the unskilled, another for the semi-skilled, and a very refined structure for the training of various grades of qualified and supervisory labour power.

(iii) The continuation schools in practice
(a) Frankfurt

The Frankfurt-am-Main municipal obligatory Schools for Adults were considered to be a model of this sort of training and stratification. The compulsory three-year courses, comprising six hours per week of instruction in either the mornings or the evenings, were divided up not only according to the various 'trade' groupings, such as 'foundries' and 'workshops', but also according to the levels of skills that would be taught. Thus, the 'workshops' group, which comprised the teaching of locksmithing, tinsmithing, fitting and mechanics, was further sub-divided into (1) special courses for each particular trade; (2) trade group classes; and (3) general classes for the unskilled workers. In addition to this distinct specialisation of training according to trade and skill, the DMV reported that the pupils were 'again divided as regards capacity and progress made':

> A grading is carried out in all the classes in order to prevent gifted students being held back by those who may be incapable or indolent. There are three grades of 'quality', namely, first, second and third. If it should be found that pupils are not eligible even for the lowest or third class, they are put into a preparatory class. In this manner, the school represents itself as a graduate school of four classes, with corresponding parallel classes.[104]

It should not be surprising that the DMV lauded such specialised training and lamented that 'Unfortunately but few schools have such an extensive programme as this'.[105] The DMV's encouragement of the Frankfurt model was aided by the emphasis this school placed on encapsulating its instruction in terms of producerist images of labour, particularly at the apprenticeship level. As the union noted:

> . . . technology is given from the day a young man enters on his apprenticeship, and commences by reviewing his life in the home of his parents (the home and the school—their important bearing on the physical and intellectual development of the apprentice). . . The next step is the workshop, where the pupil is. . . acquainted with the several conditions of his trade and the management and equipment of the workshop, also with the outside course of the working day (duration, legal regulations about the time of working, factory regulations, the

necessity of these regulations in regard to juvenile workers). After that, in the third course, he is instructed in the knowledge of the raw materials and the articles of consumption, the various ores and their origin and metallurgical production. . . With the fourth step he is introduced to the domain of machinery. Here he is taught about the implements of work, the tools, operators [sic: operations], technical auxiliary instruments, power machines, generators and power-centres. The fifth step embraces the chapter on working men's achievements—the division of labour, the various kinds of workpeople. . . the advantages of the division of labour, then the wages, the dependence of the wages upon the conditions of economic life and labour, the personal education, accomplishment, and capability of the workman; further, the insurance arrangements in the German Empire, the dangers and the necessary assistance in case of accidents (first aid), legal regulations, theoretical and practical instruction.[106]

Frankfurt's metal apprentices, the brighter ones at least, who could afford the fees, could also attend one of the city's municipal trade schools. Instruction was again on a part-time basis for six hours per week, and entrance was generally conditional on the pupil either passing the school's entrance examination or having completed two years of high school. The specialised trades catered for were turning, toolmaking, ironfounding, tinsmithing, fitting and electrical engineering. The schools also took in some boys between the ages of twelve and fourteen and provided them with preparatory apprenticeship instruction in drawing, geometry and modelling. If the afternoon was fine and the teachers were in a good mood, then there was also the opportunity of 'drawing from life', as the local Palm Gardens and the Zoo were placed at the disposal of the school.[107]

The equivalent of the *Höhereschule* in Frankfurt was the Royal Engineers' School. It was under the control of the Ministry for Trade and Commerce. The courses were designed around four stages, each lasting six months. Instruction was full-time, about forty-two hours per week, and the pupil had to possess a good elementary education as well as have four years of workshop experience behind him in order to be admitted. The courses concentrated on the most important areas of machine drawing, design and electro-technology. Thus the pupil studied mechanics, electrical engineering, the uses and elements of machinery, physics, chemistry, mathematics, as well as factory business practices. Laboratory experiments were also undertaken and visits were made to works, 'so that students may learn something about the plant used in large firms'.[108]

(b) Stettin and Breslau

If we turn from Frankfurt, in the Hesse region of central Germany, to Stettin, in the north-east of the *Reich*, a similarly stratified system of public, technical education was in existence by 1910. In fact, on 1 April of that year, an obligatory school for adults was opened. Before the opening of the school a number of Guild schools (*Innungsschulen*) supplied the needs of the various trades. Technical schools had also been founded with the cooperation of the local Horticultural Society, the Merchant Guilds and the Vulcan Engineering Company for the training of apprentices. These schools ceased to exist with the founding of the obligatory school. In three of the five sections of the school given over to the metal trades pupils were trained in tinsmithing, coppersmithing, engine building and turning for both small workshops and factories (Sections II and III), while Section V was wholly committed to the training of unskilled young men.[109] Stettin, however, could not match Frankfurt's facilities for the training of the higher grades of labour-power, as it did not have the resources to establish *Industrieschulen* or *Höhereschulen*. Breslau, in the south-east of the Reich, on the other hand, had six *Industrieschulen* by 1911, comprising 182 teachers who were professionally trained and 27 practical instructors. The schools were completely given over to the training of apprentices for the compulsory three-year period, but in contrast to most other schools the hours of instruction per week were twice as long, between eleven and thirteen hours. The city also provided a general continuation school for the training of the unskilled and semi-skilled.[110]

(c) Bavaria and Saxony

The state of Bavaria and the Kingdom of Saxony probably came closest to Frankfurt's model of industrial training, this time on a regional basis. In Bavaria's main industrial centres, Nuremberg, Schwabach and Augsburg, all comprising large heavy engineering firms, obligatory schools were in existence. The courses were for six hours per week, and the future unskilled and semi-skilled were especially catered for. In the metal trades courses, they were familiarised with the technologies in use in factories and were taught the 'three R's'. Apprenticed metal workers in Nuremberg were provided with four specialised courses—for metal founding and moulding; metal burning and spinning (nickel-platers); boilermaking and coppersmithing; and gilding. There were also equally specialised courses for mechanics, tinsmiths and fitters. Such highly specialised training was designed to provide the leading firms with their rank and file *ouvriers d'art,* while these firms themselves undertook the training of the higher grades of labour power.[111] This is described in further detail below. Though Schwabach did not have either an *Industrieschule* or a *Höhereschule,* its obligatory school comprised many of their features. The three-year course for metal workers was completely theoretical and intended to complement the practical instruction received at their place of work. As the following outline of the subjects taught over the three-year period shows, the practical training of the hyper-qualified was meant to be complemented by the inculcation of productive-efficiency values and of the worker's role within the Empire.

TABLE 28

The general order of subjects taught at the Schwabach Obligatory School for Adults

FIRST YEAR

1. History of trade or profession.
    Origin of handwork.
    Development in towns.
    Guilds, etc.

2. Order in the trade and life of the State.
    Apprenticeship and all appertaining thereto.
    Insurance, sick and accident.

3. Hygiene in all its branches.
    Air spaces, ventilation etc.
    Apparatus for protection from injuries, infection, dust, etc.
    First Aid.

SECOND YEAR

1. History of trade.
    Decline of handwork.
    Legal fixing of trade freedom.
    Decline of Guild.
    Machinery and its effects on trade.
    Rise of working class.

2. Order in State.
    Invalid Insurance, Accident Insurance, etc., contracts, protections.
    Worker's place in family and community.
    Duties and rights of members of community.
    Elections and offices of honour.

3. Hygiene, bodily heat, digestion.
    Tobacco and alcohol: their effect on the body.
    Deleterious effects of excessive sport, cycling, wrestling, etc.

THIRD YEAR

1. History of trade. Means of bettering the position of small masters, wage-earners.
    Co-operative societies, companies.
    Trade and commerce in present time.

2. Order in the State.
    Worker as citizen.
    Government of State and Empire.
    Tasks of the State and Empire.
    Duties and rights of a citizen.

3. Hygiene.
    Care of skin and body.
    Housing, clothing.
    The most important trade illnesses.
    Digestive process.

TABLE 28 *(Cont)*

THIRD YEAR (Cont)

Circulation of blood.

Source:
'Schools for Adults in Germany', presented by Alexander Schlicke for the *Deutsche Metallarbeiter Verband*, 1911, in *Industrial Training also Internationalism,* compiled by Charles Hobson, Secretary of the British Section, p. 32.

As in America, the attempt to inculcate solid bourgeois values for the hyper-qualified was an integral component of industrial training. Schwabach was not alone in this, as the study of 'citizens' rights and duties' was an obligatory subject in all the technical schools; though Schwabach's commitment to the study of the 'deleterious effects of excessive sports' and the 'care of skin and body' may have indicated a stronger impulse towards the mobilisation of all resources towards 'efficient' production.[112] Similarly, the Augsburg Municipal School for Adults provided their metalworker apprentices with courses in 'public political education'. In this case, however, more attention was given to training in practical supervisory functions, such as arithmetic, calculation, book-keeping and correspondence, for the 281 metal apprentices enrolled during the year 1909–1910.[113] Peter Lundgreen is doubtful whether such study was, in fact, related to the 'needs' of capitalist industry. For him, the emphasis given to political education was 'appropriate. . . only to the Prussian subject within a political system well known for its feudal and authoritarian traits'.[114] It is futile, however, to consider political education in this light or to see it as something to be contrasted with specifically technical instruction designed to fill the needs of industry. This form of instruction has to be seen as part of a total phenomenon, and not one limited to 'feudal' Germany. The values propounded were bourgeois rather than feudal. And even if they were not liberal, they were certainly efficiency orientated and most definitely related to the 'authoritarian traits' or the capitalist-organised factory.

If we turn to Saxony's technical schools, it is possible to detect three broad streams. The obligatory schools in Leipzig, Aue-im-Erzgebirge, Bautzen and Dresden looked after the training of the unskilled, while the various *Industrieschulen* in these towns took care of the needs of the higher grades of labour power. The Bautzen school provided day courses for apprentices and if a youth was articled with a firm then it generally picked up the bill for the fees. The classes were given in the morning and on Sundays, so that the boy could be available for work in the afternoon. The Aueim-Erzgebirge *Industrieschule* concentrated on various forms of finishing training for apprentices and assistants, with an emphasis on geometric drawing and trade calculation. The town also had a special

'Trade School for Tinsmiths and Fitters'. Dresden's obligatory School for Adults had *Industrieschulen* integrated into its structure and bore many similarities to Frankfurt's. Specialised training and streaming were rigorously followed and the school also provided courses of instruction for future office clerks and commercial men, for four hours per week.[115]

Table 29 summarises the information available on these schools in other regions of Germany and what they were designed to achieve for the local metal workforce. The training in these areas was again broadly based and highly specialised, with the characteristic emphasis on the training of hyper-qualified and supervisory labour, as can be seen from the evidence concerning the Stuttgart and Baden schools. One Baden school had an interesting historical dimension which should be drawn out. It will be seen that in Oberstein, located in the Grand Duchy of Oldenburg, one of the courses available was the installation and management of a small watch factory for future supervisors. Baden also used watch-making for training sections of the labour force. This custom went back to the 1840s when the first school for watchmakers was established. The original aim was to defend the housebound craft in the face of 'foreign' competition. Cheaper imports from Switzerland and other German states were threatening the future of the trade and had also forced the introduction of a tariff. By the early 1900s, however, the school was placing much more of its resources into management and supervisory education: a clear example of how far the new professional managerial hierarchy had developed and of its ability to immerse itself in a traditional craft.[116]

TABLE 29

Summary of the technical schools for metalworkers under eighteen in Württemberg, Baden, the Grand Duchy of Oldenburg, Elberfeld-Barmen and Hamburg, 1911

WÜRTTEMBERG:

Trade-Educational Act, 1906
Trade Schools were to be established in places where there were more than 30 apprentices in a trade. Instruction for seven hours per week during the day.

Stuttgart

Obligatory Day School
For the unskilled and apprentices in instrument making, founding, turning, electrical engineering, machine building, machine designing, moulding, electro-plating, grinding, mechanics, metal punching, boiler making, copper and black-smithing, tinplating, and electro-fitting. Designed to familiarise unskilled and semi-skilled with metal work and to provide advanced training for apprentices.

TABLE 29 *(Cont)*

Stuttgart

Voluntary Professional School
For machine designing, tool making and tool designing. Instruction in geometric design, sculpting, freehand drawing for draughtsmen and electrical engineering. Designed for new *ouvriers d'art.*

Esslingen

Trade School 1909
700 students in 1911. Designed to produce practical and theoretically trained supervisory staff. Courses in fine mechanics and metal work, and also book-keeping, bills of exchange, legal knowledge and calculation.

Gmund

Trade School and the *Royal School for Precious Metal Industry*
Emphasis on design, drawing and commercial-factory knowledge.

BADEN:
Pforzheim

Trade School
Compulsory for all under eighteen. Special emphasis on training new *ouvriers d'art.* Instruction in design, workshop arithmetic, business calculation electircal engineering, magnetism, galvanising and batteries.

GRAND DUCHY OF OLDENBURG:
Oberstein

Industrial School for Adults
Emphasis on training apprentices, especially in electrical engineering. Course also given in installation and management of a small watch factory directed at future supervisors. Also, theoretical instruction in the management of large concerns.

ELBERFELD-BARMEN:

Royal United Engineers' School
Evening courses, eight to ten hours per week for apprentices and assistants in mechanical and electrical engineering.

HAMBURG:

Trade Schools
By 1910, six schools devoted to machine building and electrical engineering. Also, schools for ship-building, tinplating and coppersmithing. Over 3,000 students attending summer and winter courses.

Source:
Derived from 'Schools for Adults in Germany', presented by Alexander Schlicke for the *Deutsche Metallarbeiter Verband,* 1911, in *Industrial Training also Internationalism,* compiled by Charles Hobson, Secretary of the British Section, pp. 40-60.

The background to the teaching staff in these schools also bears out this argument. In Prussia, for instance, during the years 1904–08 the number of qualified draughtsmen, technicians and engineers teaching in the trade schools almost doubled, rising from 670 to 1,222. Professional public school teachers, of course, were the overwhelming majority of teachers, and their ranks rose from 8,532 to 12,068. In contrast to these two groups, the number of handicraft workers who were teachers grew from 516 to only 753. In fact, this was a substantial relative fall in their numbers given the expansion of trade school education at this time.[117]

As should also be apparent from the description of these schools, they generally only catered for young male metal workers. Girls did have to attend obligatory schools, but the climate of the time prevented them from undertaking almost any sort of formal training in metal work. Where girls could attend a trade school, as in Stuttgart, they were more likely to be found 'studying' housework. This was also combined with courses in German, arithmetic and book-keeping, which were directed towards clerical work. If girls and women could gain employment in the metal trades, it was generally obtained by them taking up lowly white-collar positions as typists and clerks.[118] The metal industry itself, at least until the Great War, remained the preserve of males, especially in the heavier branches of the industry, as can be illustrated by referring to the age and sexual composition of the workforce in Düsseldorf between the years 1900-1913. Though both the iron and steel and engineering branches experienced a small decline in the adult male workforce, this was largely accounted for by an increase in boy labour, rising from 4.9% to 7.4% in the engineering branch and from 4.5% to 6.4% in the iron and steel branch. Furthermore, only the steel branch experienced a substantial increase in the number of female employees 16 and over, from 1.6% to 5.3%.

(iv) Training in the plants

The London County Council's accurate perception of the rigid stratification of industrial training in Germany can be further complemented by referring to developments in plant-based training. Two sorts of formal training have to be accounted for here: one for the more traditional grades of skilled labour and another for the new *ouvriers d'art* and supervisory personnel. Both were organised *via* the few remaining apprenticeships made available by the larger metal enterprises. In the case of the new *ouvriers d'art* and supervisory personnel, we can consider the training offered by two large Bavarian based firms—(1) The United Machine Factory of Augsburg-Nuremberg and, (2) The Siemens-Schuckert Works, Nuremberg. Apprentices at the United Machine Factory were undertaking four courses over three to four years for approximately twelve hours per week by 1911. This freed them for attending the local obligatory schools

TABLE 30

The age and sex composition of Düsseldorf's metal trades workforce, 1900 and 1913

Year	Total Workforce	Adult Male	Percent	Females 16 and over	Percent	Males 14 to 16 Percent		Females 14 to 16 Percent	
				Engineering Trades					
1900	7,443	7,058	94.8	16	0.2	366	4.9	2	0.03
1913	12,290	11,124	90.5	204	1.7	906	7.4	29	0.23
				Iron and Steel Trades					
1900	10,686	9,984	93.4	174	1.6	482	4.5	46	0.40
1913	11,368	10,014	88.2	606	5.3	724	6.4	12	0.10

Source:
Derived and calculated from: Bericht über den Stand und die Verwaltung der Gemeinde-Angelegenbeiten für die Stadt Düsseldorf, 1900/1913, Stadtarchiv, Düsseldorf.

for adults. Their instruction contained a strong emphasis on the development of supervisory knowledge, such as elementary business calculation and job design. The Siemens-Schuckert school placed an equally strong emphasis on business calculation, with the study of bills of exchange, book-keeping, arithmetic, health and sanitation. The students also received an all-round instruction in the theory and techniques of production through the study of algebra, geometry, physics, mechanics, chemistry, electro-techniques and drawing. An experimental workshop was connected with this school and there students were taught machine construction and fine mechanics.[119] At the *Benrather Maschinenfabrik, AG.*, in Düsseldorf, similar courses for the instruction of hyper-qualified technical workers were organised in cooperation with the trade schools run by the City Council. The firm provided both instruction rooms and training workplaces at its plant, and the students were systematically taken through all phases of the theory and practice of the production process, including manufacture, transport and marketing. Examinations were conducted in each subject and after a year's general technical and theoretical instruction the students specialised in various areas of production management.[120]

At the other extreme of the apprenticeship system was the training for the older grades of skilled labour, which were now becoming hyper-specialised. H. Reichelt's description of this sort of apprenticeship training at one of Berlin's large engineering plants in 1907 can be taken as an illustration. He observed that in the large firms, the few remaining manual apprenticeships generally fell into three categories: for machine builders, fitters and planers, and millers. It is noticeable here that apprentice turners were no longer seen as a separate entity of skilled labour. We shall note some of the consequences of this below, but it can be emphasised that the skill content of turning was considered to bear more resemblance to the lower, even more specialised skills of semi-skilled workers than to the hyper-specialised skills of millers and planers, etc. For the apprentices *(Lehrlinge)* at the enterprise Reichelt studied, the training period lasted for three to four years. Only the machine-building apprenticeships, however, received the necessary all-round training which was essential for their future utility to the firm. As can be seen in Table 31, machine-building apprentices spent no longer than eight months in one branch of the trade. The training was fairly evenly spread: eight months each on fitting, turning, milling and planing, and six months each on pattern-making and moulding. The fitting, planing and milling apprentices, by contrast, spent at least two-thirds of their three-year training period specialising in only one branch of the trade: in the case of fitters, twenty-four months on fitting; and for planing and milling apprentices, twenty-seven months on planing, milling and gear milling.[121] Dr Ernst Günther spotlighted a similar pattern of highly specialised industrial training in the Bavarian metal industry, especially at the Siemens-Schuckert Works, which complemented its programme of hyper-qualified training for the new *ouvriers d'art* with a very specialised form of training for the older grades of skilled workers.[122] It should not be thought that in these cases the training lacked quality or was completely empirical; rather, practical instruction was complemented by theoretical training at work and school, while the skills developed, though highly specialised, were of a high standard.[123] A universal milling machine operator, for example, required well-developed theoretical and practical skills to be good at his job, even if he could not, or was not allowed to, turn his hand to anything else.

TABLE 31

Number of months spent on various branches of metalwork for machine builders, fitters, and planers and millers at one large engineering works in Berlin, 1907

Machine building Apprenticeship		Fitting Apprenticeship		Planing and Milling Apprenticeship	
Fitting	8 months	Fitting	24 months	Fitting	6 months
Turning	8 months	Turning	3 months	Planing & Milling	24 months
Planing & Milling	8 months	Planing & Milling	3 months	Gear Milling	3 months
Assembling	4 months	Grinding & Polishing	3 months	Smithing & Tempering	3 months
Grinding & Polishing	3 months	Smithing & Tempering	3 months		
Gear Milling	2 months				
Smithing & Tempering	3 months				
Patternmaking	6 months				
Founding	6 months				
TOTAL	48 months		36 months		36 months

Source:
H. Reichelt, *Die Arbeitsverhältnisse in einem Berliner Grossbetrieb der Maschinenindustrie,* Leonhard Simion, Berlin, 1907, pp. 32–4.

It is immediately apparent that both these highly stratified forms of training were no longer vehicles for job promotion *within a plant,* as they could be during the nineteenth century when shortages of skilled labour-power encouraged employers to train their semi- and unskilled workers up to the higher grades of labour power. Even if the training during the nineteenth century was specialised and *dependent* on the employer distributing his technical intelligence, it at least offered the possibility of mobility up the job hierarchy as workers picked up more skills through experience. By contrast, during the early years of the twentieth century mobility was completely dependent on the possibility of a youth being able to make the *horizontal* transition from the obligatory school, trade school and technical college to the factory posts of unskilled assistant, specially skilled machinist, new *ouvrier d'art*, white-collar technician and manager. The addition of this new, public dimension to the capitalist regulation of skill not only serviced the technical needs of an industry dominated by less than one hundred monopolistic concerns, but also underwrote the class character of their now bureaucratic and professional technical intelligence.

5. *Job turnover and the new 'nomads'*

As far as the industrial metalworkers as a whole were concerned, they found that their mouthpiece, the *Deutsche Metallarbeiter Verband,* had a very ambiguous attitude to what was taking place. As we have seen, it encouraged publicly-based training, particularly when it emphasised producerist images of labour. Yet the Union was also very concerned that such training was not necessarily associated with an increase of skills for the workforce as a whole. When the International Congress of the Metalworkers' Federation met in Paris in 1900, the DMV revealed an 1895 survey which showed that for every thousand metalworkers in employment there were 377 'untrained' workers in the foundries, 577 in small machine, instrument and apparatus plants, and 700 in tin ware factories.[124] Less ambiguous, however, was the response of the manual workforce. Three distinct patterns emerged. As in the past, many of the unskilled wandered from factory to factory, lifting, carrying or driving machinery, demonstrating not only their revolt against the hyper-qualification and specialisation of labour, but also in search of better prospects or as a result of economic recessions.[125] Joining their ranks, as well, was a new kind of 'nomad', whose existence sent shivers down the spines of employers and bourgeois intellectuals. He was a 'skilled' worker driven to wander for many of the same reasons, but primarily animated by his own coherent revolt against the monotony and specialisation of labour. His attitude to work, his youthfulness and his militant desire to move from plant to plant were all seen as threatening the capitalist regulation of skill and undermining the employer's supremacy over his *Arbeitsgemeinschaft* or 'community of work'. It was a response which was seen to be militant and radical, not so much because these workers were labour 'aristocrats' seeking to maintain or restore their 'lost' relationship with the totality of the labour process, but because they wanted to *learn*, gain additional qualifications and experience, and in fact use their specialised dexterities as levers to *establish* a total relationship with the labour process. In other words, to defend and advance the economic integrity of their labour power.

Richard Ehrenberg, in the widely read journal, *Archiv für exacte Wirtschaftsforschung* (Thünen-Archiv) was instrumental in drawing attention to who these new nomads were and what they were trying to do. He spoke of them wanting to establish 'a feeling for the machine' *(mit der Maschine fühlen)* in his *Schwäche und Stärkung neuzeitlicher Arbeitsgemeinschaften,* which appeared in the journal in 1910.[126] He referred to an anonymous turner, whose work had been effectively reduced to semi-skilled labour, who wanted to be able to work 'with a full understanding for his job'. In fact, this turner argued that one should only work if a worker had this knowledge, for only then would he be able to be 'proud of his art'.[127] Having received his early specialised training at one of Stettin's steam engine works, he came to the conclusion that in order to be able to learn how to turn every piece of a steam engine then he would have to go on a 'waltz'.[128] Ehrenberg's commentary was filled with such examples, and concluded that, 'it is certain' that these workers 'wander in order to learn', both out of a certain sense of 'recklessness' *(aus Leichtsinn)* and an 'aversion' *(aus Unlust)* to specialisation.[129] Marie Bernays and Alfred Weber, in their *Auslese und Anpassung* studies, also drew attention to the high rates of job turnover for the unskilled and specialised skilled workers. Bernays, though, was more concerned to contain exaggerated bourgeois fears of these nomads. It was certainly true, she argued, that job turnover was high, but it generally took place within one industrial city or at most in the surrounding district.[130] Yet, as Alfred Weber pointed out in 1912, it was one thing for the unskilled to wander from plant to plant, it was quite another matter for hyper-specialised fitters, turners, millers and planers to take a 'waltz', applying and accumulating the skills of their branch in complete opposition to the design of the workforce envisaged by employers and the state. They had no intention of allowing themselves to become 'chained to one position' like 'Promethean slaves' as the semi-skilled workers were. They had no intention of allowing their skills to remain purely job specific, or even worse, circumscribed to the use of only one machine.[131]

There is a large body of evidence to show high rates of job turnover in the German metal industry, but it has to be handled with care. A number of large concerns in Bavaria's metal industry, for example, experienced both relatively high levels of job turnover and job stability. If we take five years of labour service as an indication of job stability, then at the United Machine Factory, Augsburg, 54.1% of the workforce had been with the firm for less than five years at the end of 1903. The firm employed 2,572 workers at this time and amongst this number 18.1% had been with the firm for more than fifteen years, while 27.1% had given between five and fifteen years of service. At the top end of the labour service hierarchy

5.3% had been with the firm between twenty-five and forty-eight years.[132] At the Locomotive Factory of Kraus & Co., the proportion of workers who had served more than five years was even higher. At the end of 1906, the firm employed 1,180 workers, of which 55.2% had served between five and twenty-five years. At the top end of the service hierarchy, some 5.9% had been with the firm for more than twenty-five years, while at the bottom 38.9% had been with the firm for less than five years.[133] Of the explanations advanced to account for this, Ernst Günther suggested that the remoteness of Bavaria's metal industry from the great centres of Berlin and the Rhineland forced employers to hold onto the workforces they had so laboriously built up.[134] At face value, this explanation has many similarities to that advanced by Antonio Gramsci to explain the rise of an 'organic' workforce at the Ford plants in Detroit. But, as the figures themselves suggest, this would be an extreme conclusion to reach, as nearly half of the workforce at the two plants had been there for less than five years. Certainly, remoteness must be considered an important factor in any explanation of relative labour stability in this region. At the same time, however, job stability was encouraged by these firms, like many others, training their own *ouvriers d'art,* who stayed with a firm for many years, if not for life, gradually assuming higher semi-managerial positions as technicians and foremen. A number of hyper-qualified fitters employed at these two plants were particularly brought on to assume such functions.[135] Such small numbers, though, cannot account for the entire phenomenon. The most likely explanation for both job stability and job turnover at these two plants is one which takes into consideration the position of the specialist semi-skilled workers. Bernays observed that the majority of semi-skilled workers were little influenced by the desire to wander, as they remained locked into the skills they had acquired in one factory.[136] Rather than constituting an homogeneous stratum of workers whose skills were easily interchangeable, they found themselves locked into a hierarchy of finely differentiated skills not separately exchangeable from plant to plant. If they left, then in all probability they would sink back into the ranks of the unskilled and have to climb up the ladder again.[137] At the Daimler Motor Works, for instance, it was the semi-skilled turners who found themselves locked into these positions, while the unskilled *Hilfsarbeiter* and the specialised *Handwerker*—fitters, patternmakers and machine builders—'wandered' and 'waltzed'.[138] This restriction on mobility was further exacerbated in Bavaria by the region's remoteness from the great centres of Berlin and the Rhineland. There were just fewer opportunities for metalworkers to move around, unless they decided to migrate from one side of the country to another.[139]

The Promethean character of semi-skilled labour was further reinforced by the development of surplus labour populations, whose members stood ready to take up the position of a semi-skilled worker if he took it into his head to wander. Düsseldorf's metal trades graphically illustrated this development, as Table 32 demonstrates. In both branches of the industry these years of expansion and technical change went hand in hand with massive increases in the number of people seeking positions. It was a development which brought about a rapid decline in job placement rates. In the engineering branch, for instance, the job placement rate for every one hundred workers seeking a job declined from 64.1 in 1905 to 16.8 in 1909, rising marginally to 34.5 by 1914. As will be seen, this was brought about by a staggering increase in the number of workers seeking positions in the branch, rising from 2,223 in 1905 to 10,138 in 1914. At the same time, the number of jobs available could not keep pace with the number sought. It should also be noted that this situation was not

TABLE 32

Employment trends in Düsseldorf's metal industry. Iron, steel and engineering, 1905–1914
Iron and Steel
(including, blast furnaces, puddling, steel and rolling)

Year	Number of Positions Open	Number of Positions Sought	Number of Positions Filled	Job Placement Rate (For every 100 workers seeking a position)
1905	1,686	1,932	1,562	80.8
1906	3,527	4,253	3,297	77.5
1907	3,036	4,581	3,024	66.0
1908	1,655	4,386	1,431	32.6
1909	1,472	4,338	1,231	28.4
1910	1,428	4,226	1,063	25.1
1911	1,921	4,290	1,672	39.0
1912	2,504	5,156	2,060	39.9
1913	1,990	5,312	1,703	32.1
1914	2,171	3,854	1,802	46.8

Engineering Trades
(including foundries)

Year	Number of Positions Open	Number of Positions Sought	Number of Positions Filled	Job Placement Rate
1905	1,475	2,233	1,431	64.1
1906	2,527	5,207	2,490	47.8
1907	2,925	5,839	2,869	49.1
1908	1,105	4,294	981	22.8
1909	820	4,071	686	16.8
1910	1,098	4,204	965	22.9
1911	1,327	4,346	1,214	27.9
1912	2,027	4,853	1,793	36.9
1913	2,312	6,646	2,141	32.2
1914	3,834	10,138	3,496	34.5

Source:
Jahresbericht des Statistischen Amts der Stadt Düsseldorf, 1905–1914, Stadtarchiv, Düsseldorf.

caused by large numbers of metalworkers already in employment seeking alternative work within the branch. Düsseldorf's Statistical Office calculated that only 3% of the number of positions sought could be accounted for by metalworkers already having a job. Given such pressures from the labour market, metalworkers in employment were very vulnerable to displacement. It would not be an exaggeration to assume that this situation was largely responsible for the absence of regular strike activity in Düsseldorf's large firms, and in the Rhineland generally, during the pre-war years.[140] It should also be noted that this demand for positions in the industry was not caused by rising unemployment. Quite the contrary, it was caused by improvements to training and the specialisation of labour, which considerably broadened the supply of labour and intensified the demand for positions.

Some semi-skilled workers, though, threw caution to the winds, especially in Berlin and the Württemberg region. When Reichelt visited his Berlin enterprise during May–June 1905, he found that there were 1,332 workers employed. Of this number, 45% were in their first year of service, while 75% had served no more than five years at the plant.[141] The experience of the *Maschinenfabrik Esslingen,* in Württemberg, was very similar during the early 1900s. In 1883 the average period of service was already down to 27.72 months. By 1900, this had declined to 12.55 months and by 1914, it had reached the miserable depths of 5.38 months. Every stratum of the workforce and every age group contributed to these high rates of turnover, though like the two Bavarian firms a small proportion of the workforce (21%) had been with the firm for more than ten years in 1908.[142] At the Berlin firm the proportion of the workforce who had given more than ten years of service by 1905 was even less—11%.[143] When Reichelt sought an explanation for such high rates of turnover in Berlin, he was driven to the conclusion that its root cause was the specialised nature of training and the intensive forms of labour.[144] He compared service records and age compositions for the workforce at the Berlin firm during May–June, 1905 with those of a state-run marine factory in Kiel on 1 November, 1903.

Reichelt found that, where 75% of the workforce at the Berlin firm had served less than five years, some 55% of the Kiel workforce had given more than five years of service.[145] Furthermore, 23.7% of the workers at the marine plant were under 25 years of age, while in Berlin, the proportion was 30.7%.[146] At the other end of the age hierarchy, he found that 12.3% of the workers at the Kiel plant were over fifty years of age. By contrast, the Berlin plant had only 7.8% of its workers over fifty years of age.[147] Though both workforces can be seen to contain large numbers of young workers, the youthfulness of the workforce at the Berlin plant was even more pronounced. In 1905, 80% of the workers were aged between sixteen and thirty-five, with approximately one-third aged between twenty-one and thirty. Finally, in contrast to the marine works, the Berlin firm employed three times the proportion of young workers aged between nineteen and twenty-one.[148] In Reichelt's view, the slower pace of production at the marine works encouraged a more balanced age composition in the workforce, whereas in the privately-owned Berlin plant, workers over the age of forty were quickly weeded out. At this plant, at least, the intensive and specialised nature of labour meant that young workers gave the best years of their lives to the accumulation of capital and the over-use of their labour power, only to be thrown onto the streets when they were no longer productive.[149] If this prospect did not impress them, then they quickly sought to escape the new psycho-physical apparatus of labour by revolting with their feet. Heilwig Schomerus has found that the *Maschinenfabrik Esslingen* underwent a similar experience during the early 1900s. By 1912 approximately 80% of the workforce was less than thirty years old. In complete contrast, however, at least 80% of the firm's administrative hierarchy was over thirty.[150] This polarisation between the age composition of the workforce and the administrators of the firm had been developing since the 1880s and gave rise to generational conflicts between management and labour, or between the young workers and the older *Angestellten* and employers.[151] The implication of this, as Alfred Weber noted as early as 1912, was that the proletariat was forced to operate within a different life and work cycle from those who were the agents of the new professional, technical intelligence. Where employers, office personnel, technicians and new *ouvriers d'art* were reaching the heights of their intellectual maturity and technical skills after forty, the non-professional workers found themselves on the scrap-heap, with the last twenty years of their lives considered to be a surplus commodity.[152] Reichelt drew an even more forceful conclusion. In his view, if employers continued to 'disregard the welfare of their workers', then they would soon find their position as heads of factories under challenge from young, militant and specialised workers seeking to overturn the capitalist regulation of skill.[153]

Up to 1914, however, German metal employers had little to fear as regards the general security of their position. They had already become extremely confident members of Germany's industrial bourgeoisie during the latter half of the nineteenth century, and as far as the successful operation of their plants was concerned, they were completely attuned to the need for privately regulating the training and skills of their workers. By the early years of this century, they had also successfully grafted on a public system of training in conjunction with the state. Yet where the success of overcoming relative industrial backwardness may account for their early confidence and security, by the turn of the century more modern forces were at work. In the context of a massive wave of expansion and fixed capital investment, the structure and character of the workforce was transformed. Huge monopolistic and bureaucratically-organised firms took charge of the industry. Workers were concentrated into fewer and larger plants. New technical and economic needs emerged which had to be served, primarily in the area of *planning* the most intensive use of plant and equipment. New patterns of training in the factories and the schools were developed, which on the one hand sought to consolidate management's planning and supervisory role in the labour process and, on the other hand, would impose on the overwhelming majority of workers a more intensive and specialised use of their labour-power in direct production. Public and private professional training was organised for higher management engineers, technicians, administrative employees and supervisory personnel. At the same time, professional training for a new stratum of hyper-qualified workers, who could build machinery and maintain it in good working order, was brought to ful-filment in the plants and the schools. But this was only necessary for a small minority. For the rest, the unskilled, the semi-skilled and the new breed of highly-specialised skilled workers a more 'manual' instruction was the order of the day. Highly specialised and fragmented both inside and outside of the factory, this ranged over *familiarising* workers with the machinery they would have to intensively *use;* learning to read and effectively *carry out* instructions; and finally, 'skilfully' *operating* the machinery.

Overall, then, Germany did indeed lead the way in making the transition from a competitive and empirical system of training to one which publicly serviced the requirements of the large concerns and under-wrote the basic class structure of the *Reich.* The only shadow cast over this achievement, at least as far as employers were concerned, was the growing problem of labour turnover. But again this only affected their highly-specialised skilled workers and the unskilled. Furthermore, against the background of general union ambiguity of what the new training methods meant for workers, this phenomenon only registered how confused workers were about the structural changes occurring and how they were only slowly coming to grips with them. Employers, then, had every reason to dismiss or not even notice pessimistic critics of their professional technical intelligence.

Parts of the system of technical education, though, were not without more immediate contradictions in the pre-war period. This was especially so for the new 'technical servants' who found their ranks to be threatened by over production and their occupational status potentially degraded. There was a whiff in the air that black-coated employees could also suffer from specialisation and become 'proletarianised'. As an upwardly mobile industrial army, technicians, lower echelon engineers, draughtsmen, technicians and chemists, had to face the prospect of not only remaining wage and salary earners, but of having their positions eroded within the

labour market. In fact, it proved to be the case that the rate of production
of black-coated graduates far outpaced the growth of industry. Between
1890–91 and 1904–05, the number of students attending technical
colleges rose from 5,432 to 15,866, an increase of the order of 300%.
When combined with the many thousands who attended either university
or the special technical schools for hyper-qualified metalworkers, it
became increasingly obvious that there would not be enough places
available in industry. Such pressures in the labour market directly led to
the formation of the *Bund der technischen industrielle Beamten* (Association of Technical Officers), which by late 1905 comprised some 3,000
members. As a union, and not a professional technical 'society', it sought
to defend the economic conditions of technical employees to the extent of
demanding an eight-hour working day and an end to secrecy clauses in
labour contracts, which prevented an employee from taking up employment at another firm in the industry for several years if he decided to
leave.[154]

Such realities are hardly consistent with recent arguments that employers were as 'dependent' on their workers' skills as workers were on the
enterprise. At the beginning of this book it was described how at Platt's
textile machinery works in Britain in 1896, workers found great difficulty
in using their highly-specialised skills anywhere else, with the result that
employers developed a great mastery over the labour market and could
impose their own conditions on their men. It would seem that even some
technical employees in Germany were feeling this kind of pressure during
the early 1900s, apart from rank and file metalworkers. By 1914 we also
found some observers describing this as a 'great pity', though the 'in-
evitable' result of the bourgeoisie's expanding role in the direct production
process. By the inter-war period a more bizarre and tragic example of this
specialisation of skill and training had taken place at a Siemens assembly
shop in Germany.

In an unit room, blind women could be found assembling components
for larger assemblies. For the Siemens' management, the dexterity and
utility of these women was to be found in their very blindness, not to say
in the saving on lighting costs that their employment allowed. The women
were supplied with accommodation, could shop at the company store
and had a job for life. There is no evidence that any of these women ever
regained their sight through some good fortune. If one had, this may have
proved to be an obstacle to further employment, for when a Japanese
electrical engineering team came to Germany and visited the plant, they
were apparently convinced by the Siemens' management that they could
not replicate such work, as only highly-skilled blind women could perform
it. The moral of this tale is not, as one sociologist, Charles Sabel, would
have us believe, how a far-sighted enterprise became as 'dependent' on
their 'blind women at work', as the women were on the company.[155] The

real moral is, as we found Peter Mathias saying at the very beginning of this work, how 'every society needs the support of myths which buttress values important to its way of life', values which preclude this tale from becoming a source of 'disaffection' or 'an agency for subverting contemporary values'. For our sociologist, the tale represents 'a kind of dignity that makes plausible the dream of a better world'.[156] The truth, however, bears a remarkable resemblance to the fable of Menenius Agrippa, a fifth-century Roman patrician, who sought to convince the plebeians not to raze his regime. Drawing an analogy between the State and the human body, he suggested that the patricians were the stomach and the plebeians were the limbs. The limbs were necessary to feed the stomach, and if the stomach did not receive sustenance then the limbs, too, would lose all their powers and die. It appears that the plebeians were convinced that they were mere fragments of their own body and so did not attempt to rip out their own stomachs. It requires no leap of imagination to see how this popular fable bears on the experience of the blind women at Siemens in the 1930s. The Roman patrician and his recalcitrant plebeians may have had a more materialistic conception of the relationship between the mind and limb, but the Siemens' management learnt how to perfect one-sided specialities, at the expense of a whole woman's working capacity. They had learnt, in Marx's words, 'to make a speciality of the absence of all development'.[157] In the period described in this story, the 'crippled monstrosity' of an individual's labour power proved to be largely unusable outside of the employer's factory. By the 1930s a special handicap could also be pressed into the service of specialised labour. Here, dexterity in a specialised activity, component assembly, took on a spatial and bodily shape, fulfiling the degradation of labour in an unlit room where only the blind could work. Here, too, the stomach continued to be fed by the limbs; but unlike the fairy tale propounded by our neo-Taylorist sociologist, this story has no happy ending. It offers no recourse to a 'dignity' that would make 'plausible the dream of a better world'. It offers only subjugation or revolt.

NOTES

1. *Report of the London County Council on Trade and Technical Education in Germany and France*, London County Council, London, 1914, pp. 2, 8.
2. See G. Neuhaus, *Die berufliche und soziale Gliederung des deutschen Volks*, Berlin, 1911, p. 73. The phrase 'engineering proper' refers to the *Maschinen-industrie* in Germany, as distinct from the larger category of 'engineering and allied trades', which came under the heading of *Industrie Maschinen, Instrumente und Apparate* in the various national and local censuses.
3. See *Bericht über den Stand und die Verwaltung der Gemeinde-Angelegenheiten für die Stadt Düsseldorf*, 1900–13, Stadtarchiv, Düsseldorf.
4. *ibid.*, 1913.
5. *ibid.*, 1913.

6. *ibid.*, 1900/1913.
7. See Eckhard Brockhaus, *Zusammensetzung und Neustruktierung der Arbeiter-klasse vor dem ersten Weltkrieg*, p. 12.
8. *ibid.*, p. 14.
9. See *Bericht über den Stand und die Verwaltung der Gemeinde-Angelegenheiten für die Stadt Düsseldorf*, 1900–13, Stadtarchiv, Düsseldorf.
10. See Jürgen Kocka, 'Entrepreneurs and Managers in German Industrialization', *Cambridge History of Europe, Vol. VII, Pt. 1, The Industrial Economies*, pp. 558–9; and see also by the same author, *Unternehmensverwaltung und Angestelltenschaft am Beispiel Siemens, 1897-1914, passim.*
11. See Deutsche Metallarbeiter Verband, *Die Schwereisenindustrie*, DMV (Berlin), 1912, p. 105. See also C. Matschoss, *Ein Jahrhundert deutscher Maschinenbau, 1819-1919*, Julius Springer, Berlin, 1922, p. 191 ff; W.H. Dooley, 'Engineering Methods in Germany and America', *Cassier's Magazine*, Vol. XL, May 1911, p. 62, for a description of the firm, Messrs Haniel and Lueg, Düsseldorf, which employed 2,000 people in 1911. See also, A. Schröter and W. Becker, *Die deutsche Maschinenindustrie in der industriellen Revolution*, pp. 214-79 for a discussion of earlier concentration movements in the engineering industry.
12. See Jürgen Kocka, 'The Rise of Modern Industrial Enterprise in Germany', in Alfred Chandler Jr. and Herman Daems, eds., *Managerial Hierarchies*, Harvard University Press, Cambridge, Mass., 1980, Table 3.1, p. 79.
13. 'Report on the General Condition of Trade in Germany', 1913, International Metalworkers' Federation Congress, Berlin, 1913, in *Industrial Training also Internationalism*, compiled by Charles Hobson, Secretary of the British Section, p. 527.
14. *ibid.*, p. 527.
15. J. Carr and W. Taplin, *A History of the British Steel Industry*, Basil Blackwell, Oxford, 1962, p. 240.
16. Kurt Wiedenfeld's *Ein Jahrhundert rheinischer Montanindustrie, 1815-1915*, A. Marcus and E. Webers Verlag, Bonn, 1916, pp. 143-8 and *passim.*
17. See Simon Kuznets, 'Quantitative Aspects of the Economic Growth of Nations, VI: Long-Term Trends in Capital Formation Proportions', in *Economic Development and Cultural Change*, IX, No. 4, Pt. II, July 1961, Table 3, p. 10.
18. *ibid.*, Table 3, p. 10.
19. See W.G. Hoffman (with Franz Grumbach and Helmut Hesse), *Das Wachstum der Deutschen Wirtschaft seit der Mitte des 19. Jahrhundert*, Springer Verlag, Berlin, 1965, Table 10, p. 44.
20. *ibid.*, p. 26.
21. *ibid.*, p. 35.
22. For a further discussion of these points, see W.G. Hoffman, 'Long-Term Growth and Capital Formation in Germany', in F.A. Lutz, ed., *The Theory of Capital*, Proceedings of a Conference held by the International Economics Association, Macmillan, London, 1961, pp. 126-7.
23. See Duncan Burn, *An Economic History of Steel Making, 1865-1939*, p. 88 ff., and T. Vogelstein, 'Die rheinisch-westfälische Montan- und Eisenindustrie', *Schriften des Vereins für Socialpolitik*, Vols. 105-106, 1903, p. 82. To the best of my knowledge there is no present-day study of the 1895-1905 boom and bust and its impact on German society. German historical studies are sadly lacking here, with the exception of an article by Dieter Groh, who seems to have literally fallen into this area and, lacking any hard evidence, has put together a most interesting argument of which more is spoken later. Groh's article is entitled, 'The Intensification of Work and Industrial Conflict in Germany, 1896-1914', *Politics and Society*, Nos. 3-4, 1978, pp. 349-98.

24. See Carr and Taplin, *op. cit.*, p. 186. These two writers also join the ranks of a non-German contingent who appreciate the importance of this period.
25. *ibid.*, p. 186.
26. *ibid.*, Table XXXI, p. 184.
27. See Paul Steller, 'Die Maschinenindustrie Deutschlands', *Schriften des Vereins für Socialpolitik*, Nos. 107-108, 1903, p. 7.
28. *ibid.*, pp. 44-6.
29. *ibid.*, pp. 1-74.
30. See Dr Josef Loewe, 'Die Elektrotechnische Industrie', *Schriften des Vereins für Socialpolitik*, Nos. 107-108, pp. 77-8.
31. See P. Steller, 'Die Maschinenindustrie Deutschlands', *loc. cit.*, p. 10. See also Jürgen Kocka, *Unternehmensverwaltung und Angestelltenschaft am Beispiel Siemens, 1847-1914, passim.*
32. See Dr J. Loewe, 'Die Elektrotechnische Industrie', *loc. cit.*, pp. 80-1.
33. *ibid.*, pp. 85-6.
34. *ibid.*, pp. 84-5.
35. *ibid.*, pp. 84-5.
36. See Duncan Burn, *op. cit.*, p. 88.
37. See Paul Steller, 'Die Maschinenindustrie Deutschlands', *op. cit.*, pp. 12-13.
38. See T. Vogelstein, 'Die rheinisch-westfälische Montan- und Eisenindustrie', *loc. cit.*, pp. 97-9.
39. *ibid.*, p. 123.
40. See Paul Steller, 'Die Maschinenindustrie Deutschlands', *loc. cit.*, p. 10.
41. See Dr Rolf Wagenführ, 'Die industriewirtschaftlichen. . .', *Sonderhefte des Instituts für Konjunkturforschung*, Vol. 31, Berlin 1933, p. 9.
42. Paul Steller, 'Die Maschinenindustrie Deutschlands', *loc. cit.*, pp. 15-16.
43. See Otto Bosselmann, 'Erzbergbau und Eisenindustrie in Lothringen-Luxemburg', *Schriften des Vereins für Socialpolitik*, Vol. 105-106, p. 50.
44. *ibid.*, p. 50.
45. See Burn, *op. cit.*, p. 89.
46. See T. Vogelstein, 'Die rheinisch-westfälische Montan- und Eisenindustrie', *loc. cit.*, pp. 85-7, 131.
47. *ibid.*, pp. 33-4.
48. *ibid.*, p. 64.
49. See Paul Steller, 'Die Maschinenindustrie Deutschlands', *loc. cit.*, pp. 44-6.
50. T. Vogelstein, 'Die rheinisch-westfälische Montan- und Eisenindustrie', *loc. cit.*, pp. 99-100.
51. Dr J. Loewe, 'Die Elektrotechnische Industrie', *loc. cit.*, pp. 101, 103, 139-40.
52. See T. Vogelstein, 'Die rheinisch-westfälische Montan- und Eisenindustrie', *loc. cit.*, pp. 115-16, for further information on cartel organisations in the Rhineland. For a description of the growth of cost consciousness amongst employers during the early 1900s and the implications this had for management strategies in the workplace see Jürgen Kocka, 'Industrielles Management: Konzeptionen- und Wirtschaftsgeschichte, *Vierteljahreschrift für Sozial- und Wirtschaftsgeschichte*, Vol. 56, No. 3, 1969, pp. 332-72, esp. p. 357.
53. See Dieter Groh, 'The Intensification of Work and Industrial Conflict in Germany, 1896-1914', *loc. cit., passim.*
54. See Jürgen Tampke, *The Ruhr and Revolution: The Revolutionary Movement in the Rhenish-Westphalian Industrial Region*, ANU Press, Canberra, 1978, p. 12.
55. Dr F. Syrup, 'Die gesetzliche Begrenzung der Arbeitszeit erwachsener männlicher Arbeiter unter besonderer Berücksichtigung der Grössindustrie, *Archiv für exacte Wirtschaftsforschung*, Bd. 4, Heft 4, 1912, p. 537. See also Walter

Schmitz, 'Regelung der Arbeitszeit und Intensität der Arbeit', *Archiv für exacte Wirtschaftsforschung*, Vol. 3, No. 2, 1911, pp. 165–328.

56. Syrup, *loc. cit.*, Tables I–II, pp. 538–9; and Tables III–IV, pp. 540–1.

57. See correspondence between the Rhineland metal employers and the Düsseldorf *Regierungspräsident*, 1909–11, *Hauptstaatsarchiv* Düsseldorf (D.H.St.A.), *Arbeitsschutz in der Grosseisenindustrie*, 33389. *Gutehoffnungshütte*, Oberhausen, to *Regierungspräsident*, 20/11/1909.

58. *ibid.*, *Gutehoffnungshütte*, Oberhausen, to *Regierungspräsident*, 20/11/1909.

59. *ibid.*, *Guthoffnungshütte*, Oberhausen, to the *Regierungspräsident*, 20/11/1909.

60. *ibid.*, *Düsseldorfer Rohren und Eisen Walzwerke* to *Regierungspräsident*, 16/2/1909.

61. *ibid.*, *E. Bocking & Co.*, to the *Regierungspräsident*, 16/4/1909, 15/6/1909, 18/6/1909.

62. *ibid.*, *Düsseldorfer Rohren und Eisen Walzwerke* to the *Regierungspräsident*, 16/2/1909.

63. For a general analysis of the evolution of management consciousness in Germany at this time, particularly in the fields of job calculation, accountancy, industrial administration and business organisation, see Kocka, 'Industrielles Management', *loc. cit.*, pp. 347–54.

64. *Balcke, Tellering & Co., AG.*, to the *Königlichen Gewerbsinspektor*, 17/3/1909. D.H.St.A., *Arbeitsschutz in der Grosseisenindustrie*, 33389. For the Krupp example cited above, see *ibid.*, *Friedrich Krupp, AG*, Essen to the *Regierungspräsident*, 16/2/1909.

65. *ibid.*, *Hannsche Werke AG.*, to the *Königlichen Gewerbe-Inspektor*, 31/3/1909.

66. *ibid.*, *Hannsche Werke AG.*, to the *Regierungspräsident*, Düsseldorf, 8/3/1909. See also letter to same, 17/2/1909.

67. *ibid.*, *Rheinische Stahlwerke*, Duisburg-Meiderich, to the *Regierungspräsident*, 4/10/1909.

68. See H. Reichelt, *Die Arbeitsverhältnisse in einem Berliner Grossbetrieb der Maschinenindustrie*, Leonhard Simion, Berlin, 1907, p. 26.

69. See Tampke, *op. cit.*, p. 12.

70. Hans Ehrenberg, *Die Eisenhüttentechnik und der deutsche Hüttenarbeiter*, p. 113.

71. Otto Jeidels, *Die Methoden der Arbeiterentlöhnung in der rheinisch-westfälischen Eisenindustrie*, p. 106. See also Elaine Glovka Spencer, 'Between Capital and Labour: Supervisory Personnel in Ruhr Heavy Industry Before 1914', *Journal of Social History*, Vol. 9, No. 2, Winter 1975, pp. 179–80.

72. Dora Landé, 'Arbeits- und Lohnverhältnisse in der Berliner Maschinenindustrie zu Beginn des 20 Jahrhundert', *Schriften des Vereins für Socialpolitik*, Nos. 133–134, 1910, p. 329.

73. A starting point for the interested reader or student concerning the new systems of pay and job calculation is the nine-volume survey by the *Centralverein für das Wohl der Arbeitenden Klassen*, published between 1906 and 1909. The survey covered the evolution of new work processes, methods of wage payment and the introduction of job and enterprise calculation for the entire heavy metal industry, with reports on Berlin, the Rhineland, Bavaria, Silesia, Hanover and the Lorraine. We have already referred to Fritz Schulte's *Die Entlöhnungsmethoden in der Berliner Maschinenindustrie* (1906), Otto Jeidel's *Die Methoden der Arbeiterentlöhnung in der rheinisch-westfälischen Eisenindustrie* (1907), Cl. Heiss' *Die Entlöhnungsmethoden in der Berliner Feinmechanik* (1909), and H. Reichelt's *Die Arbeitsverhältnisse in einem Berliner Grossbetrieb der Maschinenindustrie* (1907), which comprise four volumes of the survey. The other volumes are: Ernst Günther, *Die Entlöhnungsmethoden in der*

Bayrischen Eisen und Maschinenindustrie, Leonhard Simion, 1908; Walter Timmerman, *Die Entlöhnungsmethoden in der Hannoverschen Eisenindustrie*, Leonhard Simion, Berlin, 1906; Bruno Simmerbach, *Die Entlöhnungsmethoden in der Eisenindustrie Schlesians*, Leonhard Simion, 1906; O. Bosselmann, *Entlöhnugnsmethoden in der suedwest deutsch-luxemburgischen Eisenindustrie*, Leonhard Simion, Berlin, 1906; and Waldemar Follos, *Lohn und Arbeitsverhältnisse in der Berliner Metallindustrie*, Leonhard Simion, Berlin, 1907.

74. Elaine Glovka Spencer, 'Between Capital and Labour: Supervisory Personnel in Ruhr Heavy Industry Before 1914', *loc. cit.*, p. 185.

75. See André Pelletan, 'Les écoles techniques allemandes', *Revue de Métallurgie*, Vol. 3, No. 11, November 1906, pp. 589, 606.

76. *ibid.*, p. 606.

77. *ibid.*, p. 589.

78. 'Schools for Adults in Germany', presented by Alexander Schlicke for the *Deutsche Metallarbeiter Verband*, December, 1911, in *Industrial Training also Internationalism*, 1915, International Metalworkers' Federation, compiled by Charles Hobson, Secretary of the British Section, pp. 55-6.

79. André Pelletan, 'Les écoles techniques allemandes', *loc. cit.*, 1906, p. 591. See also E. Leduc, 'L'organisation syndicale et technique en Allemagne', *Bulletin de la Société d'Encouragement pour l'Industrie Nationale*, Vol. 105, October 1909, pp. 232-3.

80. Pelletan, 'Les écoles techniques allemandes', *loc. cit.*, p. 591. The right to grant diplomas, however, was not easily acquired. A major and prolonged controversy had first to take place between the colleges and the traditional universities with respect to their respective functions and roles in national scientific development—theoretical and applied. For this story see Karl-Heinz Manegold, *Universität, Technische Hochschule und Industrie*, Duncker and Humblot, Berlin, 1970, pp. 249-305.

81. See Pelletan, 'Les écoles techniques allemandes', *loc. cit.*, p. 590.

82. *ibid.*, p. 598 ff. See also E. Leduc, 'L'organisation syndicale et technique en Allemagne', *loc. cit.*, p. 239 ff, for a description of the mechanical laboratories at Charlottenburg and the testing laboratories at Gross-Lichterfelde in Berlin. The British magazine, *The Engineer*, also gives a good description of the Dresden laboratories, the mechanical equipment for which was often provided by leading firms in the area, such as Deutz Gas Motor Works. See 'The Dresden Technical High School', *The Engineer*, Vols. 101-102, January 26, 1906, pp. 101-2.

83. Pelletan, 'Les écoles techniques allemandes', *loc. cit.*, p. 590.

84. *ibid.*, p. 593.

85. *ibid.*, p. 594.

86. *ibid.*, pp. 596-97. For a general discussion of German higher technical education from an English point of view, see A.P.M. Fleming and R.W. Bailey, *Engineering as a Profession*, pp. 246-9.

87. See 'Aussprüch des Vereines deutscher Ingenieure über Hochschule- und Unterrichtsfragen, beschlossen in Jahre 1906', *Zeitschrift des Vereines Deutscher Ingenieure*, Vol. LI, No. 8, February 23, 1907, pp. 299-304; see also O. Taaks, 'Zweiter Bericht des Deutschen Ausschusses für technisches Schulwesen', *Zeitschrift des Vereines Deutscher Ingenieure*, Vol. LIV, No. 25, 18 June 1910, pp. 1050-2.

88. See Committee on Industry and Trade (Balfour Committee), *Industrial and Commercial Efficiency*, HMSO, London, 1927, p. 260. By 1910 there were at least 501 commercial schools *(Kaufmännische Fortbildungsschulen)* with an enrolment of approximately 65,000 students. This was, of course, a quite small number when compared with the technical continuation schools, which at this

time comprised 1,877 schools and a student population of 327,000. These will be described in more detail below, but it cannot be doubted that commercial education received a shot in the arm during the last few years before the War. See Jürgen Kocka, 'Entrepreneurs and Managers in German Industrialisation', *loc. cit.*, p. 573.

89. Jürgen Kocka, *Angestellte zwischen Faschismus und Demokratie. Zur politischen Sozialgeschichte der Angestellten: U.S.A., 1890-1914, im internationalen Vergleich*, Göttingen, 1977, pp. 131-2.

90. See 'Schools for Adults in Germany', presented by Alexander Schlicke for the *Deutsche Metallarbeiter Verband*, December 1911, *loc. cit.*, p. 17.

91. See Frederick William Roman, *The Industrial and Commercial Schools of the United States and Germany: A Comparative Study*, G.P. Putnam's Sons, New York, 1915, p. 3.

92. See 'Schools for Adults in Germany', presented by Alexander Schlicke for the *Deutsche Metallarbeiter Verband*, December 1911, *loc. cit.*, pp. 65-6.

93. *ibid.*, p. 13. In the smaller towns evening classes were more often the rule. See *ibid.*, p. 15.

94. For historians, there is also a major difficulty in actually categorising and comparing these schools by type, either for the different regions in Germany or internationally. In a number of German states the schools could be called industrial continuation schools or trade schools. It is also the case that English translations of the names of trade schools falsely convey their activities. Hence, it must be understood that the title of a particular type of trade school may presuppose that it carries out several functions, at times specialising in training particular grades of workers, at other times training both higher and lower grades of manual and supervisory labour. The only way through this maze is to look at what a trade school actually did in a region or town and then categorise its place within the structures of training as a whole.

95. See 'Schools for Adults in Germany', presented by Alexander Schlicke for the *Deutsche Metallarbeiter Verband*, December 1911, *loc. cit.*, pp. 17-19. For further background information on the formation of trade schools in the various states, see Roman, *op. cit.*, pp. 32-59.

96. Roman, *op. cit.*, p. 132.

97. *ibid.*, p. 77 ff.

98. *ibid.*, pp. 80-3.

99. See 'Schools for Adults in Germany', presented by Alexander Schlicke for the *Deutsche Metallarbeiter Verband*, December 1911, *loc. cit.*, p. 13.

100. W.H. Dooley, 'Engineering in Germany and America', *Cassier's Magazine*, Vol. XL, May 1911, p. 68.

101. *ibid.*, pp. 67-8.

102. Roman, *op. cit.*, pp. 119-21.

103. See W.H. Dooley, 'Engineering in Germany and America', *loc. cit.*, pp. 67-8. See also O. Taaks, 'Zweiter Bericht des Deutschen Ausschusses für technisches Schulwesen', 1910, *loc. cit.*, pp. 1050-2.

104. See 'Schools for Adults in Germany', presented by Alexander Schlicke, for the *Deutsche Metallarbeiter Verband*, December 1911, *loc. cit.*, p. 20.

105. *ibid.*, p. 14.

106. *ibid.*, p. 14.

107. *ibid.*, pp. 21-2.

108. *ibid.*, p. 22. See also p. 23.

109. *ibid.*, pp. 23-4.

110. *ibid.*, pp. 25-6. For a further discussion on the variations in the quality and extent of technical training in the different states, see Roman, *op. cit.*, p. 134 ff.

111. 'Schools for Adults in Germany', presented by Alexander Schlicke for the *Deutsche Metallarbetier Verband*, December 1911, *loc. cit.*, pp. 30-1.
112. *ibid.*, see pp. 14-15, 25, 30-1.
113. *ibid.*, p. 34.
114. Peter Lundgreen, 'Industrialization and the Educational Formation of Manpower in Germany', *Journal of Social History*, Vol. 9, No. 1, Fall 1975, p. 174.
115. 'Schools for Adults in Germany', presented by Alexander Schlicke for the *Deutsche Metallarbetier Verband*, December 1911, *loc. cit.*, pp. 37-40.
116. See Frank Hauerkamp, *Staatliche Gewerberförderung im Grossherzogtum Baden*, pp. 188-247.
117. See Roman, *op. cit.*, p. 149.
118. See 'Schools for Adults in Germany', presented by Alexander Schlicke for the *Deutsche Metallarbeiter Verband*, December 1911, *loc. cit.*, p. 45. See also Roman, *op. cit.*, pp. 109-18.
119. 'Schools for Adults in Germany', presented by Alexander Schlicke for the *Deutsche Metallarbeiter Verband*, December 1911, *loc. cit.*, p. 31.
120. See C. Matschoss, *Ein Jahrhundert deutscher Maschinenbau, 1819-1919*, p. 259; *Maschinenbauschule, Düsseldorf*, D.H.St.A., 379, EIV, IV 13/421, 1909. For a description of a similar school for metalworkers run by Krupp and other firms in conjunction with the municipal council in Essen, see *Maschinenbauschule, Essen*, D.H.St.A., 366, 1906-08; 367, 1909-11; 368, 1912-13; EIV, IV 13/411.
121. H. Reichelt, *op. cit.*, pp. 32-4.
122. Ernst Günther, *op. cit.*, pp. 202-6, and Anlage IV, pp. 220-30.
123. Reichelt, *op. cit.*, p. 35.
124. See 'Report on the Position and Organisation of the Metalworkers associated with the International Metallurgist Congress, Paris, 1900: German Metal Industry', presented by Alexander Schlicke, in *Industrial Training also Internationalism*, 1915. International Metalworkers' Federation, compiled by Charles Hobson, Secretary of the British Section, pp. 206-7.
125. See Marie Bernays, 'Berufswahl und Berufsschicksal des modernen Industriearbeiters', *Archiv für Sozialwissenschaft und Sozialpolitik*, Bd. 36, 1912, pp. 889-90 for a discussion of the mobility of the *Hilfsarbeiter* at the Daimler Motor Works.
126. Richard Ehrenberg, 'Schwäche und Stärkung neuzeitlicher Arbeitsgemeinschaften', *Archiv für exacte Wirtschaftsforschung*, Bd. III, 1911, p. 517.
127. *ibid.*, p. 517.
128. *ibid.*, p. 518.
129. *ibid.*, p. 517.
130. Bernays, *loc. cit.*, pp. 887-8.
131. See Alfred Weber, 'Berufsschicksal der Industriearbeiter', *Archiv für Sozialwissenschaft und Socialpolitik*, Bd. 34, Heft 2, 1910, pp. 393-4. After the passage of nearly seventy years, the historian J.J. Lee, offers a more soothing interpretation of this sort of job changing. In his view, turnover for the skilled workers was only a 'substitute for formal career guidance'. See J.J. Lee, 'Labour in German Industrialization', *Cambridge Economic History of Europe*, Vol. VIII, Pt. 1, p. 461.
132. See Ernst Günther, *op. cit.*, p. 7.
133. *ibid.*, p. 7. See also Lawrence Schofer, *The Formation of a Labor Force, Upper Silesia, 1865-1914*, University of California Press, Berkeley, 1975, p. 126 ff., for a description of similar patterns of long service and high labour turnover in the mines and steel mills in Silesia during the early 1900s.
134. Ernst Günther, *op. cit.*, p. 8.
135. *ibid.*, Tables 57-5, p. 138. In his study of the Ruhr town of Bochum, David

Crew had also found that a small proportion of skilled metalworkers assumed lower managerial and clerical posts in the industry after many years of service with a firm. See David Crew, 'Definitions of Modernity: Social Mobility in a German Town, 1880-1901', in Peter N. Stearns and Daniel J. Walkowitz, eds., *Workers in the Industrial Revolution,* Transaction Books, New Brunswick, New Jersey, 1974, Table 4, p. 305.

136. Bernays, *loc. cit.,* p. 892.
137. Weber, *loc. cit.,* pp. 393-4.
138. Bernays, *loc. cit.,* pp. 888-9. For a contrary explanation, see J.J. Lee, *loc. cit.,* p. 463. Lee suggests that when specialised skilled workers stayed put in a big firm, they did so because of their identification with the sophisticated machinery. Peter Stearns, however, has a much more realistic appreciation of this. See his *Lives of Labour: Work in a Mature Industrial Society,* Croom Helm, London, 1975, pp. 242-7 and esp. pp. 244-5.
139. Günther, *op. cit.,* p. 8.
140. Jeidels, after visiting many large firms in the region and in Düsseldorf during 1906-07, discovered that there had been very few strikes in the large firms over the previous twenty years, even taking into account the 1905 strike wave. Any strike activity that did take place was generally limited to only one section of the workforce in a plant, and never involved workers in an entire region under-taking collective action. Most activity was limited to small groups of workers in small shops and in areas outside the big cities, that is in Barmen, Remscheid and Solingen, rather than in Düsseldorf, Cologne and Duisberg. As Jeidels put it: 'The rarity of strikes is therefore a sign of weak resistance in the large firms of the Rhine-Westphalian region.' See Jeidels, *op. cit.,* pp. 148, 150-3.
141. Reichelt, *op. cit.,* p. 12.
142. See Heilwig Schomerus, *Die Arbeiter der Maschinenfabrik Esslingen. Forschun-gen zur Lage der Arbeiterschaft im 19 Jahrhundert,* Letta-Cotta, Stuttgart, 1977, Table 41, pp. 166, 168.
143. Reichelt, *op. cit.,* p. 12.
144. *ibid.,* p. 11.
145. *ibid.,* Table 6, pp. 13, 127.
146. *ibid.,* Tables 3-4, pp. 124-5.
147. *ibid.,* Tables 3-4, pp. 124-5.
148. *ibid.,* Table 3, p. 124.
149. *ibid.,* p. 11.
150. Schomerus, *op. cit.,* Table 47, p. 201.
151. *ibid.,* p. 196.
152. Weber, *loc. cit.,* p. 388. See also Richard Ehrenberg, 'Das Arbeitsverhältnis als Arbeitsgemeinschaft', *Archiv für exacte Wirtschaftsforschung,* Bd. II, 1907-09, p. 176 ff.
153. Reichelt, *op. cit.,* p. 11.
154. See *The Engineer,* Vols. 99-100, 24 November 1905, pp. 517-18; and Herr Hummell's 'Die gewerkschaftlichen Organisationen der Industrie, inbesondere der industriellen Beamten', *Zeitschrift des Vereines Deutscher Ingenieure,* Vol. 49, No. 43, 28 October 1905, pp. 1758-9.
155. Charles Sabel, *Work and Politics: The Division of Labour in Industry,* pp. 98-9.
156. *ibid.,* p. xii.
157. Karl Marx, *Capital,* Vol. 1, p. 470.

CONCLUSIONS

'Feudalisation', 'professionalisation', 'bourgeoisification'—whatever the terms used by observers and participants to explain the changes to skill compositions and training methods in the European metal industry at the beginning of this century, they all sought to highlight the growing differentiation, specialisation and polarisation of mental and manual faculties used in production. Certainly, as a *technical ensemble* the changes were very *differentiated*. Skills and training methods were broken up, recomposed and allotted to new personnel. They were at once enriched and impoverished, transformed and diluted, abolished and newly created. There was no technical homogeneity about the evolving structure of managerial technical intelligence or of the hierarchies of labour-power. Furthermore, managerial technical intelligence did not become an exclusively mental activity. Quite the contrary, the *specialisation* of faculties used in the planning and execution of the product resulted in a refined hierarchy of directors and agents incorporating the skills of both manual and mental labour in their activities, especially *via* the labour of the technician, chemist, metallurgist, new *ouvrier d'art,* and other 'professional' employees. Neither was manual labour, or the labour-power applied in the direct production process, completely degraded to an exclusively physical activity. Professional disqualification from the directive, supervisory and technical responsibilities of production certainly took place, but these changes did not produce an undifferentiated mass or homogeneous class of automatons. The new hyper-specialised workers were testimony to this—skilled at their tasks and drawing on the new psycho-physical apparatus of labour, they were rewarded with as much nervous as physical fatigue. For those who would never admit their now complete exclusion from the labour of superintendence and management and an all-round technical knowledge of their special trade, there was the possibility of following the example of the waltzing turner, or of bludgeoning a foreman for a change to a different machine, as J.T. Murphy did, or formally attempting to counter-regulate skills and training through trade union organisation and the creation of trade union schools, as British and French workers did.

As a *social ensemble,* however, none of this prevented the forging of a formal and professional 'intellectual potency' at one pole of society.[1] The faculties of mental and manual labour were increasingly *polarised* around the professional qualification of management and the dequalification of proletarian labour. We do not have to highlight the impact of machine technology on the faculties used in production to account for these changes. There was definitely no technical reason why a minority should tend to professionally monopolise the directive and scientific functions of labour as a specialised activity, while the overwhelming majority of work-people should be actively disqualified from the formal technical knowledge associated with their labour. There was also no technical reason why the rate and sequence of the movement of mind and limb should be dissociated from active intelligence. Only a social and economic explanation can fully account for these changes, and especially why enterprises had to establish more intensive forms of dominion over the organisation and training of labour-power during this first phase of transition to a more monopolistic capitalism.[2]

As employers became aware of the economic consequences of their huge investment in plant and machinery, they sought to shift the emphasis of their training methods from those which were based on fragmented managerial hierarchies and labour-intensive production strategies to those which would ensure a greater centralisation of managerial power, a more intensive use of fixed capital and an optimal maintenance of machinery. As a result, various public training schemes were developed to complement the private regulation of training, particularly for management engineers, technical and supervisory personnel, and hyper-qualified skilled workers. No longer was it possible to rely exclusively on an empirical and competitive private regulation of training inside the factory. No longer was it possible to allow the workforce spontaneously to accumulate specialised and not so specialised skills through the experience of factory work *per se*. As the needs of enterprises changed, as the workforce became concentrated into larger plants and as profitable output came to depend on the intensive use of machinery, public apparatuses of professional training had to be fashioned for the labour of supervision, management and the maintenance of machinery.

David Noble has a claim on our attention here, for he too, in his own excellent study of the rise of professional management in America at this time suggests that the social dimension is paramount. In his view, 'the increasing capitalist monopolisation of, and control over, production, and the diminishing autonomy and cost of labour. . . made possible the most efficient reorganisation of the production process by the capitalist, and thus the maximisation of profitable output'.[3] These changes, as we have seen, were also at work in the metal industry in Britain, France and Germany.

Undoubtedly this encouraged a strong sense of 'professional' dequalification amongst some workers with a craft heritage, even though their craft had been effectively regulated by employers for several generations. Edouard Dolléans has poignantly illustrated these sentiments in the case of France. The destruction of a sense of 'task' and its place in the total structure of work meant the disappearance of a most important element in the 'joy of labour'. Labour ceased to be a 'source of individual satisfaction', for labour had ceased to be its animator.[4] The new regulation of skills established by the middle of the last century meant not only that workers felt 'disintegrated' within the enterprise, hence giving rise to a sense of detachment from work, they also felt a sense of isolation from society and the nation as a whole, thus giving rise to sentiments of 'inferiority' and 'deficiency'.[5] But, as distinct from earlier waves of 'great fear' that engulfed the workforce, some workers were aware that this was no fulfilment of a continuous process of 'deskilling'. The changes taking place were novel and unusual. The worker poet, Alfred Williams, spoke of workers being kept 'in a state of continual agitation and suspense' by a supervisory staff that had been 'doubled or trebled', and of himself becoming more 'pliable' and 'plastic'. But it was not only the poet who could grasp the totality of a new psycho-physical apparatus of labour and the sense of agitation to mind and limb which was a consequence of its operation. Jean Latapie, one of the leaders of the French Federal Union of Metallurgical Workers, speaking at the St Etienne Congress of his Union in September 1901, conveyed to the delegates that 'the increasing progress of the machine in industry, and of scientific discoveries, modify indefinitely the modes of production, intensify, divide and subdivide labour. . . to such a point that proper tradesmen are eliminated more and more and reduced to simple auxiliaries of the machine and mere specialists'.[6] Such an understanding of the new and more intensive forms of psycho-physical labour laid the basis for a more progressive response to the capitalist regulation of skill. If the consequence of these 'methods of capitalist exploitation' was the confinement of workers 'in narrow lines', putting 'speciality against speciality', then it followed from a consideration of these 'facts' that it was of 'inestimable utility for the workers to realise the concentration of their forces and the unification of their action'.[7]

For a future *Fédération des Métaux*, under Merrheim's leadership, this comprised the arduous task of pulling together all the areas of specialised expertise in the metal industry—moulders, fitters, turners, machinists, metallurgists, coppersmiths, etc.—a task not completed until 1913.[8] In Germany, the relative absence of a craft heritage made the unification of specialised competences all the easier. The mighty *Deutsche Metallarbeiter Verband* comprising industrial, trade, and 'craft' sections was a veritable army with half a million members by 1913.[9] In Britain, amalgamation committees were formed in the late 1900s in the engineering unions, particularly in the ASE; but in this case the movement for unification could not yet overcome the craft legacy of entrenched sectional unionism.[10] Yet, even if progressive responses were protracted in France, rapid in Germany and relatively blocked in Britain, there could be no doubt that many workers were beginning to question, if not challenge, the new mirage of 'professional' labour and its associated illusion that technical and material progress generated social and moral progress *for all.* Though this story is the subject of another work, it can be noted here that when many middle-class observers pointed to the problem of progress possibly endangering social stability in the long term, they were only bearing witness to the fact that workers were themselves beginning to turn their *minds* to the subject of their right of access to skills and training programmes in order to safeguard their own human dignity and economic security. Skill may be an ensemble of qualitatively different mental and manual attributes, but by the early years of this century it had also become a major social and political question—it was now a class issue in the fullest sense of the term. The public and private training schemes in operation by 1914 structurally altered how proletarian metalworkers could obtain access to both scientific knowledge of production and positions within the factory's hierarchy. With ever more of the higher technical and supervisory positions filled horizontally by employees with a professional-extra-factory training, the vast majority of workers found themselves increasingly locked into specialised tasks and positions which were neither interchangeable between plants nor able to be used as building blocks for upward mobility within an enterprise.

At this time, though, any sustained challenge to managerial technical intelligence lay in the future rather than in the present. Only as a result of the long pre-war and wartime experience of the specialisation of training and skill did the newly consolidated Amalgamated Engineering Union, for example, set out in its 1920 Charter the demand that all workers should receive a formal public and factory-based training which would allow everyone to be able to set up, inspect and operate a number of different machines. This was to be done irrespective of whether a worker was actually allowed to undertake these varied tasks by an employer. It was the Union's view that no-one should be punished for the recomposition of skills and training. In 1914, however, the public and private institutions for training the workforce only demonstrated how pervasive was the influence of 'professional management' on the workplace and society at large. The depth of intensity of this movement varied from country to country. In Britain it took shape by combining traditional factory-based training with an exclusive and very effective public and private educational system for the highest grades of labour-power. France adopted a similar structure, though it was slower in providing a public infrastructure for the training of its workforce. But once this came into existence, after 1911, it showed a number of more progressive features than the British system, particularly in the area of training upper-echelon managers and introducing compulsory part-time public instruction for the entire workforce below the age of eighteen. Where a weakness was apparent was in the systematic provision of state education for future middle-class technicians and lower-echelon managers.

In contrast to these two countries, Germany established public and private structures for the training of all social classes in the workforce. At first, this was generated during the latter half of the nineteenth century by the extensive development of industry in an historically more backward setting; but, by the turn of the century, the modern pressures of fixed capital expansion lay at the heart of the changes to skill compositions and training methods, as was the case in Britain and America.

Many of the features of these systems of industrial training are very much with us today, particularly their highly-stratified structures which directly mobilise the classes of our own society into socially exclusive trade schools, technical colleges, polytechnics, universities and management schools. That the powerful example of 'Americanism' provided a climate of opinion for these changes to take root and flower need not be denied. Indeed, it must be emphasised. But, it must be added that the transformation of skill compositions and training methods was not American in inspiration. The inspiration grew out of the similar and comparable experience of all three countries. Furthermore, even America, in providing Europe with a 'unifying idea' of professional management, had to take second place to the ensemble of public and private technical institutions and training methods developing in Germany.

We need not then obey the dictates of an historical tradition which would have us constantly ask, 'why should countries. . . so close to each other' in terms of culture and languages 'have developed systems of training which differed so greatly one from another?'.[11] These words, penned by Professor Floud in 1982, comprise the most up-to-date expression of an interpretation which has long outlived its utility. If this story has fulfilled its task, it has been to show that it is no longer possible to assess industrial training methods from a quantitative perspective, so that nations can be graded on a homogeneous scale of success or failure. The experiences of America, Britain, France and Germany cannot be assessed in terms of either the Americans' neglect of formal industrial training and their reliance on purely private and plant-specific skills; or of the Germans' fetish for state-inspired training schemes, which were designed more generally to 'fit future workers for any job appropriate to the skills which they have learned'; or of the French and British somehow occupying a position in between these two extremes; with the British, for example, concentrating on plant training and evening schools, in order to produce a workforce with general skills easily transportable from factory to factory.[12] These are myths, and any writer burdened by them is led off into all sorts of contradictory positions. Professor Floud, for instance, is compelled to admit that, in the case of Germany, public and compulsory training, allegedly designed to produce a workforce with transportable skills, was in fact so highly specialised that workers were unable to move out of their fixed positions, either within the plant or outside of it.[13] It is also a myth to distinguish between part-time and full-time training and assume that, as a consequence of this, vertical mobility was a greater possibility under the part-time British and French models than under the full-time German and American models.[14] In the first instance, in none of the countries examined here was a full-time education possible, except for the very highest grades of managerial labour-power. In the case of Germany, this was possible for engineers, metallurgists, chemists, draughts-men and an array of technical personnel; in Britain, France and America, the net was tightened and included only the pinnacle of the managerial and technical labour force: managers, chemists, and upper-echelon engineers. For the rest, training was part-time, either on the job, in factory schools or in sandwich courses organised between the school and the factory. Certainly, the scope and intensity of part-time education differed amongst the various national metal industries and within the European states themselves. The British concentrated on evening tuition, while the French, Germans and Americans focused their activities on part-time day tuition. Neither system, though, structurally encouraged vertical mobility for the workforce as a whole. True, the British and American systems, in contrast to the German and French, allowed workers to follow up their training past the age of eighteen, and this allowed some to obtain super-visory positions as a result of promotion from the 'ranks'. But sadly this phenomenon has all the qualities of defining buoyancy in terms of the rate of descent to the sea bed: for workers *as a class* were now increasingly excluded from vertical mobility both within the plant or between plants.

This leads to our second major conclusion in evaluating the substance of national differences. In no way can they be so blown up as to be only accountable in terms of the indigenous power of a national culture. What came to be held in common has proved to be of greater historical import-ance than the differences. Certainly, uneven development played a great role in shaping the various roads that were followed to a more professional production management. However, in no way did the French, as a national entrepreneurial class, distrust their workers more than the Germans or the British, let alone the Americans. It cannot be concluded, therefore, that French industry was more hierarchical and frozen than its British or German versions.[15] We must, of course, emphasise the various national and political lineages in the making of a trained labour force, but giving a national identity to training programmes is a long way from assuming that their content and aims were remarkably different. It was definitely not the case that the division of labour in the German metal industry, for example, was constructed around a hierarchy of training and qualifica-tions. Mr Trebilcock is correct when he suggests that 'it is impossible to dispute the judgment that the German educational system was tailored, with unusual precision, to industrial needs. The narrow division of labour employed in German factories did in fact require highly specialised (or tightly focused) technicians'.[16] Qualifications were, indeed, dependent upon the division of labour. How far this was unique to Germany is another matter, and how far such a specialised system of training was merely the 'required' *technical product* of the division of labour is surely contentious.

Where Mr Trebilcock is inaccurate, though, is on the question of international comparisons. In his view, the German system 'did indeed score heavily' when measured against 'the British education provision, with its more or less comprehensive divorce between technology and science, industry and universities', France, too, 'failed' in the 'application of science to practical problems'.[17] This story, by contrast, does not substantiate an interpretation based on profound qualitative differences in the training of the workforce and the application of science in the European metal industry. It has been suggested, however, that in the case of Britain, even if engineering management was professionalised, this proved to be so exclusive as to be next to useless. In other words, the cocoon was so tightly spun as to prevent any tendency towards a sustainable professionalisation of production management. The evidence for this is that in Germany and America such huge numbers of engineers were being produced that the British effort was feeble by comparison. In the early 1900s, for example, some commentators quote that 14,130 engineering students attended university in the USA in 1906 and that 7,130 did so in Germany. In Britain, however, only 1,433 students were enrolled in engineering courses at university during the same year. Michael Sanderson concludes from these data that 'we' were backward as a nation.[18]

Yet such a royal 'we' of deficiency is not as self-evident as may at first appear. In Germany and America, students of engineering at universities were not just brought on to fill the ranks of upper managerial cadres, as in Britain. Their training was also meant to supply the needs of the lower technical and scientific strata in the factories. In Britain, on the other hand, these ranks were filled by the technical colleges and secondary technical institutes, which emphasised evening classes and one-day-a-week formal tuition, combined with on-the-job training.

A further problem with such an argument is that it fails to appreciate the historical context which shaped the diploma fetishes so characteristic of the German and American systems of industrial training. The rapid expansion, not to say overproduction, of university-trained engineers and technical personnel in these two countries only served to highlight the problems of employers having to carve out a professional managerial domain against the background of either an 'oppressive' system of contracting or an historically chronic shortage of trained managerial and technical labour-power. In America, as well, an exclusive university training for engineers had a distinct ideological role to play in supplanting producerist images of labour and management so closely associated with contracting. Britain was not forced to face these problems to the same extent and, as a result, university education was not called upon to play the same expansive role in training engineers for all levels in the managerial hierarchy. This did not make the British system any the more backward or regressive than its American and German counterparts. In fact, it made for a technically more flexible higher education system, and one less likely to endanger socially the class structure of the factory by over-producing graduate engineers with little prospect of filling the very highest positions. Yet even in emphasising these cultural and national differences, one cannot fail to see the common experience that was weaving together the training of a workforce and its management across national boundaries.

Finally, this story has sought to make a number of more general points. Several Marxist and neo-Taylorist authors have been criticised for failing to appreciate the two-fold character of skill and training, i.e. their technical and social dimensions as it were. Consequently, they are only able to assess changes to skill compositions in terms of unilinear scales, whether they be of deskilling or upgrading, and can envisage nothing more than the workforce becoming either more homogeneous or more differentiated and stratified. Yet if many historians and sociologists have been constrained by theories which can only seek out the complete degradation of labour or the 'valuable', 'considerable' and 'genuine' skills of the machine tender and maintenance worker, we have found a process where skills were at once made technically more differentiated and socially more polarised around the contrary interests of employers and workers. But, if both perspectives are unable to reveal the full import of the re-composition of skills and training methods taking place at this time, it is unnecessary to labour our critique of the Marxist position. From a social point of view the primary issue has been well understood.

The importance of Harry Braverman's legacy must be emphasised here. He, like Marx, understood the primacy and quality of capital's social relations of production: of workers being pressed into the service of expanding an employer's profitable output; of capital having to accumulate incessantly and, therefore, having constantly to transform technologies, skills and training methods; and of capital never allowing the 'working population' to assume a permanent 'shape'.[19] It has been this perspective which has allowed us to lay bare the driving force behind the professionalisation of production management in the European and American metal industries at the beginning of this century: the shift towards a more monopolistic capitalism, whose scientific, economic and technical needs called forth the addition of a new public dimension to the regulation of skill and training. Of the four countries studied, all were subject to similar pressures to professionalise the structure of production management, from the managers at the pinnacle of an enterprise through to the new hyper-qualified workers. In the European and American metal industries, at least, capitalist conditions of production now enforced a public as well as a private separation between the directive and scientific functions of mental labour and 'unprofessional' manual labour. For those who made up the ranks of the unprofessionals, this was truly the age of *la grand petité.*

NOTES

1. The phrase is taken from Alfred Sohn-Rethel. See his 'Technische Intelligenz zwischen Kapitalismus und Sozialismus', in Richard Vahrenkamp, ed., *Technologie und Kapital,* Edition Suhrkamp, Frankfurt-am-Main, 1973, pp. 11-38.
2. An interesting discussion from this point of view is Frank Deppe's, ' "Alte" und "neue" Arbeiterklasse', in *ibid.,* pp. 73-93, especially pp. 75-80.
3. David Noble, *America by Design,* p. 259.
4. Edouard Dolléans, *Histoire du Travail en France,* Tome 1, p. 149.
5. *ibid.,* p. 150.
6. See Jean Latapie, Secretary, 'Report of the Federal Union of Metallurgical Workers of France to the International Metallurgists' Congress, Amsterdam, 1904', in *Industrial Training also Internationalism,* compiled by Charles Hobson, Secretary of the British Section, 1915, p. 314.
7. *ibid.,* pp. 313-14.
8. See Dolléans, *op. cit.,* p. 42.
9. See G.D.H. Cole, *The World of Labour,* Macmillan, London, 1928, pp. 176-80, and 'Report of the German Metallurgists' Federation to the International Metalworkers' Federation, Amsterdam, 1904', *loc. cit.,* pp. 294-5.
10. See James Hinton, *The First Shop Stewards' Movement,* pp. 172-3, 283-5. See also Alistair Reid's *The Division of Labour in the British Shipbuilding Industry, passim.*
11. See Roderick Floud, 'Technical Education 1850-1914: Speculations on Human Capital Formation', in L. Jörberg and N. Rosenberg, eds., *Technological Change, Employment and Investment,* Eighth International Economic History Congress, Budapest, 1982. Published by the Department of Economic History, Lund University, Sweden, 1982, p. 85.
12. *ibid.,* pp. 87-9.
13. *ibid.,* p. 86.
14. *ibid.,* p. 92.
15. See Charles Sabel, *Work and Politics: The Division of Labour in Industry,* pp. 24-5.
16. See Clive Trebilcock, *The Industrialisation of the Continental Powers, 1780-1914,* p. 64.
17. *ibid.,* p. 63.
18. See Michael Sanderson, *The Universities and British Industry,* p. 24. See also Göran Ahlström, *Engineers and Industrial Growth,* Croom Helm, London, 1982, pp. 82-5, for a more recent reaffirmation of this position.
19. Harry Braverman, *Labour and Monopoly Capital,* pp. 20, 27.

ACKNOWLEDGEMENTS

I should like to thank those who have given me their time, support, criticism and help, especially Stuart Macintyre and Leslie Hannah. Barry Supple and Roy Hay made detailed page-by-page criticism. Let me also thank those who have given money, resources and consideration; the German Historical Institute in London provided a grant for a year's research in Düsseldorf and Bremen; the British Institute in Paris provided for six months study there; St John's College, Cambridge, helped with travel expenses; and the Ellen McArthur Fund provided financial support for Mrs Hazel Hedge to type the final draft. I should like to thank the chief librarian and staff of the Cambridge University Library, the Sheffield City Library, the Stadtarchiv and Hauptstaatsarchiv in Düsseldorf and the Bibliothèque Nationale in Paris. Finally, two people have seen this work grow from an idea into a printed volume; to them this work is dedicated.

SELECT BIBLIOGRAPHY

GENERAL

Industrial Training also Internationalism, from 1883 to 1913, compiled by Charles Hobson, Secretary of the British Section (International Metalworkers' Federation) and issued by the authority of the advisory committee, Hudson and Son, Birmingham, 1915.

GREAT BRITAIN

Official Publications

Annual Report of the Chief Inspector of Factories and Workshops, 1908, Cd. 4664, *Parliamentary Papers*, Vol. XXI, 1909.

Annual Report of the Chief Inspector of Factories and Workshops, 1909, Cd. 5191, *Parliamentary Papers*, Vol. XXVIII, 1910.

Committee on Industry and Trade (Balfour Committee), *Industrial and Commercial Efficiency*, Vols. 1 and 2, HMSO, London, 1927-28.

———————————————— *Survey of Industrial Relations*, HMSO, London, 1926.

——————————————*Survey of Metal Industries*, HMSO, London, 1928.

Report of an Enquiry by the Board of Trade into Working Class Rents in the United Kingdom, 'Sheffield', Accounts and Papers, 46, 1906, Cd. 3864, Vol. CVII.

Report of Minutes of Evidence Taken Before the Truck Committee, 1908-09, Cd. 4444, *Parliamentary Papers*, Vol. XLIX, 1908.

Report of the Royal Commission on the Poor Laws and Relief of Distress, Appendix Vol. VIII, Minutes of Evidence, Cd. 5066, 1910, *Parliamentary Papers*, Vol. XLVIII, 1910.

Royal Commission on Trade Disputes and Combinations, Minutes of Evidence together with Index and Appendices, Cd. 2826, 1906, *Parliamentary Papers*, Vol. LVI, 1906.

Tenth Report from the Royal Commission on Trade Unions, Minutes of Evidence, 1867-68, Cd. 3980-VI, Vol. XXXIX, *British Parliamentary Papers*, Vol. 9, *Industrial Relations*, Irish University Press, Shannon,

Ireland, 1970.
Third Census of Production, Vol. 3, HMSO, London, 1933.

Journals and Newspapers

Cassier's Magazine
Economic Journal
The Engineer
Engineering
Engineering Review
Fielden's Magazine
The Institution of Electrical Engineers, Proceedings
Institution of Mechanical Engineers, Proceedings
Iron and Coal Trades Review
Ironmonger
Journal of the Iron and Steel Institute
Page's Weekly
Sheffield Daily Telegraph
Sheffield and Rotherham Independent
Yorkshire Post

Contemporary books

W.J. Ashley, *Scientific Management and the Engineering Situation,* Sidney Ball Memorial Lecture, 1922, OUP, London, 1922.

Lord Askwith, *Industrial Problems and Disputes,* Murray, London, 1922.

Charles Babbage, *On the Economy of Machinery and Manufactures* (1832), John Murray, London, 1846.

John Batey, *Science of Works Management,* Scott, Greenwood and Son, London, 1914.

R.A. Bray, *Boy Labour and Apprenticeship,* Constable, London, 1911.

F.G. Burton, *The Commercial Management of Engineering Works,* Second Edition, The Scientific Publishing Co., Manchester, 1905.

S.J. Chapman, ed., *Labour and Capital after the War,* John Murray, London, 1918.

E.P. Cheney, *Industrial and Social History of England,* Macmillan, London, 1901.

G.D.H. Cole, *Self Government in Industry,* Bell and Sons, London, 1917.
————— , *The World of Labour,* Macmillan, London, 1928.

N.B. Dearle, *Industrial Training,* King, London, 1914.

Barbara Drake, *Women in the Engineering Trades,* Fabian Research Department, Allen and Unwin, London, 1917.

E.T. Elbourne, *Factory Administration and Accounts* (1914), Longmans, London, 1919.

Empire Mining and Metallurgical Congress, *Proceedings, Part IV, Metallurgy of Iron and Steel, Section C of Congress. 3-6 June 1924*, Cleveland House, London, 1925.

Sir William Fairbairn, *A Treatise on Mills and Millwork, Part 1. On the Principles of Mechanism and on Prime Movers*, Longman, Green, Roberts and Green, London, 1864.

A.P.M. Fleming and J.G. Pearce, *Principles of Apprentice Training: with Special Reference to the Engineering Industry*, Longmans, Green and Co., London, 1916.

A.P.M. Fleming and R.W. Bailey, *Engineering as a Profession: scope, training and opportunities for advancement*, John Long, London, 1913.

London County Council, *Report on the Apprenticeship Question, Minutes of the Education Committee of the London County Council, February 24, 1909*, LCC, London, 1909.

Patrick McGeown, *Heat the Furnace Seven Times More: An Autobiography*, Hutchinson, London, 1967.

H.E. Morgan, *Munitions of Peace: Our Preparedness for the Trade War*, Nisbet and Co., London, 1916.

J.T. Murphy, *New Horizons*, John Lane, London, 1942.

E.A. Pratt, *Trade Unions and British Industry*, John Murray, London, 1904.

D.F. Schloss, *Methods of Industrial Remuneration*, Third Edition, Williams and Northgate, London, 1898.

D. Smith and P.C.N. Pickworth, *Engineers' Costs and Economical Workshop Production*, Emmott, London, 1914.

Sidney and Beatrice Webb, *The History of Trade Unionism* (1911), Longmans, London, 1920.

————————————— , *Industrial Democracy*, Longmans, London, 1919.

Alfred Williams, *Life in a Railway Factory* (1915), Newton Abbot, London, 1969.

Other books and articles

Göran Ahlström, *Engineers and Industrial Growth*, Croom Helm, London, 1982.

D.H. Aldcroft, ed., *The Development of British Industry and Foreign Competition, 1875-1914*, George Allen and Unwin, London, 1968.

W.H.G. Armytage, *The Rise of the Technocrats: A Social History of Engineering*, Faber and Faber, London, 1976.

Maxine Berg, ed., *Technology and Toil*, CSE Books, London, 1979.

Gerhard Brandt, *Gewerkschaftliche Interessenvertretung und sozialer Wandel. Eine soziologische Untersuchung über die Entwicklung der*

Gerwerkschaften in der britischen Eisen-und Stahlindustrie, 1886-1917, E.V.A., Frankfurt, 1975.

Keith Burgess, 'Technological Change and the 1852 Lock-Out in the British Engineering Industry', *International Review of Social History*, Vol. XIV, Pt. 2, 1969.

——————, 'Trade Union Policy and the 1852 Lock-Out in the British Engineering Industry', *International Review of Social History*, Vol. 17, Pt. 3, 1972.

Duncan Burn, *An Economic History of Steel Making, 1867-1939*, CUP, Cambridge, 1940.

J. Carr and W. Taplin, *A History of the British Steel Industry*, Basil Blackwell, Oxford, 1962.

R.O. Clarke, 'The Dispute in the British Engineering Industry, 1897-98: An Evaluation', *Economica*, No. 94, May 1957.

G.D.H. Cole and Raymond Postgate, *The Common People, 1746-1946*, Methuen, London, 1949.

François Crouzet, *The Victorian Economy*, translated by A.S. Forster, Methuen and Co. Ltd., London, 1982.

Tony Elger, 'Valorisation and "Deskilling", A Critique of Braverman', *Capital and Class*, No. 7, Spring 1979.

Frederick Engels, *The Condition of the Working Class in England in 1844*, in Karl Marx and Frederick Engels, *Collected Works*, Vol. 4, Lawrence and Wishart, London, 1976.

Charlotte Erickson, *British Industrialists: Steel and Hosiery, 1850-1950*, National Institute of Economic and Social Research. Economic and Social Studies, CUP, Cambridge, 1959.

C. Feinstein, *National Income, Expenditure and Output of the United Kingdom*, CUP, Cambridge, 1972.

Roderick Floud, *The British Machine Tool Industry, 1850-1914*, CUP, Cambridge, 1976.

Roderick Floud and D.N. McCloskey, eds., *The Economic History of Britain*, 2 Vols., CUP, Cambridge, 1981.

Robert Gray, *The Labour Aristocracy in Victorian Edinburgh*, Clarendon Press, Oxford, 1976.

Roy Hay, 'The British Business Community, Social Insurance and the German Example', in W.J. Mommsen, ed., *The Emergence of the Welfare State in Britain and Germany*, Croom Helm, London, 1981, pp. 107-32.

James Hinton, *The First Shop Stewards' Movement*, Allen and Unwin, London, 1973.

E.J. Hobsbawm, *Industry and Empire*, Penguin, London, 1974.

John Humphrey, 'Labour Use and Labour Control in the Brazilian Automobile Industry', *Capital and Class*, No. 12, Winter 1980-81.

David S. Landes, *The Unbound Prometheus: Technological Change and*

Industrial Development in Western Europe from 1750 to the Present, CUP, Cambridge, 1970.

A.L. Levine, *Industrial Retardation in Britain, 1880-1914*, Weidenfeld and Nicolson, London, 1967.

Karl Marx, *Capital*, Vol. 1 (1867), Penguin, London, 1976.

Peter Mathias, 'Business History and Management Education', *Business History*, Vol. XVII, January 1975.

Peter Mathias and M.M. Postan, eds., *The Cambridge Economic History of Europe, Vol. VII, The Industrial Economies: Capital, Labour and Enterprise, Pts. 1 and 2*, CUP, Cambridge, 1978.

Peter Mathias, *The First Industrial Nation: An Economic History of Britain, 1700-1914*, Methuen and Co., London, 1969.

D.N. McCloskey, ed., *Essays on a Mature Economy: Britain after 1840*, Methuen and Co., London, 1971.

Joseph Melling, ' "Non-Commissioned Officers": British Employers and their Supervisory Workers, 1880-1920', *Social History*, Vol. 5, No. 2, May 1980.

W. Minchinton, *The British Tinplate Industry, A History*, Clarendon Press, Oxford, 1956.

B.R. Mitchell and P. Deane, *Abstract of British Historical Statistics*, CUP, Cambridge, 1962.

B.R. Mitchell, *European Historical Statistics, 1750-1970*, Macmillan, London, 1975.

Charles More, *Skill and the English Working Class, 1870-1914*, Croom Helm, London, 1980.

P.W. Musgrave, *Technical Change, the Labour Force and Education. A Study of the British and German Iron and Steel Industries, 1860-1964*, Pergamon Press, Oxford, 1967.

Sidney Pollard, 'British and World Shipbuilding', *Journal of Economic History*, Vol. XVII, No. 3, 1957.

——————, *The Genesis of Modern Management*, Arnold, London, 1956.

——————, 'Wages and Earnings in the Sheffield Trades, 1851-1914', *Yorkshire Bulletin of Economic and Social Research*, Vol. VI, 1954.

Alastair Reid, 'Politics and Economics in the Formation of the British Working Class: A Response to H.F. Moorehouse', *Social History*, Vol. 3, No. 3, October 1978.

Paul Robertson and Sidney Pollard, *The British Shipbuilding Industry, 1870-1914*, Harvard University Press, Cambridge, Mass., London, 1979.

Eric Roll, *An Early Experiment in Industrial Organisation, being a history of the firm Boulton and Watt* (1930), Frank Cass and Co., London, 1968.

Charles Sabel, *Work and Politics: The Division of Labour in Industry*,

CUP, Cambridge, 1982.

Raphael Samuel, 'The Workshop of the World: Steam Power and Hand Technology in mid-Victorian Britain', *History Workshop*, No. 3, Spring, 1977.

Michael Sanderson, *The Universities and British Industry, 1850-1970*, Routledge and Kegan Paul, London, 1972.

———————— , ed., *The Universities in the Nineteenth Century*, Routledge and Kegan Paul, London, 1975.

S.B. Saul, 'The American Impact upon British Industry', *Business History*, Vol. 3, 1960.

——— , 'The Market and the Development of Mechanical Engineering Industries in Britain, 1860-1914', *Economic History Review*, Vol. XX, 1967.

——— , 'The Motor Industry in Britain in 1914', *Business History*, Vol. 5, 1962.

——— , *Technological Change: the United States and Britain in the Nineteenth Century*, Methuen, London, 1970.

Gareth Stedman-Jones, 'Class Struggle and Industrial Revolution', *New Left Review*, No. 90, March–April, 1975.

Clive Trebilcock, ' "Spin-Off" in British Economic History', *Economic History Review*, Second Series, Vol. 22, No. 3, December 1969.

Jonathan Zeitlin, 'Craft Control and the Division of Labour: Engineers and Compositors in Britain, 1890-1930', *Cambridge Journal of Economics*, Vol. 3, No. 3, September 1979.

GERMANY

Archives

Düsseldorf Hauptstaatsarchiv, Castle Kalkum: *Arbeitsschutz in der Gross-eisenindustrie, 1909-11*, File No. 33389.

Stadtarchiv, Düsseldorf: *Bericht über den Stand und die Verwaltung der Gemeine-Angelegenheiten, für die Stadt Düsseldorf, 1900-14*.

—————————————— : *Jahresbericht des Statistischen Amts der Stadt Düsseldorf für die Jahre 1904 bis 1914*.

Journals

Archiv für exacte Wirtschaftsforschung (Thünen-Archiv).
Archiv für Sozialwissenschaft und Sozialpolitik.
Schriften des Vereins für Socialpolitik.
Stahl und Eisen.
Technik und Wirtschaft, Monatschrift des Vereines deutscher Ingenieure.
Zeitschrift des Vereines Deutscher Ingenieure.

Contemporary books

T.C. Banfield, *Industry of the Rhine,* 2 Vols., 1846–48, *Series II, Manufactures,* C. Cox, London, 1846–48.

Deutsche Metallarbeiter Verband, *Die Schwereisenindustrie,* DMV, Berlin, 1912.

Hans Ehrenberg, *Die Eisenhüttentechnik und der deutsche Hüttenarbeiter,* J.G. Cotta'sche Buchhandlung, Münchener Volkswirtschaftliche Studien 80–81, Stuttgart and Berlin, 1906.

Ernst Günther, *Die Entlöhnungsmethoden in der Bayrischen Eisen und Maschinenindustrie,* Centralverein für das Wohl der arbeitenden Klassen, Leonhard Simion, Berlin, 1907.

Cl. Heiss, *Die Entlöhnungsmethoden in der Berliner Feinmechanik,* Centralverein. . ., Leonhard Simion, Berlin, 1909.

Otto Jeidels, *Die Methoden der Arbeitentlöhnung in der rheinisch-westfälischen Eisenindustrie,* Centralverein. . ., Leonhard Simion, Berlin, 1907.

C. Matschoss, *Ein Jahrhundert deutscher Maschinenbau, 1819–1919,* Julius Springer, Berlin, 1922.

——————, *Männer der Technik,* Verein Deutscher Ingenieure, Berlin, 1925.

H. Reichelt, *Die Arbeitsverhältnisse in einem Berliner Grossbetrieb der Maschinenindustrie,* Centralverein. . ., Leonhard Simion, Berlin, 1907.

Frederick William Roman, *The Industrial and Commercial Schools of the United States and Germany, A Comparative Study,* G.P. Putnam's Sons, New York, 1915.

Fritz Schulte, *Die Entlöhnungsmethoden in der Berliner Maschinenindustrie,* Centralverein. . ., Leonhard Simion, Berlin, 1906.

Walter Timmerman, *Die Entlöhnungsmethoden in der hannoverschen Eisenindustrie,* Centralverein. . ., Leonhard Simion, Berlin, 1906.

Kurt Wiedenfeld, *Ein Jahrhundert rheinischer Montanindustrie, 1815–1915,* A. Marcus and E. Webers Verlag, Bonn, 1916.

Other books and articles

Guido Baldi, 'Theses on the Mass Worker and Social Capital', *Radical America,* Vol. 6, No. 3, May–June, 1972.

Max Barkhausen, 'Government Control and Free Enterprise in Western Germany and the Low Countries in the Eighteenth Century', in Peter Earle, ed., *Essays in European Economic History, 1500–1800,* Clarendon Press, Oxford, 1974.

H. Beau, *Das Leistungswissen der frühindustriellen Unternehmertums in Rheinland und Westfälen,* Cologne, 1959.

Sergio Bologna, 'Class Composition and the Theory of the Party at the

Origin of the Workers Councils' Movement', in *The Labour Process and Class Strategies,* Pamphlet 1, CSE Books, London, 1976, pp. 68–91.

Eckhard Brockhaus, *Zusammensetzung und neustruktierung der Arbeiterklasse vor dem ersten Weltkrieg,* Trikont Verlag, Munich, 1975.

Ralph Dahrendorf, *Class and Class Conflict in Industrial Society,* Routledge and Kegan Paul, London, 1959.

Frank Deppe, ' "Alte" und "neue" Arbeiterklasse', in Richard Vahrenkamp, ed., *Technologie und Kapital,* Edition Suhrkamp, Frankfurt-am-Main, 1973.

W. Fischer, 'Innerbetrieblicher und sozialer Status der frühen Fabrikarbeiterschaft', *Forschungen zur Sozial- und Wirtschaftsgeschichte,* Vol. VI, 1964.

Alexander Gerschenkron, 'Economic Backwardness in Historical Perspective', in Bert F. Hoselitz, ed., *The Progress of Underdeveloped Areas,* University of Chicago Press, Chicago and London, 1969, pp. 3–29.

Dieter Groh, 'Intensification of Work and Industrial Conflict in Germany 1896–1914', *Politics and Society,* Vol. 8, Nos. 3–4, 1978.

Frank Hauerkamp, *Staatliche Gewerberförderung im Grossherzogtum Baden unter besonderer Berücksichtigung der Entwicklung des Gewerblichen Bildungswesen im 19. Jahrhundert,* Verlag Karl Alber, Freiburg/ Munich, 1979.

Walter G. Hoffman, Franz Grumbach and Helmut Hesse, *Das Wachstum der Deutschen Wirtschaft seit der Mitte des 19 Jahrhundert,* Springer Verlag, Berlin, 1965.

W.G. Hoffman, 'Long-Term Growth and Capital Formation in Germany' in F.A. Lutz, ed., *The Theory of Capital,* Proceedings of a Conference held by the International Economic Association, D C Hague, Macmillan, London, 1961.

Hartmut Kaelble, 'From Family Enterprise to the Professional Manager: the German Case', in Eighth International Economic History Congress, Budapest, 1982, B. 89, *From Family Firm to Professional Management: Structure and Performance of Business Enterprise;* Organiser: L. Hannah, Akadémiai Kiado, Budapest, 1982.

Jürgen Kocka, *Unternehmensverwaltung und Angestelltenschaft am Beispiel Siemens, 1847–1914,* Ernst Klett Verlag, Stuttgart, 1969.

Witold Kula, *An Economic Theory of the Feudal System, Towards a Model of the Polish Economy,* NLB, London, 1976.

S. Kuznets, 'Quantitative Aspects of the Economic Growth of Nations: II, Industrial Distribution of National Product and Labour Force', in *Economic Development and Cultural Change,* Supplement to Vol. V, No. 4, July 1957.

————, 'Quantitative Aspects of the Economic Growth of Nations: VI, Long-Term Trends in Capital Formation Proportions', in *Economic*

Development and Cultural Change, Vol. IX, No. 4, Part II, July 1961.

Erhard Lucas, *Zwei Formen von Radikalismus in der deutschen Arbeiterbewegung*, Verlag Roter Stern, Frankfurt, 1976.

Peter Lundgreen, *Bildung und Wirtschaftswachstum im Industrialisierungprozess des 19. Jahrhundert*, Berlin, 1973.

—————————, 'Industrialization and the Educational Formation of Manpower in Germany', *Journal of Social History*, Vol. 9, No. 1, Fall 1975.

Karl-Heinz Manegold, *Universität, Technische Hochschule und Industrie. Eine Beitrag zur Emanzipation der Technik im 19. Jahrhundert unter besonderer Berücksichtigung der Bestrebungen Felix Kleins*, Duncker and Humblot, Berlin, 1970.

Karl-Heinz Roth, *Die 'andere' Arbeiterbewegung und die Entwicklung der kapitalistischen Repression von 1800 bis zur Gegenwart*, Trikont Verlag, Munich, 1973.

Lawrence Schofer, *The Formation of a Labour Force in Upper Silesia, 1865-1914*, University of California Press, Berkeley, 1975.

—————————, 'Patterns of Worker Protest: Upper Silesia 1865–1914', *Journal of Social History*, Vol. 4, 1972.

Heilwig Schomerus, *Die Arbeiter der Maschinenfabrik Esslingen. Forschungen zur Lage der Arbeiterschaft im 19. Jarhundert*, Letta-Cotta, Stuttgart, 1977.

—————————, 'Ausbildung und Aufsteigsmöglichkeiten württembergischer Metallarbeiter 1850 bis 1914 am Beispiel der Maschinenfabrik Esslingen', in Ulrich Engelhardt, Volker Sellin and Horst Stucke, eds., *Soziale Bewegung und politische Verfassung*, Ernst Klett Verlag, Stuttgart, 1975, pp. 372–93.

A. Schröter and W. Becker, *Die deutsche Maschinenbauindustrie in der industriellen Revolution*, Akademie, East Berlin, 1962.

Alfred Sohn-Rethel, 'Technische Intelligenz zwischen Kapitalismus und Sozialismus', in Richard Vahrenkamp, ed., *Technologie und Kapital*, Edition Suhrkamp, Frankfurt-am-Main, 1973, pp. 11–38.

Elaine Glovka Spencer, 'Between Capital and Labour: Supervisory Personnel in Ruhr Heavy Industry Before 1914', *Journal of Social History*, Vol. 2, No. 2, Winter 1975.

Peter Stearns, 'The Unskilled and Industrialization', *Archiv für Sozial Geschichte*, Bund XVI, 1976.

Peter Stearns and Daniel Walkowitz, eds., *Workers in the Industrial Revolution*, Transaction Books, New Brunswick, New Jersey, 1974.

Clive Trebilcock, *The Industrialization of the Continental Powers, 1780–1914*, Longman, London, 1981.

R. Wagenführ, 'Die industriewirtschaftlichen Entwicklungstendenzen der deutschen und internationalen Industrieproduktion 1860 bis 1932', *Sonderhefte des Instituts für Konjunkturforschung*, Vol. 31, Berlin,

1933.

FRANCE

Journals

Bulletin de l'Association des anciens élèves de l'École des Mines de Paris.
Bulletin de l'Association pour le développement de l'Enseignement technique.
Bulletin de la Société d'Encouragement pour l'Industrie Nationale.
Bulletin de la Société de l'Industrie minérale.
Mouvement socialiste.
Revue générale des Sciences.
Revue de Métallurgie.
Revue Psychologique.
Statistique de l'Industrie minérale.

Contemporary books

M. Briat, *L'enseignement professionnel: rapport fait au nom de la Commission permanente du Conseil supérieur du Travail,* Imprimerie Nationale, Paris, 1905.

J.H. Cagninacci, *L'instruction professionnelle de l'ouvrier,* Paris, 1910.

Georges Friedmann, *Problèmes humains du machinisme industriel,* NRF, Gallimard, Paris, 1946.

Josefa Ioteyko, *The Science of Labour and its Organisation,* Routledge, London, 1919.

——————— , *La science du travail et son organisation,* F. Alcon, Paris, 1917.

London County Council, *Report of the London County Council on Trade and Technical Education in Germany and France,* LCC, London, 1914.

Alphonse Merrheim, *La métallurgie, son origine, son développement,* Paris, 1913.

Other books and articles

Frederick B. Artz, 'L'enseignement technique en France pendant l'époque révolutionnaire, 1789–1815', *Revue Historique,* Vol. CXCVII, July–September 1946, October–December 1946.

Fernand Braudel, *Capitalism and Material Life, 1400–1800,* Fontana/Collins, Glasgow, 1974.

Rondo Cameron, with F. Mendels and J.P. Ward, eds., *Essays in French Economic History,* Richard D. Irwin, Illinois, 1970.

——————— , 'Economic Growth and Stagnation in France, 1815–

1914', *Journal of Modern History*, Vol. XXX, No. 1, March 1958.

——————— , *France and the Economic Development of Europe*, Princeton University Press, Princeton, New Jersey, 1961.

François Caron, *Histoire de l'exploitation d'un grand reséau: La Compagnie du Chemin de Fer du Nord, 1846-1937*, Ecole Pratique des Hautes Etudes, Paris, 1973.

F. Crouzet, et al., eds., *Essays in European Economic History*, St. Martins Press, New York, 1969.

——————— , 'French Economic Growth in the Nineteenth Century Reconsidered', *History*, No. 59, 1974.

——————— , 'Recherches sur la production d'armements en France, 1815–1913, *Revue Historique*, No. 231, 1974.

——————— , 'Remarque sur l'industrie des armements en France (du milieu du XIXe siècle à 1914)', *Revue Historique*, No. 231, 1974.

Adeline Daumard, 'Les élèves de l'École polytechnique de 1815 à 1848', *Revue d'histoire moderne et contemporaine*, Vol. V, 1958.

Edouard Dolléans and Gérard Dehove, *Histoire du travail en France: mouvement ouvrier et législation sociale. Des origines à 1919*, Tome 1, Editions Domat Montchrestien, Paris, 1953.

A.L. Dunham, *Industrial Revolution in France, 1815-1848*, Exposition Press, New York, 1955.

Claude Fohlen, 'The Industrial Revolution in France, 1700–1914', in Carlo M. Cippola, ed., *Fontana Economic History of Europe*, Vol. IV, Fontana, London, 1970.

M. Freyssenet, *La division capitaliste du travail*, Savelli, Paris, 1977.

Bertrand Gille, 'La formation du prolétariat dans l'industrie sidérurgique française', *Revue d'histoire de la sidérurgie*, Tome IV, No. 4, October–December, 1963.

——————— , *Les origines de la grande industrie métallurgique en France*, Editions Domat Montchrestien, Paris, 1947.

——————— , 'Paulin Talabot, recherches pour une biographie', *Revue d'histoire des mines et de la métallurgie*, Tome II, No. 1, 1970.

———————, *La sidérurgie française au XIXe siècle, recherches historiques*, Librairie Droz, S.A., Geneva, 1968.

Gerd Hardach, 'Les pròblemes de main-d'oeuvre à Decazeville', *Revue d'histoire de la sidérurgie*, Tome VIII, No. 1, 1967.

———————, *Der soziale Status des Arbeiters in der Frühindustrialisierung. Eine Untersuchung über die Arbeitnehmer in der französische eisenschaffenden Industrie zwischen 1800 und 1870*, Duncker and Humblot, Berlin, 1969.

Herbert Heaton, *Economic History of Europe*, Harper and Row, New York, 1969.

J.M. Laux, *In First Gear: The French Automobile Industry to 1914*, McGill-Queens University, Montreal, 1967.

Yves Lequin, 'La formation du prolétariat industriel dans la région lyonnaise au XIX siècle: approches méthodologiques et premiers résultats', *Le mouvement social*, No. 97, October–December 1976.

M. Lévy-Leboyer, 'Le patronat française a-t-il été malthusien', *Le mouvement social*, No. 88, 1974.

S. Lilley, 'Social Aspects of the History of Science', *Archives Internationales d'Histoire des Sciences*, Année 2, 1948-49.

Robert R. Locke, 'Drouillard, Benoist et Cie', *Revue d'histoire de la sidérurgie*, Tome VIII, No. 4, 1967.

Val R. Lorwin, *The French Labour Movement*, Harvard University Press, Cambridge, Mass., 1954.

Marc Maurice, François Sellier and Jean-Jacques Silvestre, 'La production de la hiérarchie dans l'entreprise: recherche d'un effet sociétal', *Revue française de sociologie*, No. 20, April 1979.

Alberto Melucci, 'Action patronale, pouvoir, organisation. Réglements d'usine et contrôle de la main-d'oeuvre au XIXe siècle', *Le mouvement social*, No. 97, October–December 1976.

Joseph N. Moody, *French Education Since Napoleon*, Syracuse University Press, New York, 1978.

Aimée Moutet, 'Les origines du système de Taylor en France: Le point de vue patronal, 1907-1914', *Le mouvement social*, No. 93, October–December 1975.

G. Palmade, *French Capitalism in the Nineteenth Century*. Translated, with an introduction by Graeme M. Holmes, David and Charles, Newton Abbot, Devon, 1972.

F. Ponteil, *Histoire de l'enseignement en France. Les grandes étapes, 1789-1964*, Sirey, Paris, 1966.

Antoine Prost, *L'enseignement en France, 1800-1967*, Librairie Armand Colin, Paris, 1968.

Georges Ribeill, 'Les débuts de l'ergonomie en France à la veille de la Première Guerre mondiale', *Le mouvement sociale*, No. 113, October–December, 1980.

Joan Wallach Scott, *The Glassworkers of Carmaux: French Craftsmen and Political Action in a Nineteenth Century City*, Harvard University Press, Cambridge, Mass., 1974.

William H. Sewell, Jr., *Work and Revolution in France. The Language of Labor from the Old Regime to 1848*, CUP, Cambridge, 1980.

P.N. Stearns, 'Against the Strike Threat: Employer Policy Toward Labour Agitation in France, 1900-14', *Journal of Modern History*, Vol. 40, December 1968.

Margot B. Stein, 'The Meaning of Skill: The Case of the French Engine-Drivers, 1837-1917', *Politics and Society*, Vol. 8, Nos. 3-4, 1978.

Guy Thuillier, *Georges Defaud et les débuts du grand capitalisme dans la métallurgie en Nivernais au XIXe siècle*, Paris, 1953.

M. Verry, *Les laminoires ardennais. Déclin d'une aristocratie professionnelle*, Paris, 1955.

J. Vial, *L'industrialisation de la sidérurgie française, 1814-1864*, 2 Vols., Thèse pour le Doctorat ès Lettres, Mouton & Cie., Paris, 1967.

L.A. Vincent, 'Evolution de la production intérieure brute en France de 1896 à 1938', *Études et Conjoncture*, Vol. XVII, No. 2, 1962.

Denis Woronoff, 'Le monde ouvrier de la sidérurgie ancienne: note sur l'exemple française', *Le mouvement social*, No. 97, October–December 1976.

AMERICA

Journals and reports

Engineering Magazine.
Iron Age.
The Iron Review.
Iron Trade Review.
The Machinist.
Quarterly Journal of Economics.
Reports of Commissioners, Special Reports, Vols. 10-11, Education in the United States of America, Parts I-II, Cd. 837 and Cd. 1156, *Parliamentary Papers*, Vols. XXVIII and XXIX (1), 1902.

Contemporary books

Paul H. Douglas, *American Apprenticeship and Industrial Education*, Columbia University Studies in History and Economics, New York, 1915.

R.F. Hoxie, *Scientific Management and Labour*, Appleton, New York and London, 1915.

Reports of the Mosely Education Commission to the United States of America, October-December 1903, Co-operative Printing Society Limited, London, 1904.

F.W. Taylor, *Scientific Management*, Harper, New York; Western Reserve University, Cleveland, 1971.

——————— , *Shop Management* (1903), New York, London, 1947.

Other books and articles

Reinhard Bendix, *Work and Authority in Industry. Ideologies of Management in the Course of Industrialization*, University of California Press, Berkeley, London, 1974.

Harry Braverman, *Labour and Monopoly Capital: The Degradation of*

Labour in the Twentieth Century, Monthly Review Press, New York, London, 1974.

Jeremy Brecher (The Work Relations Group), 'Uncovering the Hidden History of the American Workplace', *Review of Radical Political Economics,* Vol. 10, No. 4, Winter 1978.

David Brody, *Steelworkers in America, the Non-Union Era,* Harvard University Press, Cambridge, Mass., 1960.

John Buttrick, 'The Inside Contract System', *Journal of Economic History,* Vol. 12, No. 3, Summer 1952.

M.A. Calvert, *The Mechanical Engineer in America, 1830-1910: Professional Cultures in Conflict,* John Hopkins Press, Baltimore, 1967.

Alfred D. Chandler, Jr., and Herman Daems, eds., *Managerial Hierarchies: Comparative Perspectives on the Rise of Modern Industrial Enterprise,* Harvard University Press, Cambridge, Mass., 1980.

Dan Clawson, *Bureaucracy and the Labour Process: the Transformation of U.S. Industry, 1860-1920,* Monthly Review Press, New York, 1980.

Mike Davis, 'Why the U.S. Working Class is Different', *New Left Review,* No. 123, September–October, 1980.

Philip S. Foner, *History of the Labor Movement in the United States, Vol. III, The Policies and Practices of the American Federation of Labour, 1900-1909,* International Publishers, New York, 1973.

Raymond Goldsmith, *The Flow of Capital Funds in the Post-War Economy,* Bureau of Economic Research, Columbia University Press, New York and London, 1965.

David M. Gordon, Richard Edwards and Michael Reich, *Segmented Workers, Divided Workers: The Historical Transformation of Labor in the United States,* CUP, Cambridge, 1982.

Antonio Gramsci, 'Americanism and Fordism', in Quinton Hoare and Geoffrey Nowell Smith, eds., *Selections from the Prison Notebooks of Antonio Gramsci,* International Publishers, New York, 1973.

H.J. Habakkuk, *America and British Technology in the Nineteenth Century,* CUP, Cambridge, 1962.

Jeff Henderson and Robin Cohen, 'Capital and the Work Ethic', *Monthly Review,* Vol. 31, No. 6, November, 1979.

Charles Hill, 'Fighting the Twelve-Hour Day in the American Steel Industry', *Labor History,* Vol. 15, No. 1, Winter 1974.

Clark Kerr and Abraham Siegel, 'The Structuring of the Labour Force in Industrial Society: New Dimensions and New Questions', *Industrial and Labour Relations Review,* Vol. 8, 1955.

S. Kuznets, *Capital in the American Economy,* National Bureau of Economic Research, Princeton University Press, Princeton, 1961.

————— , 'Capital Formation and Economic Growth', in, by the same author *Population, Capital and Growth,* Heinemann, London, 1973.

Edwin Layton, Jr., ed., *Technology and Social Change in America,* Harper and Row, New York and London, 1973.

Craig R. Littler, 'Understanding Taylorism', *British Journal of Sociology,* Vol. XXIX, No. 2, June 1978.

David Montgomery, 'Workers' Control of Machine Production in the Nineteenth Century', *Labor History,* Vol. 17, No. 4, Fall 1976.

M.J. Nadworny, *Scientific Management and the Unions, 1900-32: a Historical Analysis,* Harvard University Press, Cambridge, Mass., 1955.

David Nelson, *Workers and Managers: Origins of the New Factory System in the United States, 1880-1920,* University of Wisconsin Press, Wisconsin, 1975.

David F. Noble, *America by Design. Science, Technology and the Rise of Corporate Capitalism,* Alfred A. Knopf, New York, 1977.

Bryan Palmer, 'Class, Conception and Conflict: The Thrust for Efficiency— Managerial Views of Labour and the Working Class Rebellion, 1903–1922', *Review of Radical Political Economics,* Vol. 7, No. 2, Summer 1975.

Jesse S. Robinson, *The Amalgamated Association of Iron, Steel and Tin Workers,* Baltimore, 1920.

Nathan Rosenberg, 'Karl Marx on the Economic Role of Science', *Journal of Political Economy,* Vol. 82, 1974.

————————— , 'Technological Change in the Machine Tool Industry, 1840-1910', *Journal of Economic History,* Vol. 33, No. 4, December 1963.

David Stark, 'Class Struggle and the Transformation of the Labour Process: A Relational Approach', *Theory and Society,* Vol. 9, 1980.

Kathrine Stone, 'The Origin of Job Structures in the Steel Industry', in Root and Branch, eds., *The Rise of the Workers' Movements,* Fawcett Publications, Greenwich, 1975, pp. 123-58.

Peter Temin, 'Labour Scarcity and the Problem of American Industrial Efficiency in the 1850s', *Journal of Economic History,* Vol. XXVI, No. 3, September 1966.

Brinley Thomas, *Migration and Economic Growth,* CUP, Cambridge, 1954.

INDEX

Peters, Dr. Th., 172-3
Pickworth, P.C.N., 74-5
Pollard, Sidney, xxxi, 48, n. 36
Postgate, Raymond, F.
production pauses, Germany: employers' strategies concerning, 221-5; legislation for, 221; metal enterprises' response to legislation, 221, 222, 223; time studies of in various enterprises, 222-4

Reich, Michael: see skills, theories of
Reichelt, H., 224-5; apprentice training survey, 245-6; on job turnover rates, Berlin, 251-2; on employer-worker relations, 252
Reid, Alistair, xxxii
Report on the Apprenticeship Question 1909 (London County Council), 132-3
Revue de Métallurgie, xiii, xxxvii, 22, 142, 171; campaign for improved industrial training, 171, 174-5; involvement in quality specialisation, 180
Ribes-Christofle, M. de: see apprenticed labour, apprenticeships: France
Robertson, Paul, xxxi, 48, n. 36
Roll, Eric, 9
Roper, Anton, 28
Roseberry, Lord: see National Efficiency Movement, leading politicians of
Rosenberg, Nathan, 25
Rostow, Walt, 74
Roth, Karl Heinz, xxxvi
Royal Commission on the Poor Laws, 130, 131, 134, 145, 148
Royal Ordnance factories 113: managerial training in, 113-14; investigation of, 113

Sabel, Charles, 91-2, 254; see also skills, theories of
St. Etienne, 22; Unieux steelworks in, 25
Samuel, Raphael, 13-14
Samuelson, James: see skills, contemporary perceptions of: Britain
Sanderson, Michael, 109, 269
Saul, S.B., xxxi, 14, 110, 114
Schiess, Ernst, 27-8
Schlesinger, George: see German industry, contemporary views of

Schloss, David, 66, 67, 69
Schneider, Eugène, 20
Schneider, Herman, 88
Schomerus, Heilwig: workforce age composition survey, Maschinenfabrik Esslingen, 252
Schroder, Karl, 33-4
Schroter, A., 27, 28
Schulte, Fritz, xxiv, xxxvii; see also skills, contemporary, perceptions of: Germany
Schwab, Charles, 79
science, scientists in industry: application of, France, 24-6; French superiority in, 22; late development of, Britain, 26; Socrates' view of, 25
scientific management, America, xvi, xvii, 77, 78, 79; see also Hoxie, R.F., Taylor, F.W.
Segitz, Martin, 67, 68
Sellier, François, xli
Sewell, William, F., 7
Shaw, Mr Thomas, J.P.: Vice-Chairman, Sheffield Distress Committee, 148-9
Sheffield, 15, 106, 107; see also capital investment boom, metal industry, J.T. Murphy, skills, Vickers
Sheffield Distress Committee, 148; see also Shaw, Mr Thomas, J.P.
Siegel, Abraham, xl
Siemens & Halske, AG: see engineering industry, Germany—electrical branch
Silvestre, Jean-Jacques, xli
skills,
—America, American Federation of Labor craft restrictions, xvii; capitalist regulation of, 92; degradation of, 92; dequalification of, 63, 77; marxist view of, 90-1; recomposition of, 79;
—Britain, craft control collapse, 11; decline of millwrights' craft, 8-9, 46-7, n. 20; decomposition of, metal industry, 10, 11, 13; employer regulation of, xviii, xix; trade union defence of, 40; trade union regulation of, 150-1;
—France, artisan crafts: challenges to, 3; erosion of, 3; by-passing of craftmanship, xi, xii; capitalist regulation of, 188; collapse of craftmanship, 18-19; dequalification of, metal industry, 265; employer regulation of, 189; producerist images of, 188,